RICK AND MORTY

VOLUME TEN

AN ONI PRESS PUBLICATION

[adult swim]

Rick and

VOLUME TEN

***RICK AND MORTY*™** CREATED BY **DAN HARMON** AND **JUSTIN ROILAND**

RETAIL COVER BY
MARC ELLERBY AND **SARAH STERN**

ONI EXCLUSIVE COVER BY
JULIETA COLÁS

EDITED BY
SARAH GAYDOS

DESIGNED BY
KATE Z. STONE

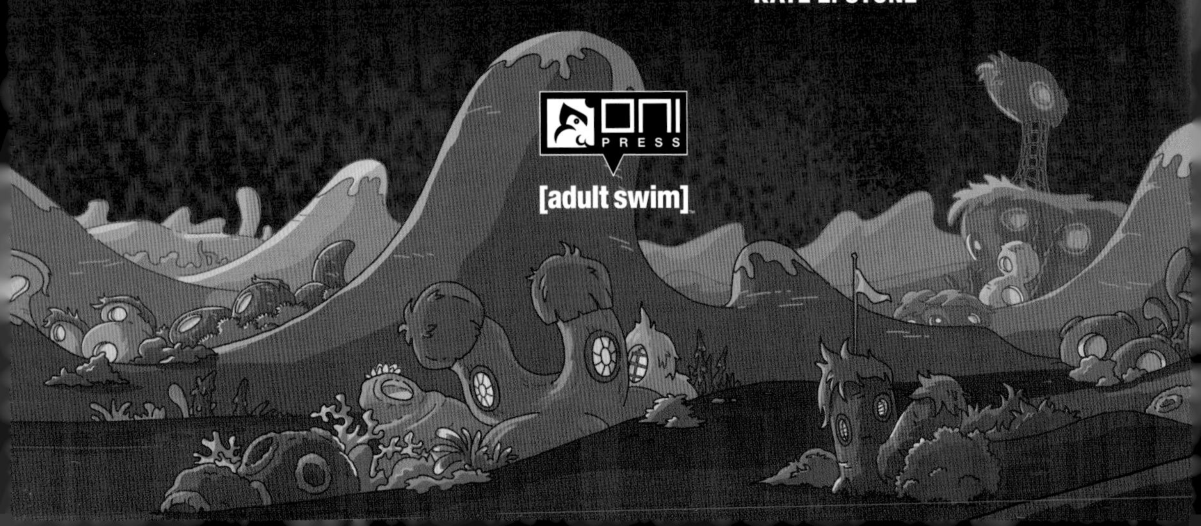

ONI PRESS
[adult swim]

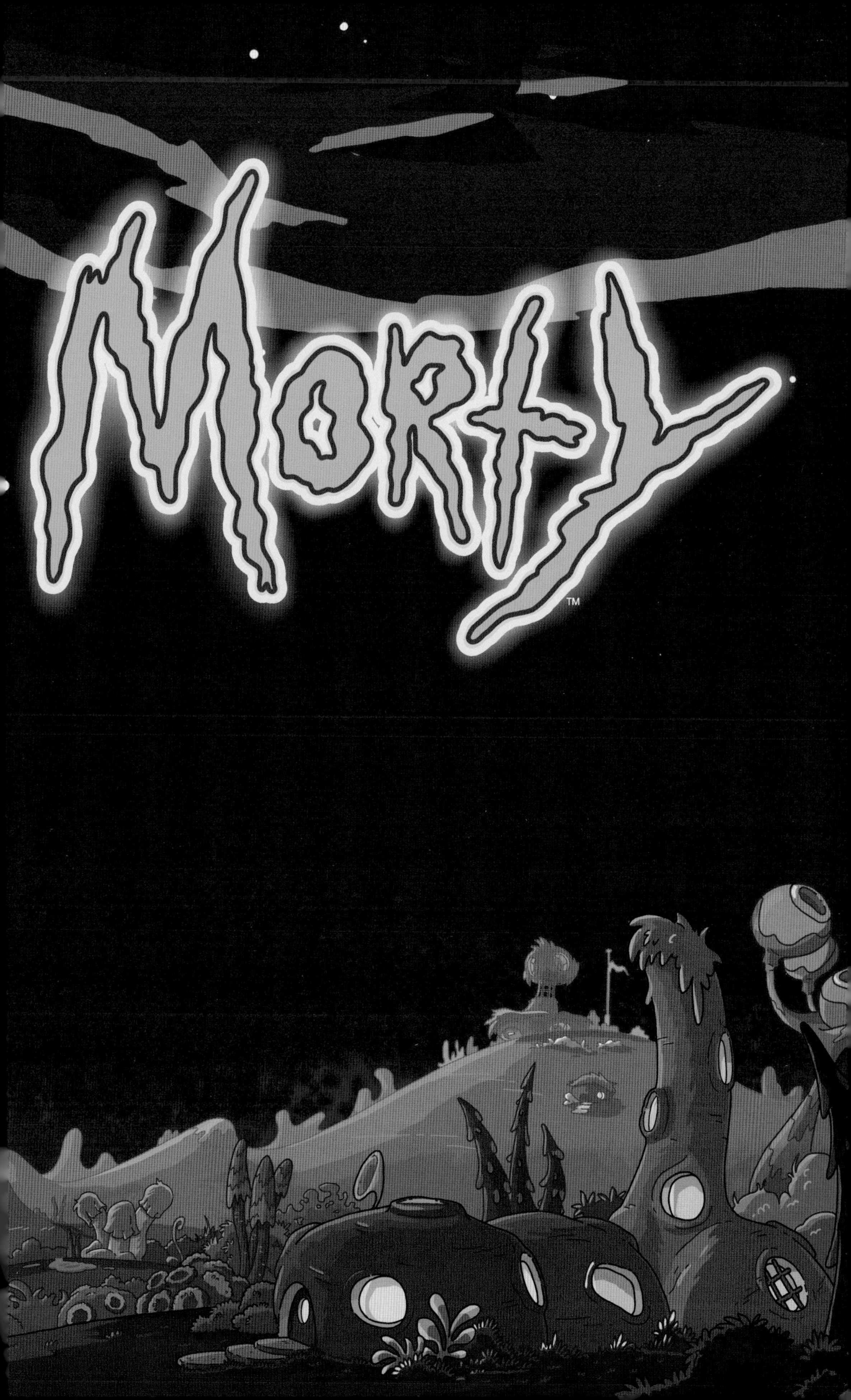
Morty™

PUBLISHED BY ONI PRESS, INC.

JOE NOZEMACK FOUNDER & CHIEF FINANCIAL OFFICER

JAMES LUCAS JONES PUBLISHER

SARAH GAYDOS EDITOR IN CHIEF

CHARLIE CHU V.P. OF CREATIVE & BUSINESS DEVELOPMENT

BRAD ROOKS DIRECTOR OF OPERATIONS

MELISSA MESZAROS DIRECTOR OF PUBLICITY

MARGOT WOOD DIRECTOR OF SALES

AMBER O'NEILL SPECIAL PROJECTS MANAGER

TROY LOOK DIRECTOR OF DESIGN & PRODUCTION

KATE Z. STONE SENIOR GRAPHIC DESIGNER

SONJA SYNAK GRAPHIC DESIGNER

ANGIE KNOWLES DIGITAL PREPRESS LEAD

ARI YARWOOD SENIOR EDITOR

ROBIN HERRERA SENIOR EDITOR

DESIREE WILSON ASSOCIATE EDITOR

KATE LIGHT EDITORIAL ASSISTANT

MICHELLE NGUYEN EXECUTIVE ASSISTANT

JUNG LEE LOGISTICS COORDINATOR

[adult swim]

ONIPRESS.COM
FACEBOOK.COM/ONIPRESS
TWITTER.COM/ONIPRESS
INSTAGRAM.COM/ONIPRESS
ADULTSWIM.COM
TWITTER.COM/RICKANDMORTY
FACEBOOK.COM/RICKANDMORTY

THIS VOLUME COLLECTS ISSUES #46-50
OF THE ONI PRESS SERIES RICK AND MORTY®.

FIRST EDITION: DECEMBER 2019

ISBN 978-1-62010-685-3
EISBN 978-1-62010-686-0
ONI EXCLUSIVE ISBN 978-1-62010-699-0

PRINTED IN CHINA.

LIBRARY OF CONGRESS CONTROL NUMBER: 2019934130

1 2 3 4 5 6 7 8 9 10

SPECIAL THANKS TO JUSTIN ROILAND, DAN HARMON, MARISA MARIONAKIS, ELYSE SALAZAR, MIKE MENDEL, JANET NO, AND MEAGAN BIRNEY.

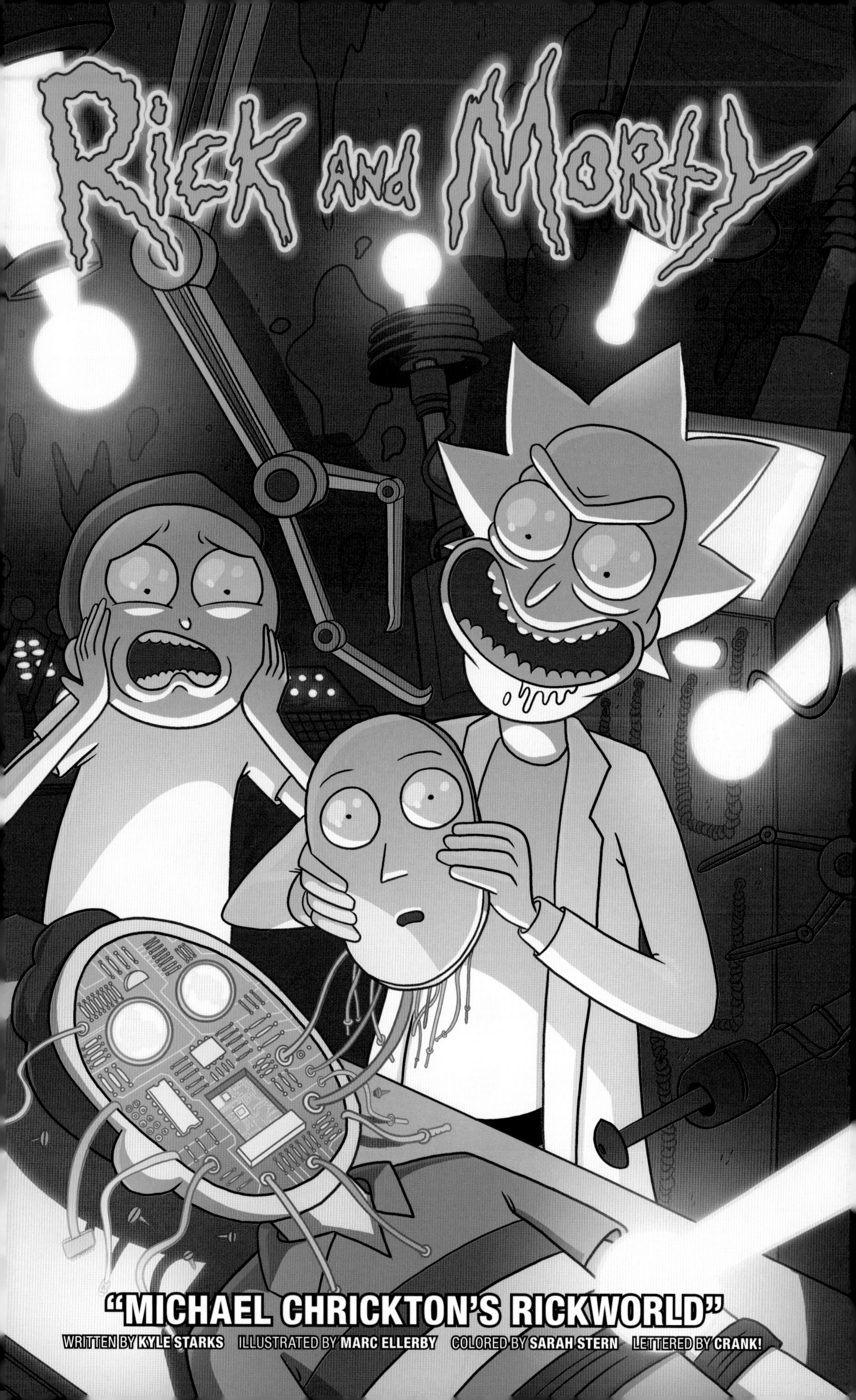
Rick and Morty

"MICHAEL CHRICKTON'S RICKWORLD"

WRITTEN BY **KYLE STARKS** ILLUSTRATED BY **MARC ELLERBY** COLORED BY **SARAH STERN** LETTERED BY **CRANK!**

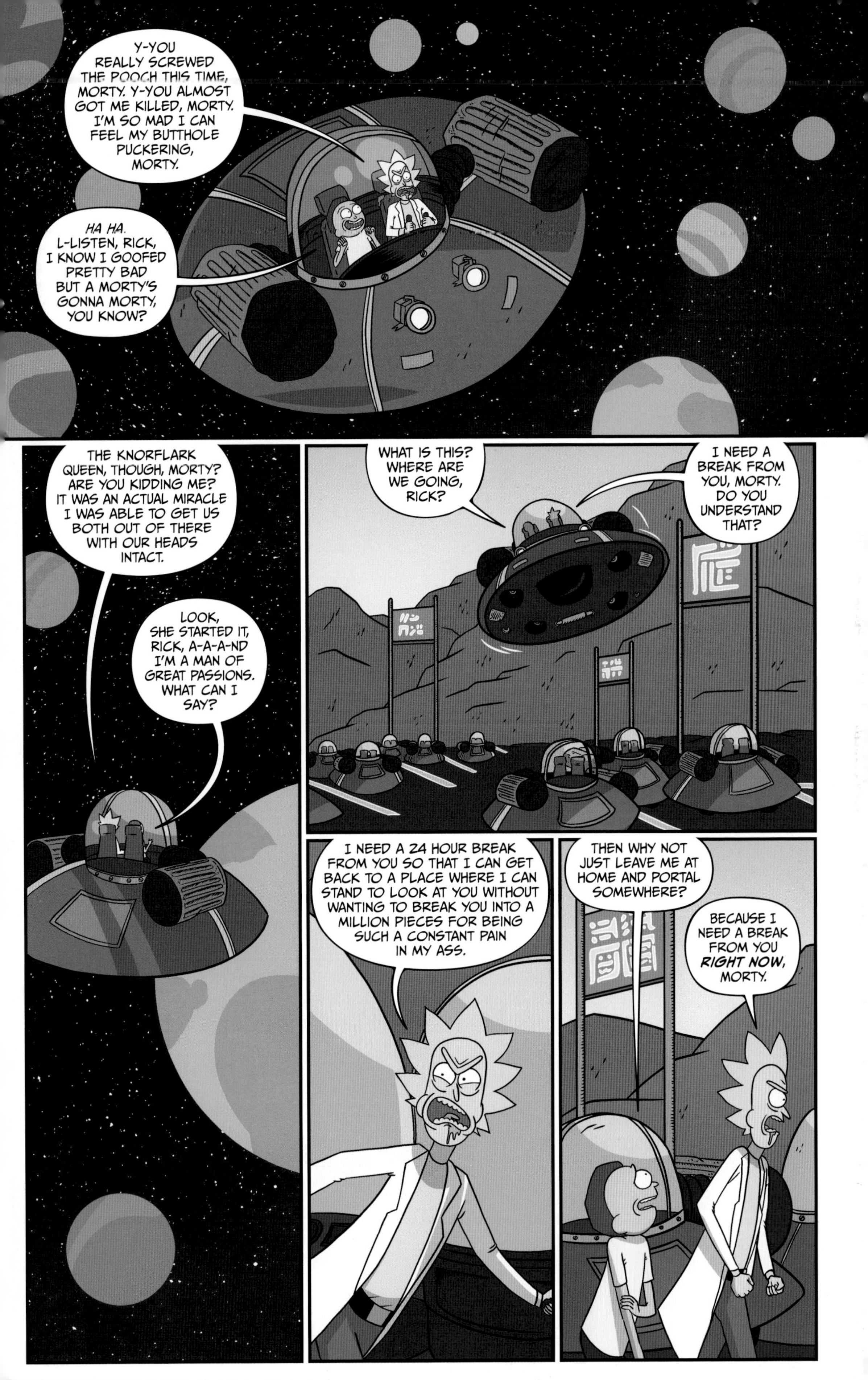
Y-YOU REALLY SCREWED THE POOCH THIS TIME, MORTY. Y-YOU ALMOST GOT ME KILLED, MORTY. I'M SO MAD I CAN FEEL MY BUTTHOLE PUCKERING, MORTY.
HA HA. L-LISTEN, RICK, I KNOW I GOOFED PRETTY BAD BUT A MORTY'S GONNA MORTY, YOU KNOW?
THE KNORFLARK QUEEN, THOUGH, MORTY? ARE YOU KIDDING ME? IT WAS AN ACTUAL MIRACLE I WAS ABLE TO GET US BOTH OUT OF THERE WITH OUR HEADS INTACT.
LOOK, SHE STARTED IT, RICK, A-A-A-ND I'M A MAN OF GREAT PASSIONS. WHAT CAN I SAY?
WHAT IS THIS? WHERE ARE WE GOING, RICK?
I NEED A BREAK FROM YOU, MORTY. DO YOU UNDERSTAND THAT?
I NEED A 24 HOUR BREAK FROM YOU SO THAT I CAN GET BACK TO A PLACE WHERE I CAN STAND TO LOOK AT YOU WITHOUT WANTING TO BREAK YOU INTO A MILLION PIECES FOR BEING SUCH A CONSTANT PAIN IN MY ASS.
THEN WHY NOT JUST LEAVE ME AT HOME AND PORTAL SOMEWHERE?
BECAUSE I NEED A BREAK FROM YOU RIGHT NOW, MORTY.

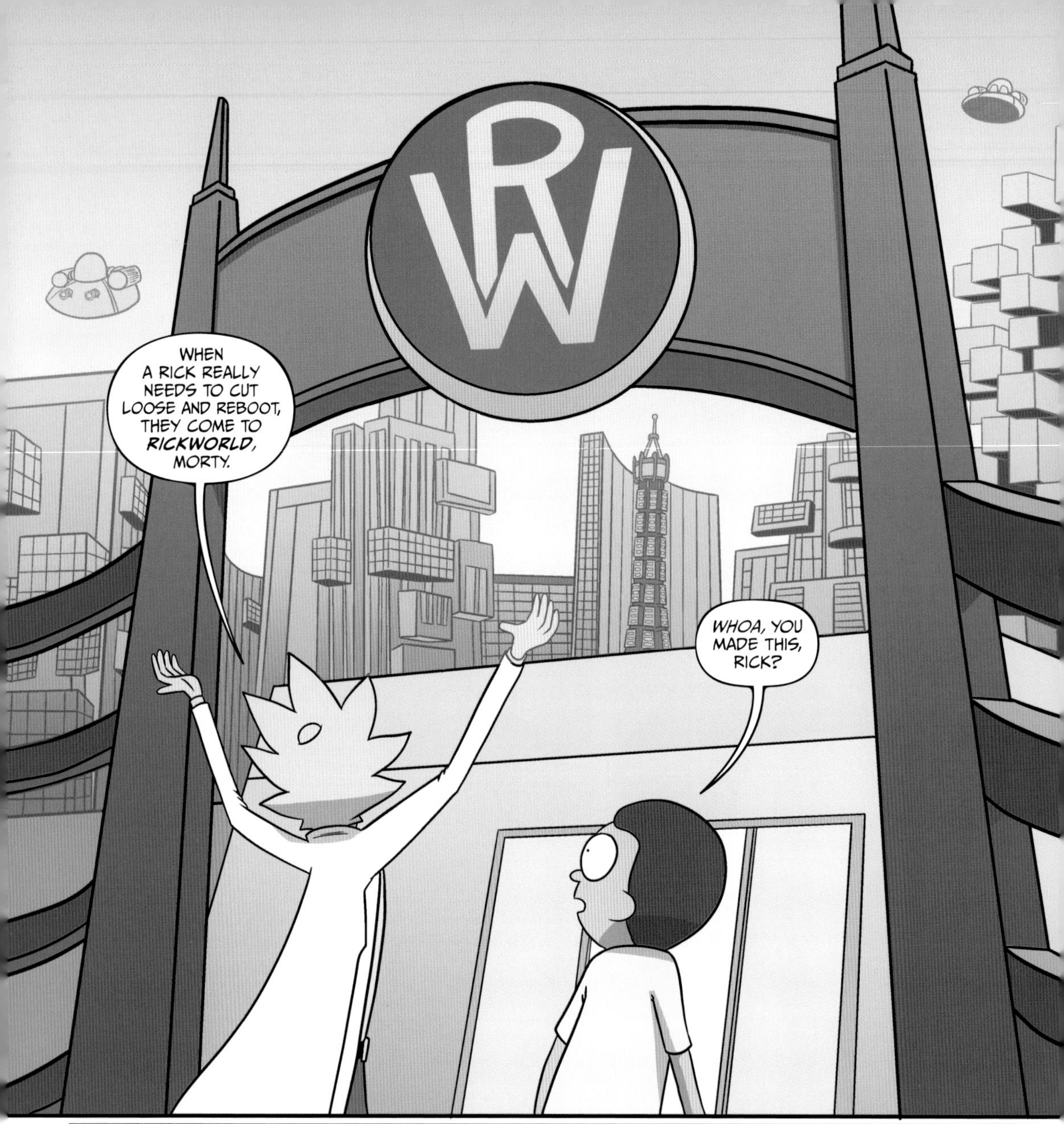
WHEN A RICK REALLY NEEDS TO CUT LOOSE AND REBOOT, THEY COME TO ***RICKWORLD***, MORTY.
WHOA, YOU MADE THIS, RICK?

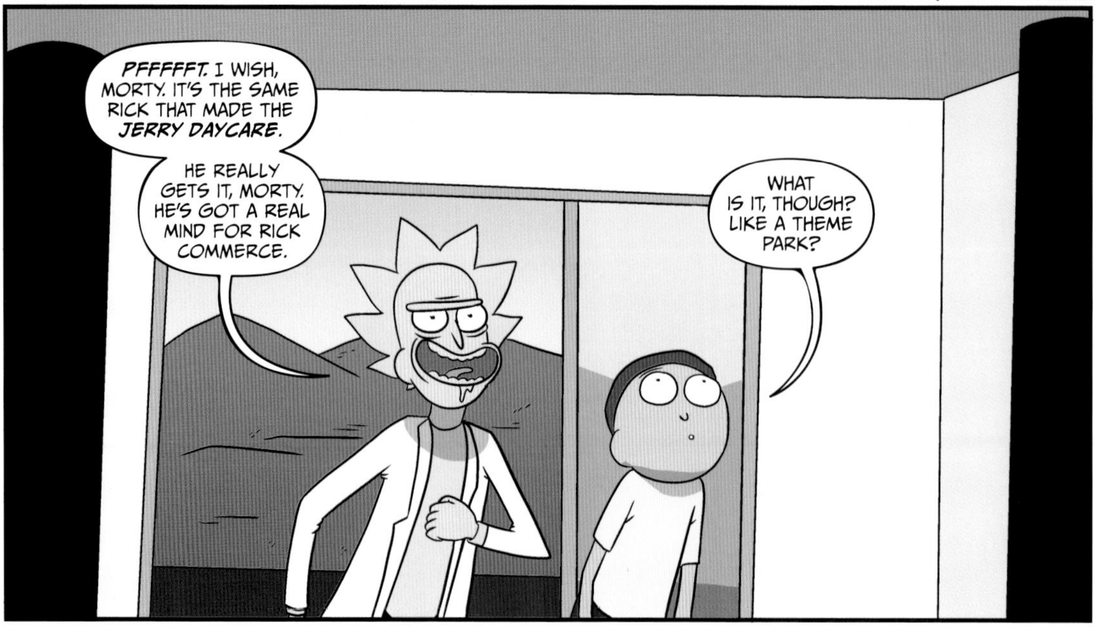
PFFFFFT. I WISH, MORTY. IT'S THE SAME RICK THAT MADE THE ***JERRY DAYCARE***.
HE REALLY GETS IT, MORTY. HE'S GOT A REAL MIND FOR RICK COMMERCE.
WHAT IS IT, THOUGH? LIKE A THEME PARK?

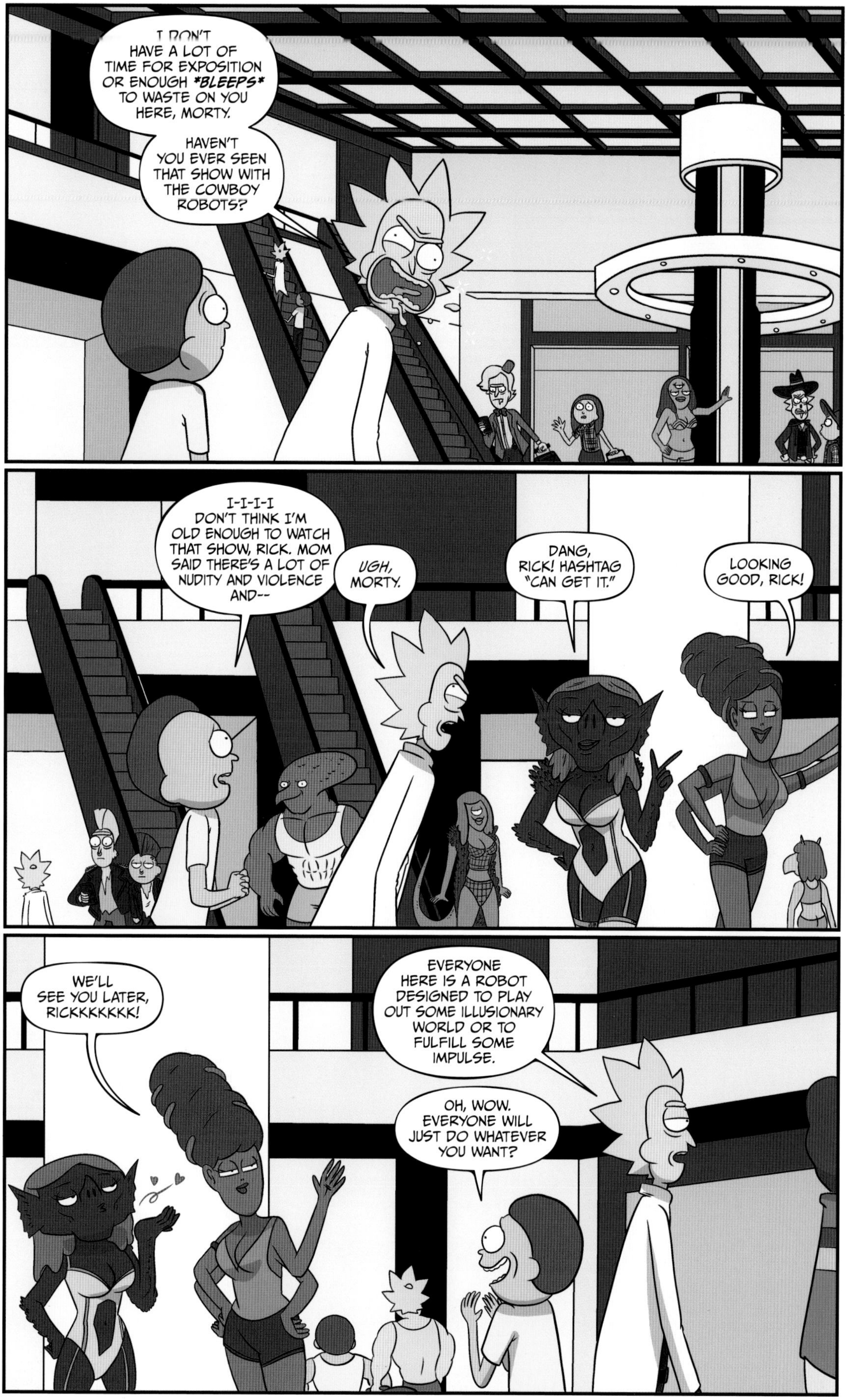
I DON'T HAVE A LOT OF TIME FOR EXPOSITION OR ENOUGH *BLEEPS* TO WASTE ON YOU HERE, MORTY.
HAVEN'T YOU EVER SEEN THAT SHOW WITH THE COWBOY ROBOTS?
I-I-I-I DON'T THINK I'M OLD ENOUGH TO WATCH THAT SHOW, RICK. MOM SAID THERE'S A LOT OF NUDITY AND VIOLENCE AND--
UGH, MORTY.
DANG, RICK! HASHTAG "CAN GET IT."
LOOKING GOOD, RICK!
WE'LL SEE YOU LATER, RICKKKKKKK!
EVERYONE HERE IS A ROBOT DESIGNED TO PLAY OUT SOME ILLUSIONARY WORLD OR TO FULFILL SOME IMPULSE.
OH, WOW. EVERYONE WILL JUST DO WHATEVER YOU WANT?

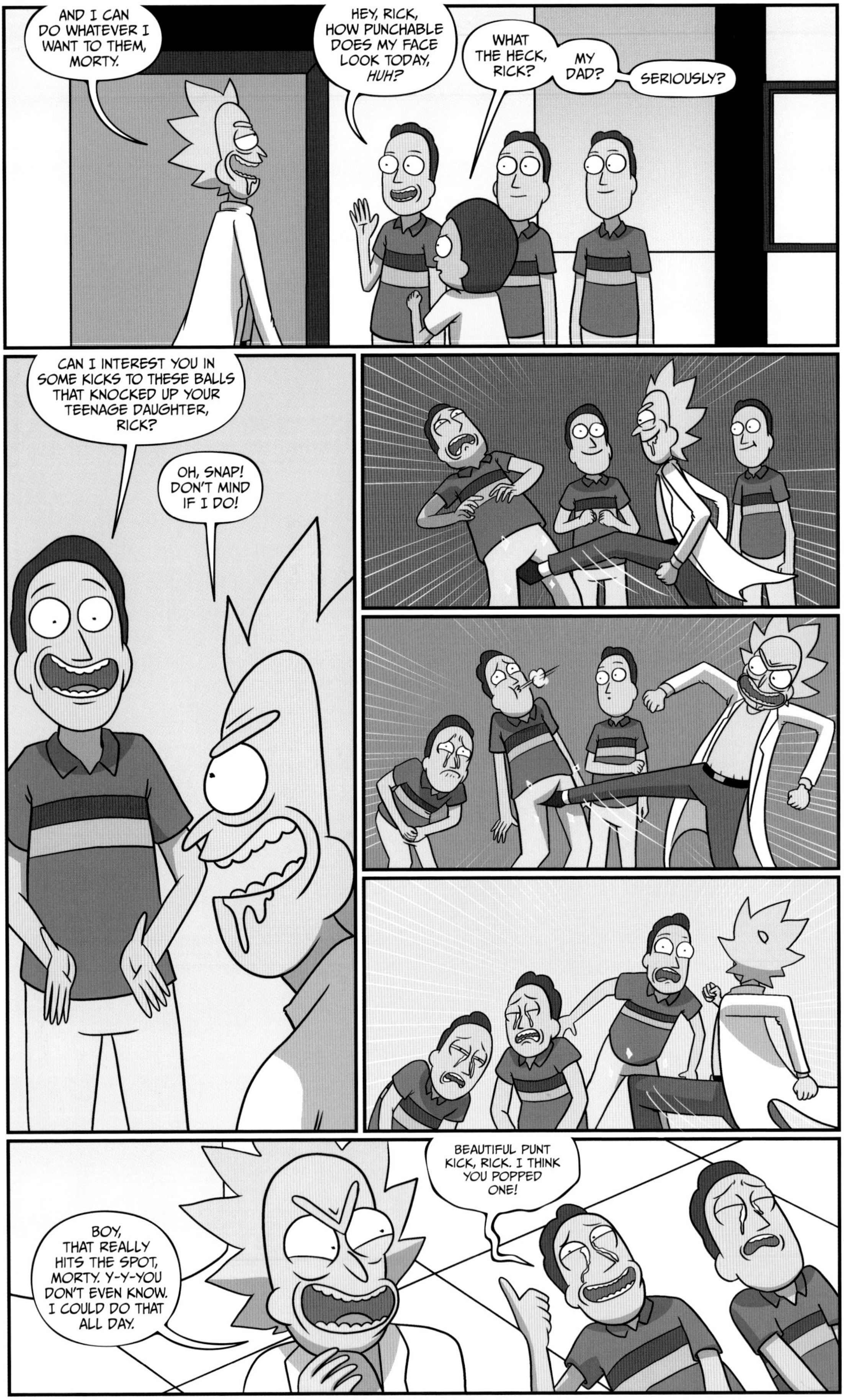
AND I CAN DO WHATEVER I WANT TO THEM, MORTY.
HEY, RICK, HOW PUNCHABLE DOES MY FACE LOOK TODAY, HUH?
WHAT THE HECK, RICK?
MY DAD?
SERIOUSLY?
CAN I INTEREST YOU IN SOME KICKS TO THESE BALLS THAT KNOCKED UP YOUR TEENAGE DAUGHTER, RICK?
OH, SNAP! DON'T MIND IF I DO!
BEAUTIFUL PUNT KICK, RICK. I THINK YOU POPPED ONE!
BOY, THAT REALLY HITS THE SPOT, MORTY. Y-Y-YOU DON'T EVEN KNOW. I COULD DO THAT ALL DAY.

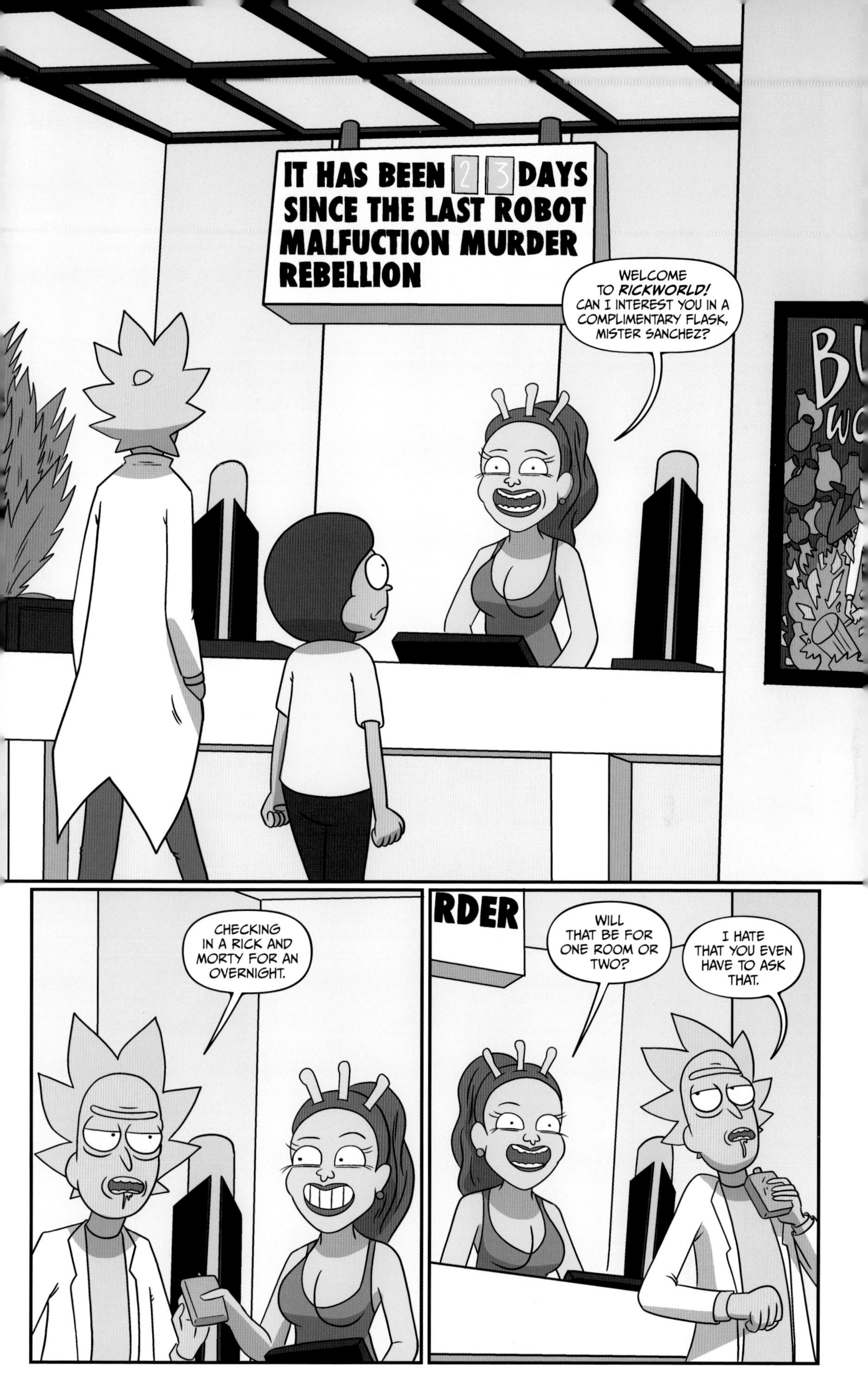
IT HAS BEEN 23 DAYS SINCE THE LAST ROBOT MALFUCTION MURDER REBELLION
WELCOME TO RICKWORLD! CAN I INTEREST YOU IN A COMPLIMENTARY FLASK, MISTER SANCHEZ?
CHECKING IN A RICK AND MORTY FOR AN OVERNIGHT.
RDER
WILL THAT BE FOR ONE ROOM OR TWO?
I HATE THAT YOU EVEN HAVE TO ASK THAT.

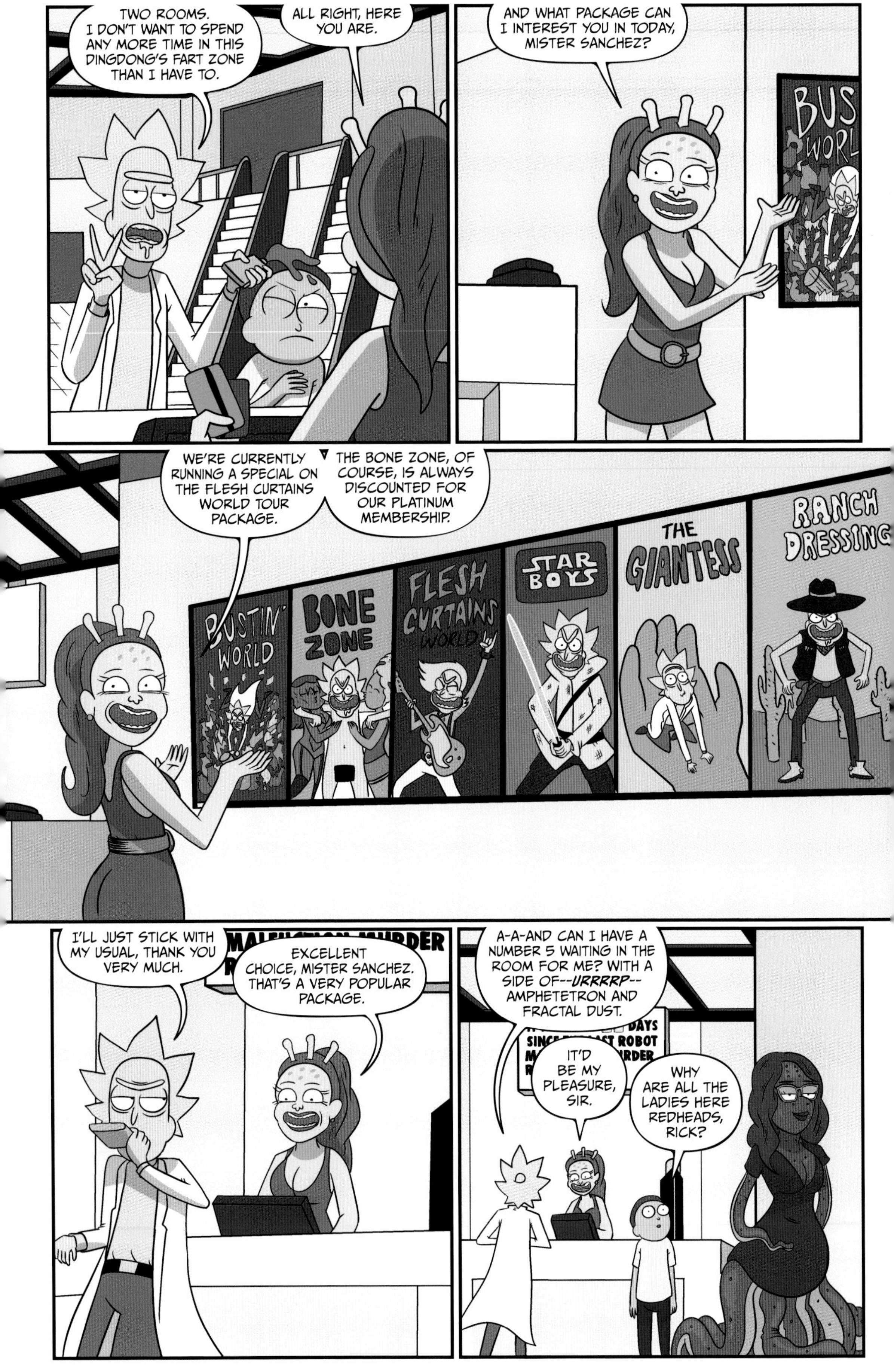
TWO ROOMS. I DON'T WANT TO SPEND ANY MORE TIME IN THIS DINGDONG'S FART ZONE THAN I HAVE TO.
ALL RIGHT, HERE YOU ARE.
AND WHAT PACKAGE CAN I INTEREST YOU IN TODAY, MISTER SANCHEZ?
WE'RE CURRENTLY RUNNING A SPECIAL ON THE FLESH CURTAINS WORLD TOUR PACKAGE.
THE BONE ZONE, OF COURSE, IS ALWAYS DISCOUNTED FOR OUR PLATINUM MEMBERSHIP.
BUSTIN' WORLD
BONE ZONE
FLESH CURTAINS WORLD
STAR BOYS
THE GIANTESS
RANCH DRESSING
I'LL JUST STICK WITH MY USUAL, THANK YOU VERY MUCH.
EXCELLENT CHOICE, MISTER SANCHEZ. THAT'S A VERY POPULAR PACKAGE.
A-A-AND CAN I HAVE A NUMBER 5 WAITING IN THE ROOM FOR ME? WITH A SIDE OF--*URRRRP*-- AMPHETETRON AND FRACTAL DUST.
IT'D BE MY PLEASURE, SIR.
WHY ARE ALL THE LADIES HERE REDHEADS, RICK?

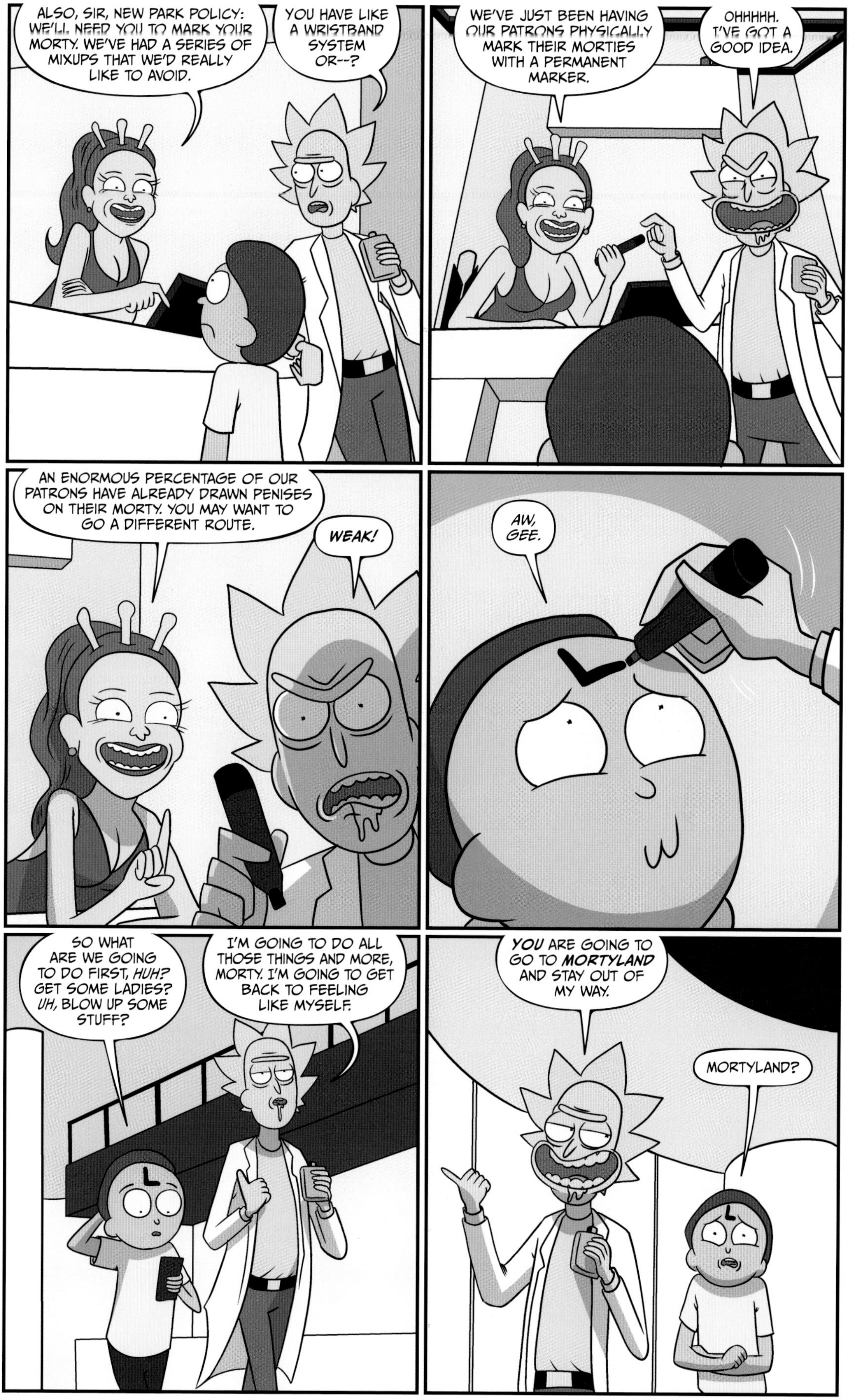
ALSO, SIR, NEW PARK POLICY: WE'LL NEED YOU TO MARK YOUR MORTY. WE'VE HAD A SERIES OF MIXUPS THAT WE'D REALLY LIKE TO AVOID.
YOU HAVE LIKE A WRISTBAND SYSTEM OR--?
WE'VE JUST BEEN HAVING OUR PATRONS PHYSICALLY MARK THEIR MORTIES WITH A PERMANENT MARKER.
OHHHHH. I'VE GOT A GOOD IDEA.
AN ENORMOUS PERCENTAGE OF OUR PATRONS HAVE ALREADY DRAWN PENISES ON THEIR MORTY. YOU MAY WANT TO GO A DIFFERENT ROUTE.
WEAK!
AW, GEE.
SO WHAT ARE WE GOING TO DO FIRST, *HUH?* GET SOME LADIES? *UH,* BLOW UP SOME STUFF?
I'M GOING TO DO ALL THOSE THINGS AND MORE, MORTY. I'M GOING TO GET BACK TO FEELING LIKE MYSELF.
YOU ARE GOING TO GO TO ***MORTYLAND*** AND STAY OUT OF MY WAY.
MORTYLAND?

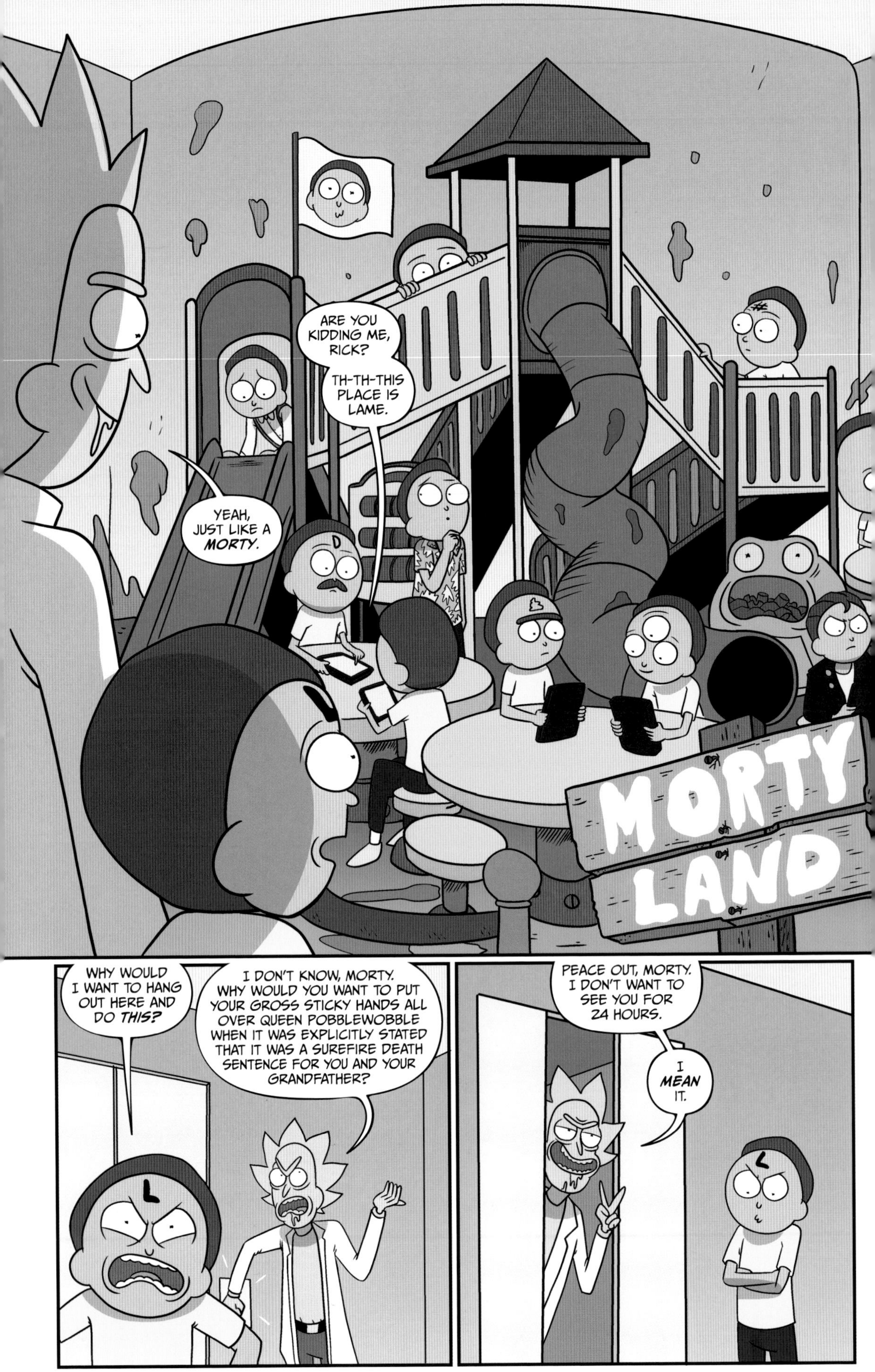
ARE YOU KIDDING ME, RICK?
TH-TH-THIS PLACE IS LAME.
YEAH, JUST LIKE A *MORTY*.
MORTY LAND
WHY WOULD I WANT TO HANG OUT HERE AND DO *THIS?*
I DON'T KNOW, MORTY. WHY WOULD YOU WANT TO PUT YOUR GROSS STICKY HANDS ALL OVER QUEEN POBBLEWOBBLE WHEN IT WAS EXPLICITLY STATED THAT IT WAS A SUREFIRE DEATH SENTENCE FOR YOU AND YOUR GRANDFATHER?
PEACE OUT, MORTY. I DON'T WANT TO SEE YOU FOR 24 HOURS.
I *MEAN* IT.

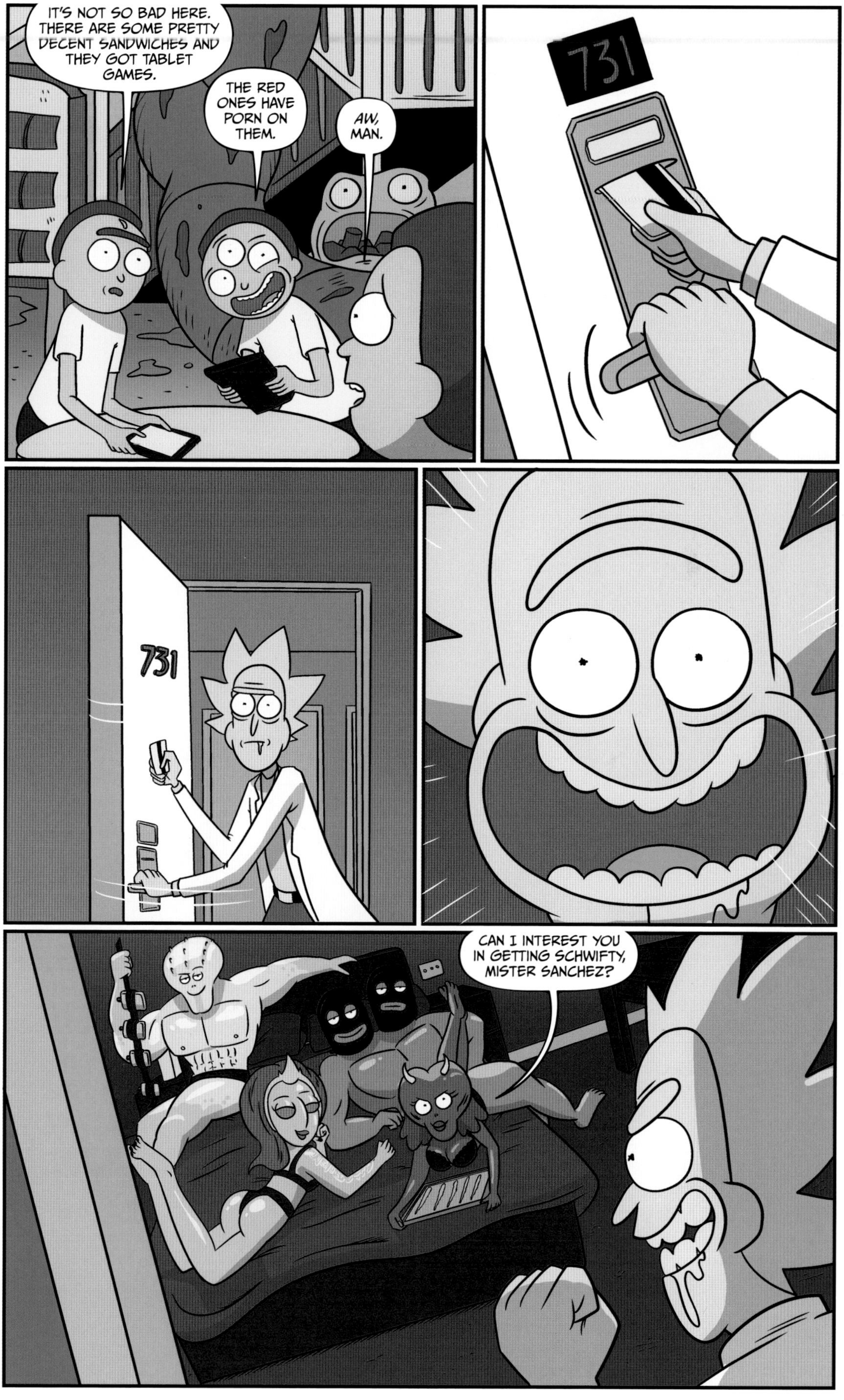
IT'S NOT SO BAD HERE. THERE ARE SOME PRETTY DECENT SANDWICHES AND THEY GOT TABLET GAMES.
THE RED ONES HAVE PORN ON THEM.
AW, MAN.
731
731
CAN I INTEREST YOU IN GETTING SCHWIFTY, MISTER SANCHEZ?

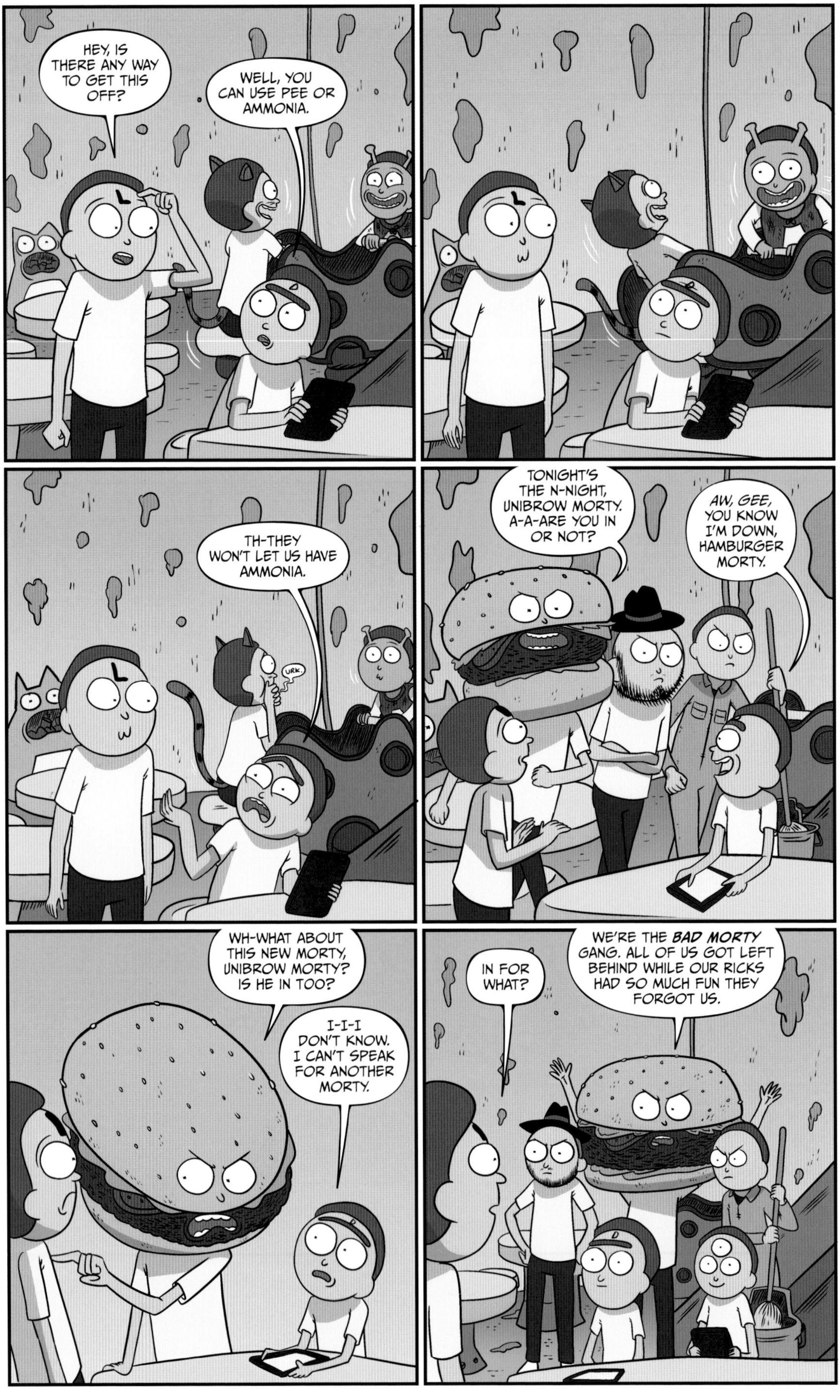
HEY, IS THERE ANY WAY TO GET THIS OFF?
WELL, YOU CAN USE PEE OR AMMONIA.
TH-THEY WON'T LET US HAVE AMMONIA.
URK.
TONIGHT'S THE N-NIGHT, UNIBROW MORTY. A-A-ARE YOU IN OR NOT?
AW, GEE, YOU KNOW I'M DOWN, HAMBURGER MORTY.
WH-WHAT ABOUT THIS NEW MORTY, UNIBROW MORTY? IS HE IN TOO?
I-I-I DON'T KNOW. I CAN'T SPEAK FOR ANOTHER MORTY.
IN FOR WHAT?
WE'RE THE BAD MORTY GANG. ALL OF US GOT LEFT BEHIND WHILE OUR RICKS HAD SO MUCH FUN THEY FORGOT US.

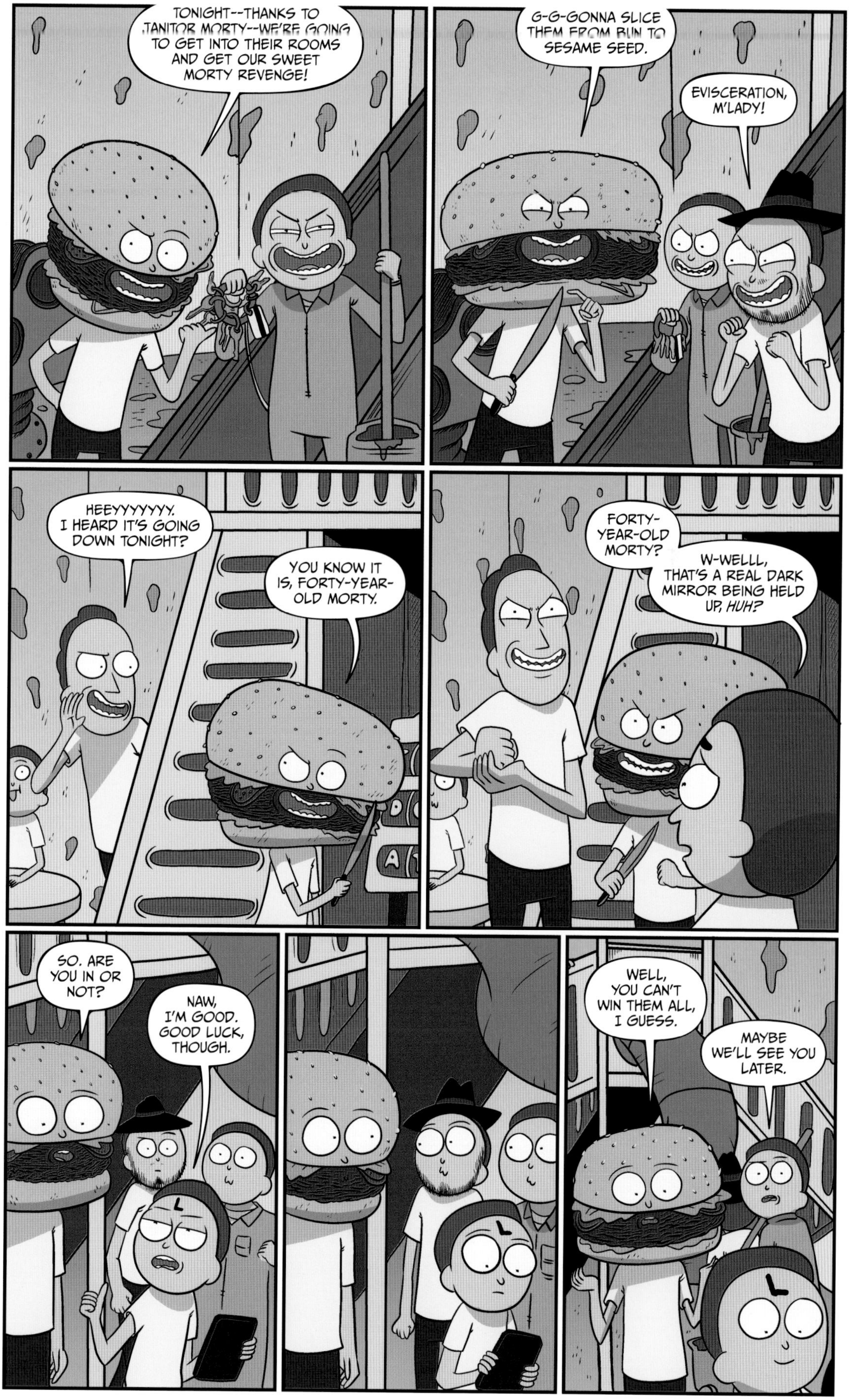
TONIGHT--THANKS TO JANITOR MORTY--WE'RE GOING TO GET INTO THEIR ROOMS AND GET OUR SWEET MORTY REVENGE!
G-G-GONNA SLICE THEM FROM BUN TO SESAME SEED.
EVISCERATION, M'LADY!
HEEYYYYYYY. I HEARD IT'S GOING DOWN TONIGHT?
YOU KNOW IT IS, FORTY-YEAR-OLD MORTY.
FORTY-YEAR-OLD MORTY?
W-WELLL, THAT'S A REAL DARK MIRROR BEING HELD UP, *HUH?*
SO. ARE YOU IN OR NOT?
NAW, I'M GOOD. GOOD LUCK, THOUGH.
WELL, YOU CAN'T WIN THEM ALL, I GUESS.
MAYBE WE'LL SEE YOU LATER.

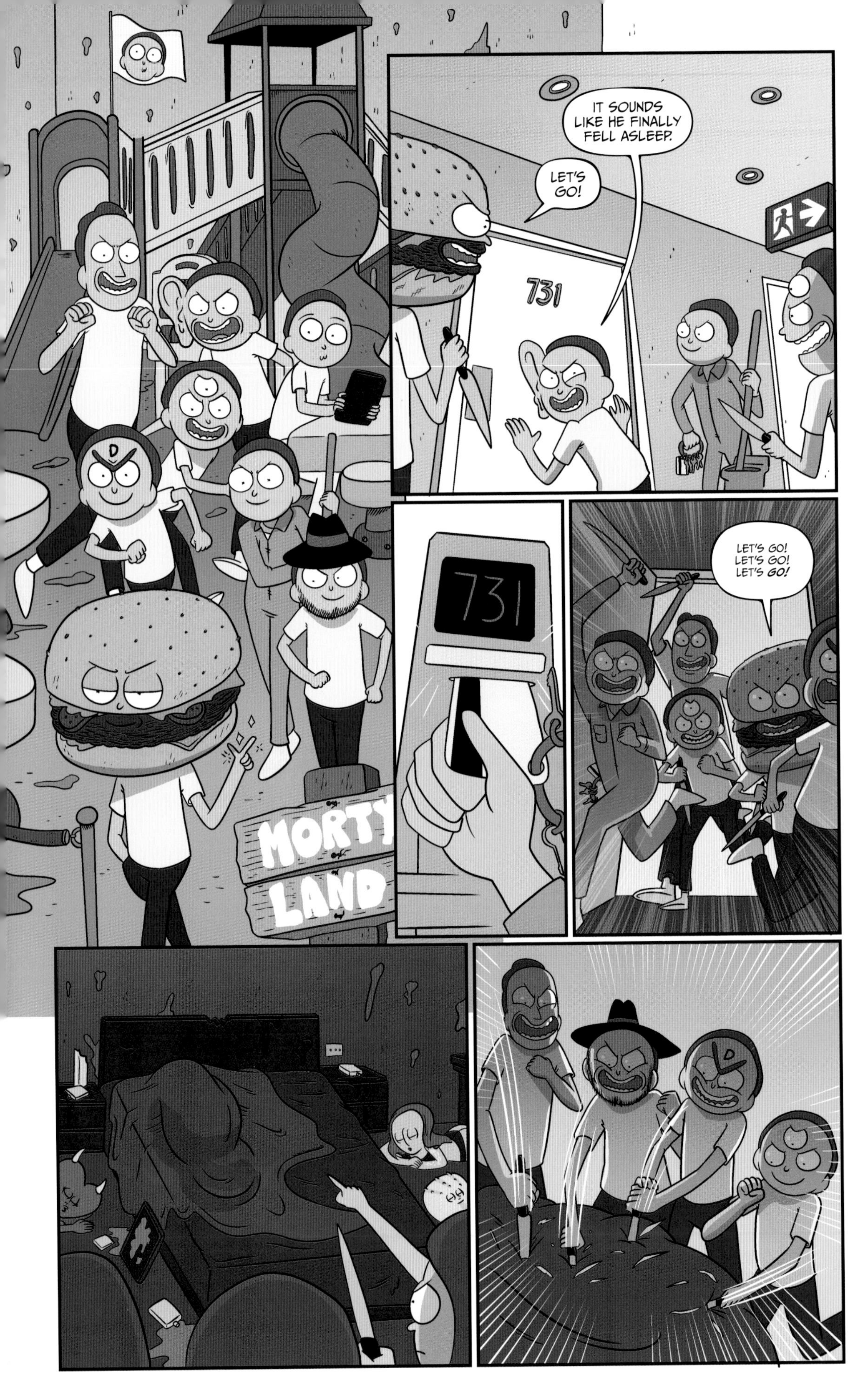
MORTY LAND
IT SOUNDS LIKE HE FINALLY FELL ASLEEP.
LET'S GO!
731
731
LET'S GO! LET'S GO! LET'S GO!

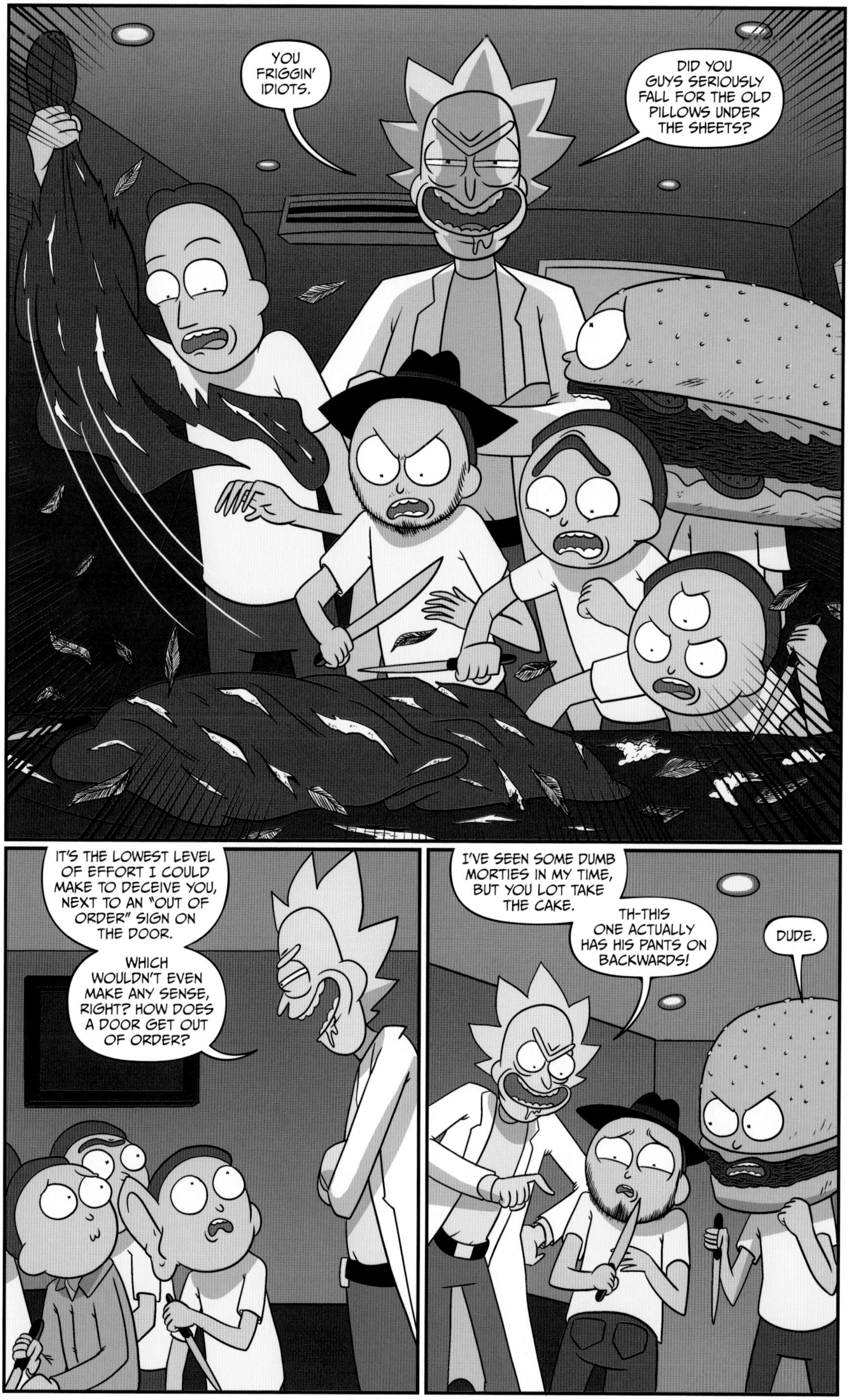
YOU FRIGGIN' IDIOTS.
DID YOU GUYS SERIOUSLY FALL FOR THE OLD PILLOWS UNDER THE SHEETS?
IT'S THE LOWEST LEVEL OF EFFORT I COULD MAKE TO DECEIVE YOU, NEXT TO AN "OUT OF ORDER" SIGN ON THE DOOR.
WHICH WOULDN'T EVEN MAKE ANY SENSE, RIGHT? HOW DOES A DOOR GET OUT OF ORDER?
I'VE SEEN SOME DUMB MORTIES IN MY TIME, BUT YOU LOT TAKE THE CAKE.
TH-THIS ONE ACTUALLY HAS HIS PANTS ON BACKWARDS!
DUDE.

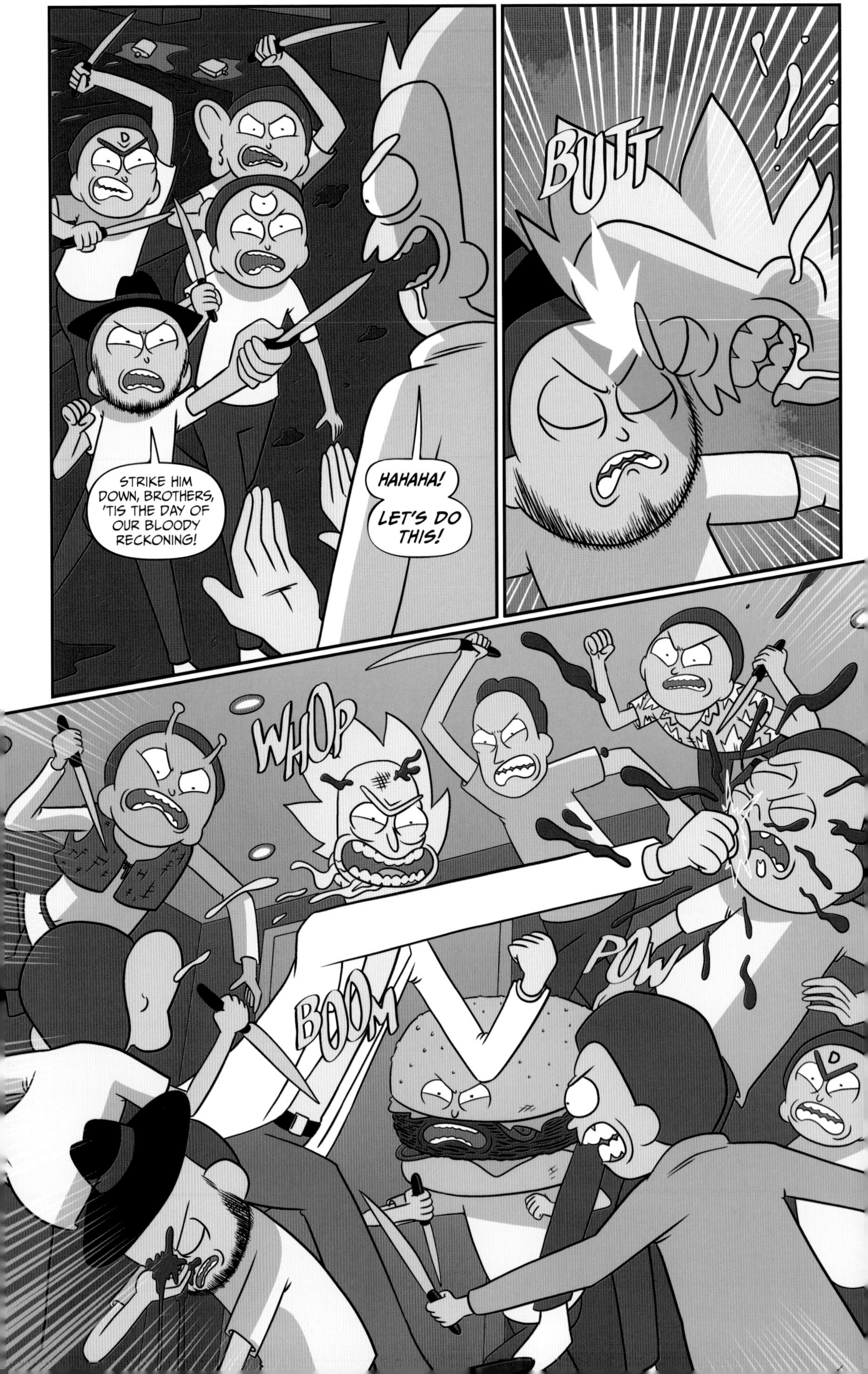
STRIKE HIM DOWN, BROTHERS, 'TIS THE DAY OF OUR BLOODY RECKONING!
HAHAHA!
LET'S DO THIS!
BUTT
WHOP
POW
BOOM

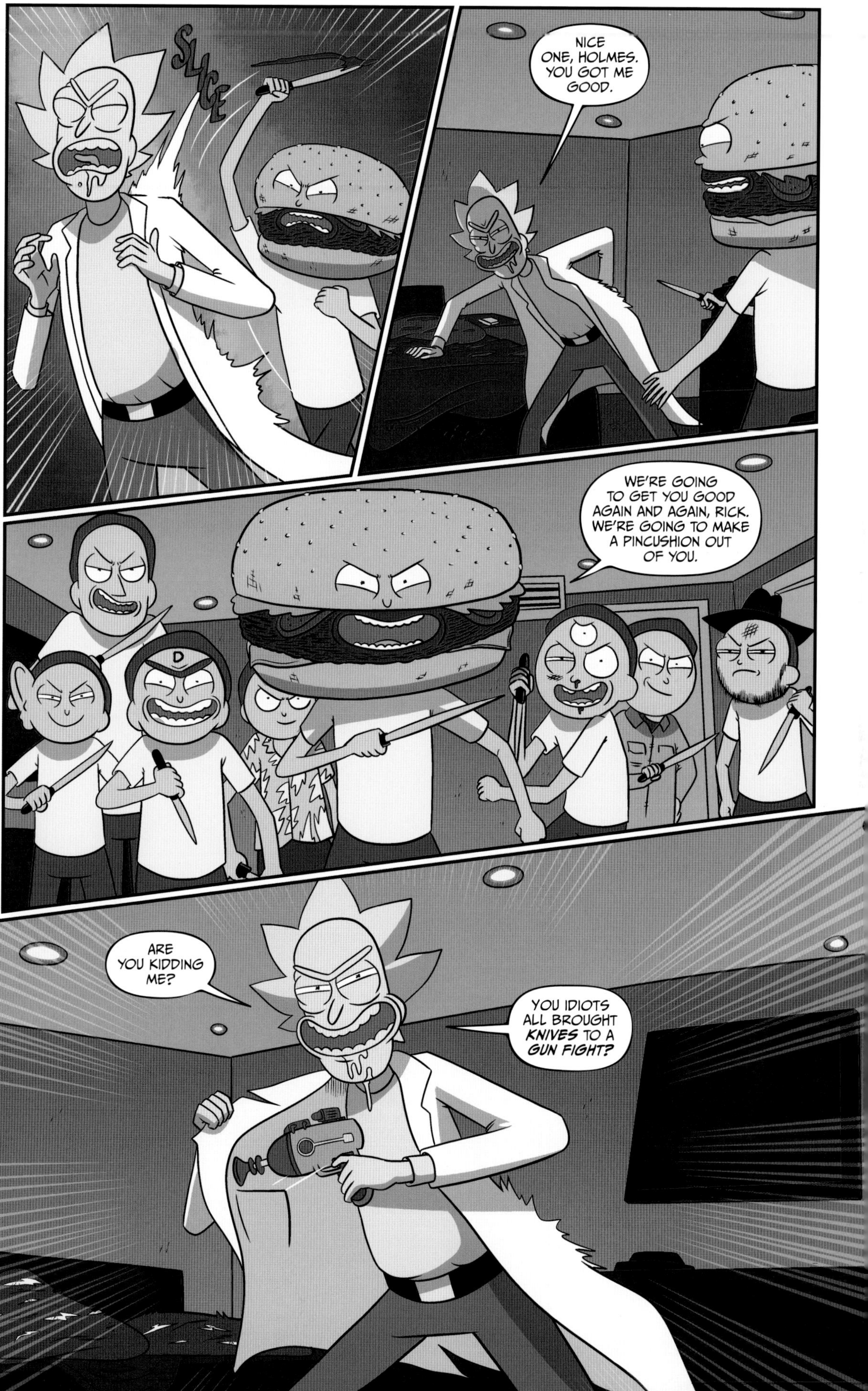
SLICE
NICE ONE, HOLMES. YOU GOT ME GOOD.
WE'RE GOING TO GET YOU GOOD AGAIN AND AGAIN, RICK. WE'RE GOING TO MAKE A PINCUSHION OUT OF YOU.
D
ARE YOU KIDDING ME?
YOU IDIOTS ALL BROUGHT *KNIVES* TO A *GUN FIGHT?*

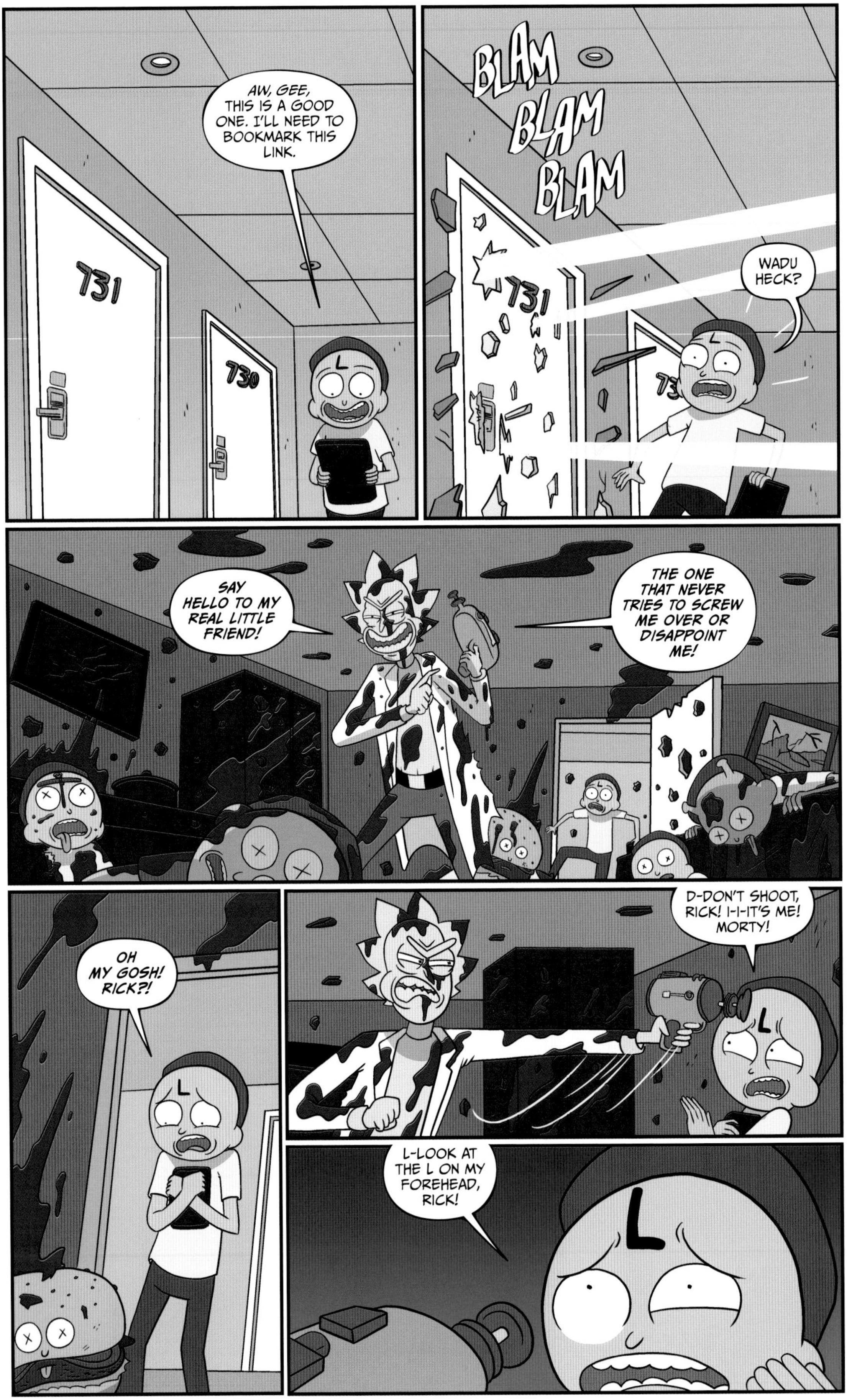
AW, GEE, THIS IS A GOOD ONE. I'LL NEED TO BOOKMARK THIS LINK.
731
730
BLAM BLAM BLAM
WADU HECK?
SAY HELLO TO MY REAL LITTLE FRIEND!
THE ONE THAT NEVER TRIES TO SCREW ME OVER OR DISAPPOINT ME!
OH MY GOSH! RICK?!
D-DON'T SHOOT, RICK! I-I-IT'S ME! MORTY!
L-LOOK AT THE L ON MY FOREHEAD, RICK!

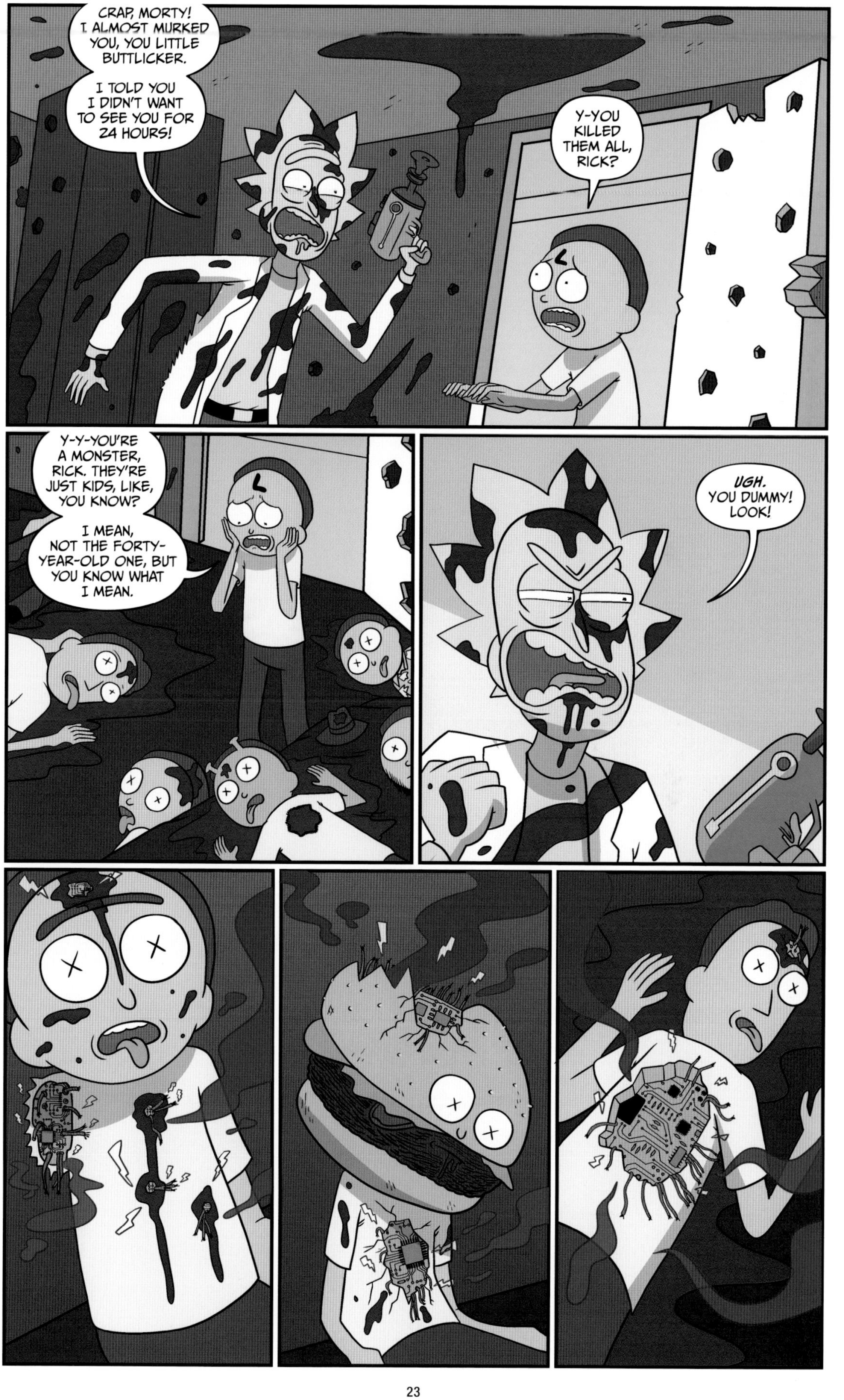
CRAP, MORTY! I ALMOST MURKED YOU, YOU LITTLE BUTTLICKER.
I TOLD YOU I DIDN'T WANT TO SEE YOU FOR 24 HOURS!
Y-YOU KILLED THEM ALL, RICK?
Y-Y-YOU'RE A MONSTER, RICK. THEY'RE JUST KIDS, LIKE, YOU KNOW?
I MEAN, NOT THE FORTY-YEAR-OLD ONE, BUT YOU KNOW WHAT I MEAN.
UGH. YOU DUMMY! LOOK!

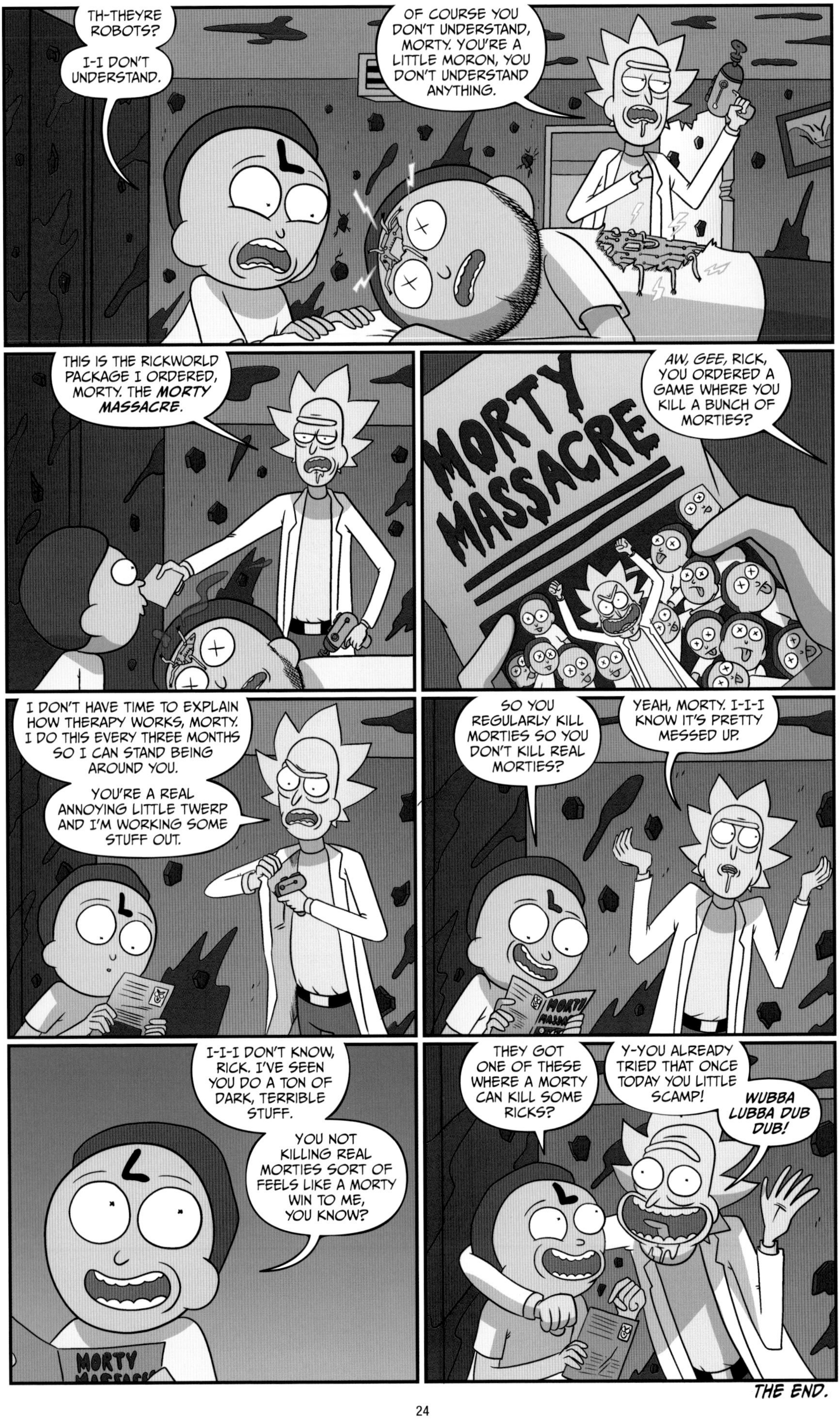
TH-THEYRE ROBOTS?
I-I DON'T UNDERSTAND.
OF COURSE YOU DON'T UNDERSTAND, MORTY. YOU'RE A LITTLE MORON, YOU DON'T UNDERSTAND ANYTHING.
THIS IS THE RICKWORLD PACKAGE I ORDERED, MORTY. THE *MORTY MASSACRE*.
MORTY MASSACRE
AW, GEE, RICK, YOU ORDERED A GAME WHERE YOU KILL A BUNCH OF MORTIES?
I DON'T HAVE TIME TO EXPLAIN HOW THERAPY WORKS, MORTY. I DO THIS EVERY THREE MONTHS SO I CAN STAND BEING AROUND YOU.
YOU'RE A REAL ANNOYING LITTLE TWERP AND I'M WORKING SOME STUFF OUT.
SO YOU REGULARLY KILL MORTIES SO YOU DON'T KILL REAL MORTIES?
YEAH, MORTY. I-I-I KNOW IT'S PRETTY MESSED UP.
I-I-I DON'T KNOW, RICK. I'VE SEEN YOU DO A TON OF DARK, TERRIBLE STUFF.
YOU NOT KILLING REAL MORTIES SORT OF FEELS LIKE A MORTY WIN TO ME, YOU KNOW?
MORTY
THEY GOT ONE OF THESE WHERE A MORTY CAN KILL SOME RICKS?
Y-YOU ALREADY TRIED THAT ONCE TODAY YOU LITTLE SCAMP!
WUBBA LUBBA DUB DUB!

THE END.

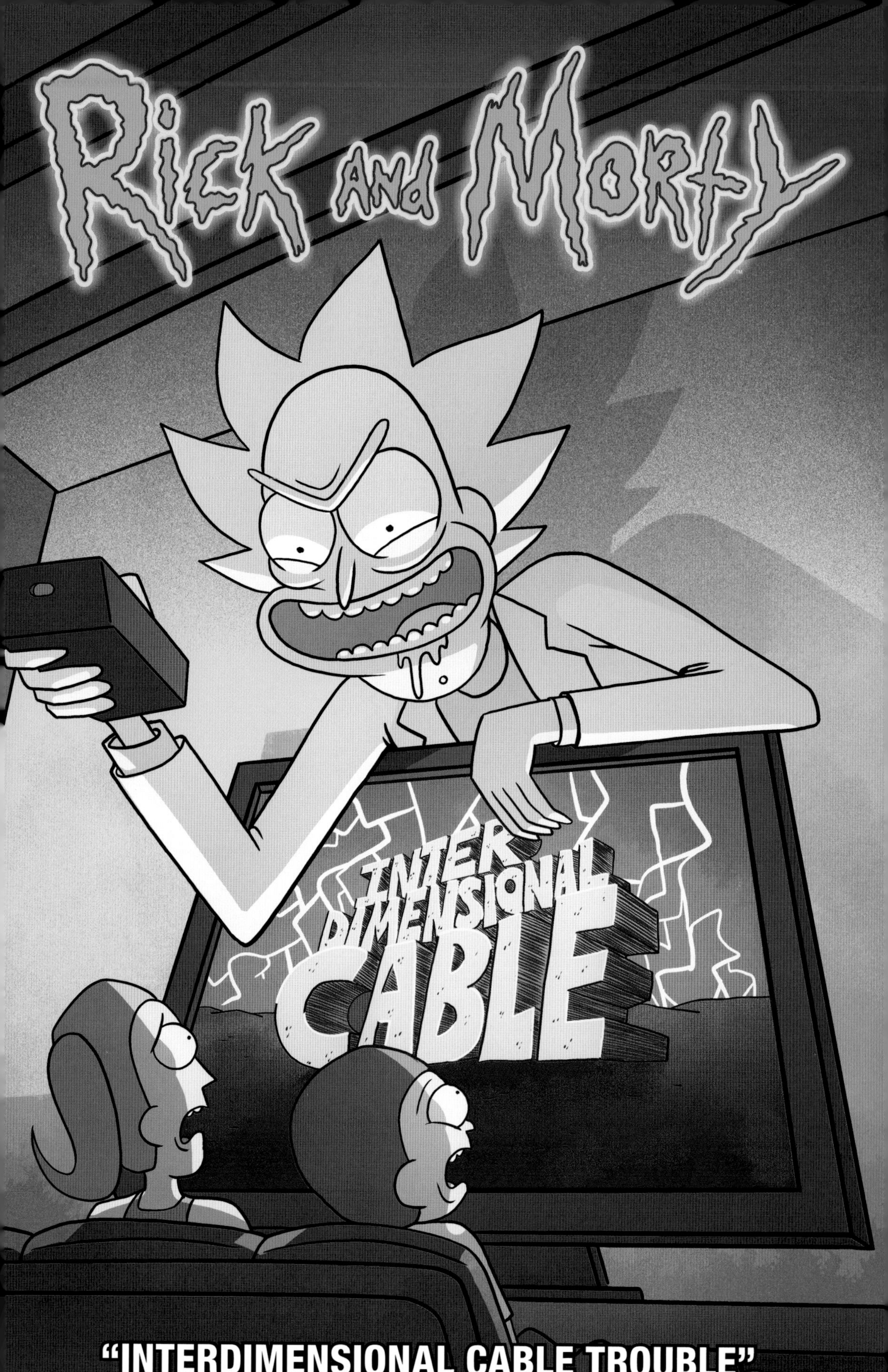
Rick and Morty™
INTER DIMENSIONAL CABLE

"INTERDIMENSIONAL CABLE TROUBLE"

WRITTEN BY **KYLE STARKS** ILLUSTRATED BY **PUESTE** COLORED BY **SARAH STERN** LETTERED BY **CRANK!**

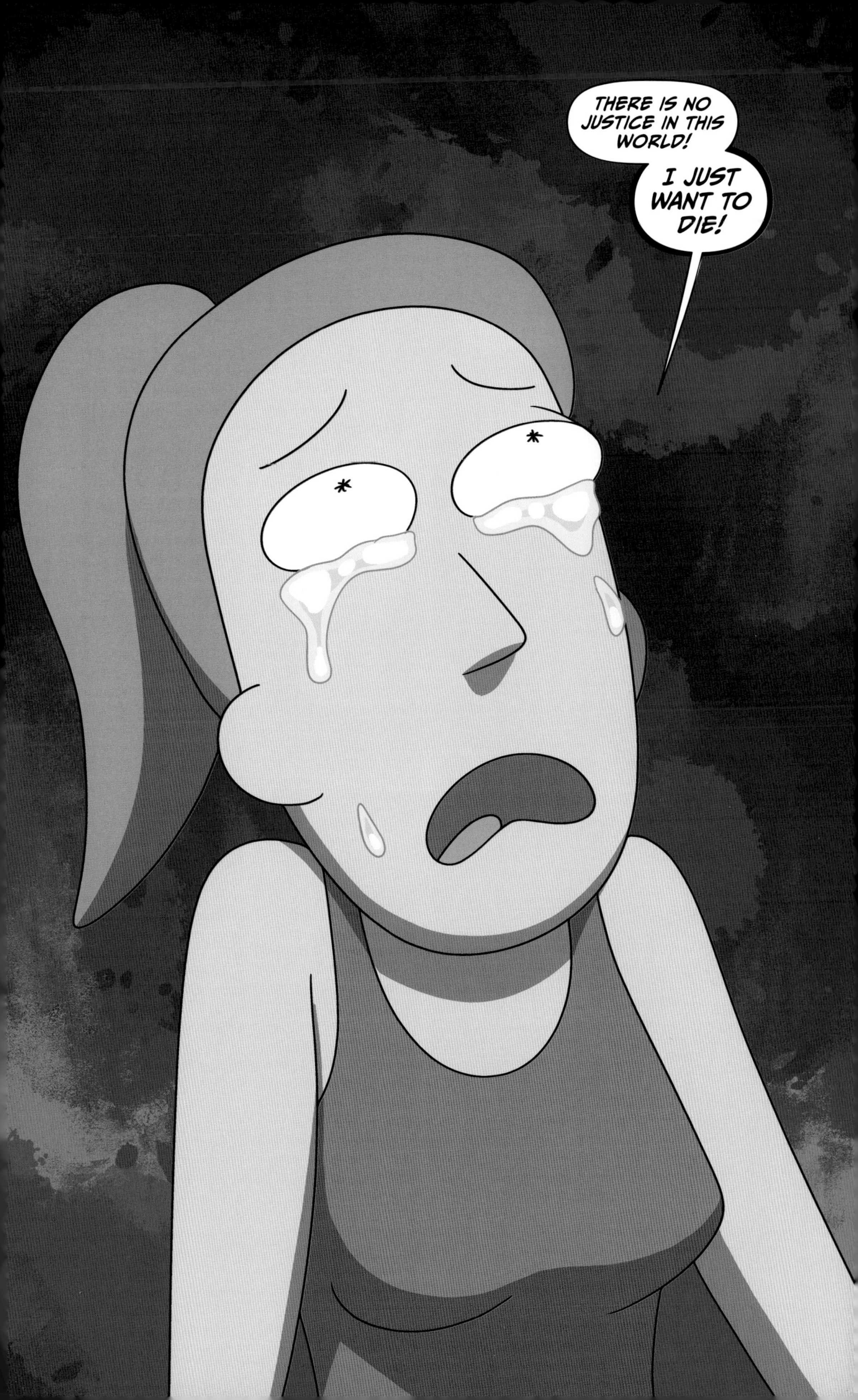
THERE IS NO JUSTICE IN THIS WORLD!
I JUST WANT TO DIE!

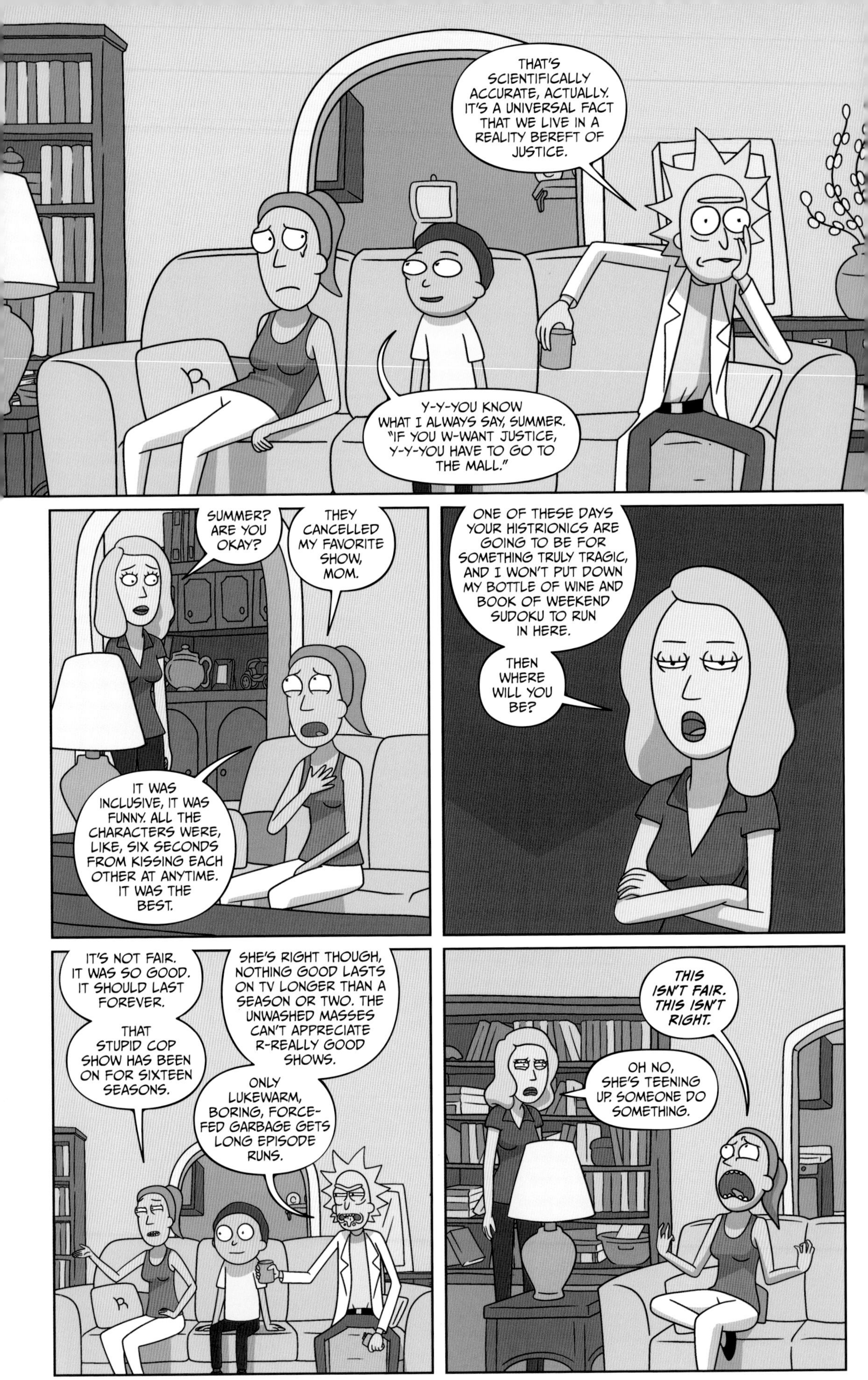
THAT'S SCIENTIFICALLY ACCURATE, ACTUALLY. IT'S A UNIVERSAL FACT THAT WE LIVE IN A REALITY BEREFT OF JUSTICE.
Y-Y-YOU KNOW WHAT I ALWAYS SAY, SUMMER. "IF YOU W-WANT JUSTICE, Y-Y-YOU HAVE TO GO TO THE MALL."
SUMMER? ARE YOU OKAY?
THEY CANCELLED MY FAVORITE SHOW, MOM.
IT WAS INCLUSIVE, IT WAS FUNNY. ALL THE CHARACTERS WERE, LIKE, SIX SECONDS FROM KISSING EACH OTHER AT ANYTIME. IT WAS THE BEST.
ONE OF THESE DAYS YOUR HISTRIONICS ARE GOING TO BE FOR SOMETHING TRULY TRAGIC, AND I WON'T PUT DOWN MY BOTTLE OF WINE AND BOOK OF WEEKEND SUDOKU TO RUN IN HERE.
THEN WHERE WILL YOU BE?
IT'S NOT FAIR. IT WAS SO GOOD. IT SHOULD LAST FOREVER.
THAT STUPID COP SHOW HAS BEEN ON FOR SIXTEEN SEASONS.
SHE'S RIGHT THOUGH, NOTHING GOOD LASTS ON TV LONGER THAN A SEASON OR TWO. THE UNWASHED MASSES CAN'T APPRECIATE R-REALLY GOOD SHOWS.
ONLY LUKEWARM, BORING, FORCE-FED GARBAGE GETS LONG EPISODE RUNS.
THIS ISN'T FAIR. THIS ISN'T RIGHT.
OH NO, SHE'S TEENING UP. SOMEONE DO SOMETHING.

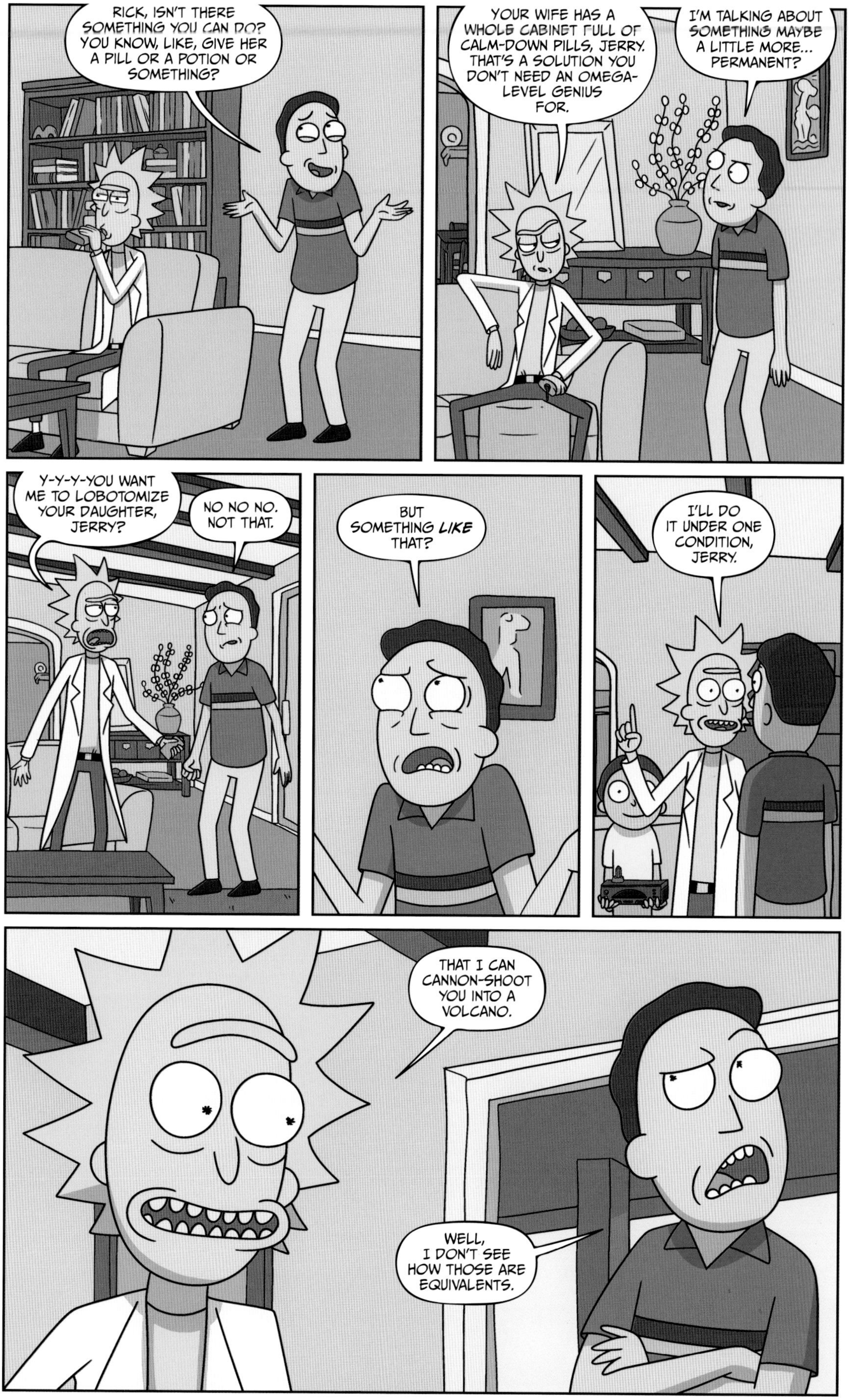
RICK, ISN'T THERE SOMETHING YOU CAN DO? YOU KNOW, LIKE, GIVE HER A PILL OR A POTION OR SOMETHING?
YOUR WIFE HAS A WHOLE CABINET FULL OF CALM-DOWN PILLS, JERRY. THAT'S A SOLUTION YOU DON'T NEED AN OMEGA-LEVEL GENIUS FOR.
I'M TALKING ABOUT SOMETHING MAYBE A LITTLE MORE... PERMANENT?
Y-Y-Y-YOU WANT ME TO LOBOTOMIZE YOUR DAUGHTER, JERRY?
NO NO NO. NOT THAT.
BUT SOMETHING *LIKE* THAT?
I'LL DO IT UNDER ONE CONDITION, JERRY.
THAT I CAN CANNON-SHOOT YOU INTO A VOLCANO.
WELL, I DON'T SEE HOW THOSE ARE EQUIVALENTS.

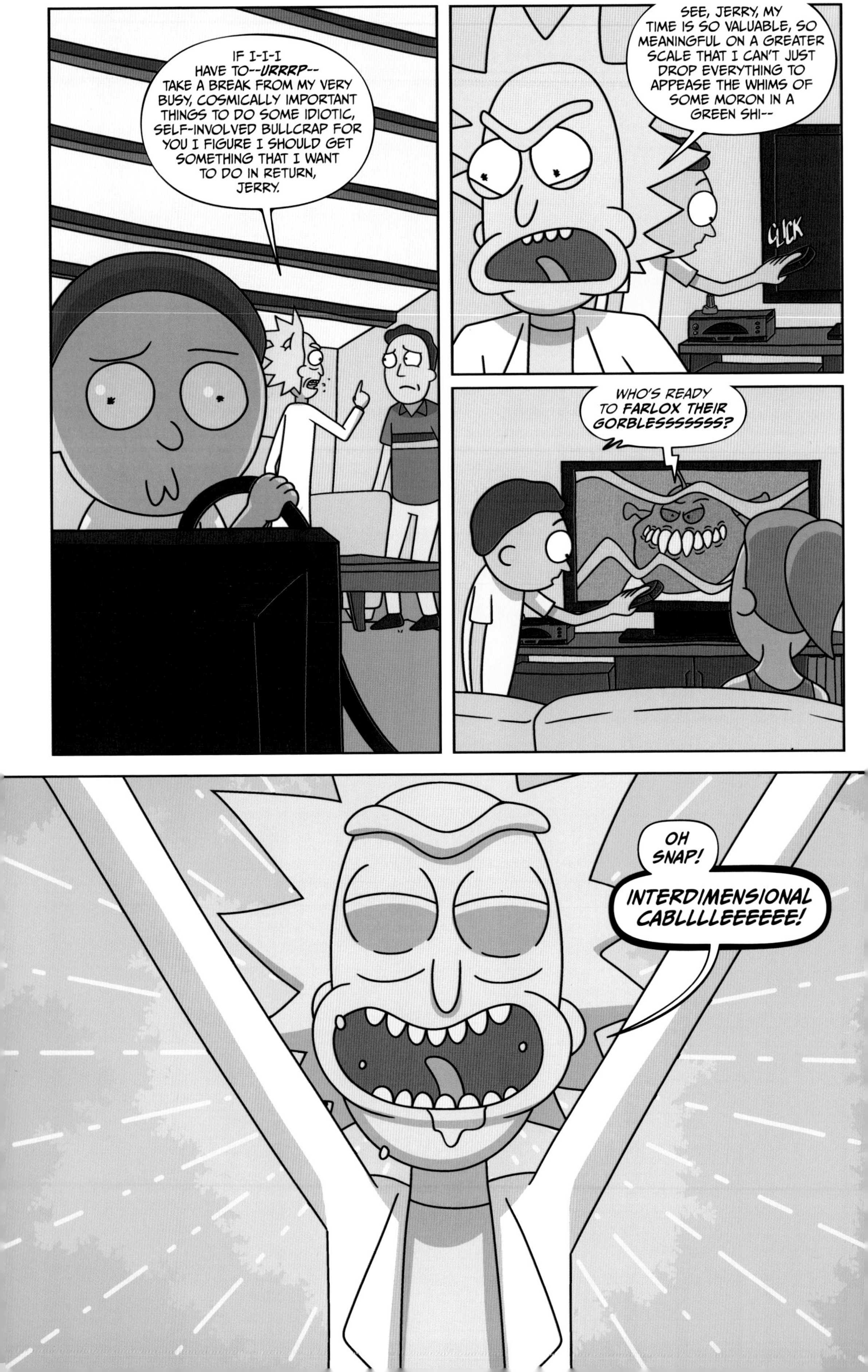
IF I-I-I HAVE TO--URRRP-- TAKE A BREAK FROM MY VERY BUSY, COSMICALLY IMPORTANT THINGS TO DO SOME IDIOTIC, SELF-INVOLVED BULLCRAP FOR YOU I FIGURE I SHOULD GET SOMETHING THAT I WANT TO DO IN RETURN, JERRY.
SEE, JERRY, MY TIME IS SO VALUABLE, SO MEANINGFUL ON A GREATER SCALE THAT I CAN'T JUST DROP EVERYTHING TO APPEASE THE WHIMS OF SOME MORON IN A GREEN SHI--
CLICK
WHO'S READY TO FARLOX THEIR GORBLESSSSSSS?
OH SNAP!
INTERDIMENSIONAL CABLLLLEEEEEE!

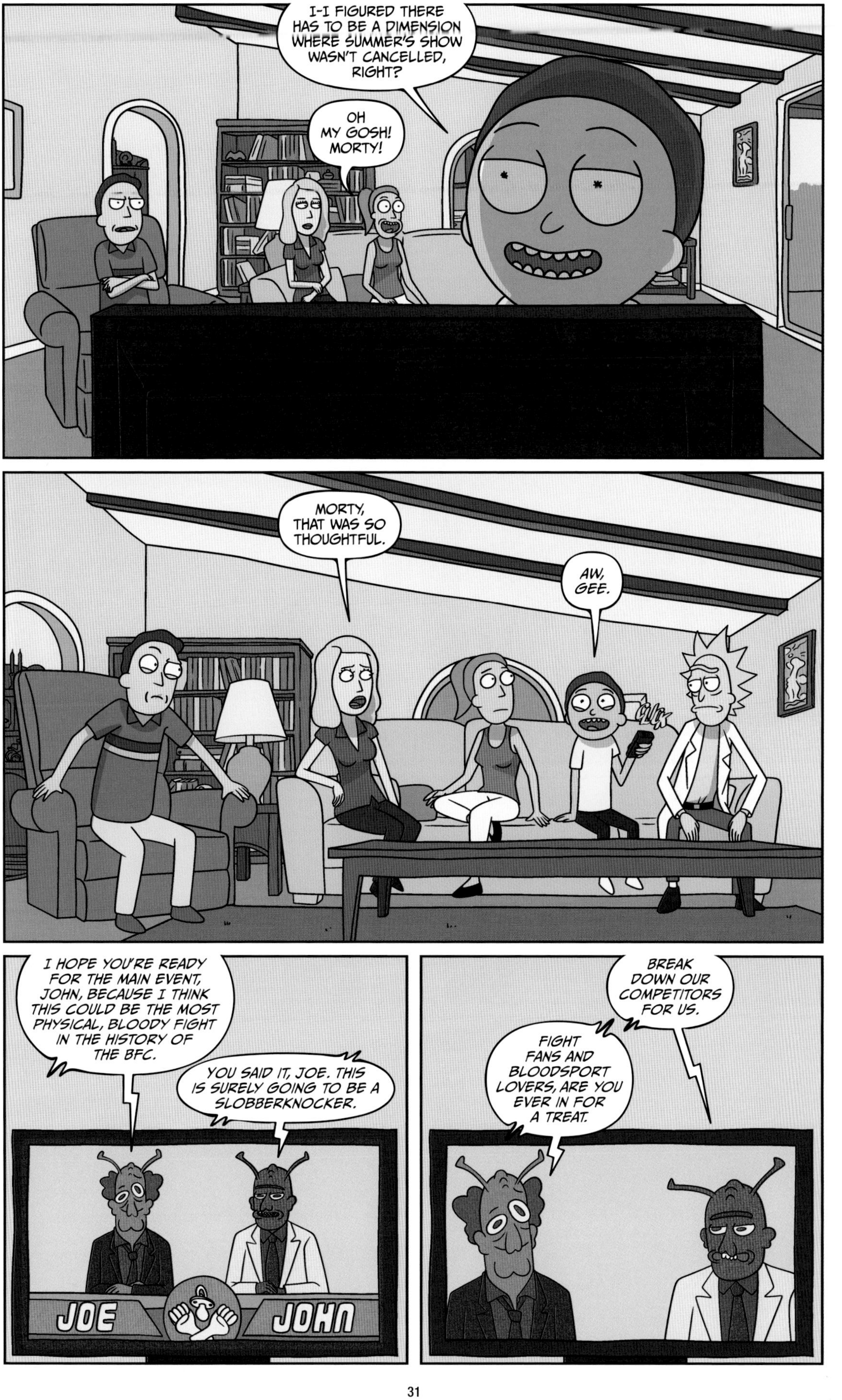
I-I FIGURED THERE HAS TO BE A DIMENSION WHERE SUMMER'S SHOW WASN'T CANCELLED, RIGHT?
OH MY GOSH! MORTY!
MORTY, THAT WAS SO THOUGHTFUL.
AW, GEE.
CLICK
I HOPE YOU'RE READY FOR THE MAIN EVENT, JOHN, BECAUSE I THINK THIS COULD BE THE MOST PHYSICAL, BLOODY FIGHT IN THE HISTORY OF THE BFC.
YOU SAID IT, JOE. THIS IS SURELY GOING TO BE A SLOBBERKNOCKER.
JOE
JOHN
FIGHT FANS AND BLOODSPORT LOVERS, ARE YOU EVER IN FOR A TREAT.
BREAK DOWN OUR COMPETITORS FOR US.

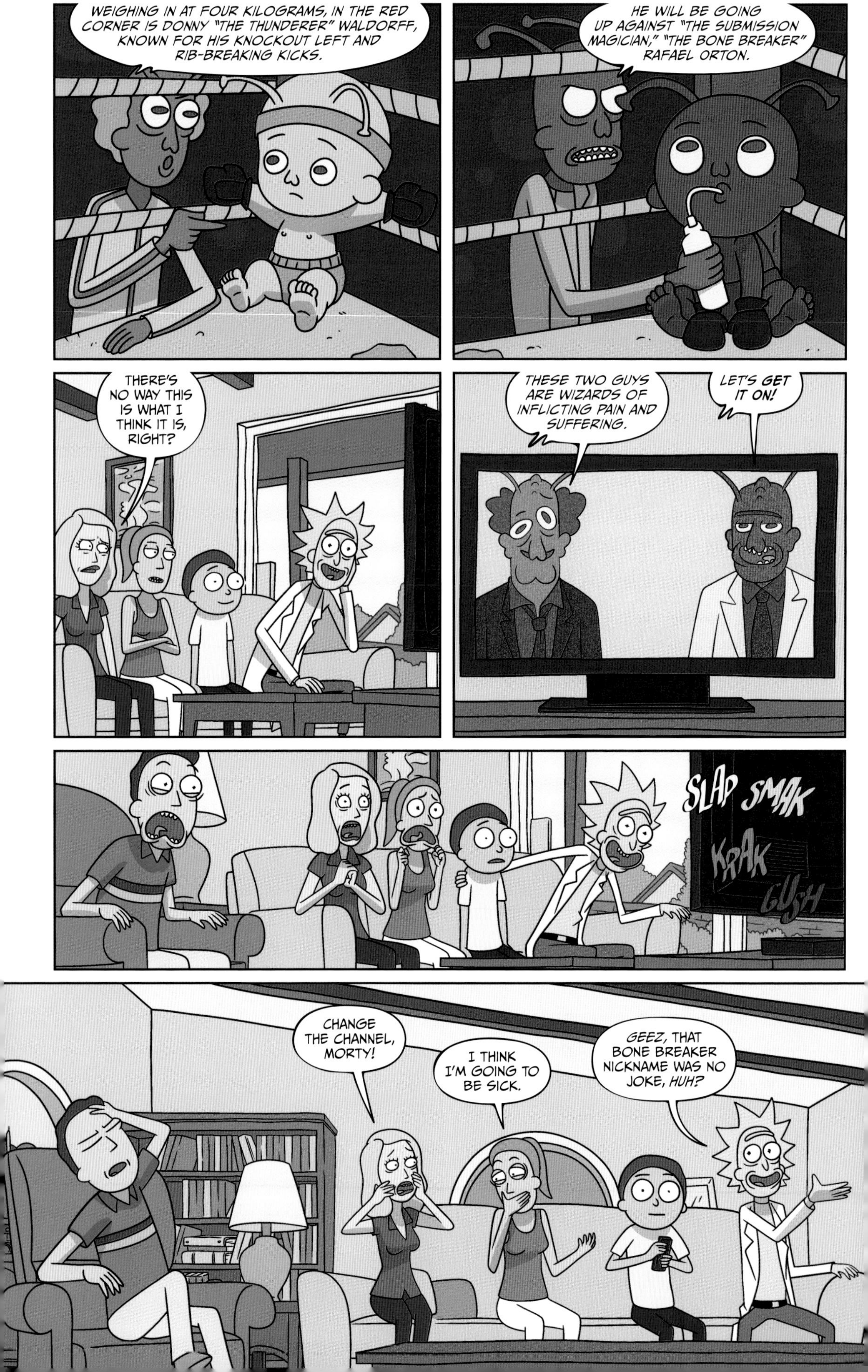

WEIGHING IN AT FOUR KILOGRAMS, IN THE RED CORNER IS DONNY "THE THUNDERER" WALDORFF, KNOWN FOR HIS KNOCKOUT LEFT AND RIB-BREAKING KICKS.
HE WILL BE GOING UP AGAINST "THE SUBMISSION MAGICIAN," "THE BONE BREAKER" RAFAEL ORTON.
THERE'S NO WAY THIS IS WHAT I THINK IT IS, RIGHT?
THESE TWO GUYS ARE WIZARDS OF INFLICTING PAIN AND SUFFERING.
LET'S GET IT ON!
SLAP SMAK
KRAK
CRUSH
CHANGE THE CHANNEL, MORTY!
I THINK I'M GOING TO BE SICK.
GEEZ, THAT BONE BREAKER NICKNAME WAS NO JOKE, HUH?

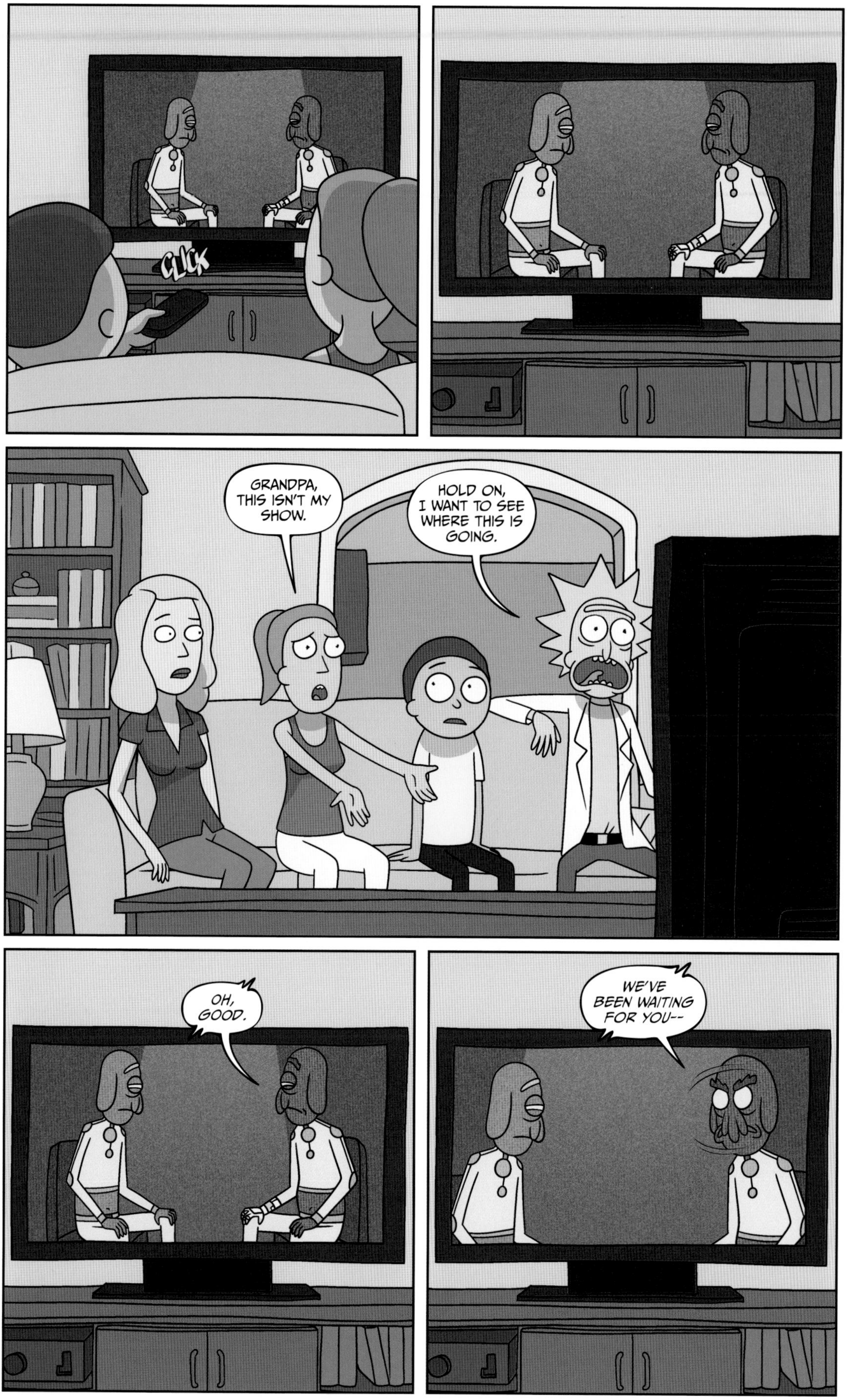
CLICK
GRANDPA, THIS ISN'T MY SHOW.
HOLD ON, I WANT TO SEE WHERE THIS IS GOING.
OH, GOOD.
WE'VE BEEN WAITING FOR YOU--

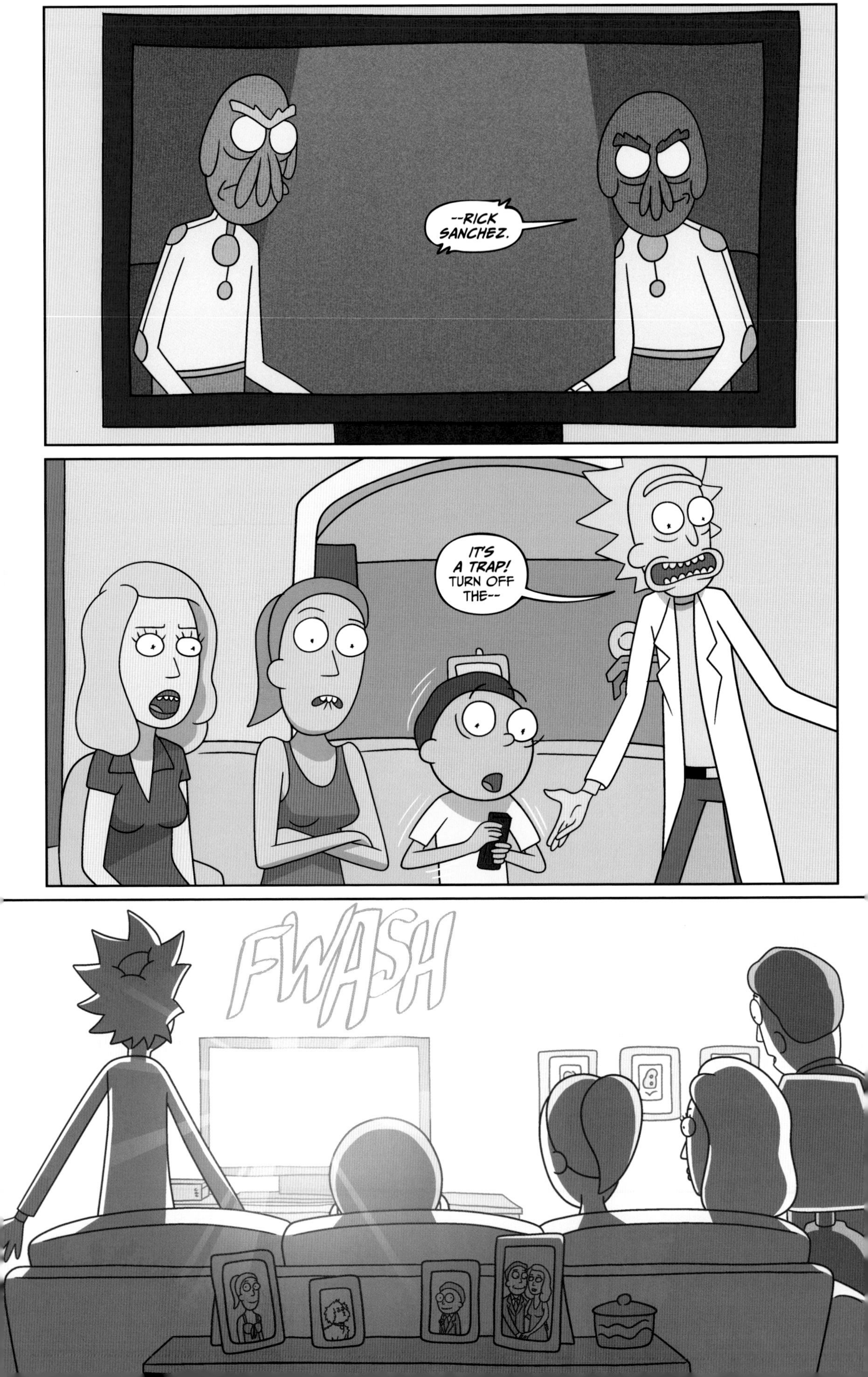
--RICK SANCHEZ.
IT'S A TRAP! TURN OFF THE--
FWASH

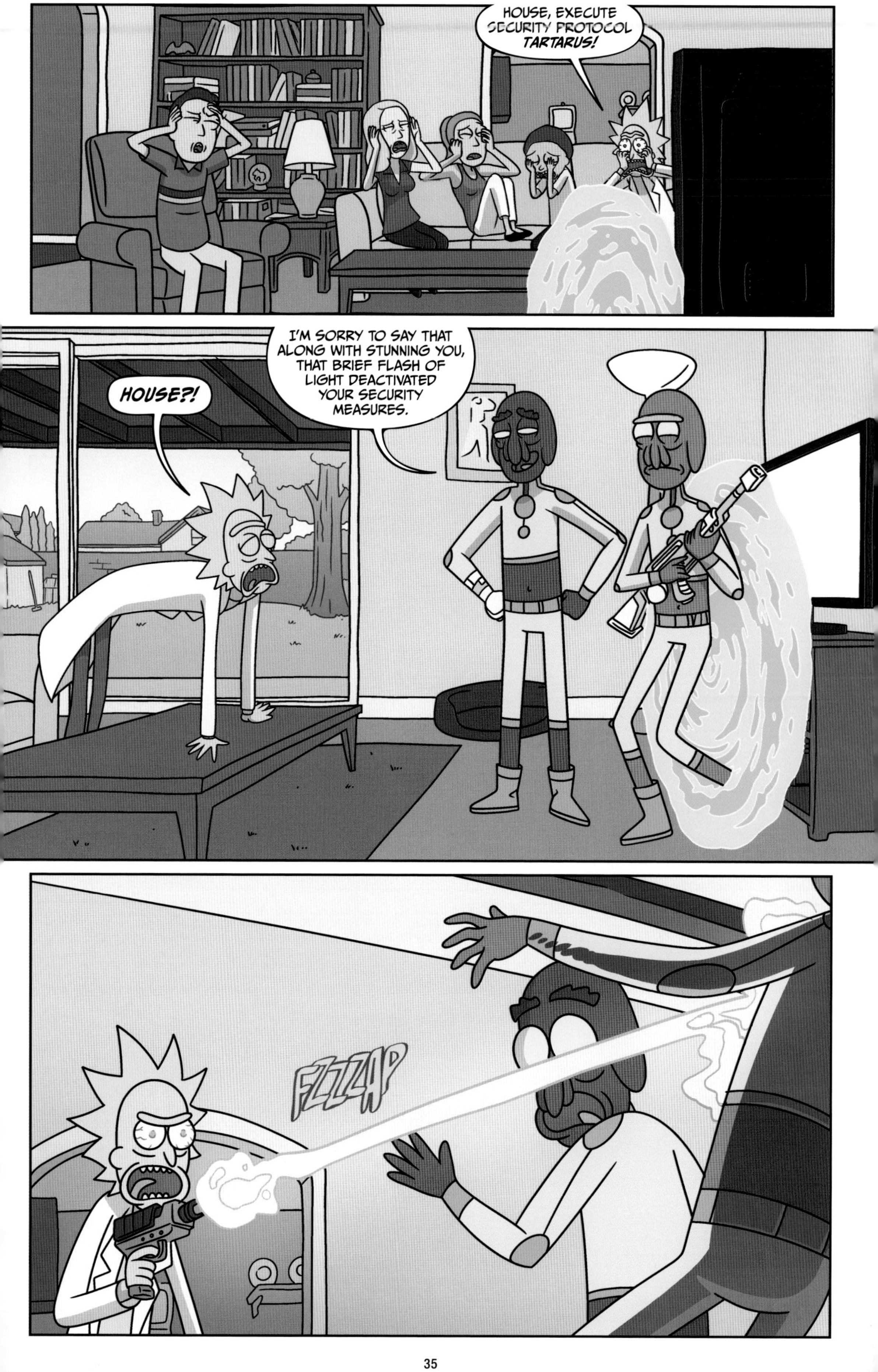
HOUSE, EXECUTE SECURITY PROTOCOL TARTARUS!
HOUSE?!
I'M SORRY TO SAY THAT ALONG WITH STUNNING YOU, THAT BRIEF FLASH OF LIGHT DEACTIVATED YOUR SECURITY MEASURES.
FZZZAP

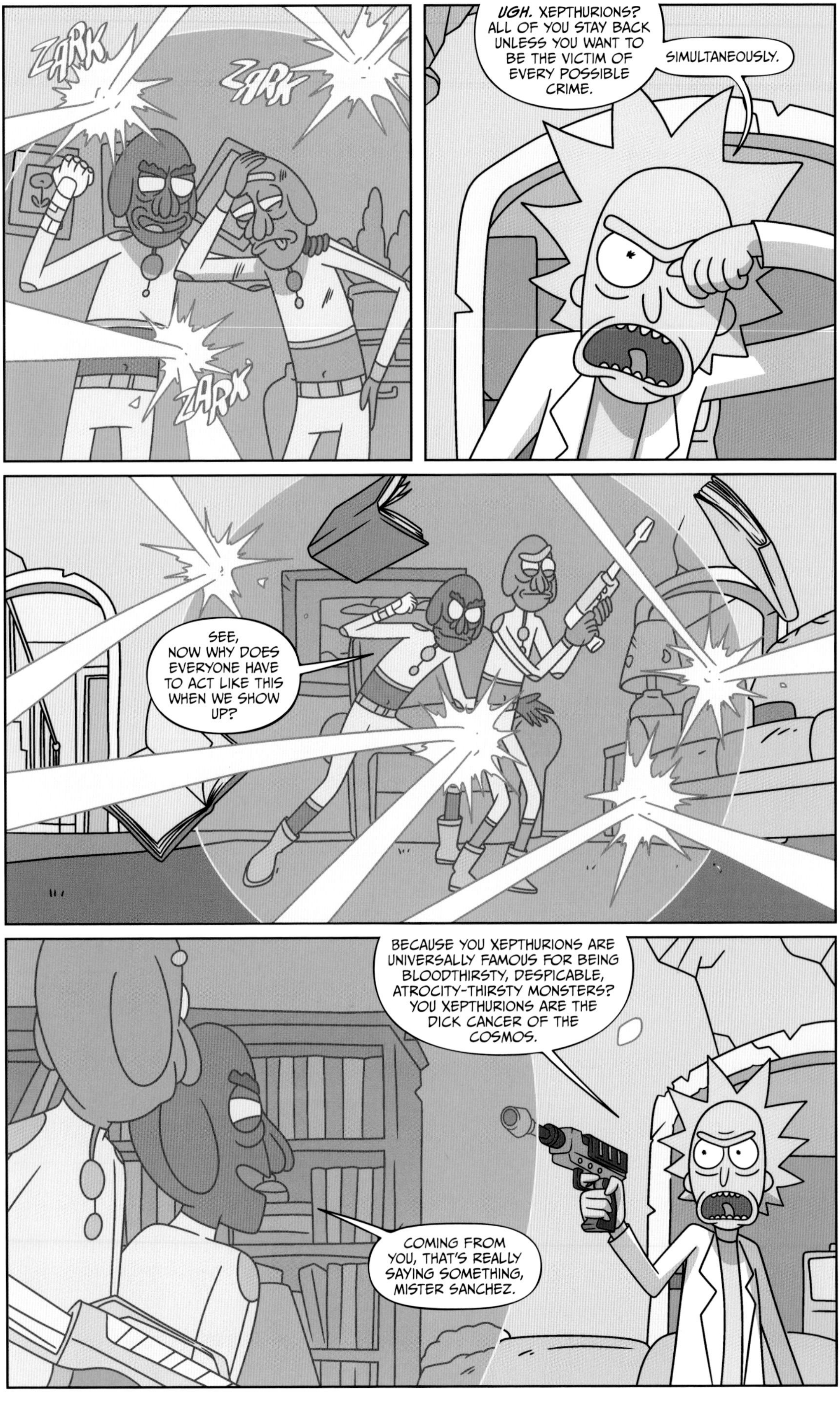
ZARK
ZARK
ZARK
UGH. XEPTHURIONS? ALL OF YOU STAY BACK UNLESS YOU WANT TO BE THE VICTIM OF EVERY POSSIBLE CRIME.
SIMULTANEOUSLY.
SEE, NOW WHY DOES EVERYONE HAVE TO ACT LIKE THIS WHEN WE SHOW UP?
BECAUSE YOU XEPTHURIONS ARE UNIVERSALLY FAMOUS FOR BEING BLOODTHIRSTY, DESPICABLE, ATROCITY-THIRSTY MONSTERS? YOU XEPTHURIONS ARE THE DICK CANCER OF THE COSMOS.
COMING FROM YOU, THAT'S REALLY SAYING SOMETHING, MISTER SANCHEZ.

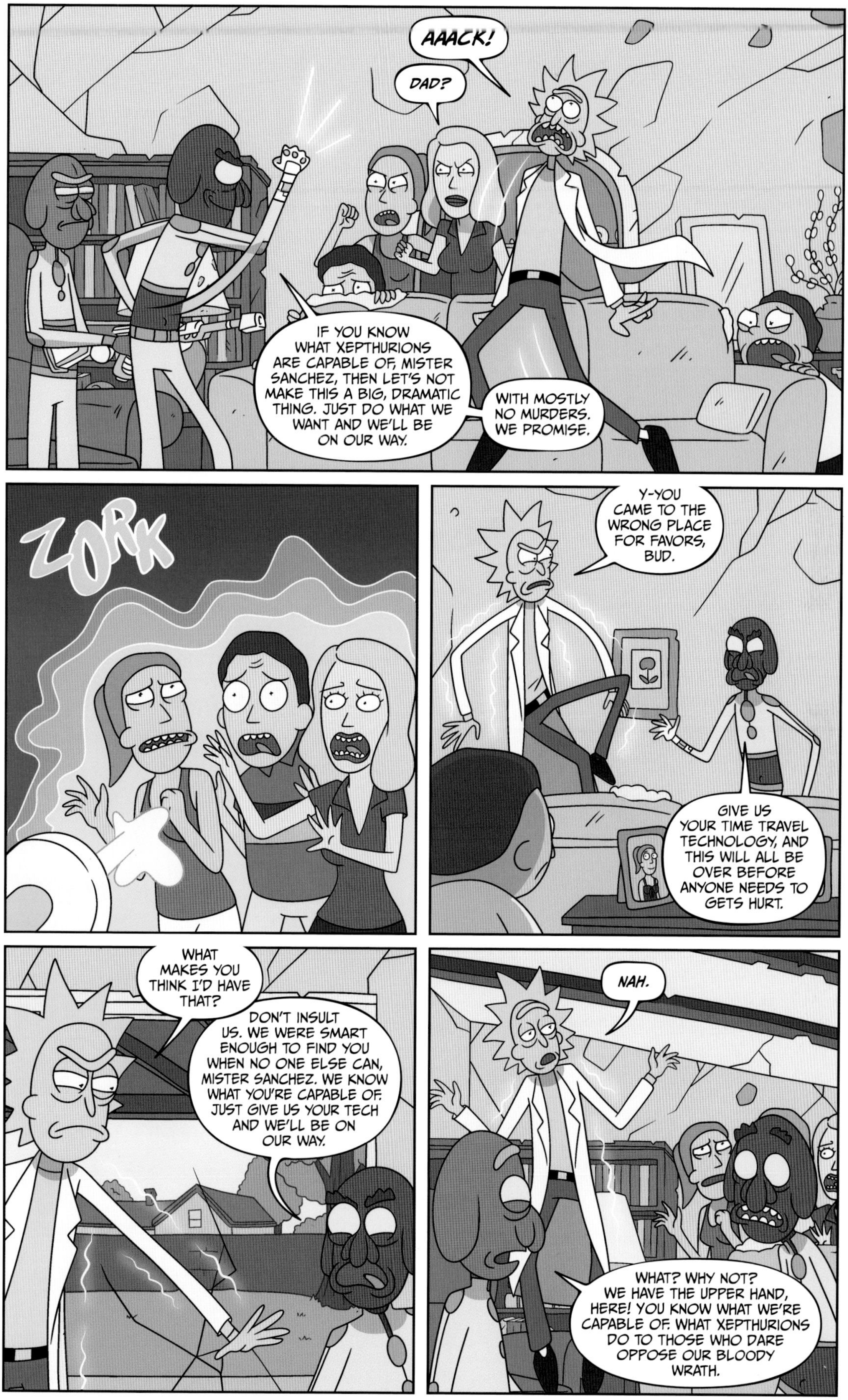
AAACK!
DAD?
IF YOU KNOW WHAT XEPTHURIONS ARE CAPABLE OF, MISTER SANCHEZ, THEN LET'S NOT MAKE THIS A BIG, DRAMATIC THING. JUST DO WHAT WE WANT AND WE'LL BE ON OUR WAY.
WITH MOSTLY NO MURDERS. WE PROMISE.
ZORK
Y-YOU CAME TO THE WRONG PLACE FOR FAVORS, BUD.
GIVE US YOUR TIME TRAVEL TECHNOLOGY, AND THIS WILL ALL BE OVER BEFORE ANYONE NEEDS TO GETS HURT.
WHAT MAKES YOU THINK I'D HAVE THAT?
DON'T INSULT US. WE WERE SMART ENOUGH TO FIND YOU WHEN NO ONE ELSE CAN, MISTER SANCHEZ. WE KNOW WHAT YOU'RE CAPABLE OF. JUST GIVE US YOUR TECH AND WE'LL BE ON OUR WAY.
NAH.
WHAT? WHY NOT? WE HAVE THE UPPER HAND, HERE! YOU KNOW WHAT WE'RE CAPABLE OF. WHAT XEPTHURIONS DO TO THOSE WHO DARE OPPOSE OUR BLOODY WRATH.

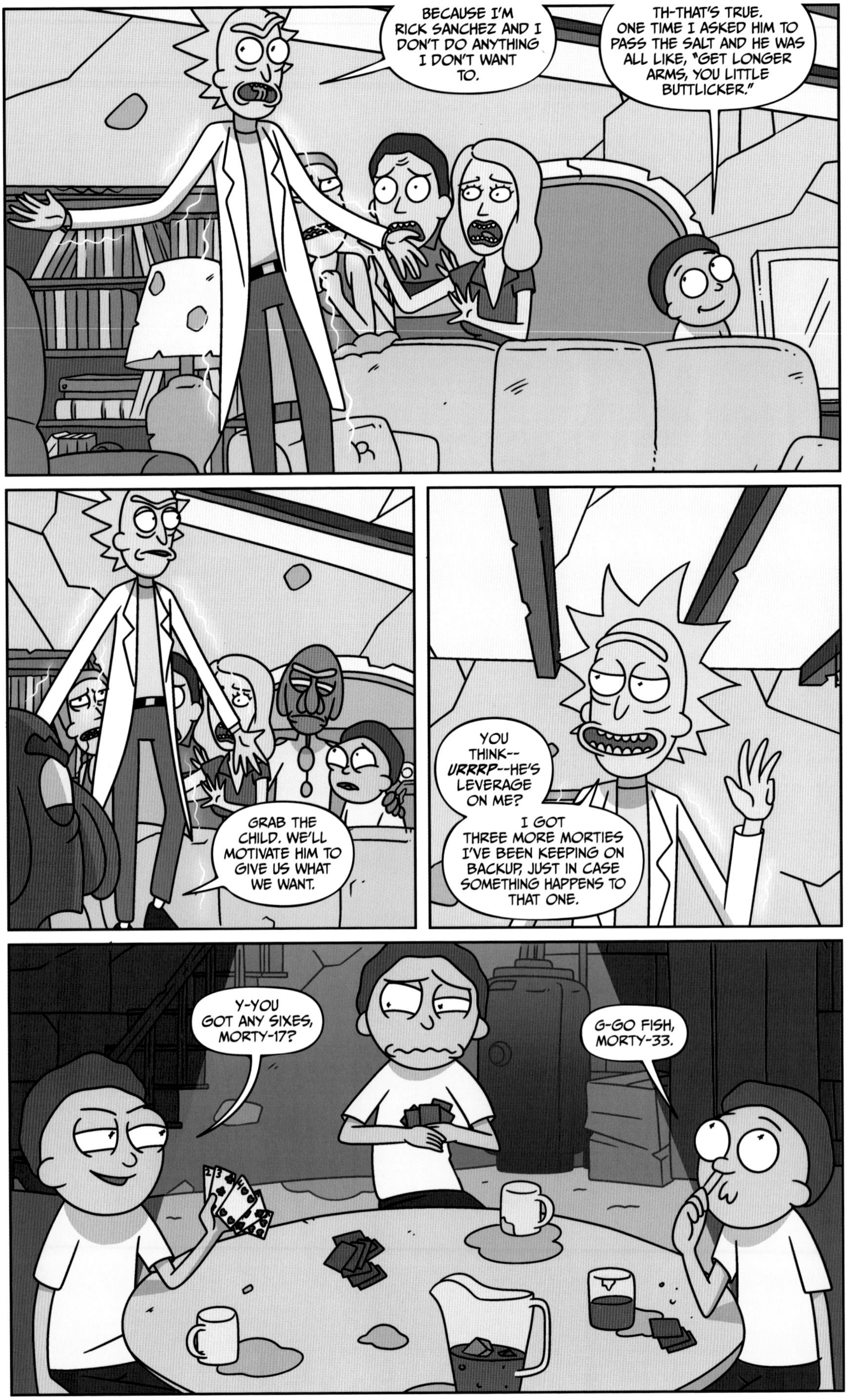
BECAUSE I'M RICK SANCHEZ AND I DON'T DO ANYTHING I DON'T WANT TO.
TH-THAT'S TRUE. ONE TIME I ASKED HIM TO PASS THE SALT AND HE WAS ALL LIKE, "GET LONGER ARMS, YOU LITTLE BUTTLICKER."
GRAB THE CHILD. WE'LL MOTIVATE HIM TO GIVE US WHAT WE WANT.
YOU THINK-- *URRRP*--HE'S LEVERAGE ON ME?
I GOT THREE MORE MORTIES I'VE BEEN KEEPING ON BACKUP, JUST IN CASE SOMETHING HAPPENS TO THAT ONE.
Y-YOU GOT ANY SIXES, MORTY-17?
G-GO FISH, MORTY-33.

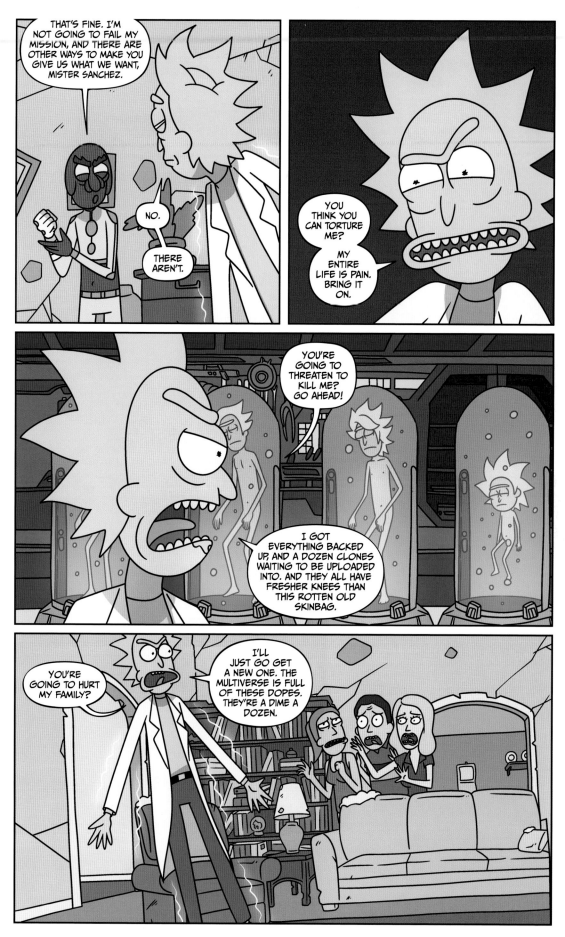

THAT'S FINE. I'M NOT GOING TO FAIL MY MISSION, AND THERE ARE OTHER WAYS TO MAKE YOU GIVE US WHAT WE WANT, MISTER SANCHEZ.

NO.

THERE AREN'T.

YOU THINK YOU CAN TORTURE ME?

MY ENTIRE LIFE IS PAIN. BRING IT ON.

YOU'RE GOING TO THREATEN TO KILL ME? GO AHEAD!

I GOT EVERYTHING BACKED UP, AND A DOZEN CLONES WAITING TO BE UPLOADED INTO. AND THEY ALL HAVE FRESHER KNEES THAN THIS ROTTEN OLD SKINBAG.

YOU'RE GOING TO HURT MY FAMILY?

I'LL JUST GO GET A NEW ONE. THE MULTIVERSE IS FULL OF THESE DOPES. THEY'RE A DIME A DOZEN.

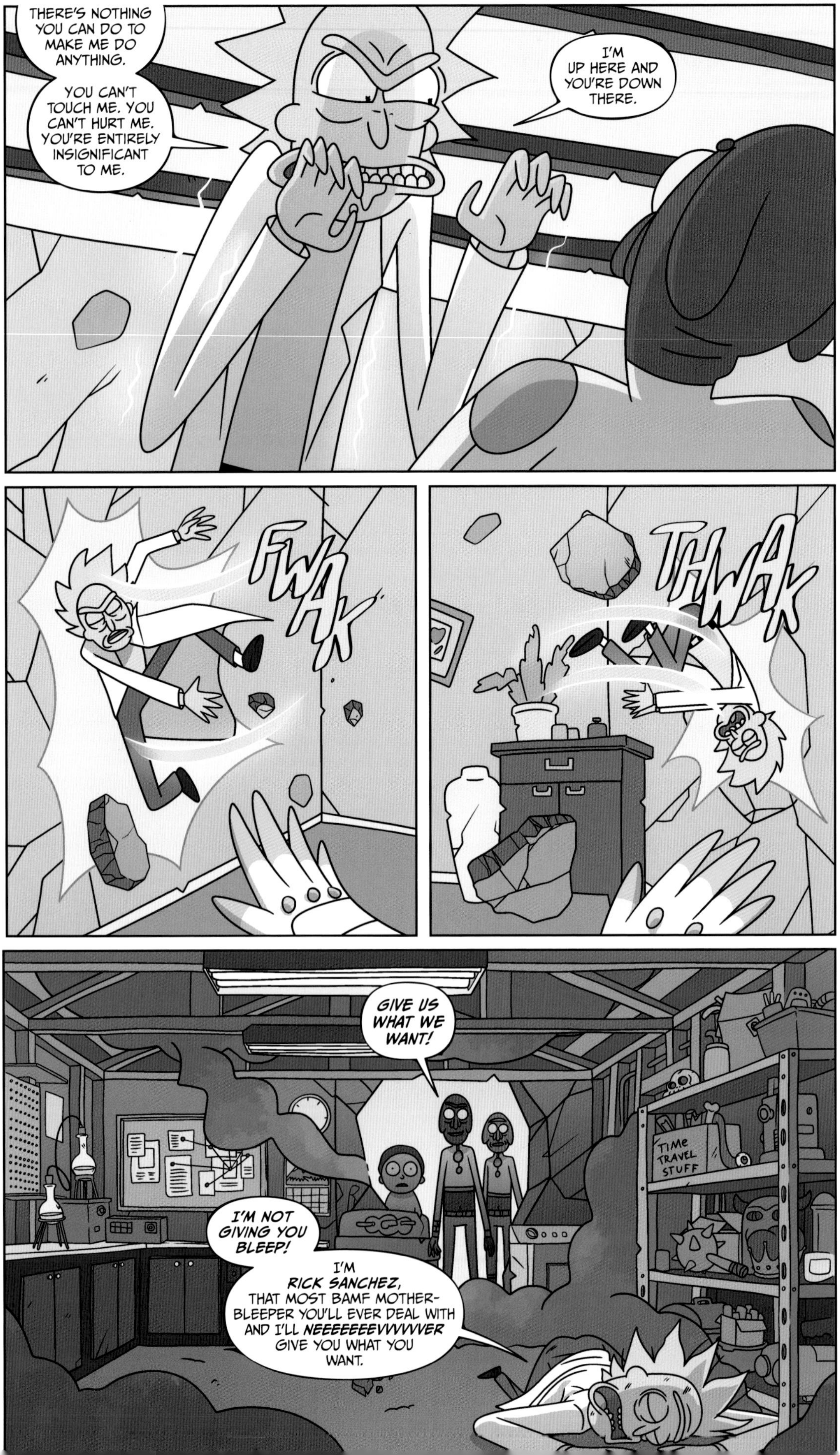
THERE'S NOTHING YOU CAN DO TO MAKE ME DO ANYTHING.
YOU CAN'T TOUCH ME. YOU CAN'T HURT ME. YOU'RE ENTIRELY INSIGNIFICANT TO ME.
I'M UP HERE AND YOU'RE DOWN THERE.
FWAK
THWAK
GIVE US WHAT WE WANT!
TIME TRAVEL STUFF
I'M NOT GIVING YOU BLEEP!
I'M RICK SANCHEZ, THAT MOST BAMF MOTHER-BLEEPER YOU'LL EVER DEAL WITH AND I'LL NEEEEEEEVVVVVVER GIVE YOU WHAT YOU WANT.

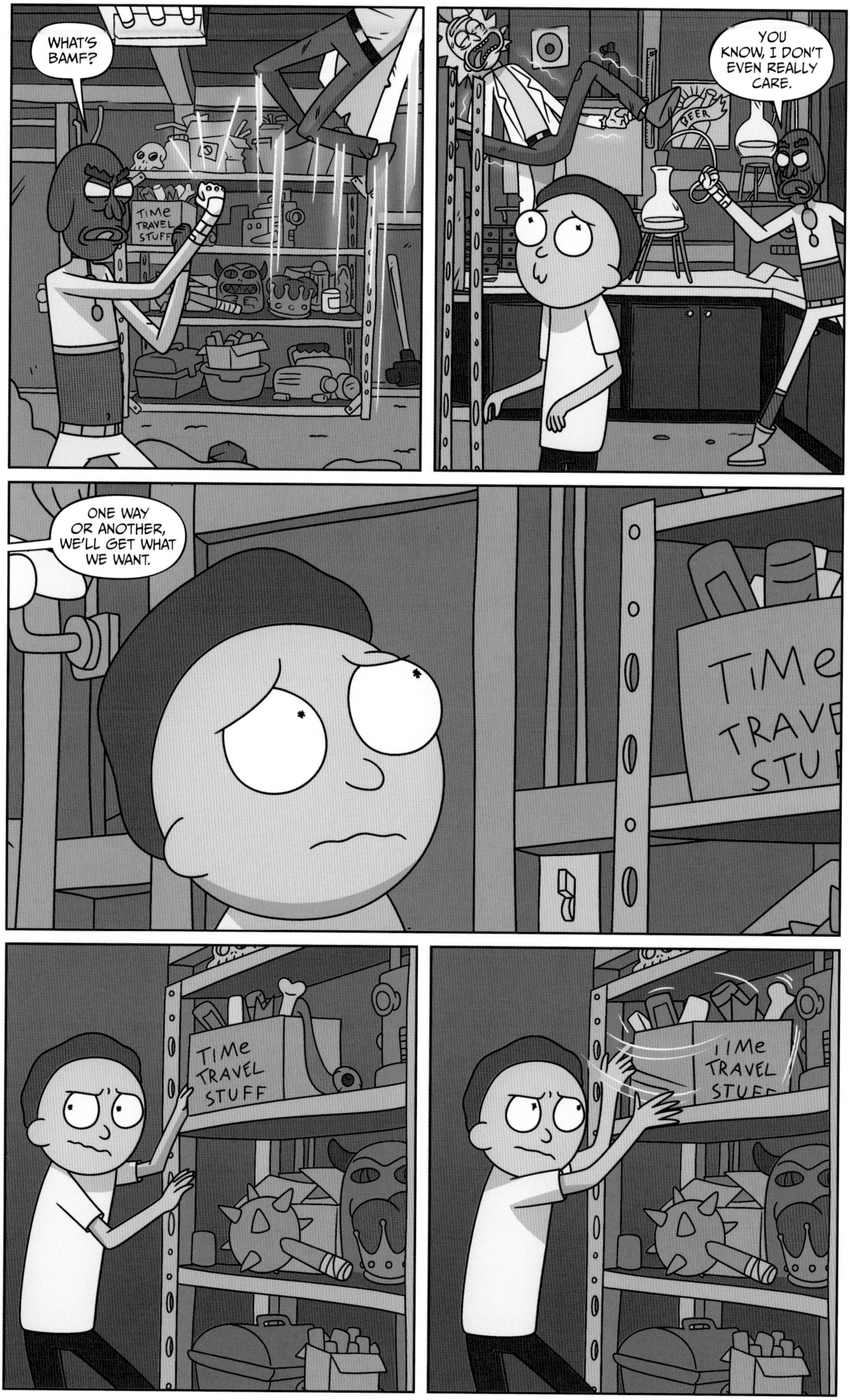
WHAT'S BAMF?
TIME TRAVEL STUFF
BEER
YOU KNOW, I DON'T EVEN REALLY CARE.
ONE WAY OR ANOTHER, WE'LL GET WHAT WE WANT.
TIME TRAVEL STUFF
TIME TRAVEL STUFF

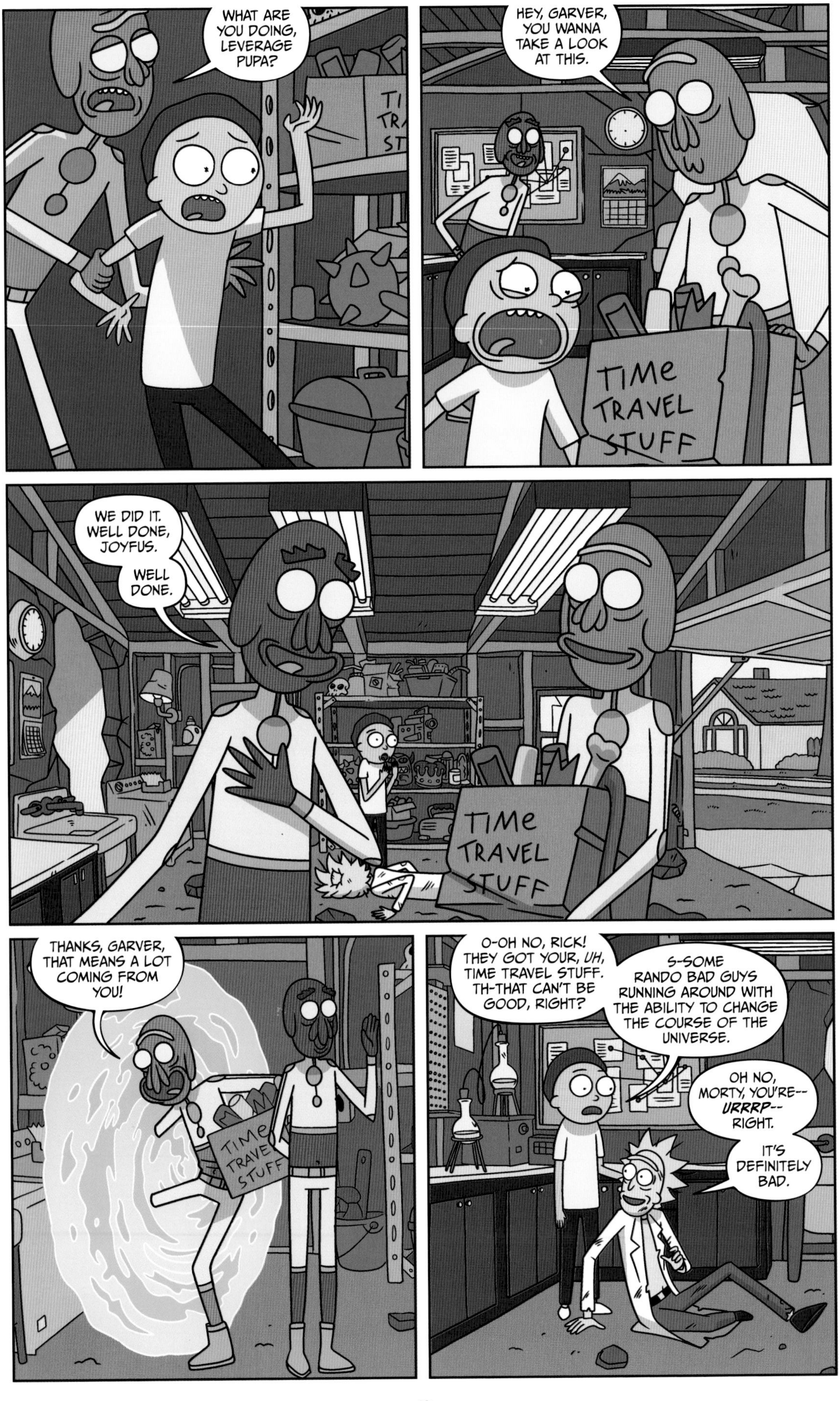
WHAT ARE YOU DOING, LEVERAGE PUPA?
HEY, GARVER, YOU WANNA TAKE A LOOK AT THIS.
TIME TRAVEL STUFF
WE DID IT. WELL DONE, JOYFUS.
WELL DONE.
TIME TRAVEL STUFF
THANKS, GARVER, THAT MEANS A LOT COMING FROM YOU!
TIME TRAVEL STUFF
O-OH NO, RICK! THEY GOT YOUR, *UH*, TIME TRAVEL STUFF. TH-THAT CAN'T BE GOOD, RIGHT?
S-SOME RANDO BAD GUYS RUNNING AROUND WITH THE ABILITY TO CHANGE THE COURSE OF THE UNIVERSE.
OH NO, MORTY, YOU'RE-- ***URRRP***-- RIGHT.
IT'S DEFINITELY BAD.

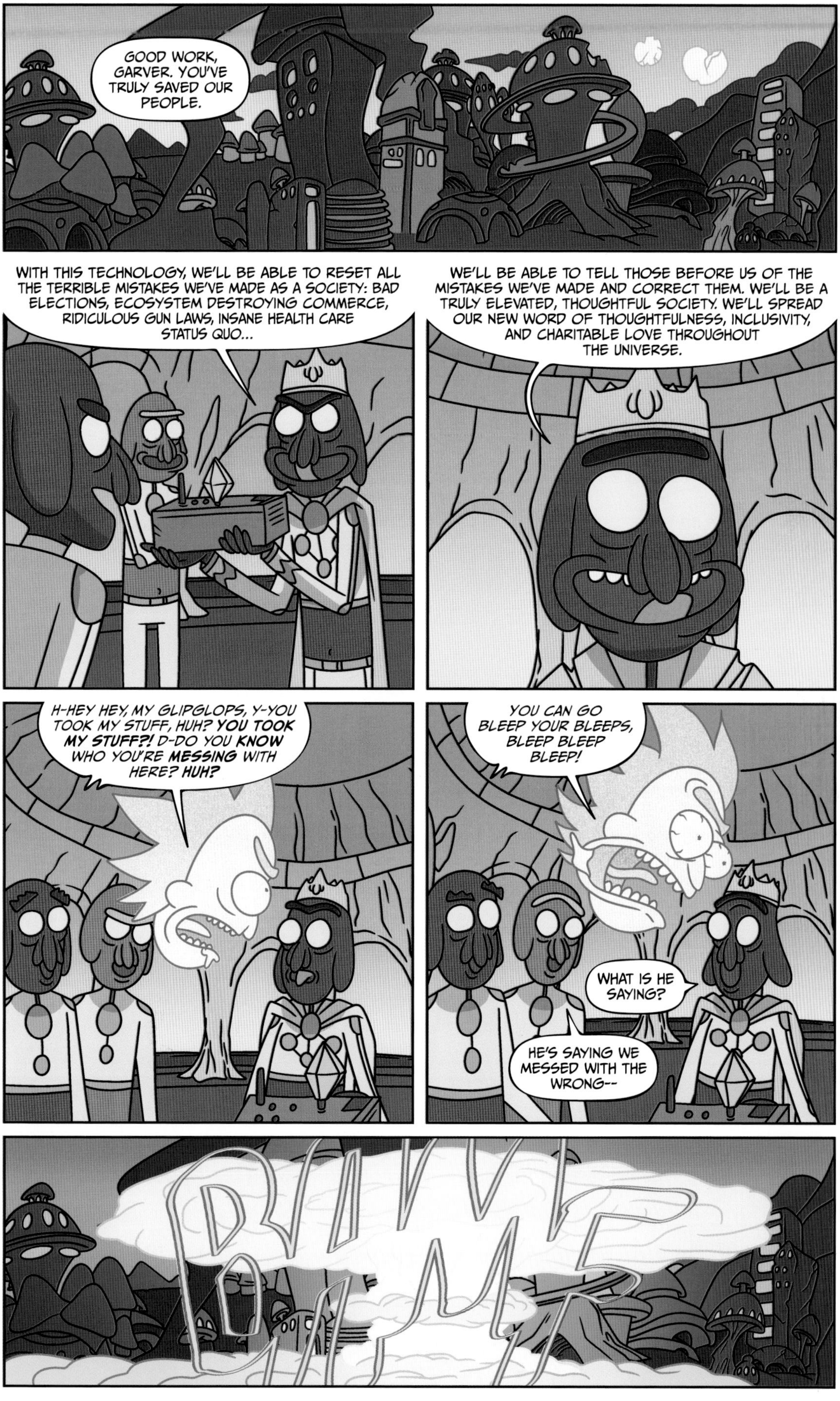
GOOD WORK, GARVER. YOU'VE TRULY SAVED OUR PEOPLE.
WITH THIS TECHNOLOGY, WE'LL BE ABLE TO RESET ALL THE TERRIBLE MISTAKES WE'VE MADE AS A SOCIETY: BAD ELECTIONS, ECOSYSTEM DESTROYING COMMERCE, RIDICULOUS GUN LAWS, INSANE HEALTH CARE STATUS QUO...
WE'LL BE ABLE TO TELL THOSE BEFORE US OF THE MISTAKES WE'VE MADE AND CORRECT THEM. WE'LL BE A TRULY ELEVATED, THOUGHTFUL SOCIETY. WE'LL SPREAD OUR NEW WORD OF THOUGHTFULNESS, INCLUSIVITY, AND CHARITABLE LOVE THROUGHOUT THE UNIVERSE.
H-HEY HEY, MY GLIPGLOPS, Y-YOU TOOK MY STUFF, HUH? **YOU TOOK MY STUFF?!** D-DO YOU **KNOW** WHO YOU'RE **MESSING** WITH HERE? **HUH?**
YOU CAN GO BLEEP YOUR BLEEPS, BLEEP BLEEP BLEEP!
WHAT IS HE SAYING?
HE'S SAYING WE MESSED WITH THE WRONG--

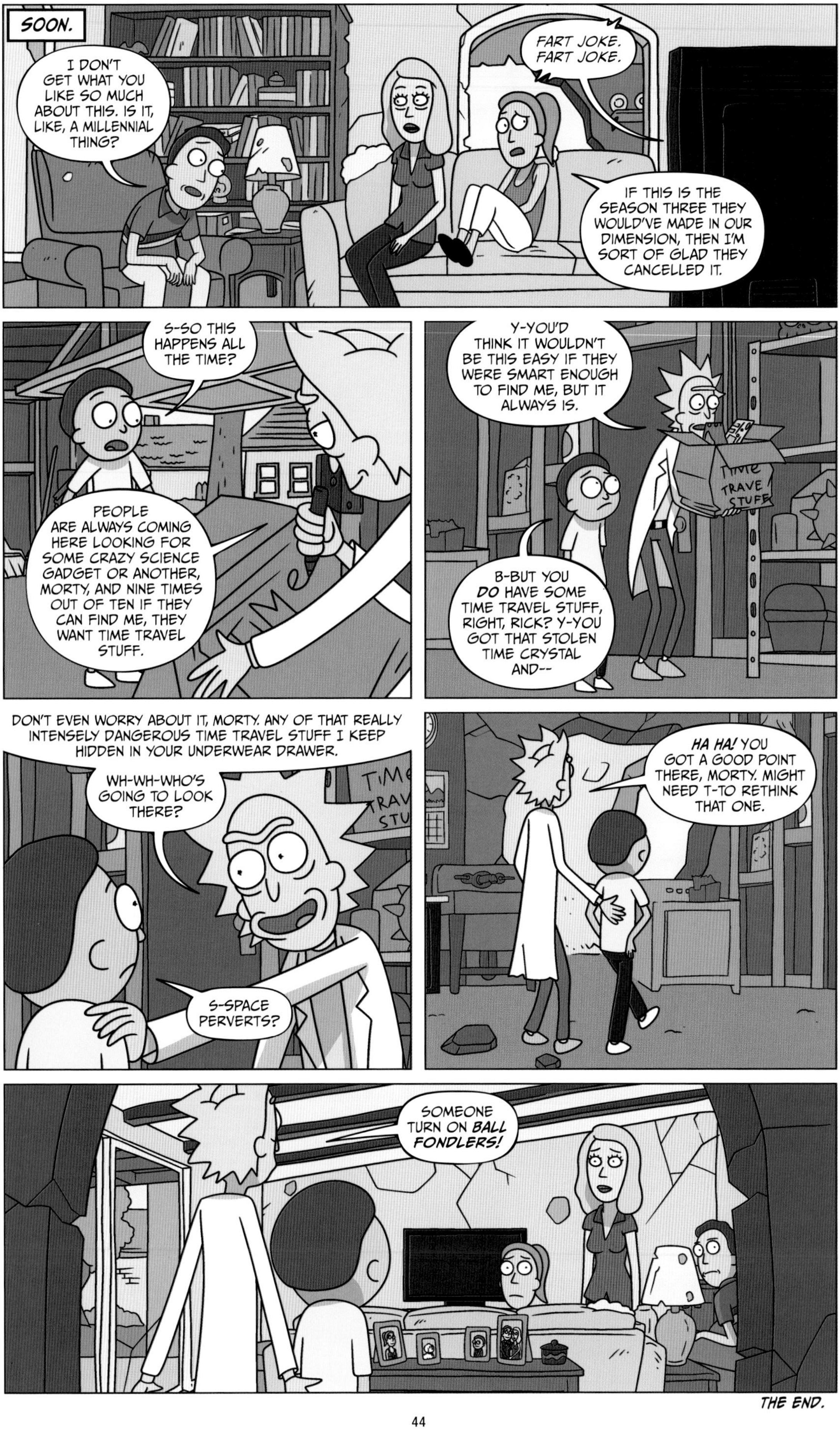
SOON.
I DON'T GET WHAT YOU LIKE SO MUCH ABOUT THIS. IS IT, LIKE, A MILLENNIAL THING?
FART JOKE. FART JOKE.
IF THIS IS THE SEASON THREE THEY WOULD'VE MADE IN OUR DIMENSION, THEN I'M SORT OF GLAD THEY CANCELLED IT.
S-SO THIS HAPPENS ALL THE TIME?
PEOPLE ARE ALWAYS COMING HERE LOOKING FOR SOME CRAZY SCIENCE GADGET OR ANOTHER, MORTY, AND NINE TIMES OUT OF TEN IF THEY CAN FIND ME, THEY WANT TIME TRAVEL STUFF.
Y-YOU'D THINK IT WOULDN'T BE THIS EASY IF THEY WERE SMART ENOUGH TO FIND ME, BUT IT ALWAYS IS.
TIME TRAVE STUFF
B-BUT YOU *DO* HAVE SOME TIME TRAVEL STUFF, RIGHT, RICK? Y-YOU GOT THAT STOLEN TIME CRYSTAL AND--
DON'T EVEN WORRY ABOUT IT, MORTY. ANY OF THAT REALLY INTENSELY DANGEROUS TIME TRAVEL STUFF I KEEP HIDDEN IN YOUR UNDERWEAR DRAWER.
WH-WH-WHO'S GOING TO LOOK THERE?
S-SPACE PERVERTS?
HA HA! YOU GOT A GOOD POINT THERE, MORTY. MIGHT NEED T-TO RETHINK THAT ONE.
SOMEONE TURN ON ***BALL FONDLERS!***
THE END.

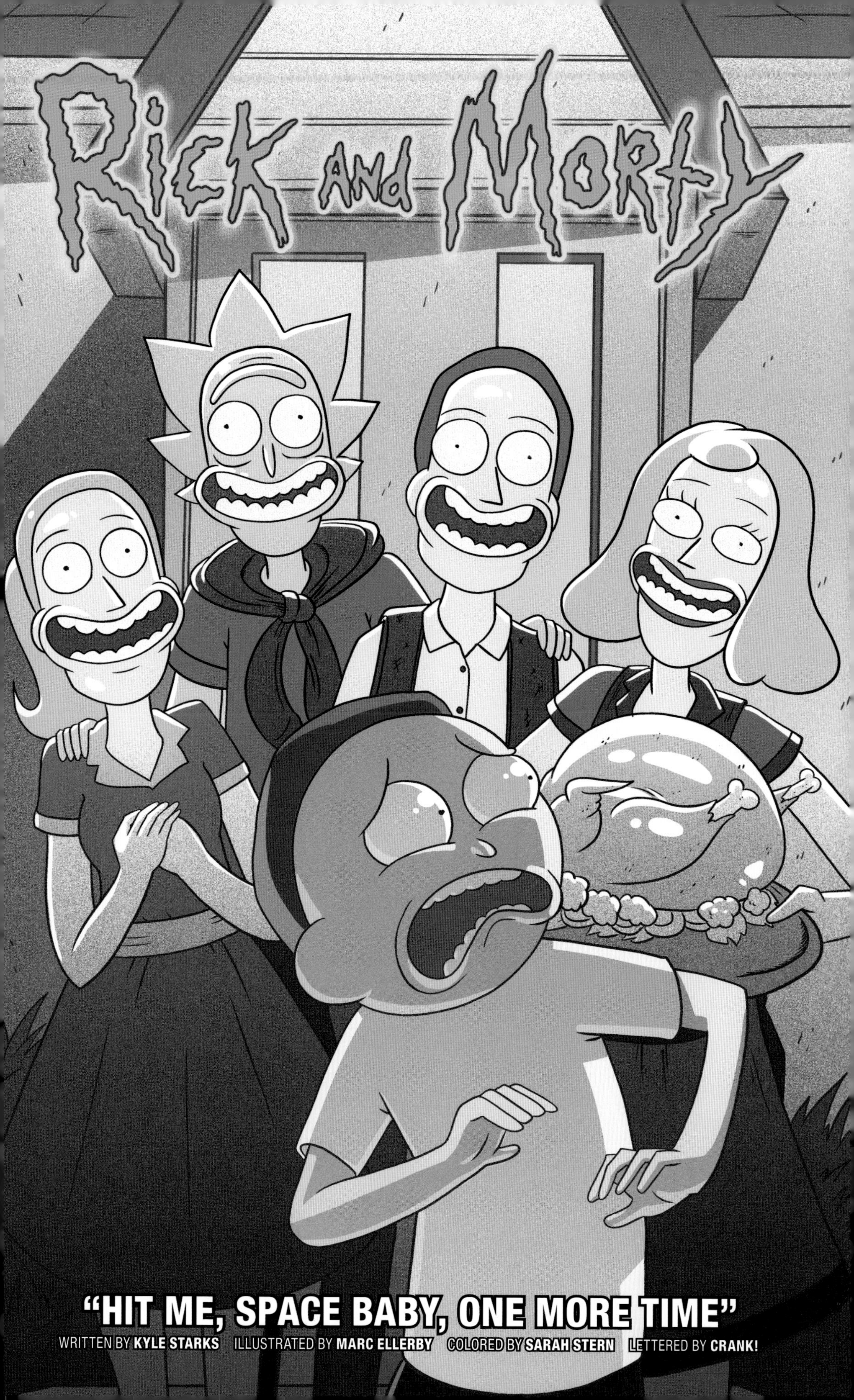
Rick and Morty

"HIT ME, SPACE BABY, ONE MORE TIME"

WRITTEN BY **KYLE STARKS** ILLUSTRATED BY **MARC ELLERBY** COLORED BY **SARAH STERN** LETTERED BY **CRANK!**

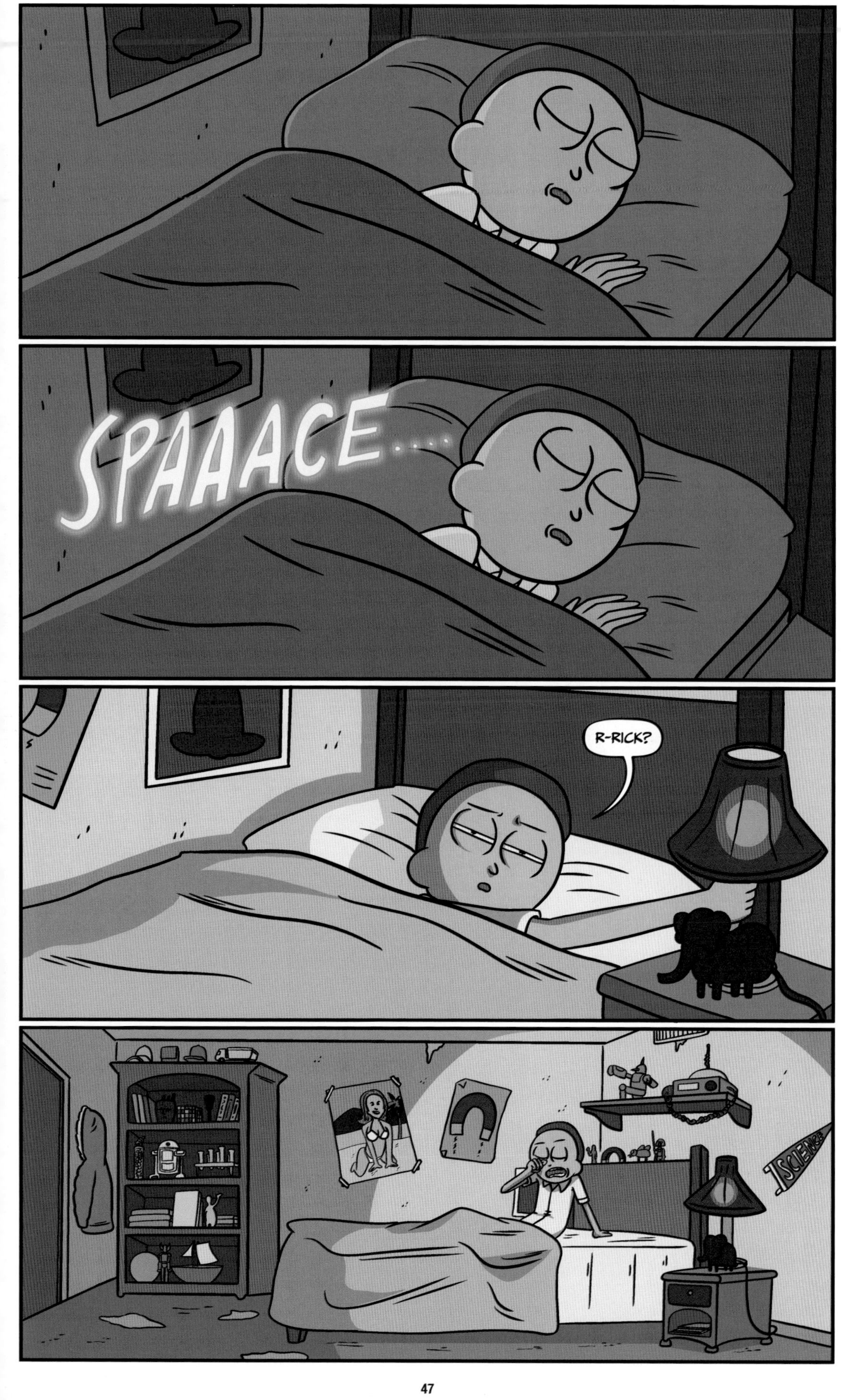
SPAAACE....
R-RICK?
SCIENCE

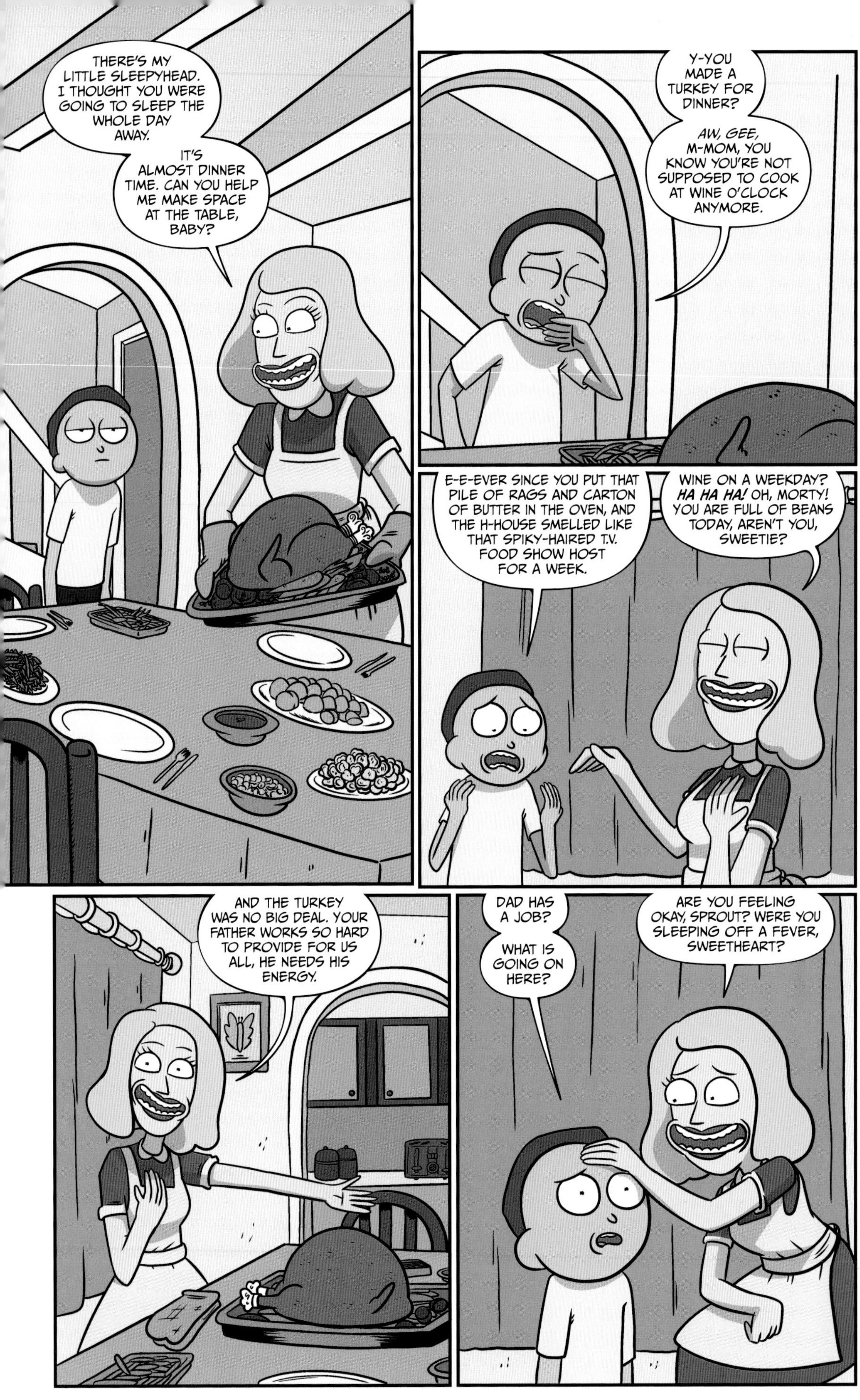
THERE'S MY LITTLE SLEEPYHEAD. I THOUGHT YOU WERE GOING TO SLEEP THE WHOLE DAY AWAY.
IT'S ALMOST DINNER TIME. CAN YOU HELP ME MAKE SPACE AT THE TABLE, BABY?
Y-YOU MADE A TURKEY FOR DINNER?
AW, GEE, M-MOM, YOU KNOW YOU'RE NOT SUPPOSED TO COOK AT WINE O'CLOCK ANYMORE.
E-E-EVER SINCE YOU PUT THAT PILE OF RAGS AND CARTON OF BUTTER IN THE OVEN, AND THE H-HOUSE SMELLED LIKE THAT SPIKY-HAIRED T.V. FOOD SHOW HOST FOR A WEEK.
WINE ON A WEEKDAY? *HA HA HA!* OH, MORTY! YOU ARE FULL OF BEANS TODAY, AREN'T YOU, SWEETIE?
AND THE TURKEY WAS NO BIG DEAL. YOUR FATHER WORKS SO HARD TO PROVIDE FOR US ALL, HE NEEDS HIS ENERGY.
DAD HAS A JOB?
WHAT IS GOING ON HERE?
ARE YOU FEELING OKAY, SPROUT? WERE YOU SLEEPING OFF A FEVER, SWEETHEART?

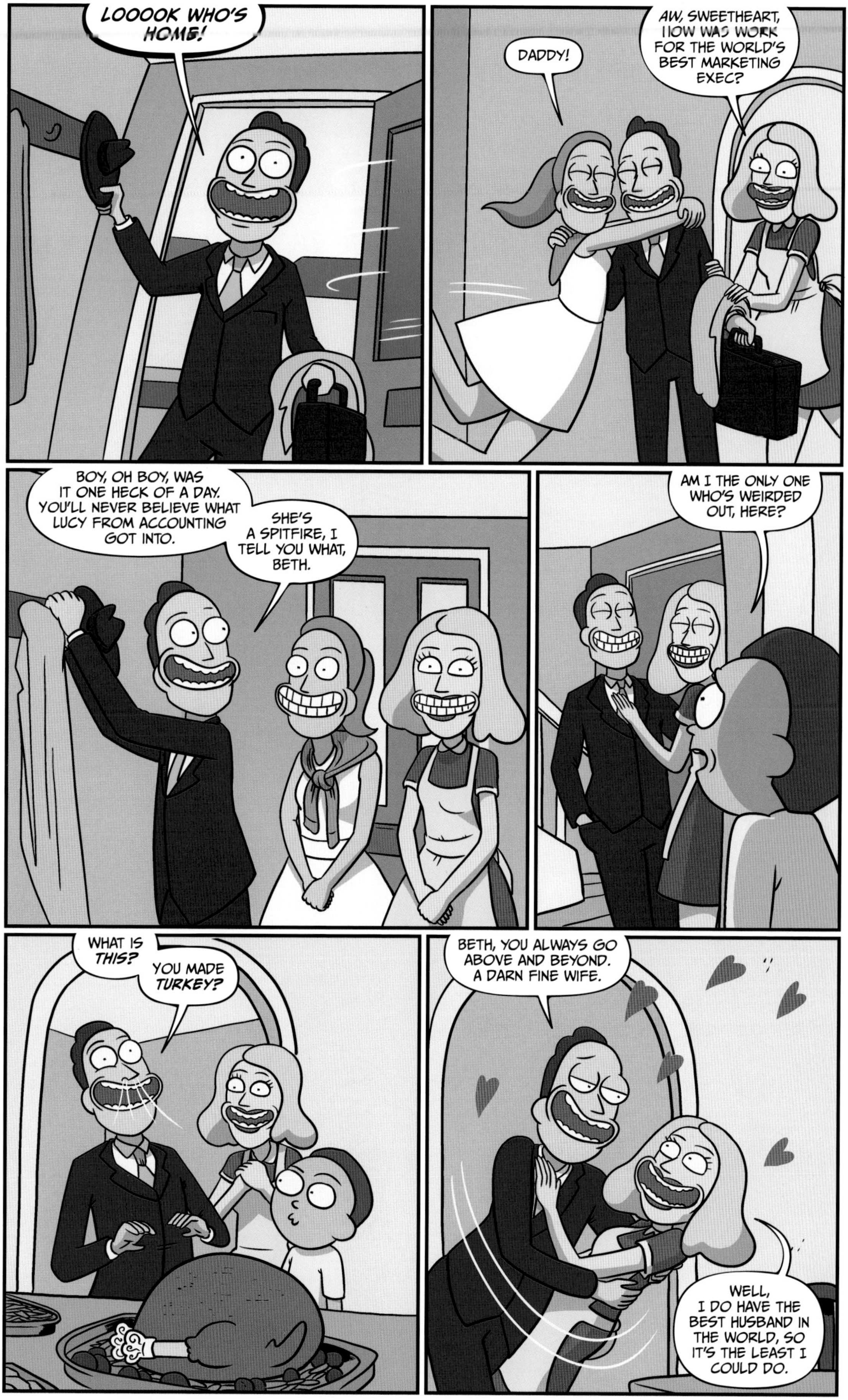
LOOOOK WHO'S HOME!
DADDY!
AW, SWEETHEART, HOW WAS WORK FOR THE WORLD'S BEST MARKETING EXEC?
BOY, OH BOY, WAS IT ONE HECK OF A DAY. YOU'LL NEVER BELIEVE WHAT LUCY FROM ACCOUNTING GOT INTO.
SHE'S A SPITFIRE, I TELL YOU WHAT, BETH.
AM I THE ONLY ONE WHO'S WEIRDED OUT, HERE?
WHAT IS *THIS?*
YOU MADE *TURKEY?*
BETH, YOU ALWAYS GO ABOVE AND BEYOND. A DARN FINE WIFE.
WELL, I DO HAVE THE BEST HUSBAND IN THE WORLD, SO IT'S THE LEAST I COULD DO.

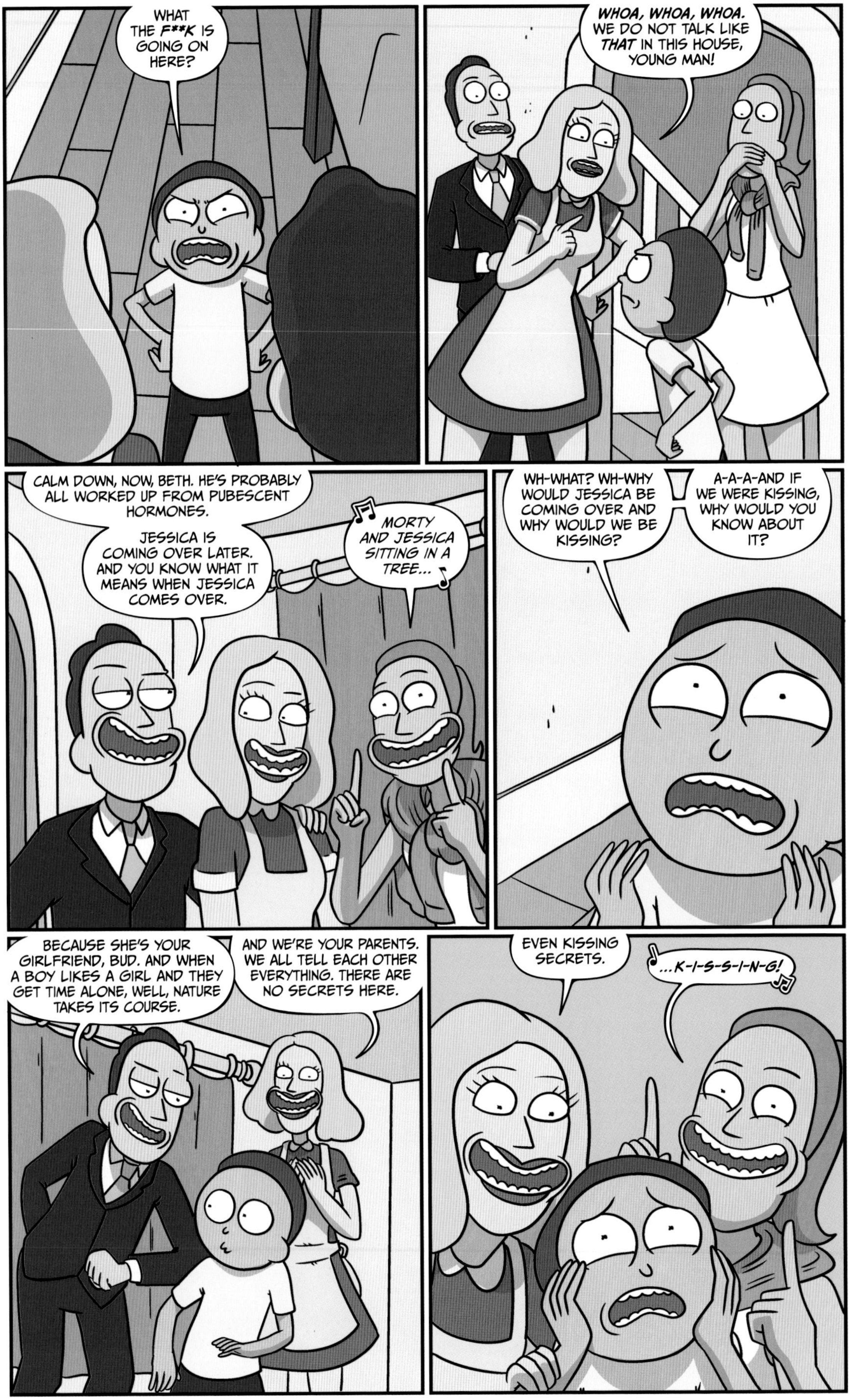
WHAT THE F**K IS GOING ON HERE?
WHOA, WHOA, WHOA. WE DO NOT TALK LIKE THAT IN THIS HOUSE, YOUNG MAN!
CALM DOWN, NOW, BETH. HE'S PROBABLY ALL WORKED UP FROM PUBESCENT HORMONES.
JESSICA IS COMING OVER LATER. AND YOU KNOW WHAT IT MEANS WHEN JESSICA COMES OVER.
MORTY AND JESSICA SITTING IN A TREE...
WH-WHAT? WH-WHY WOULD JESSICA BE COMING OVER AND WHY WOULD WE BE KISSING?
A-A-A-AND IF WE WERE KISSING, WHY WOULD YOU KNOW ABOUT IT?
BECAUSE SHE'S YOUR GIRLFRIEND, BUD. AND WHEN A BOY LIKES A GIRL AND THEY GET TIME ALONE, WELL, NATURE TAKES ITS COURSE.
AND WE'RE YOUR PARENTS. WE ALL TELL EACH OTHER EVERYTHING. THERE ARE NO SECRETS HERE.
EVEN KISSING SECRETS.
...K-I-S-S-I-N-G!

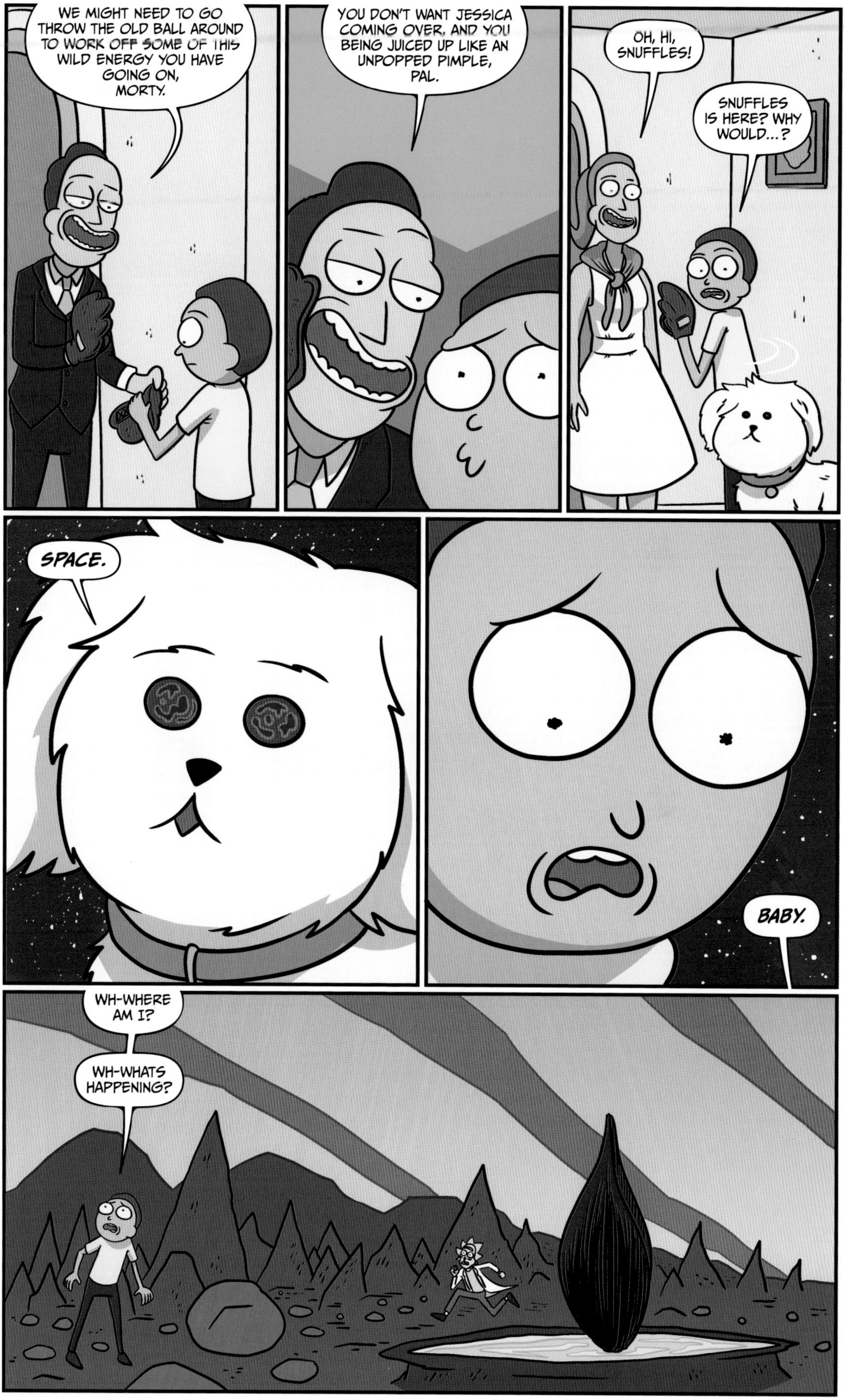
WE MIGHT NEED TO GO THROW THE OLD BALL AROUND TO WORK OFF SOME OF THIS WILD ENERGY YOU HAVE GOING ON, MORTY.
YOU DON'T WANT JESSICA COMING OVER, AND YOU BEING JUICED UP LIKE AN UNPOPPED PIMPLE, PAL.
OH, HI, SNUFFLES!
SNUFFLES IS HERE? WHY WOULD...?
SPACE.
BABY.
WH-WHERE AM I?
WH-WHATS HAPPENING?

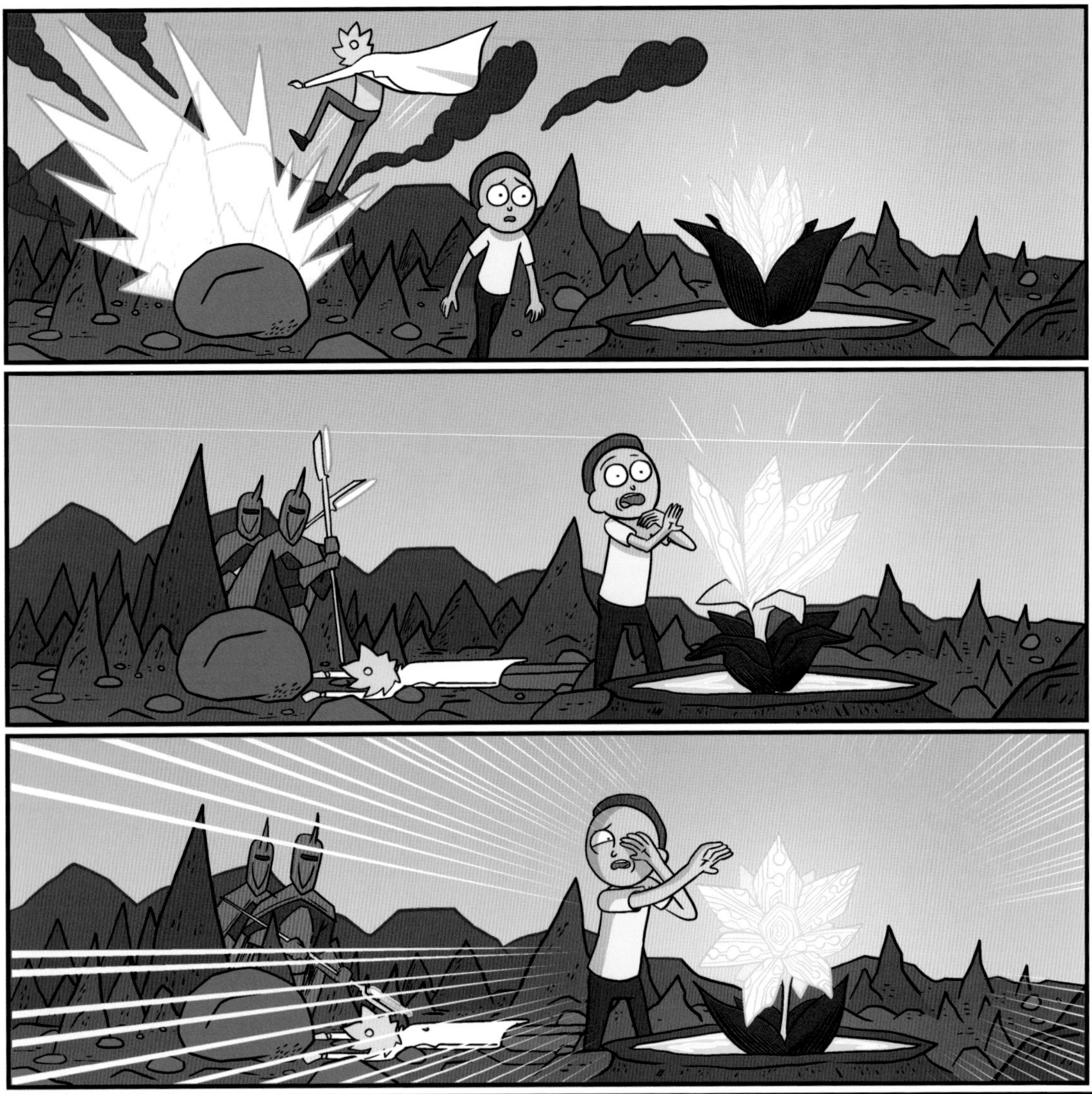

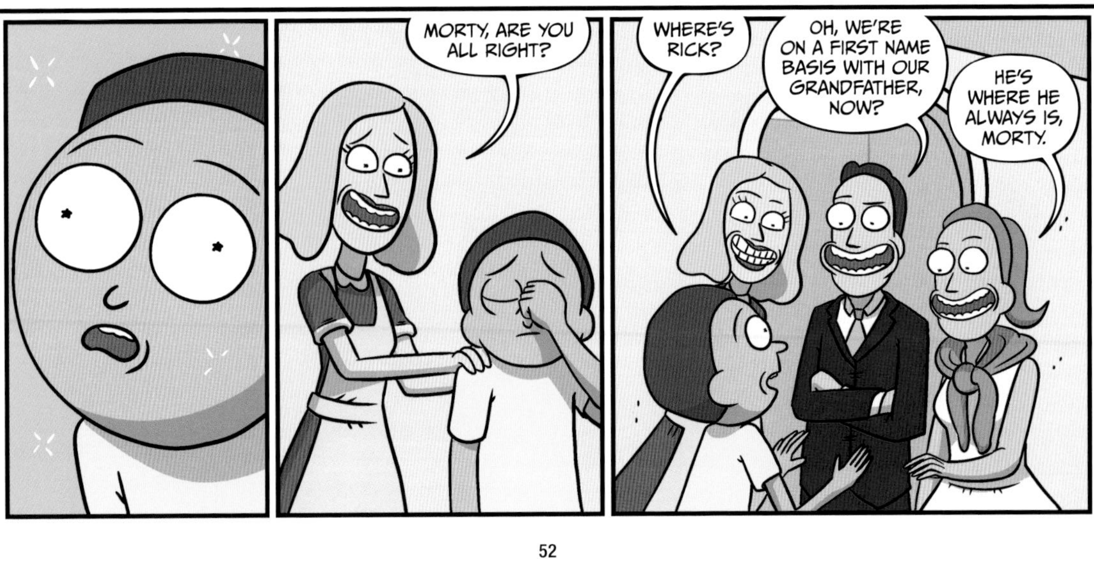
MORTY, ARE YOU ALL RIGHT?
WHERE'S RICK?
OH, WE'RE ON A FIRST NAME BASIS WITH OUR GRANDFATHER, NOW?
HE'S WHERE HE ALWAYS IS, MORTY.

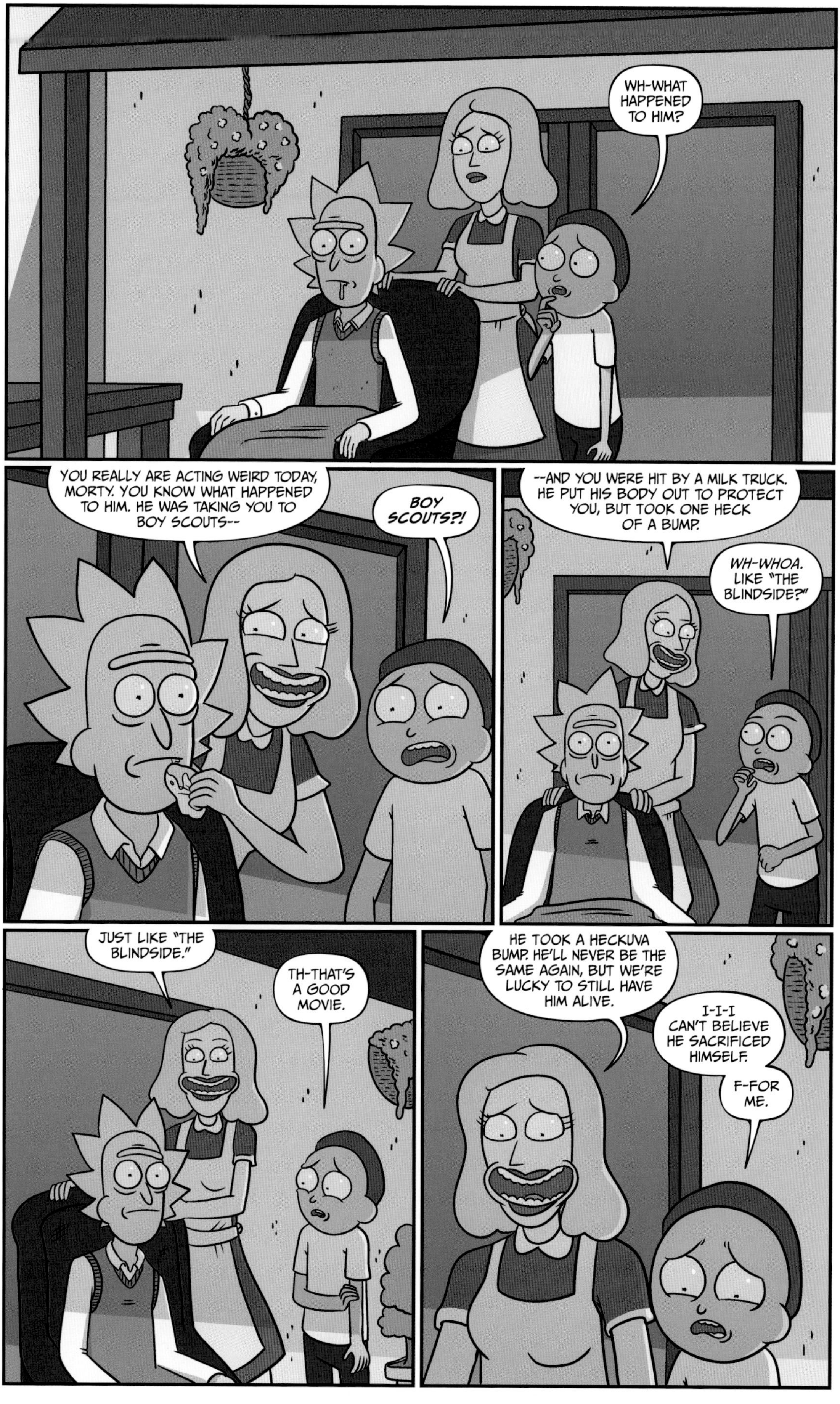
WH-WHAT HAPPENED TO HIM?
YOU REALLY ARE ACTING WEIRD TODAY, MORTY. YOU KNOW WHAT HAPPENED TO HIM. HE WAS TAKING YOU TO BOY SCOUTS--
BOY SCOUTS?!
--AND YOU WERE HIT BY A MILK TRUCK. HE PUT HIS BODY OUT TO PROTECT YOU, BUT TOOK ONE HECK OF A BUMP.
WH-WHOA. LIKE "THE BLINDSIDE?"
JUST LIKE "THE BLINDSIDE."
TH-THAT'S A GOOD MOVIE.
HE TOOK A HECKUVA BUMP. HE'LL NEVER BE THE SAME AGAIN, BUT WE'RE LUCKY TO STILL HAVE HIM ALIVE.
I-I-I CAN'T BELIEVE HE SACRIFICED HIMSELF.
F-FOR ME.

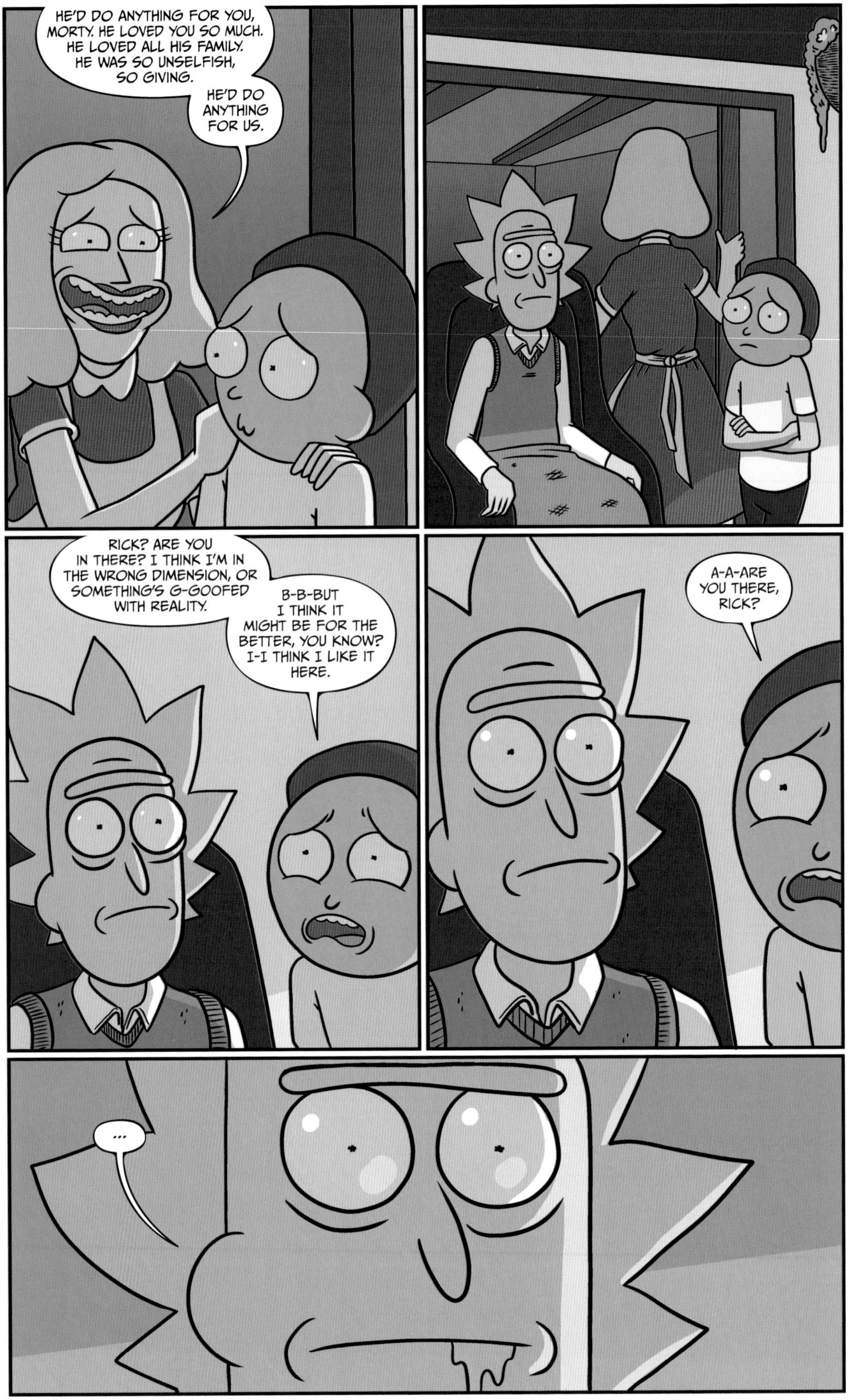
HE'D DO ANYTHING FOR YOU, MORTY. HE LOVED YOU SO MUCH. HE LOVED ALL HIS FAMILY. HE WAS SO UNSELFISH, SO GIVING.
HE'D DO ANYTHING FOR US.
RICK? ARE YOU IN THERE? I THINK I'M IN THE WRONG DIMENSION, OR SOMETHING'S G-GOOFED WITH REALITY.
B-B-BUT I THINK IT MIGHT BE FOR THE BETTER, YOU KNOW? I-I THINK I LIKE IT HERE.
A-A-ARE YOU THERE, RICK?
...

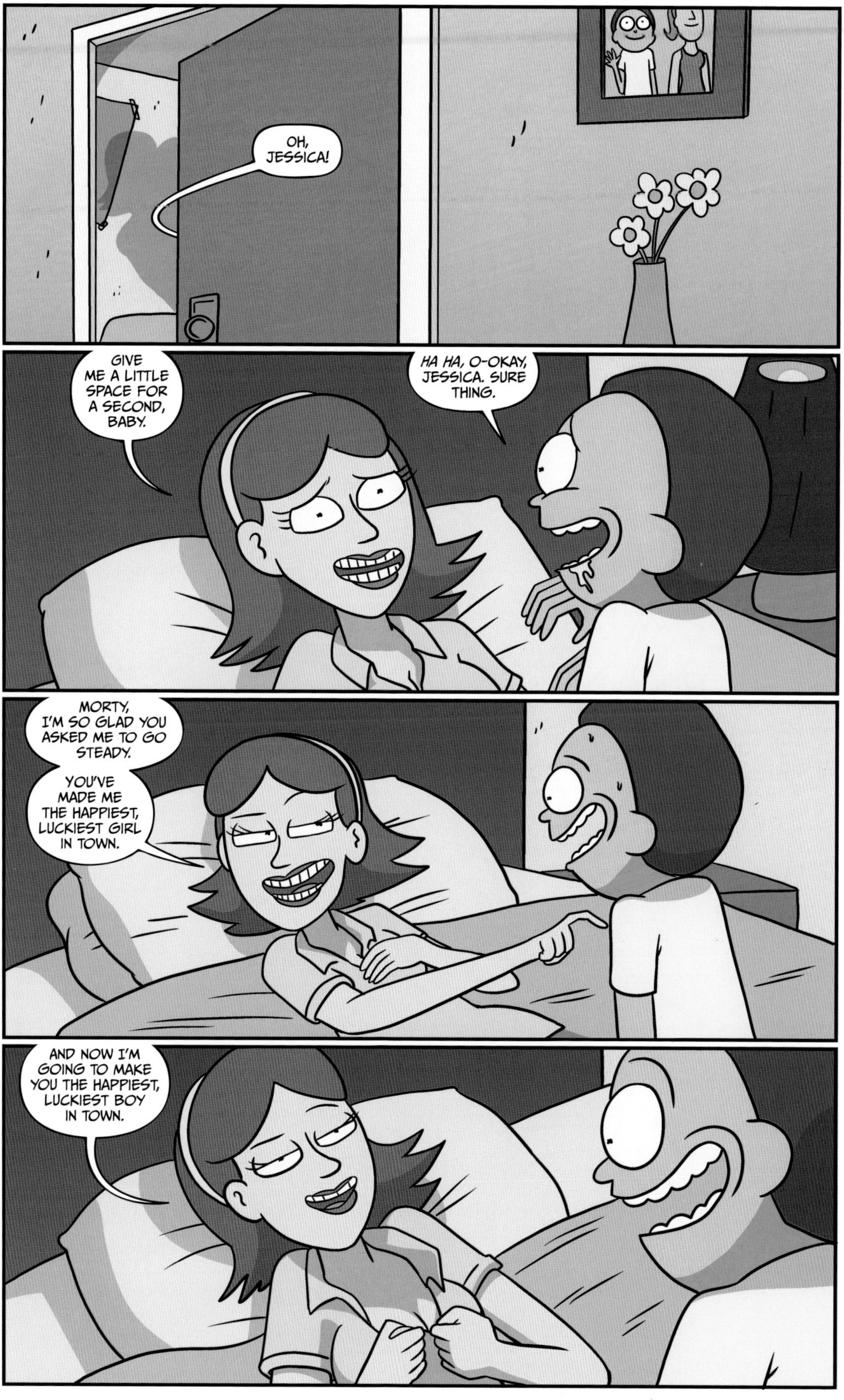
OH, JESSICA!
GIVE ME A LITTLE SPACE FOR A SECOND, BABY.
HA HA, O-OKAY, JESSICA. SURE THING.
MORTY, I'M SO GLAD YOU ASKED ME TO GO STEADY.
YOU'VE MADE ME THE HAPPIEST, LUCKIEST GIRL IN TOWN.
AND NOW I'M GOING TO MAKE YOU THE HAPPIEST, LUCKIEST BOY IN TOWN.

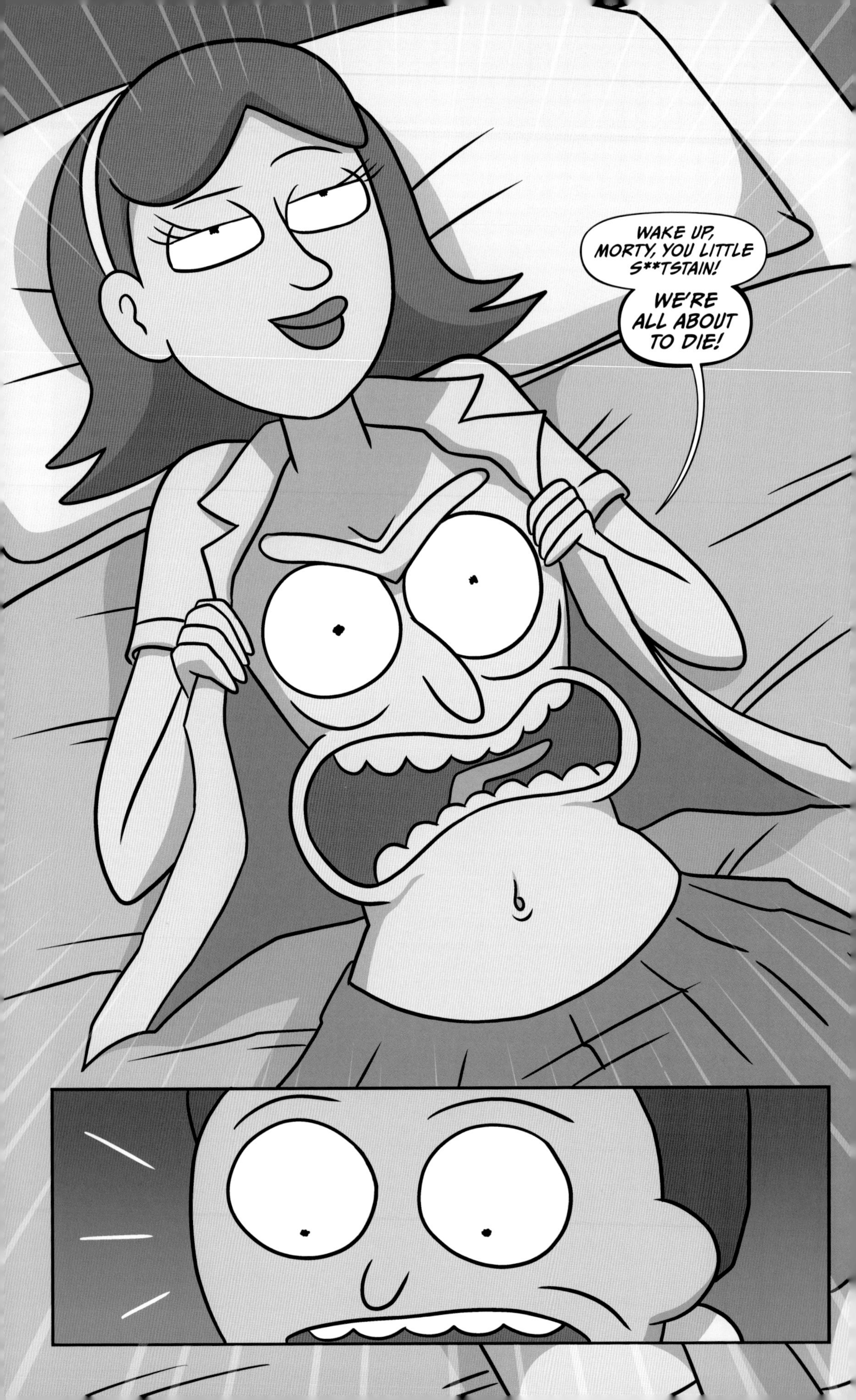
WAKE UP, MORTY, YOU LITTLE S**TSTAIN!
WE'RE ALL ABOUT TO DIE!

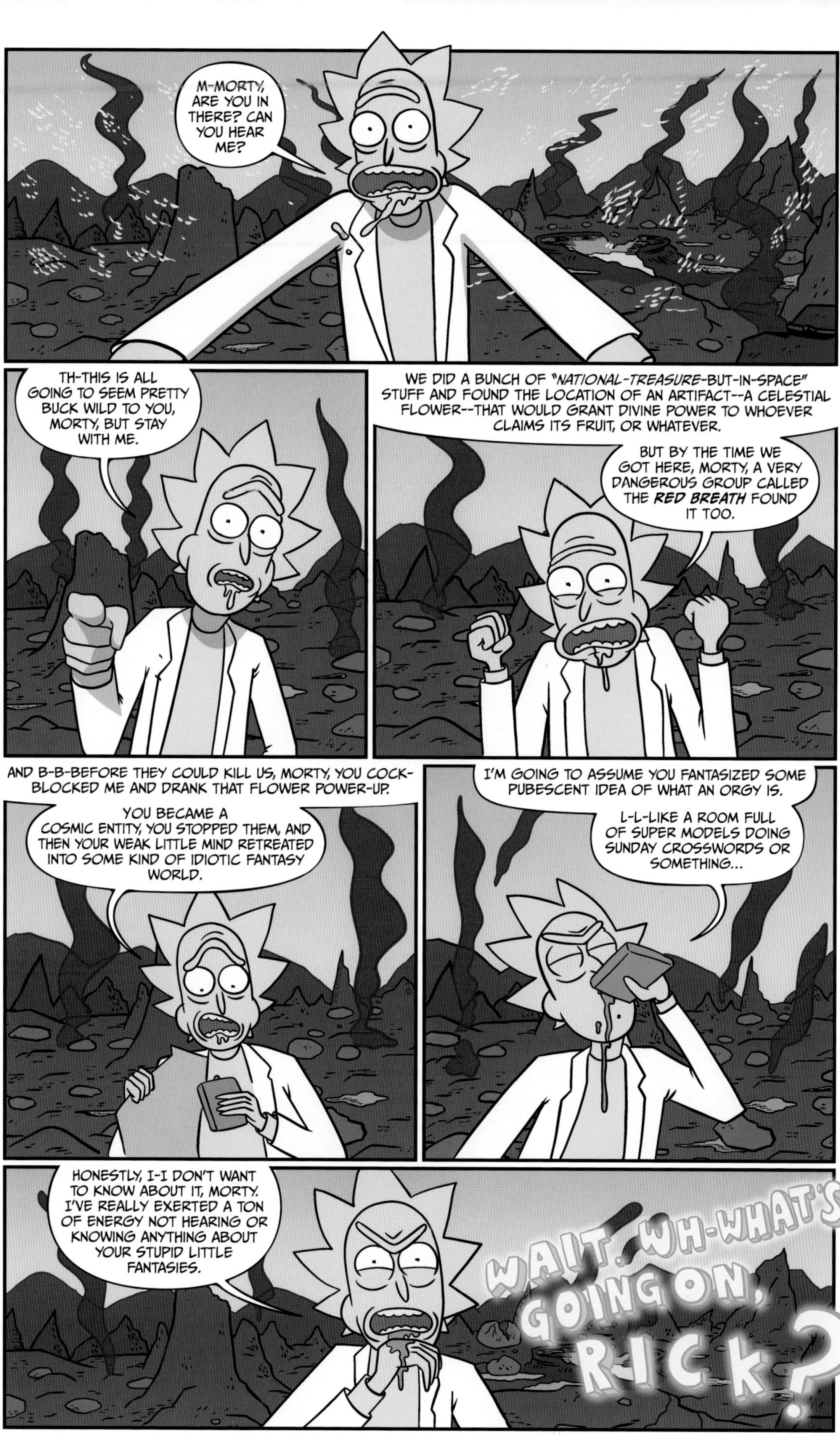
M-MORTY, ARE YOU IN THERE? CAN YOU HEAR ME?
TH-THIS IS ALL GOING TO SEEM PRETTY BUCK WILD TO YOU, MORTY, BUT STAY WITH ME.
WE DID A BUNCH OF "NATIONAL-TREASURE-BUT-IN-SPACE" STUFF AND FOUND THE LOCATION OF AN ARTIFACT--A CELESTIAL FLOWER--THAT WOULD GRANT DIVINE POWER TO WHOEVER CLAIMS ITS FRUIT, OR WHATEVER.
BUT BY THE TIME WE GOT HERE, MORTY, A VERY DANGEROUS GROUP CALLED THE RED BREATH FOUND IT TOO.
AND B-B-BEFORE THEY COULD KILL US, MORTY, YOU COCK-BLOCKED ME AND DRANK THAT FLOWER POWER-UP.
YOU BECAME A COSMIC ENTITY, YOU STOPPED THEM, AND THEN YOUR WEAK LITTLE MIND RETREATED INTO SOME KIND OF IDIOTIC FANTASY WORLD.
I'M GOING TO ASSUME YOU FANTASIZED SOME PUBESCENT IDEA OF WHAT AN ORGY IS.
L-L-LIKE A ROOM FULL OF SUPER MODELS DOING SUNDAY CROSSWORDS OR SOMETHING...
HONESTLY, I-I DON'T WANT TO KNOW ABOUT IT, MORTY. I'VE REALLY EXERTED A TON OF ENERGY NOT HEARING OR KNOWING ANYTHING ABOUT YOUR STUPID LITTLE FANTASIES.
WAIT. WH-WHAT'S GOING ON, RICK?

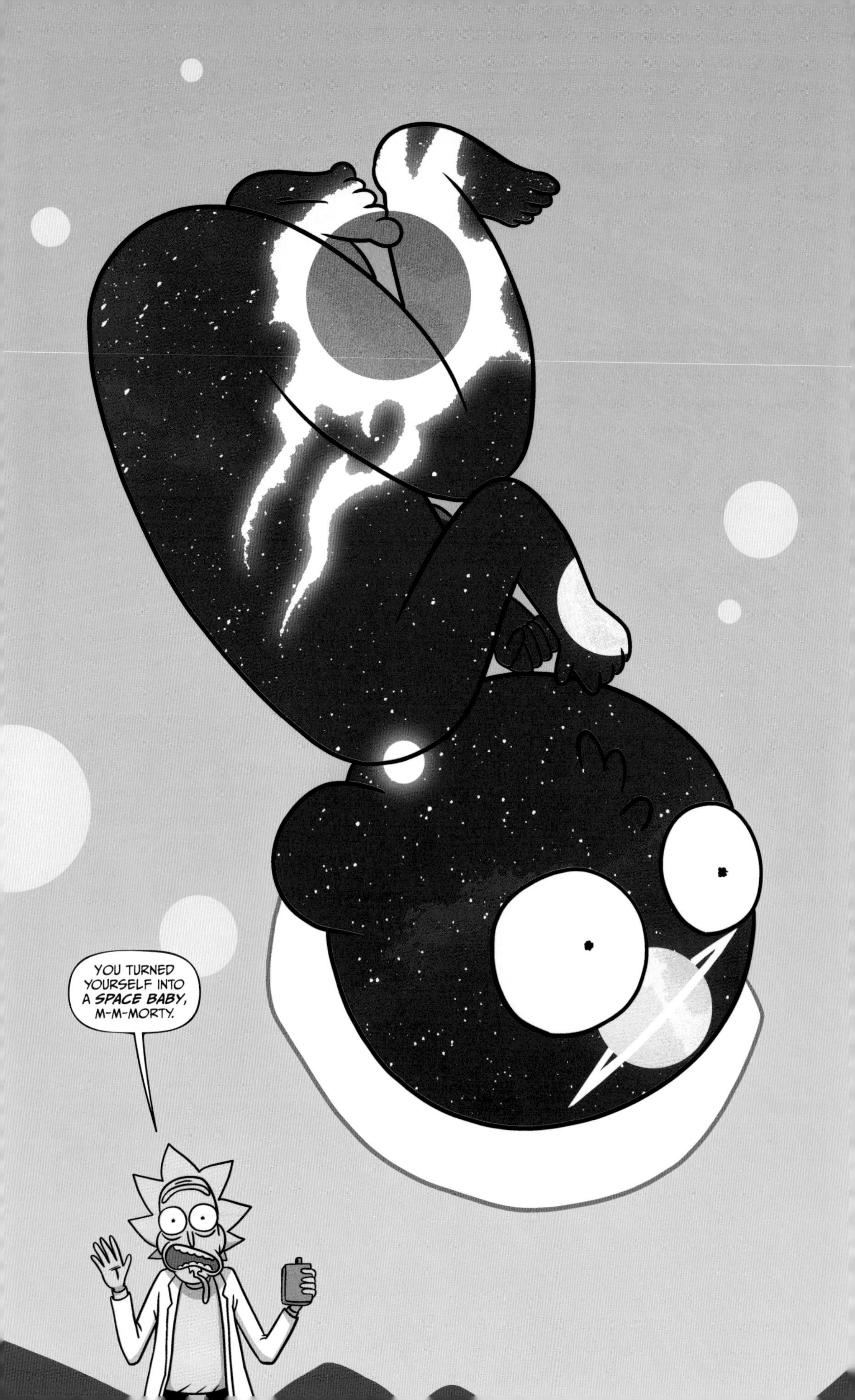
YOU TURNED YOURSELF INTO A **SPACE BABY**, M-M-MORTY.

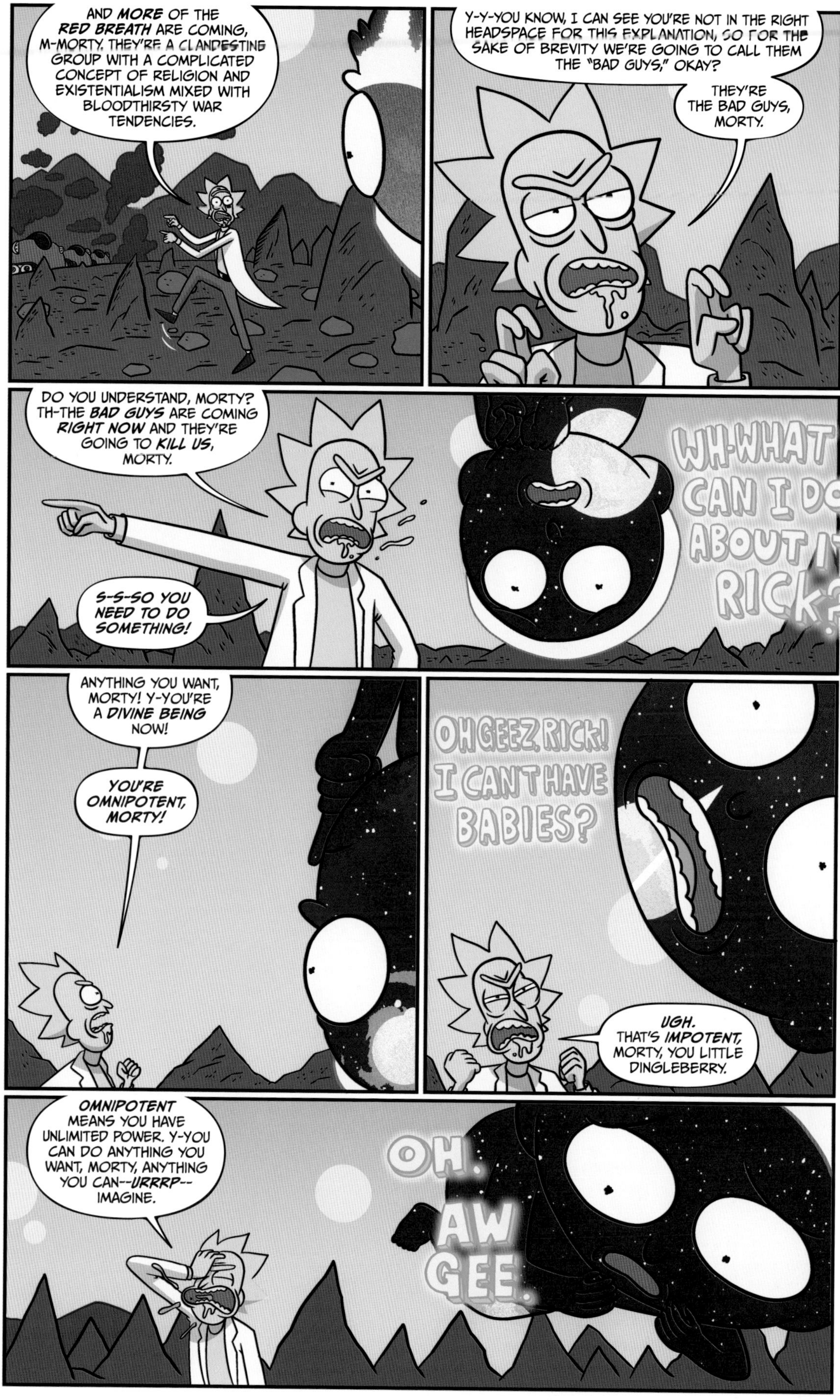
AND *MORE* OF THE *RED BREATH* ARE COMING, M-MORTY. THEY'RE A CLANDESTINE GROUP WITH A COMPLICATED CONCEPT OF RELIGION AND EXISTENTIALISM MIXED WITH BLOODTHIRSTY WAR TENDENCIES.
Y-Y-YOU KNOW, I CAN SEE YOU'RE NOT IN THE RIGHT HEADSPACE FOR THIS EXPLANATION, SO FOR THE SAKE OF BREVITY WE'RE GOING TO CALL THEM THE "BAD GUYS," OKAY?
THEY'RE THE BAD GUYS, MORTY.
DO YOU UNDERSTAND, MORTY? TH-THE *BAD GUYS* ARE COMING *RIGHT NOW* AND THEY'RE GOING TO *KILL US*, MORTY.
S-S-SO YOU NEED TO DO SOMETHING!
WH-WHAT CAN I DO ABOUT IT RICK?
ANYTHING YOU WANT, MORTY! Y-YOU'RE A *DIVINE BEING* NOW!
YOU'RE OMNIPOTENT, MORTY!
OH GEEZ RICK! I CAN'T HAVE BABIES?
UGH. THAT'S *IMPOTENT*, MORTY, YOU LITTLE DINGLEBERRY.
OMNIPOTENT MEANS YOU HAVE UNLIMITED POWER. Y-YOU CAN DO ANYTHING YOU WANT, MORTY, ANYTHING YOU CAN--*URRRP*-- IMAGINE.
OH.
AW GEE.

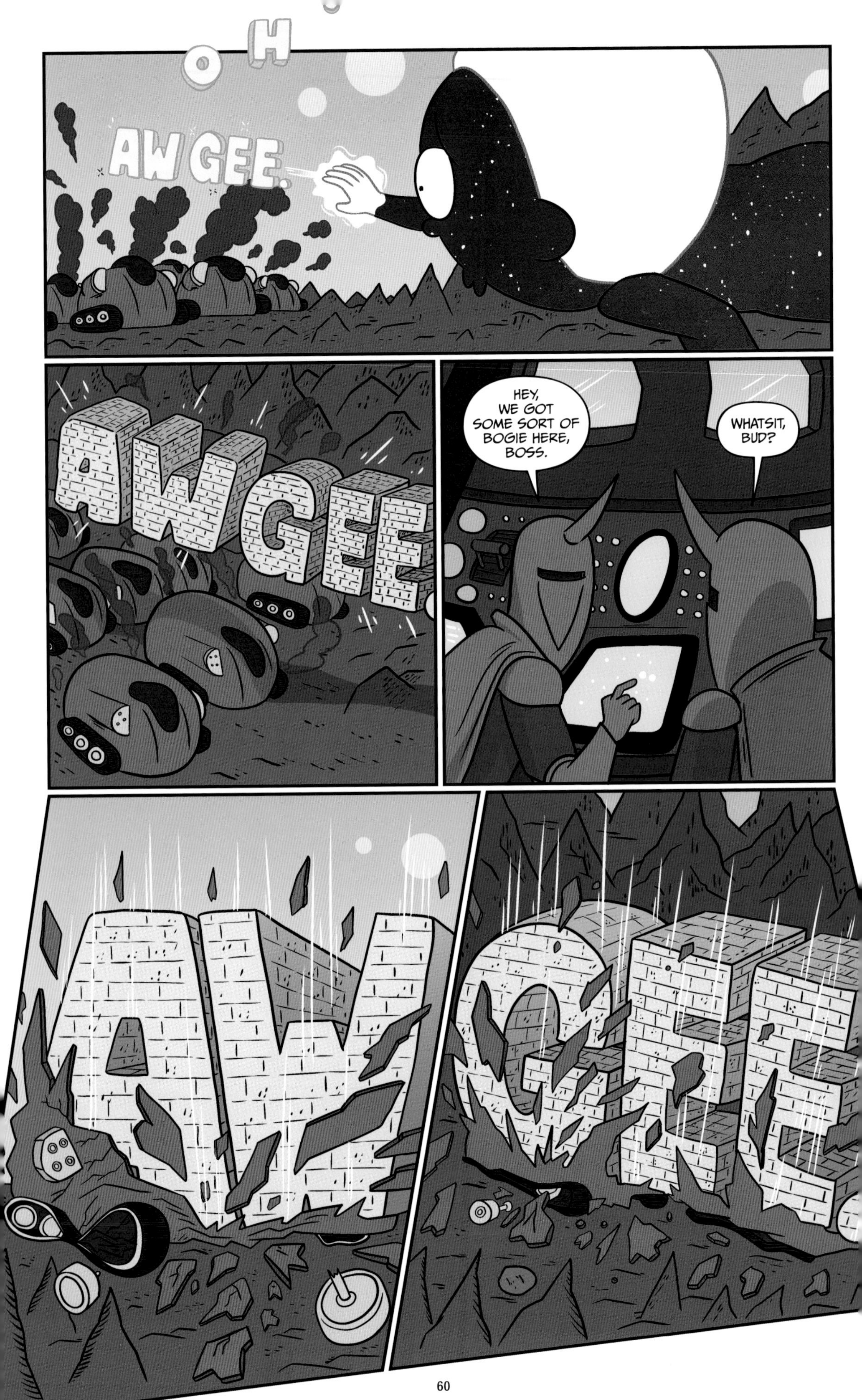
OH
AW GEE.
AWGEE
HEY, WE GOT SOME SORT OF BOGIE HERE, BOSS.
WHATSIT, BUD?
AWGEE

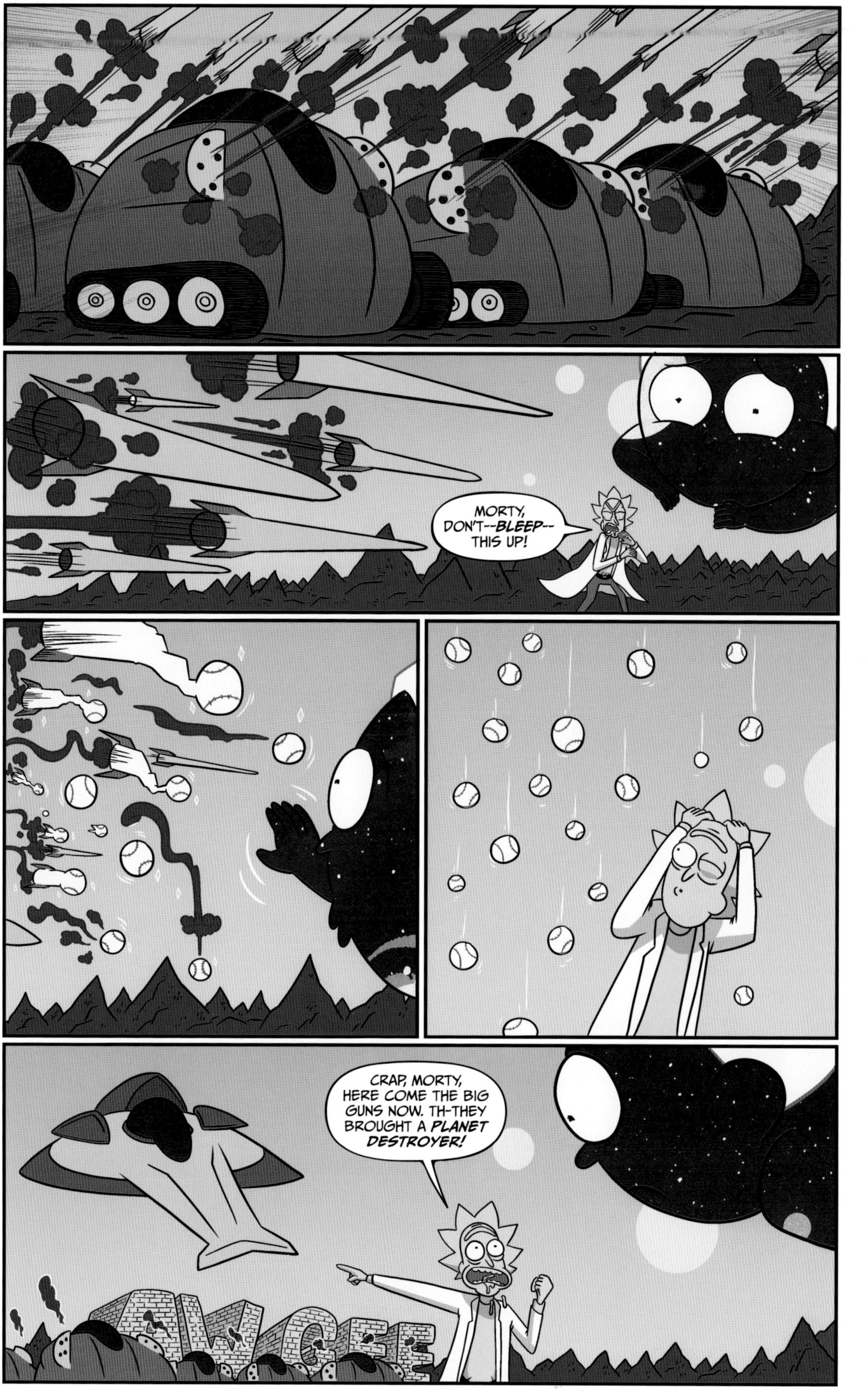
MORTY, DON'T--BLEEP-- THIS UP!
CRAP, MORTY, HERE COME THE BIG GUNS NOW. TH-THEY BROUGHT A PLANET DESTROYER!
AW GEE

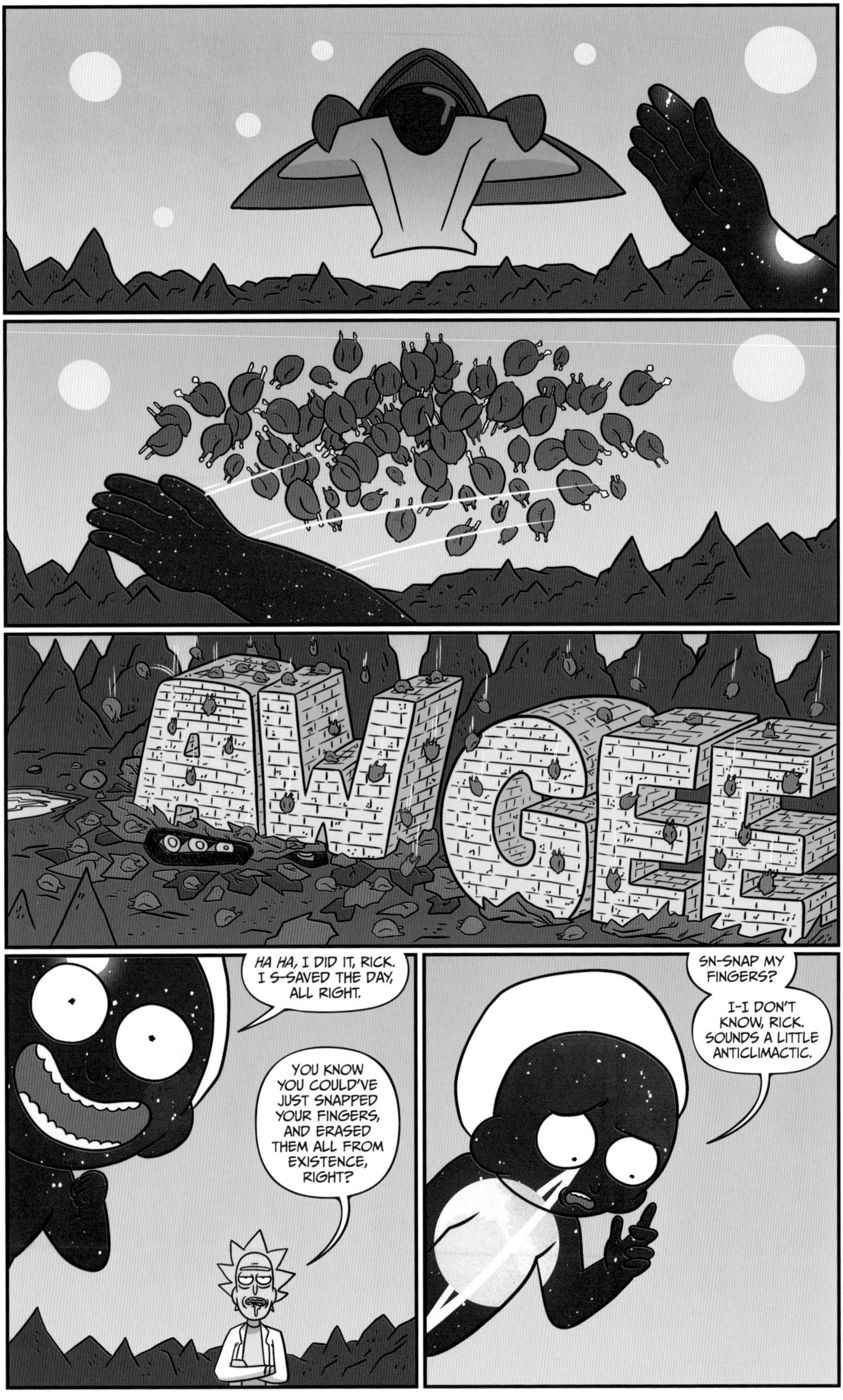
AWGEE
HA HA, I DID IT, RICK. I S-SAVED THE DAY, ALL RIGHT.
YOU KNOW YOU COULD'VE JUST SNAPPED YOUR FINGERS, AND ERASED THEM ALL FROM EXISTENCE, RIGHT?
SN-SNAP MY FINGERS?
I-I DON'T KNOW, RICK. SOUNDS A LITTLE ANTICLIMACTIC.

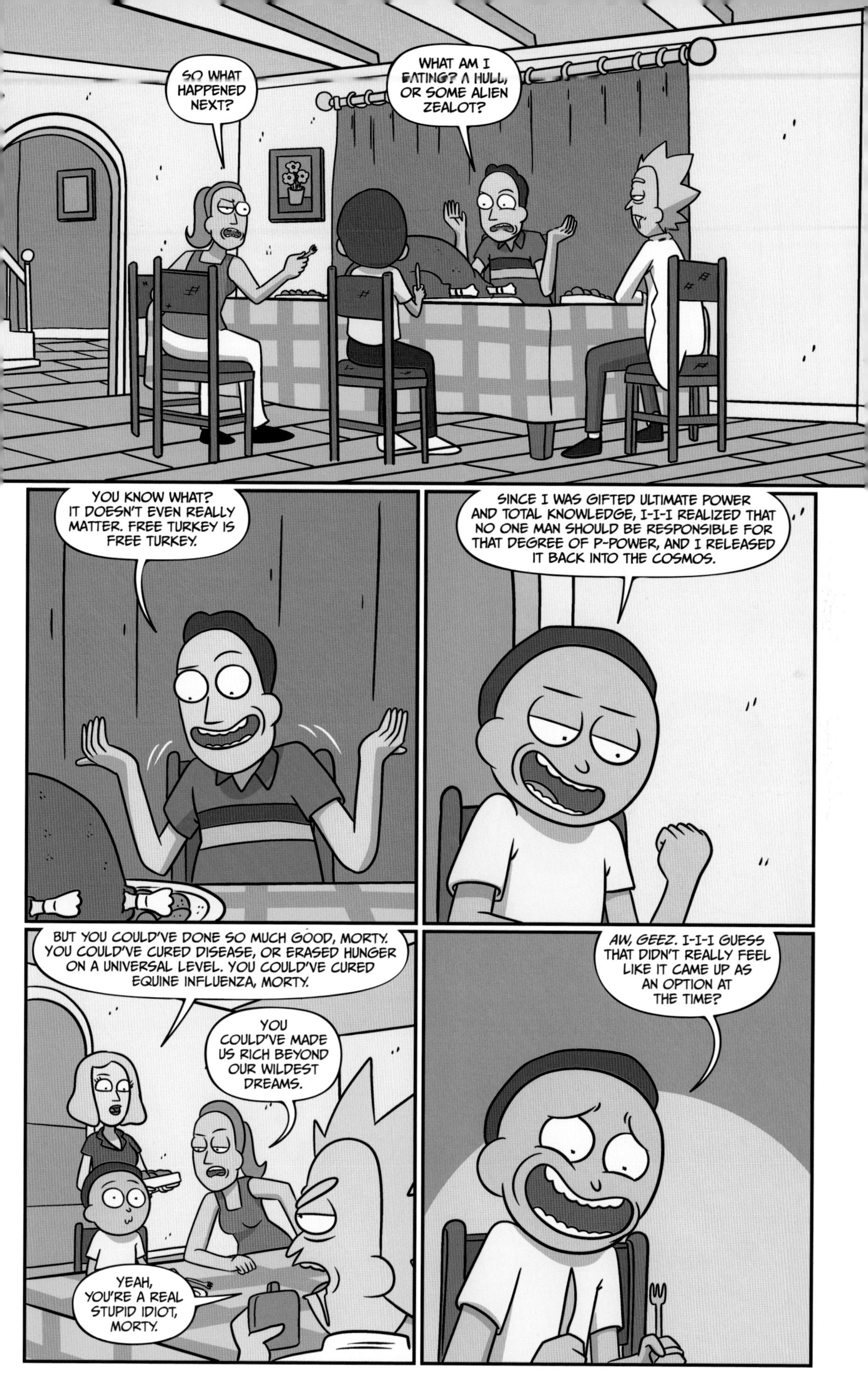
SO WHAT HAPPENED NEXT?
WHAT AM I EATING? A HULL, OR SOME ALIEN ZEALOT?
YOU KNOW WHAT? IT DOESN'T EVEN REALLY MATTER. FREE TURKEY IS FREE TURKEY.
SINCE I WAS GIFTED ULTIMATE POWER AND TOTAL KNOWLEDGE, I-I-I REALIZED THAT NO ONE MAN SHOULD BE RESPONSIBLE FOR THAT DEGREE OF P-POWER, AND I RELEASED IT BACK INTO THE COSMOS.
BUT YOU COULD'VE DONE SO MUCH GOOD, MORTY. YOU COULD'VE CURED DISEASE, OR ERASED HUNGER ON A UNIVERSAL LEVEL. YOU COULD'VE CURED EQUINE INFLUENZA, MORTY.
YOU COULD'VE MADE US RICH BEYOND OUR WILDEST DREAMS.
YEAH, YOU'RE A REAL STUPID IDIOT, MORTY.
AW, GEEZ. I-I-I GUESS THAT DIDN'T REALLY FEEL LIKE IT CAME UP AS AN OPTION AT THE TIME?

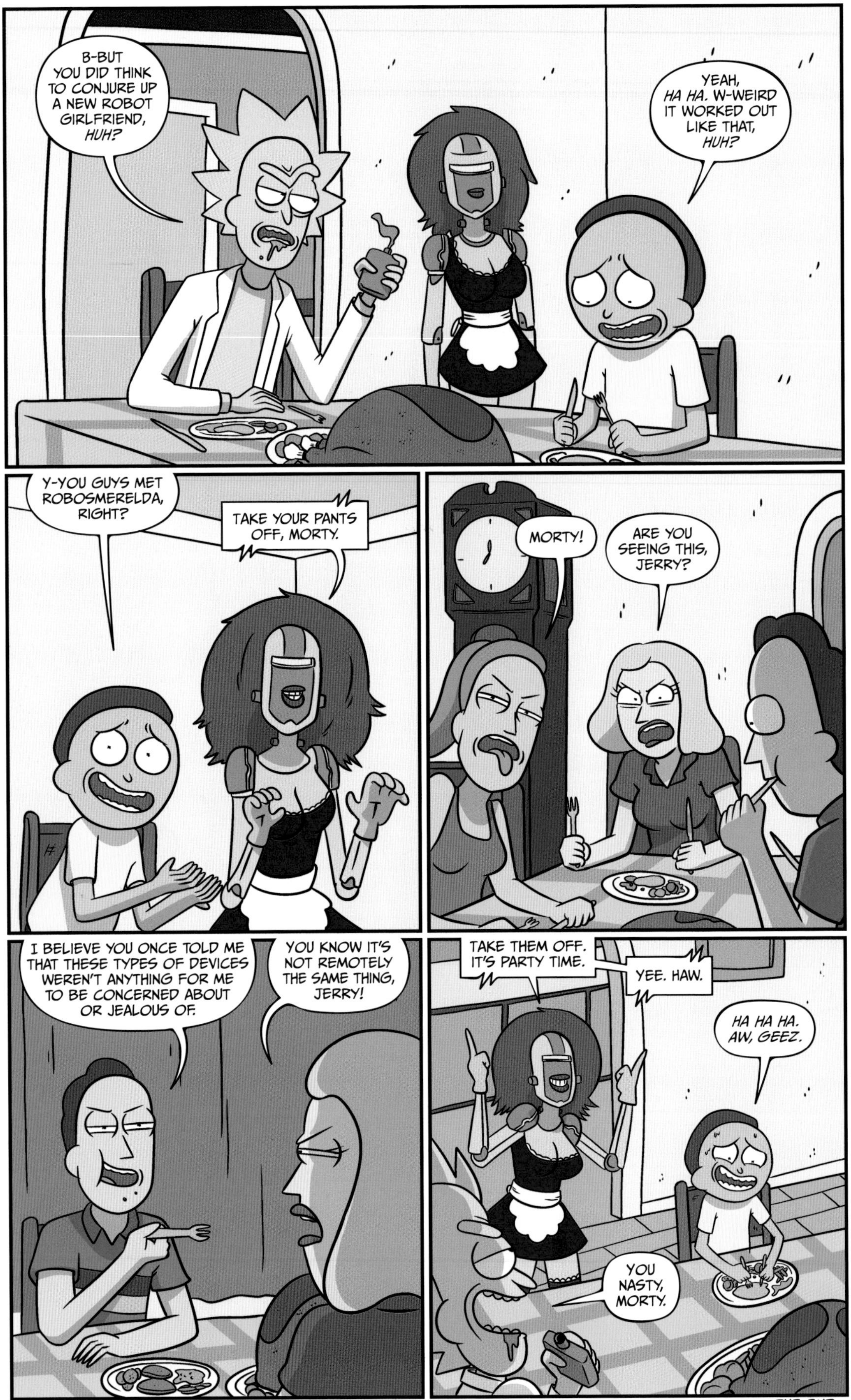

B-BUT YOU DID THINK TO CONJURE UP A NEW ROBOT GIRLFRIEND, *HUH?*
YEAH, *HA HA.* W-WEIRD IT WORKED OUT LIKE THAT, *HUH?*
Y-YOU GUYS MET ROBOSMERELDA, RIGHT?
TAKE YOUR PANTS OFF, MORTY.
MORTY!
ARE YOU SEEING THIS, JERRY?
I BELIEVE YOU ONCE TOLD ME THAT THESE TYPES OF DEVICES WEREN'T ANYTHING FOR ME TO BE CONCERNED ABOUT OR JEALOUS OF.
YOU KNOW IT'S NOT REMOTELY THE SAME THING, JERRY!
TAKE THEM OFF. IT'S PARTY TIME.
YEE. HAW.
HA HA HA. AW, GEEZ.
YOU NASTY, MORTY.

THE END.

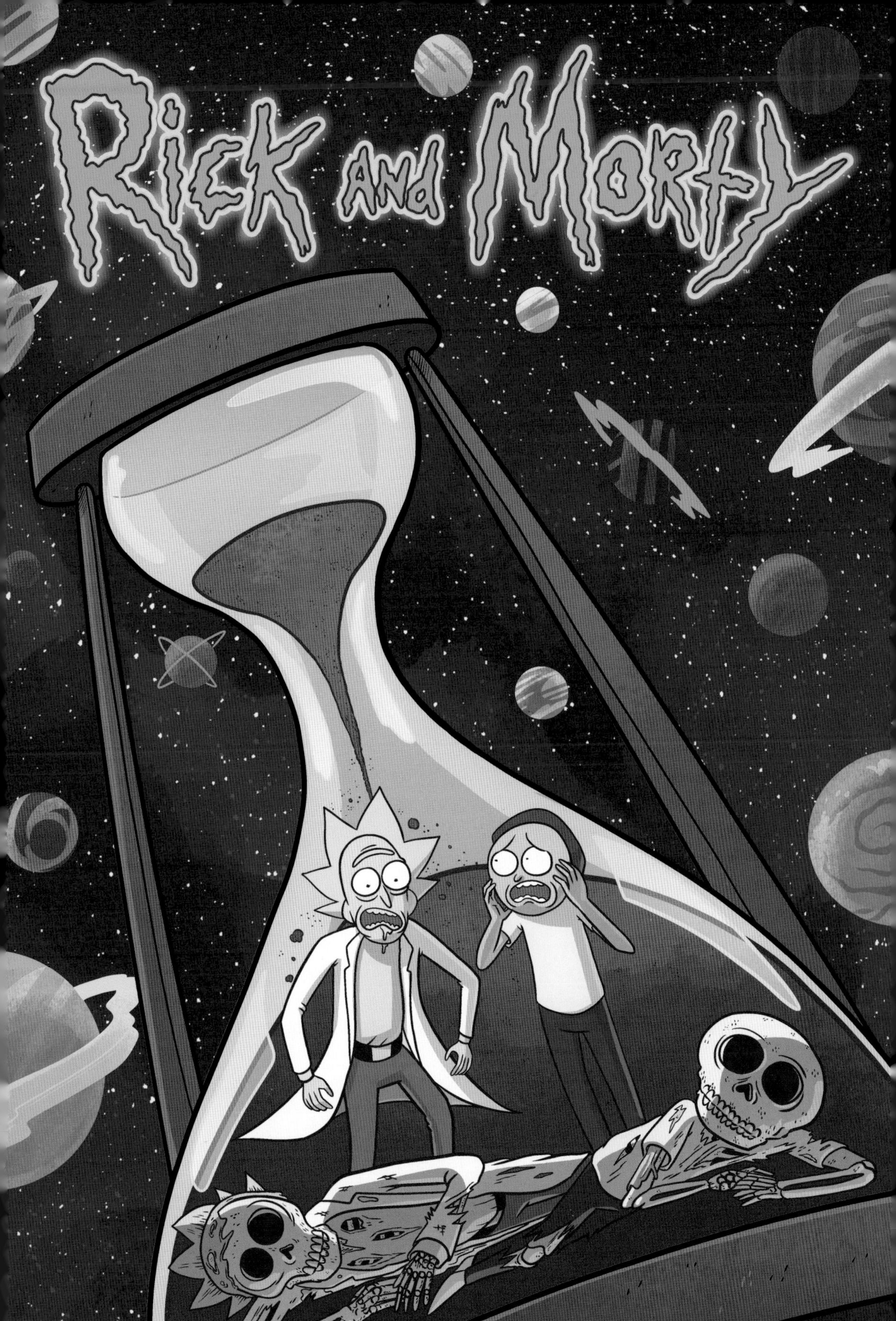
Rick and Morty

"RICKTROACTIVE"

WRITTEN BY **KYLE STARKS** ILLUSTRATED BY **MARC ELLERBY** COLORED BY **SARAH STERN** LETTERED BY **CRANK!**

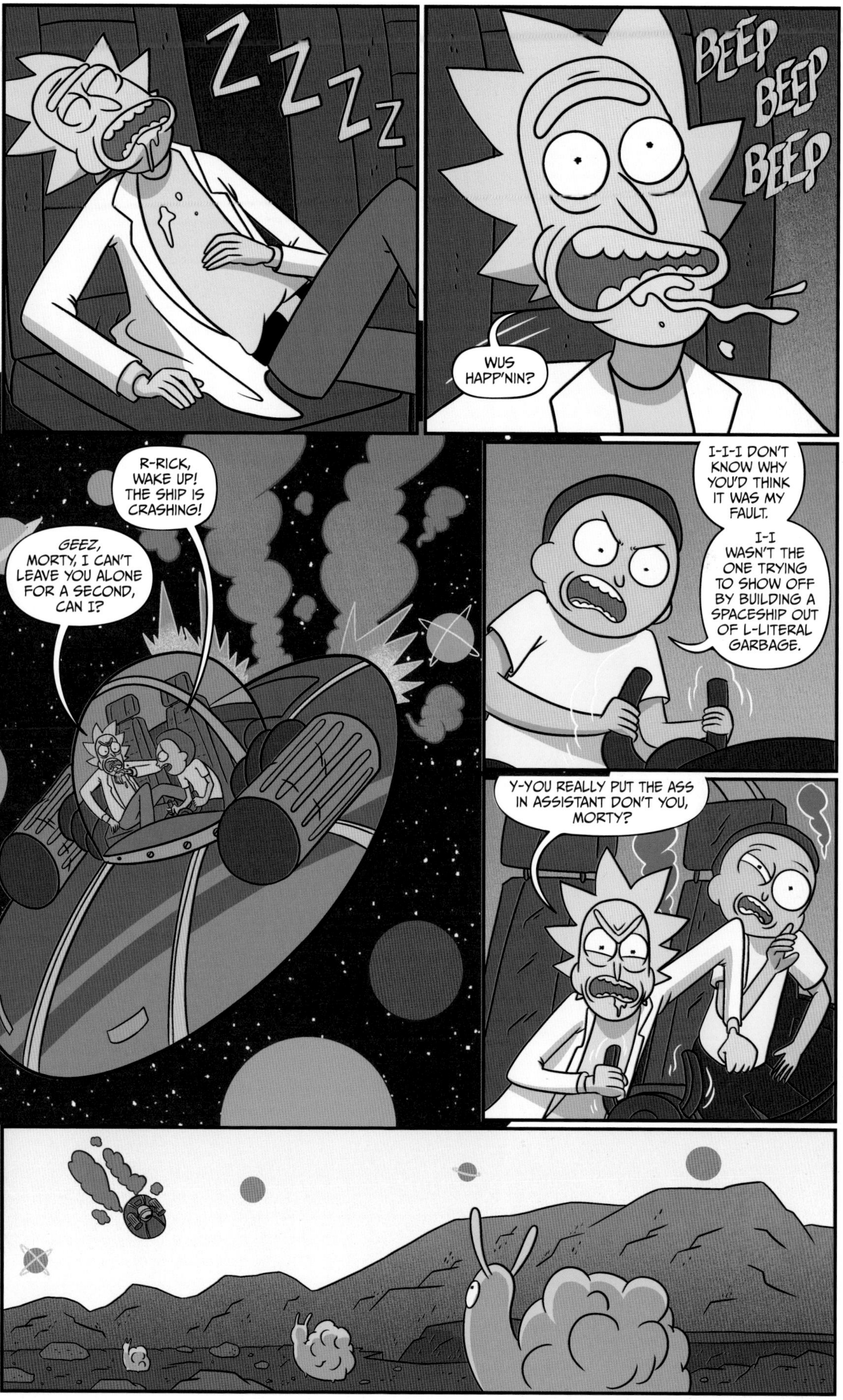
ZZZZZ
BEEP BEEP BEEP
WUS HAPP'NIN?
R-RICK, WAKE UP! THE SHIP IS CRASHING!
GEEZ, MORTY, I CAN'T LEAVE YOU ALONE FOR A SECOND, CAN I?
I-I-I DON'T KNOW WHY YOU'D THINK IT WAS MY FAULT.
I-I WASN'T THE ONE TRYING TO SHOW OFF BY BUILDING A SPACESHIP OUT OF L-LITERAL GARBAGE.
Y-YOU REALLY PUT THE ASS IN ASSISTANT DON'T YOU, MORTY?

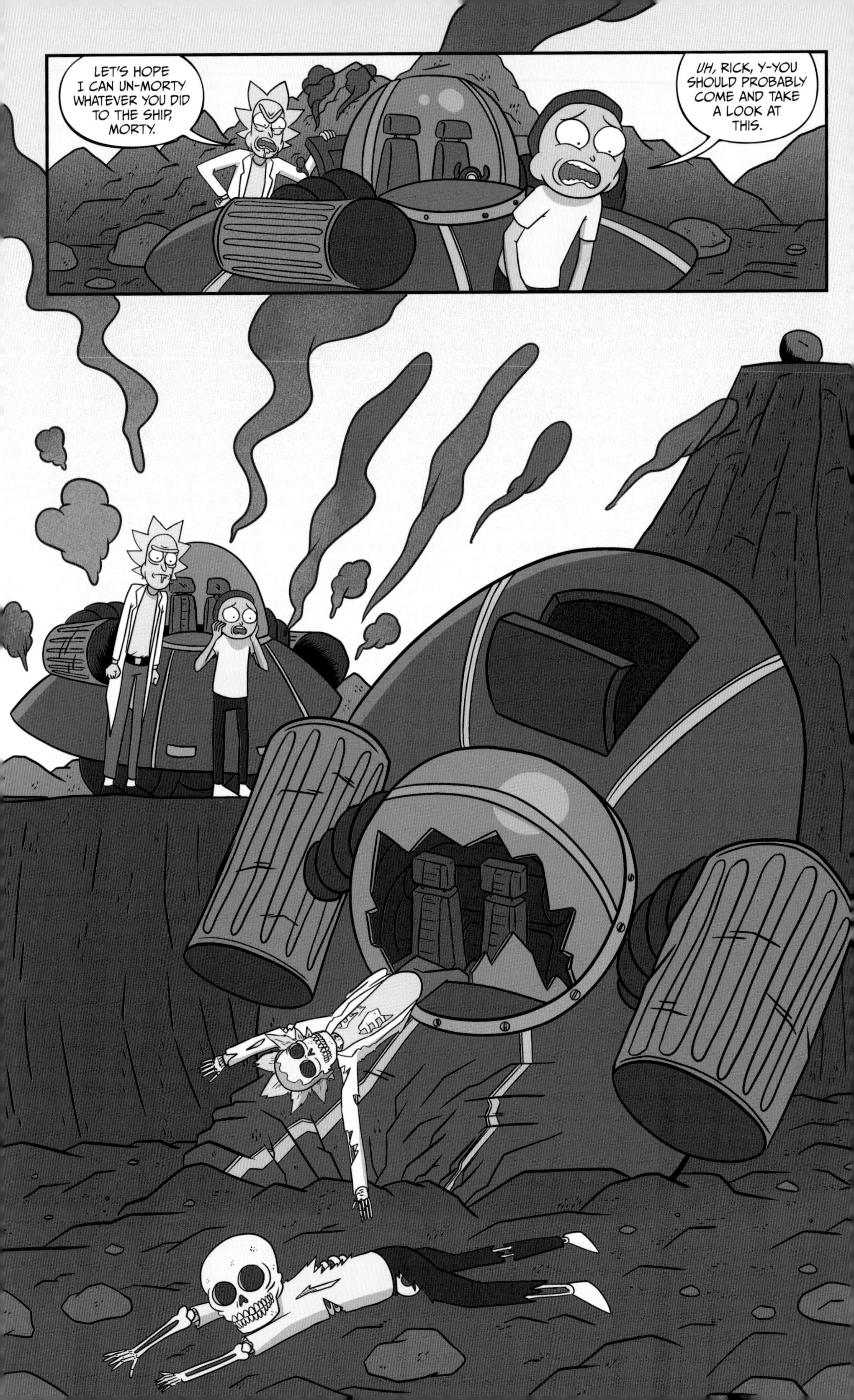
LET'S HOPE I CAN UN-MORTY WHATEVER YOU DID TO THE SHIP, MORTY.
UH, RICK, Y-YOU SHOULD PROBABLY COME AND TAKE A LOOK AT THIS.

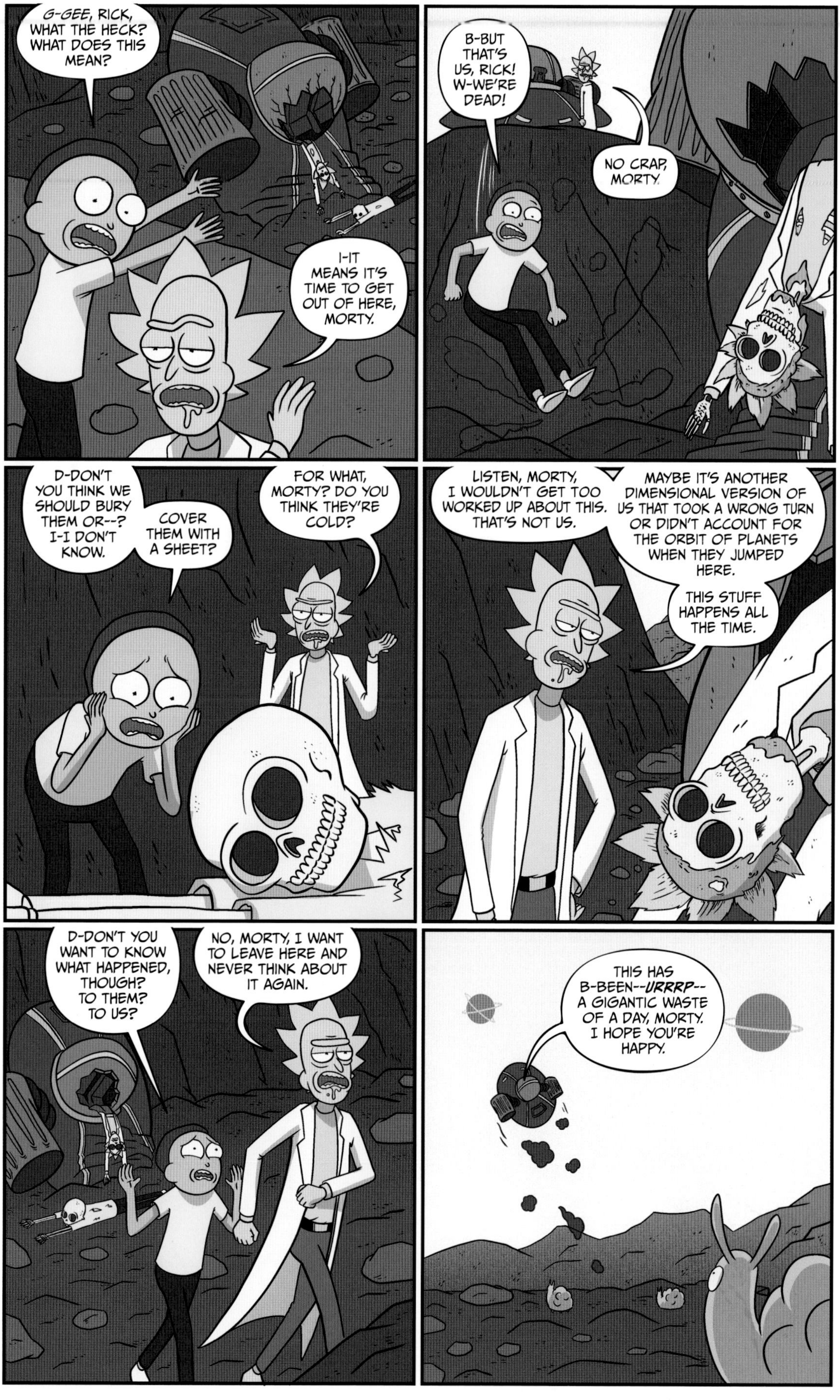
G-GEE, RICK, WHAT THE HECK? WHAT DOES THIS MEAN?
I-IT MEANS IT'S TIME TO GET OUT OF HERE, MORTY.
B-BUT THAT'S US, RICK! W-WE'RE DEAD!
NO CRAP, MORTY.
D-DON'T YOU THINK WE SHOULD BURY THEM OR--? I-I DON'T KNOW.
COVER THEM WITH A SHEET?
FOR WHAT, MORTY? DO YOU THINK THEY'RE COLD?
LISTEN, MORTY, I WOULDN'T GET TOO WORKED UP ABOUT THIS. THAT'S NOT US.
MAYBE IT'S ANOTHER DIMENSIONAL VERSION OF US THAT TOOK A WRONG TURN OR DIDN'T ACCOUNT FOR THE ORBIT OF PLANETS WHEN THEY JUMPED HERE.
THIS STUFF HAPPENS ALL THE TIME.
D-DON'T YOU WANT TO KNOW WHAT HAPPENED, THOUGH? TO THEM? TO US?
NO, MORTY, I WANT TO LEAVE HERE AND NEVER THINK ABOUT IT AGAIN.
THIS HAS B-BEEN--URRRP--A GIGANTIC WASTE OF A DAY, MORTY. I HOPE YOU'RE HAPPY.

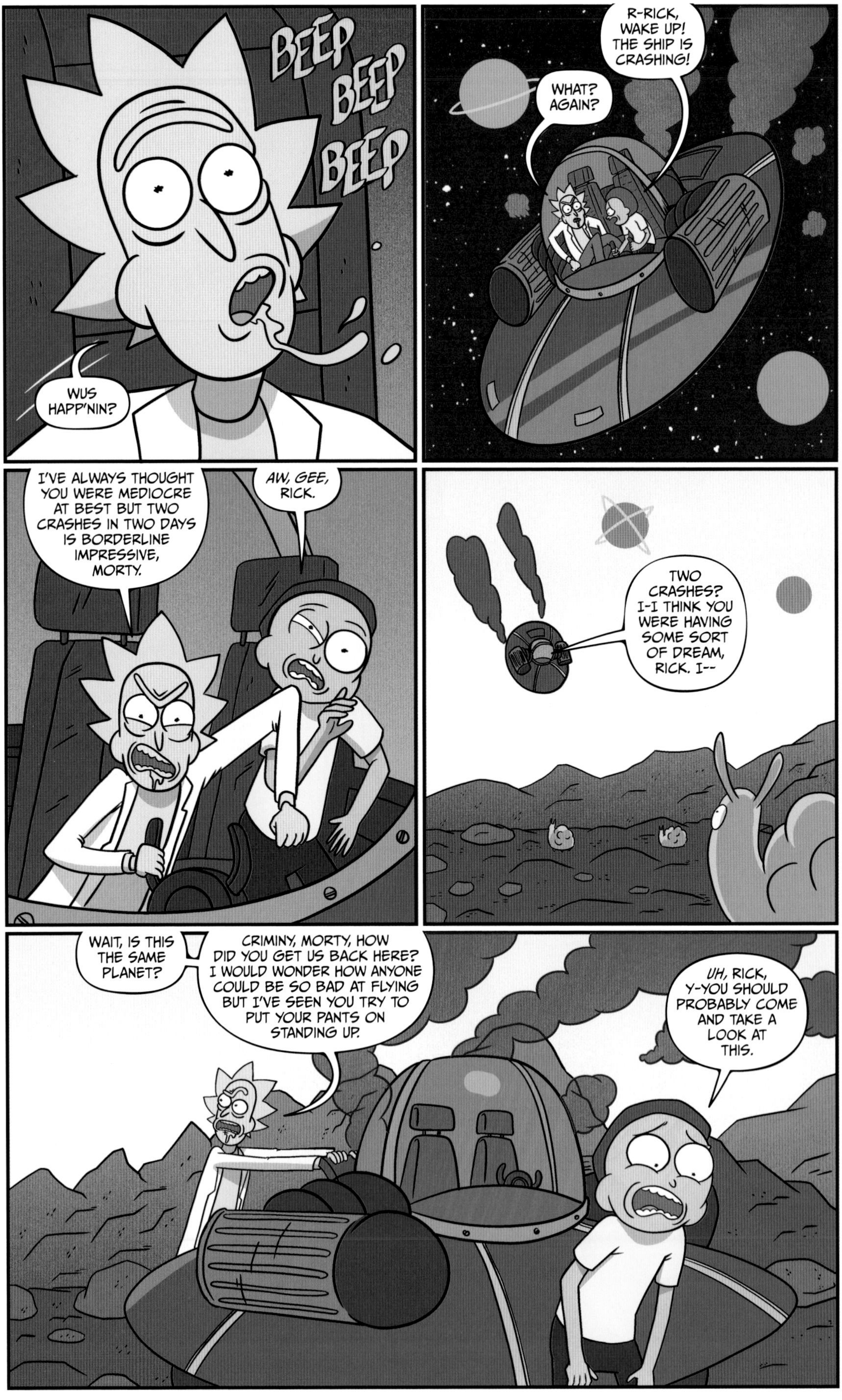

BEEP BEEP BEEP
WUS HAPP'NIN?
R-RICK, WAKE UP! THE SHIP IS CRASHING!
WHAT? AGAIN?
I'VE ALWAYS THOUGHT YOU WERE MEDIOCRE AT BEST BUT TWO CRASHES IN TWO DAYS IS BORDERLINE IMPRESSIVE, MORTY.
AW, GEE, RICK.
TWO CRASHES? I-I THINK YOU WERE HAVING SOME SORT OF DREAM, RICK. I--
WAIT, IS THIS THE SAME PLANET?
CRIMINY, MORTY, HOW DID YOU GET US BACK HERE? I WOULD WONDER HOW ANYONE COULD BE SO BAD AT FLYING BUT I'VE SEEN YOU TRY TO PUT YOUR PANTS ON STANDING UP.
UH, RICK, Y-YOU SHOULD PROBABLY COME AND TAKE A LOOK AT THIS.

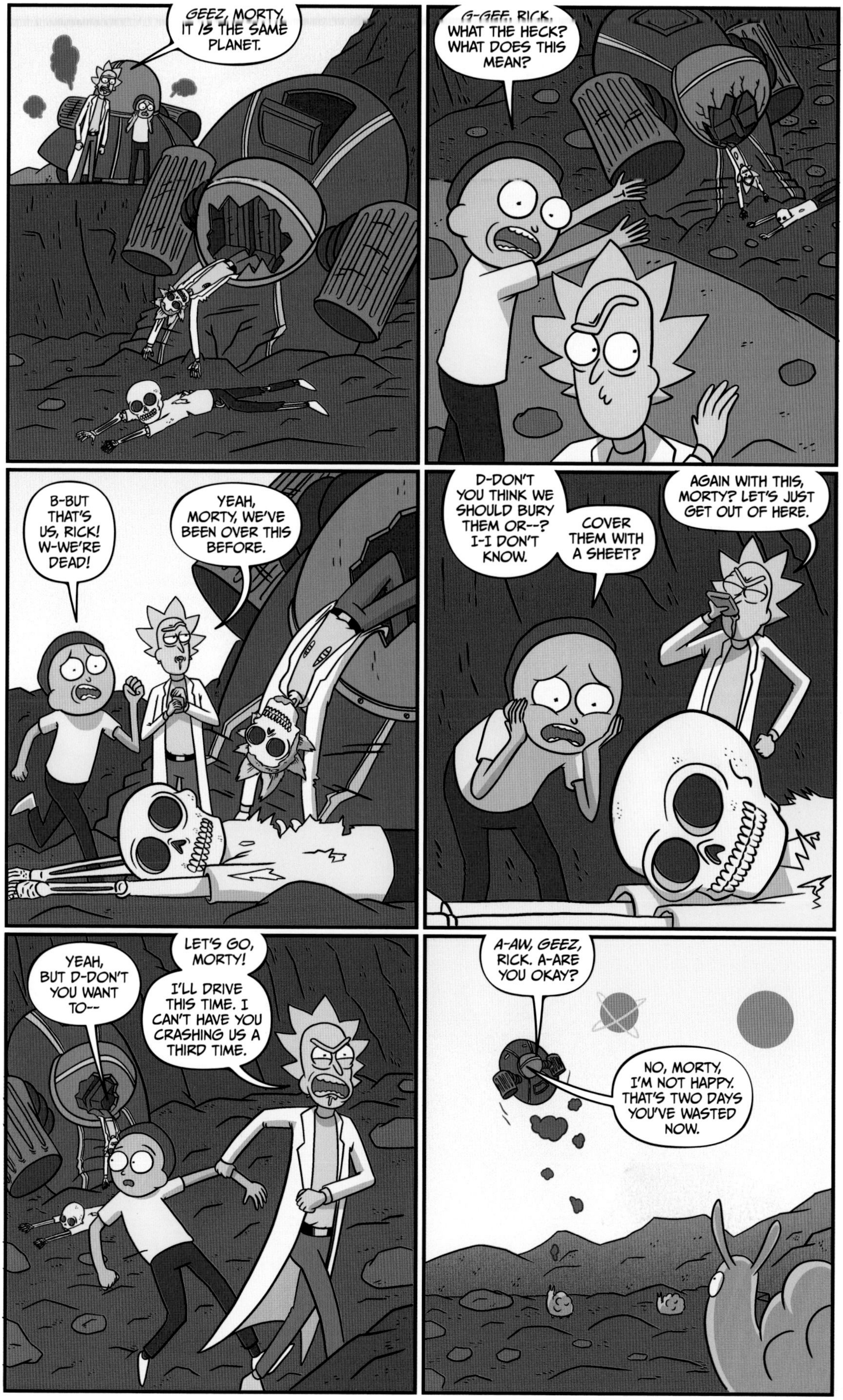
GEEZ, MORTY, IT IS THE SAME PLANET.
G-GEE, RICK. WHAT THE HECK? WHAT DOES THIS MEAN?
B-BUT THAT'S US, RICK! W-WE'RE DEAD!
YEAH, MORTY, WE'VE BEEN OVER THIS BEFORE.
D-DON'T YOU THINK WE SHOULD BURY THEM OR--? I-I DON'T KNOW.
COVER THEM WITH A SHEET?
AGAIN WITH THIS, MORTY? LET'S JUST GET OUT OF HERE.
YEAH, BUT D-DON'T YOU WANT TO--
LET'S GO, MORTY!
I'LL DRIVE THIS TIME. I CAN'T HAVE YOU CRASHING US A THIRD TIME.
A-AW, GEEZ, RICK. A-ARE YOU OKAY?
NO, MORTY, I'M NOT HAPPY. THAT'S TWO DAYS YOU'VE WASTED NOW.

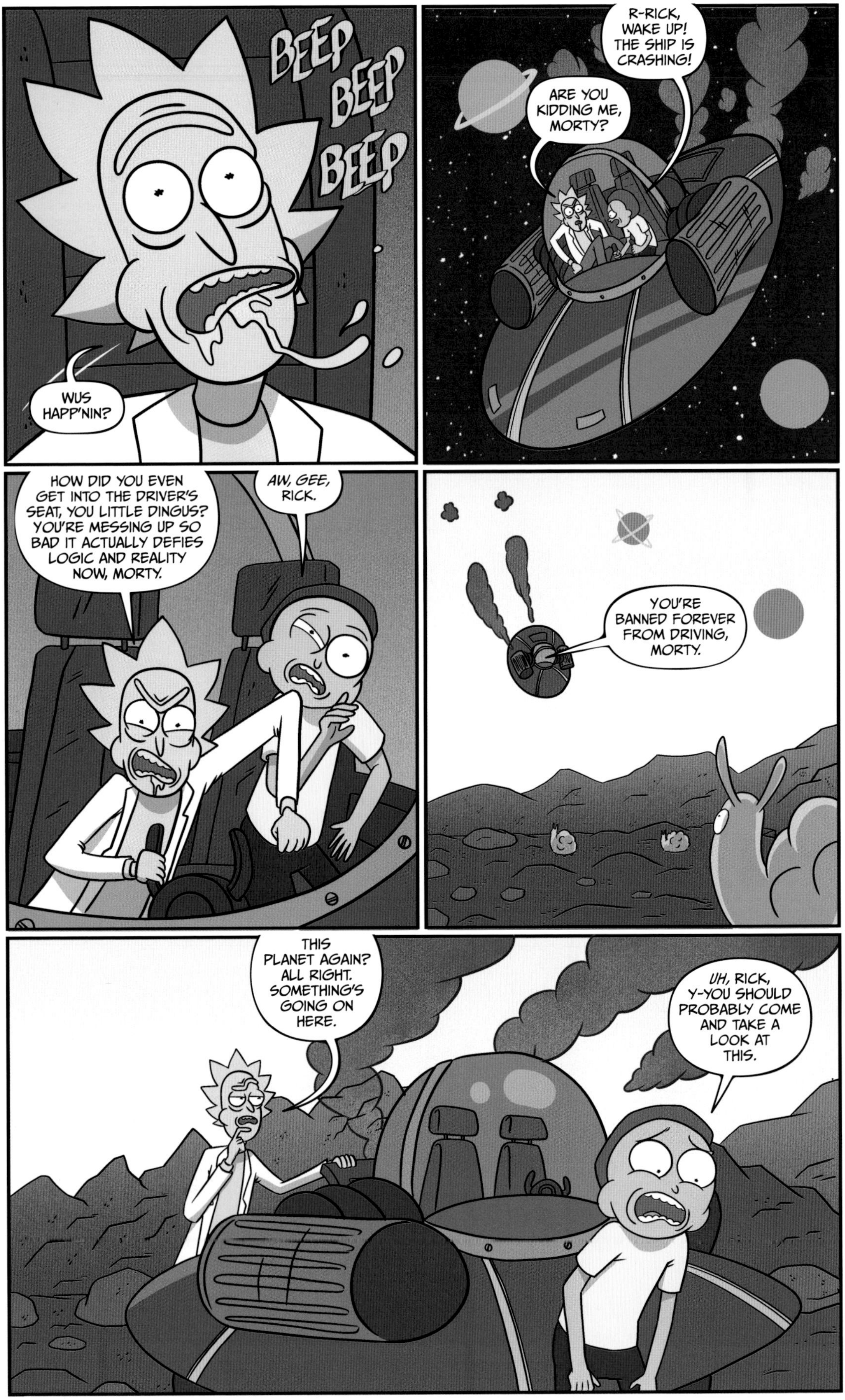
BEEP
BEEP
BEEP
WUS HAPP'NIN?
R-RICK, WAKE UP! THE SHIP IS CRASHING!
ARE YOU KIDDING ME, MORTY?
HOW DID YOU EVEN GET INTO THE DRIVER'S SEAT, YOU LITTLE DINGUS? YOU'RE MESSING UP SO BAD IT ACTUALLY DEFIES LOGIC AND REALITY NOW, MORTY.
AW, GEE, RICK.
YOU'RE BANNED FOREVER FROM DRIVING, MORTY.
THIS PLANET AGAIN? ALL RIGHT. SOMETHING'S GOING ON HERE.
UH, RICK, Y-YOU SHOULD PROBABLY COME AND TAKE A LOOK AT THIS.

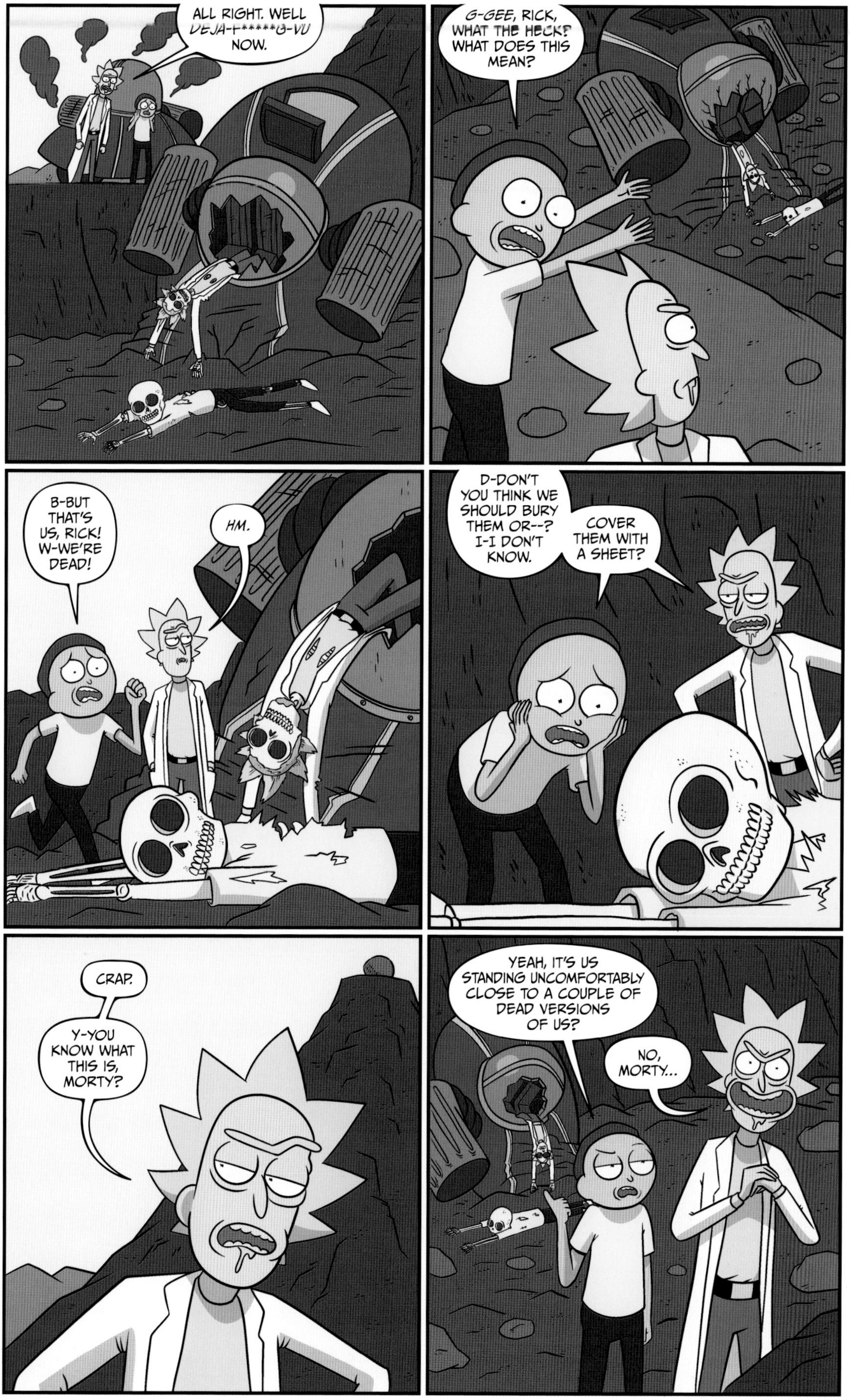

ALL RIGHT. WELL DEJA-F*****G-VU NOW.
G-GEE, RICK, WHAT THE HECK? WHAT DOES THIS MEAN?
B-BUT THAT'S US, RICK! W-WE'RE DEAD!
HM.
D-DON'T YOU THINK WE SHOULD BURY THEM OR--? I-I DON'T KNOW.
COVER THEM WITH A SHEET?
CRAP.
Y-YOU KNOW WHAT THIS IS, MORTY?
YEAH, IT'S US STANDING UNCOMFORTABLY CLOSE TO A COUPLE OF DEAD VERSIONS OF US?
NO, MORTY...

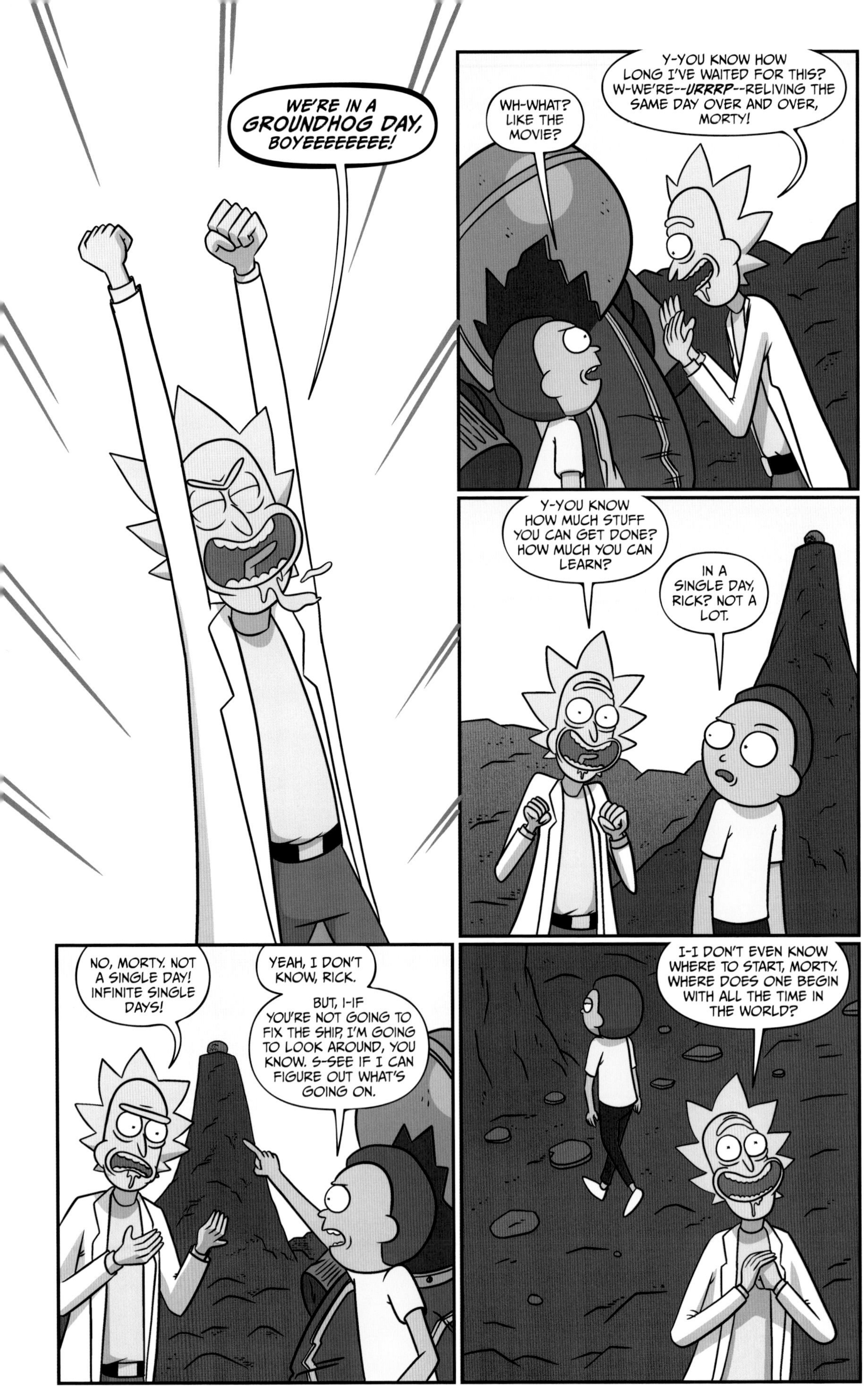
WE'RE IN A GROUNDHOG DAY, BOYEEEEEEEE!
WH-WHAT? LIKE THE MOVIE?
Y-YOU KNOW HOW LONG I'VE WAITED FOR THIS? W-WE'RE--URRRP--RELIVING THE SAME DAY OVER AND OVER, MORTY!
Y-YOU KNOW HOW MUCH STUFF YOU CAN GET DONE? HOW MUCH YOU CAN LEARN?
IN A SINGLE DAY, RICK? NOT A LOT.
NO, MORTY. NOT A SINGLE DAY! INFINITE SINGLE DAYS!
YEAH, I DON'T KNOW, RICK.
BUT, I-IF YOU'RE NOT GOING TO FIX THE SHIP, I'M GOING TO LOOK AROUND, YOU KNOW. S-SEE IF I CAN FIGURE OUT WHAT'S GOING ON.
I-I DON'T EVEN KNOW WHERE TO START, MORTY. WHERE DOES ONE BEGIN WITH ALL THE TIME IN THE WORLD?

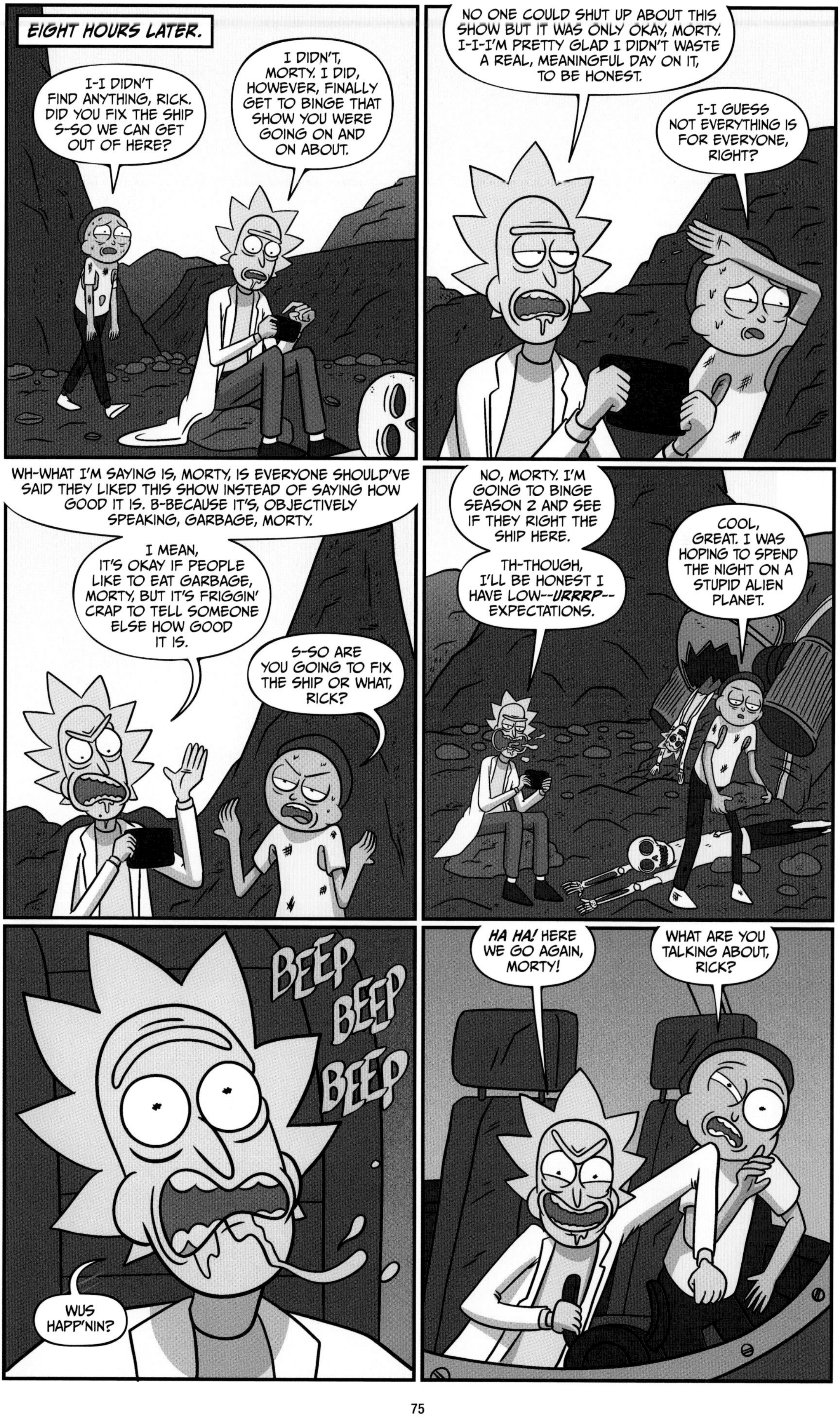
EIGHT HOURS LATER.
I-I DIDN'T FIND ANYTHING, RICK. DID YOU FIX THE SHIP S-SO WE CAN GET OUT OF HERE?
I DIDN'T, MORTY. I DID, HOWEVER, FINALLY GET TO BINGE THAT SHOW YOU WERE GOING ON AND ON ABOUT.
NO ONE COULD SHUT UP ABOUT THIS SHOW BUT IT WAS ONLY OKAY, MORTY. I-I-I'M PRETTY GLAD I DIDN'T WASTE A REAL, MEANINGFUL DAY ON IT, TO BE HONEST.
I-I GUESS NOT EVERYTHING IS FOR EVERYONE, RIGHT?
WH-WHAT I'M SAYING IS, MORTY, IS EVERYONE SHOULD'VE SAID THEY LIKED THIS SHOW INSTEAD OF SAYING HOW GOOD IT IS. B-BECAUSE IT'S, OBJECTIVELY SPEAKING, GARBAGE, MORTY.
I MEAN, IT'S OKAY IF PEOPLE LIKE TO EAT GARBAGE, MORTY, BUT IT'S FRIGGIN' CRAP TO TELL SOMEONE ELSE HOW GOOD IT IS.
S-SO ARE YOU GOING TO FIX THE SHIP OR WHAT, RICK?
NO, MORTY. I'M GOING TO BINGE SEASON 2 AND SEE IF THEY RIGHT THE SHIP HERE.
TH-THOUGH, I'LL BE HONEST I HAVE LOW--URRRP--EXPECTATIONS.
COOL, GREAT. I WAS HOPING TO SPEND THE NIGHT ON A STUPID ALIEN PLANET.
BEEP BEEP BEEP
WUS HAPP'NIN?
HA HA! HERE WE GO AGAIN, MORTY!
WHAT ARE YOU TALKING ABOUT, RICK?

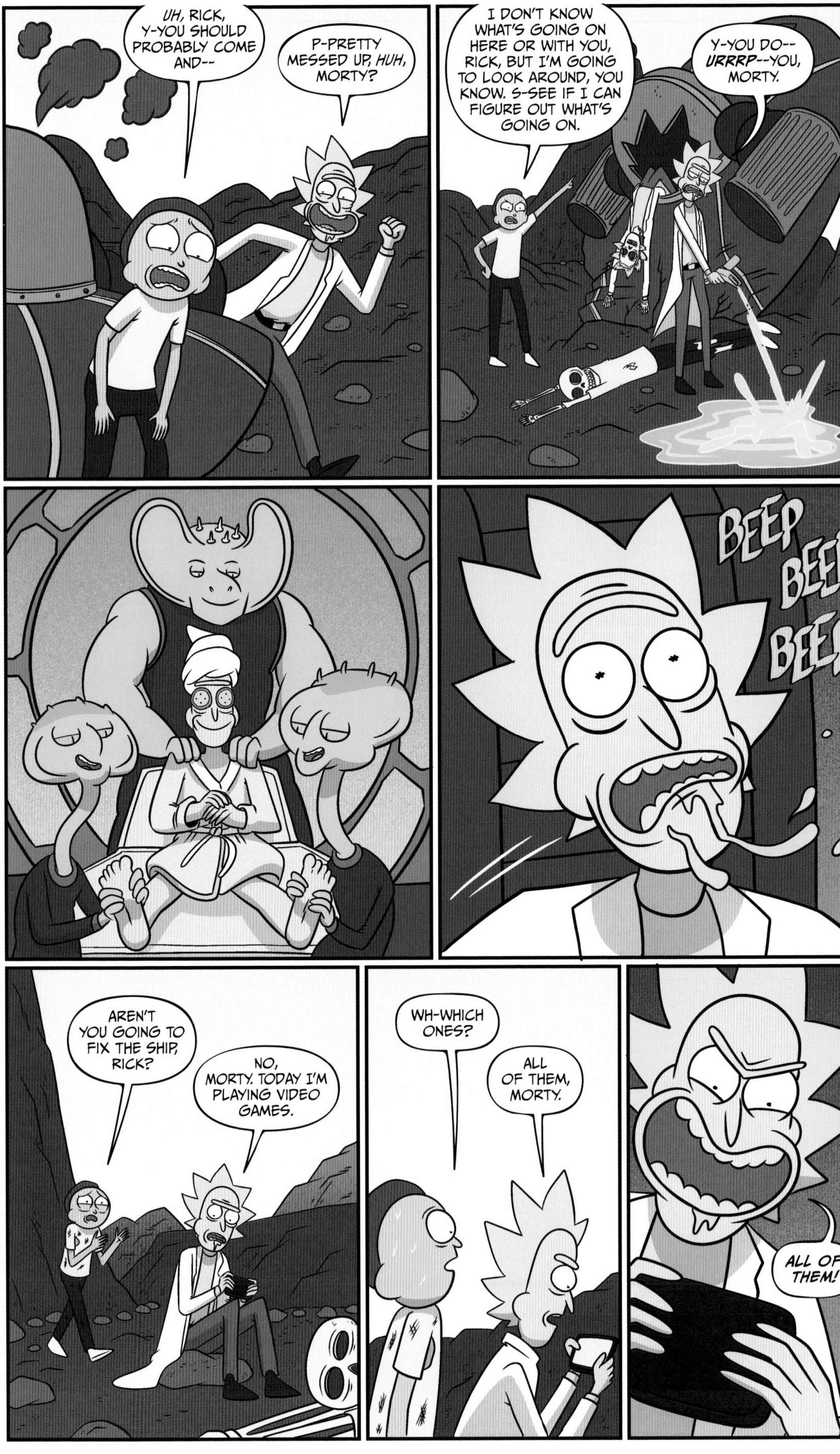

UH, RICK, Y-YOU SHOULD PROBABLY COME AND--
P-PRETTY MESSED UP, HUH, MORTY?
I DON'T KNOW WHAT'S GOING ON HERE OR WITH YOU, RICK, BUT I'M GOING TO LOOK AROUND, YOU KNOW. S-SEE IF I CAN FIGURE OUT WHAT'S GOING ON.
Y-YOU DO-- URRRP--YOU, MORTY.
BEEP BEEP BEEP
AREN'T YOU GOING TO FIX THE SHIP, RICK?
NO, MORTY. TODAY I'M PLAYING VIDEO GAMES.
WH-WHICH ONES?
ALL OF THEM, MORTY.
ALL OF THEM!

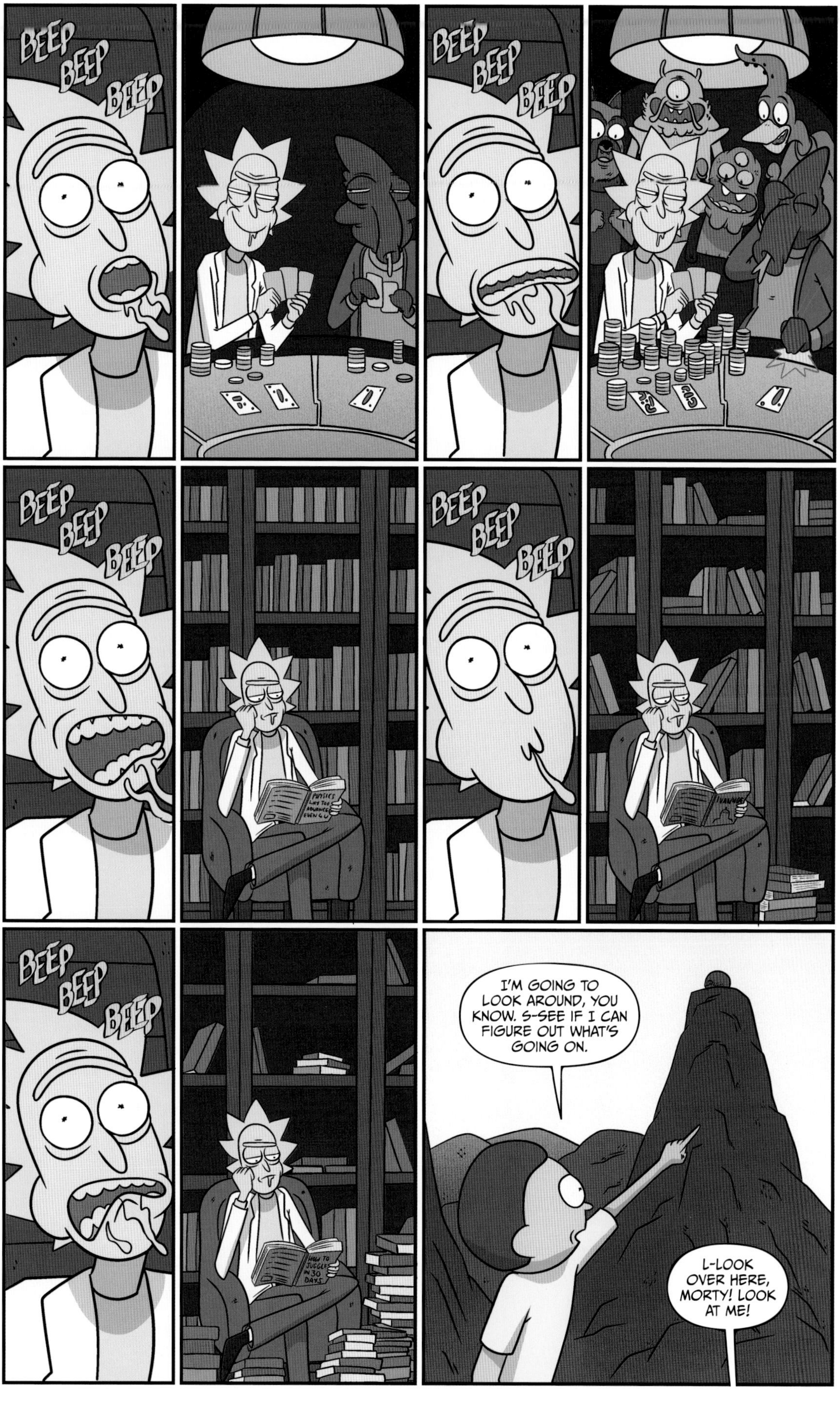
BEEP
BEEP
BEEP
BEEP
BEEP
BEEP
BEEP
BEEP
BEEP
PHYSICS WAY TOO ADVANCED EVEN 4 U
BEEP
BEEP
BEEP
IVANHOE
BEEP
BEEP
BEEP
HOW TO JUGGLE IN 30 DAYS
I'M GOING TO LOOK AROUND, YOU KNOW. S-SEE IF I CAN FIGURE OUT WHAT'S GOING ON.
L-LOOK OVER HERE, MORTY! LOOK AT ME!

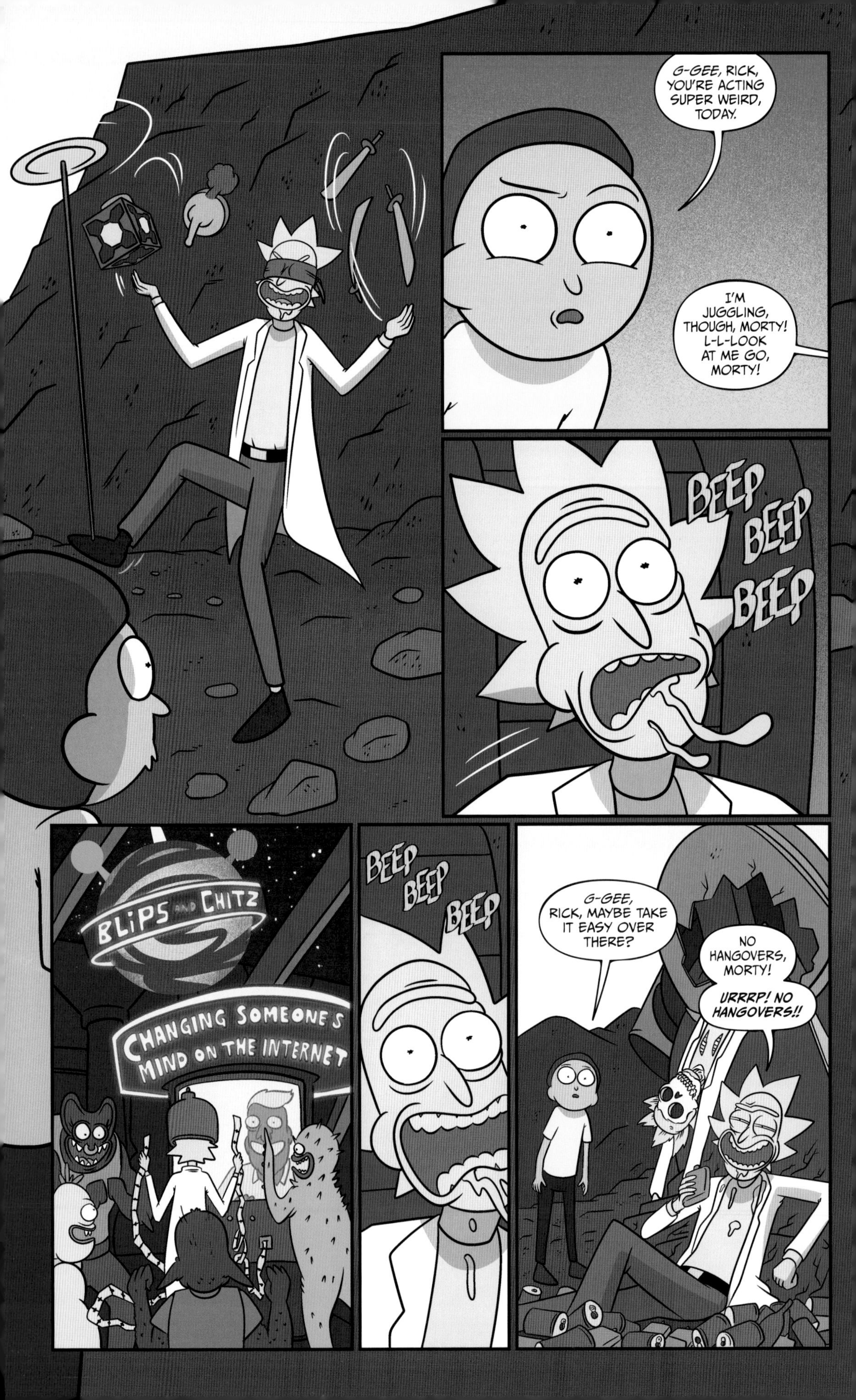
G-GEE, RICK, YOU'RE ACTING SUPER WEIRD, TODAY.
I'M JUGGLING, THOUGH, MORTY! L-L-LOOK AT ME GO, MORTY!
BEEP
BEEP
BEEP
BLIPS AND CHITZ
CHANGING SOMEONE'S MIND ON THE INTERNET
BEEP
BEEP
BEEP
G-GEE, RICK, MAYBE TAKE IT EASY OVER THERE?
NO HANGOVERS, MORTY!
URRRP! NO HANGOVERS!!

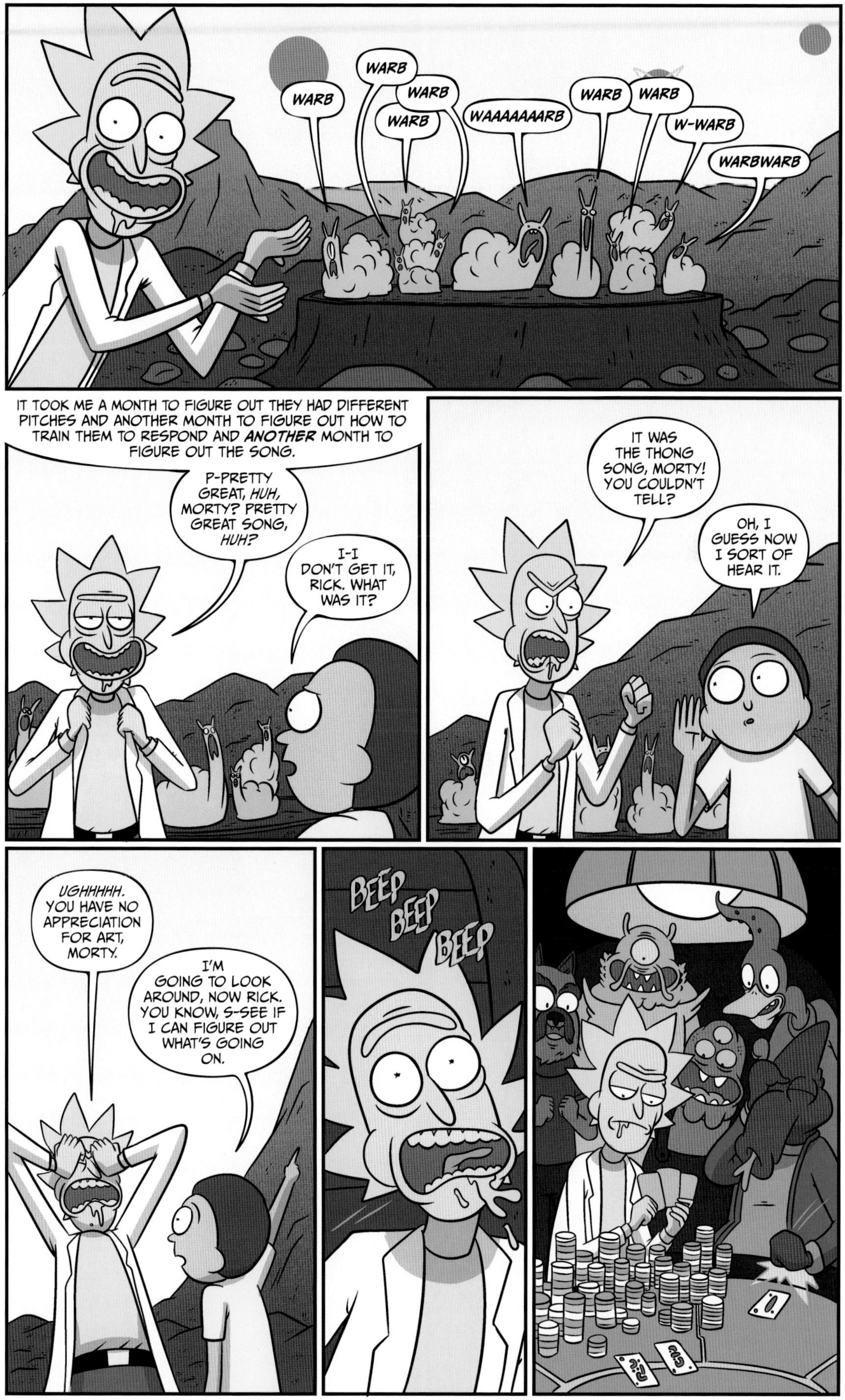
WARB
WARB
WARB
WARB
WAAAAAAARB
WARB
WARB
W-WARB
WARBWARB
IT TOOK ME A MONTH TO FIGURE OUT THEY HAD DIFFERENT PITCHES AND ANOTHER MONTH TO FIGURE OUT HOW TO TRAIN THEM TO RESPOND AND ***ANOTHER*** MONTH TO FIGURE OUT THE SONG.
P-PRETTY GREAT, *HUH*, MORTY? PRETTY GREAT SONG, *HUH?*
I-I DON'T GET IT, RICK. WHAT WAS IT?
IT WAS THE THONG SONG, MORTY! YOU COULDN'T TELL?
OH, I GUESS NOW I SORT OF HEAR IT.
UGHHHHH. YOU HAVE NO APPRECIATION FOR ART, MORTY.
I'M GOING TO LOOK AROUND, NOW RICK. YOU KNOW, S-SEE IF I CAN FIGURE OUT WHAT'S GOING ON.
BEEP
BEEP
BEEP

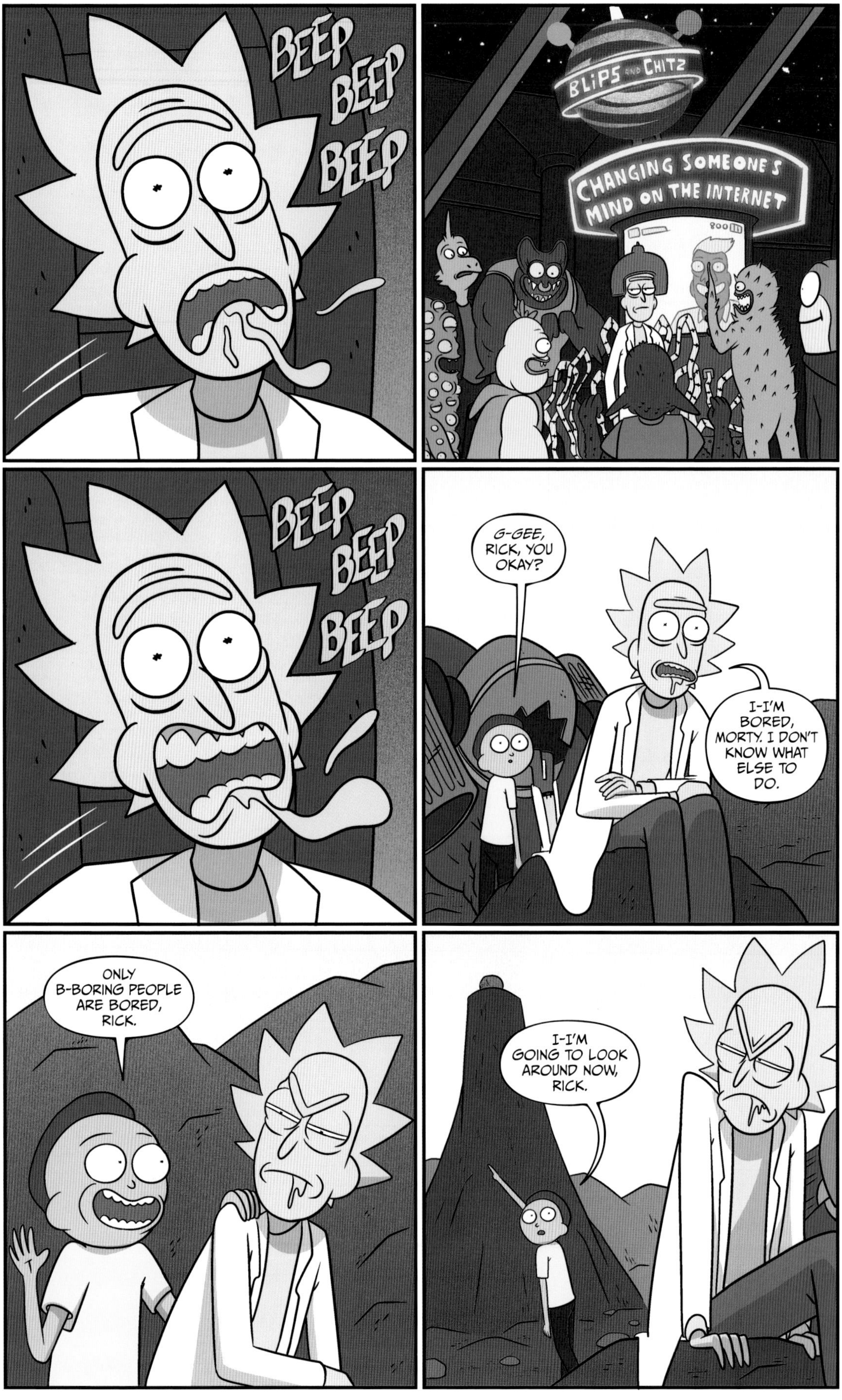
BEEP
BEEP
BEEP
BLIPS AND CHITZ
CHANGING SOMEONE'S MIND ON THE INTERNET
BEEP
BEEP
BEEP
G-GEE, RICK, YOU OKAY?
I-I'M BORED, MORTY. I DON'T KNOW WHAT ELSE TO DO.
ONLY B-BORING PEOPLE ARE BORED, RICK.
I-I'M GOING TO LOOK AROUND NOW, RICK.

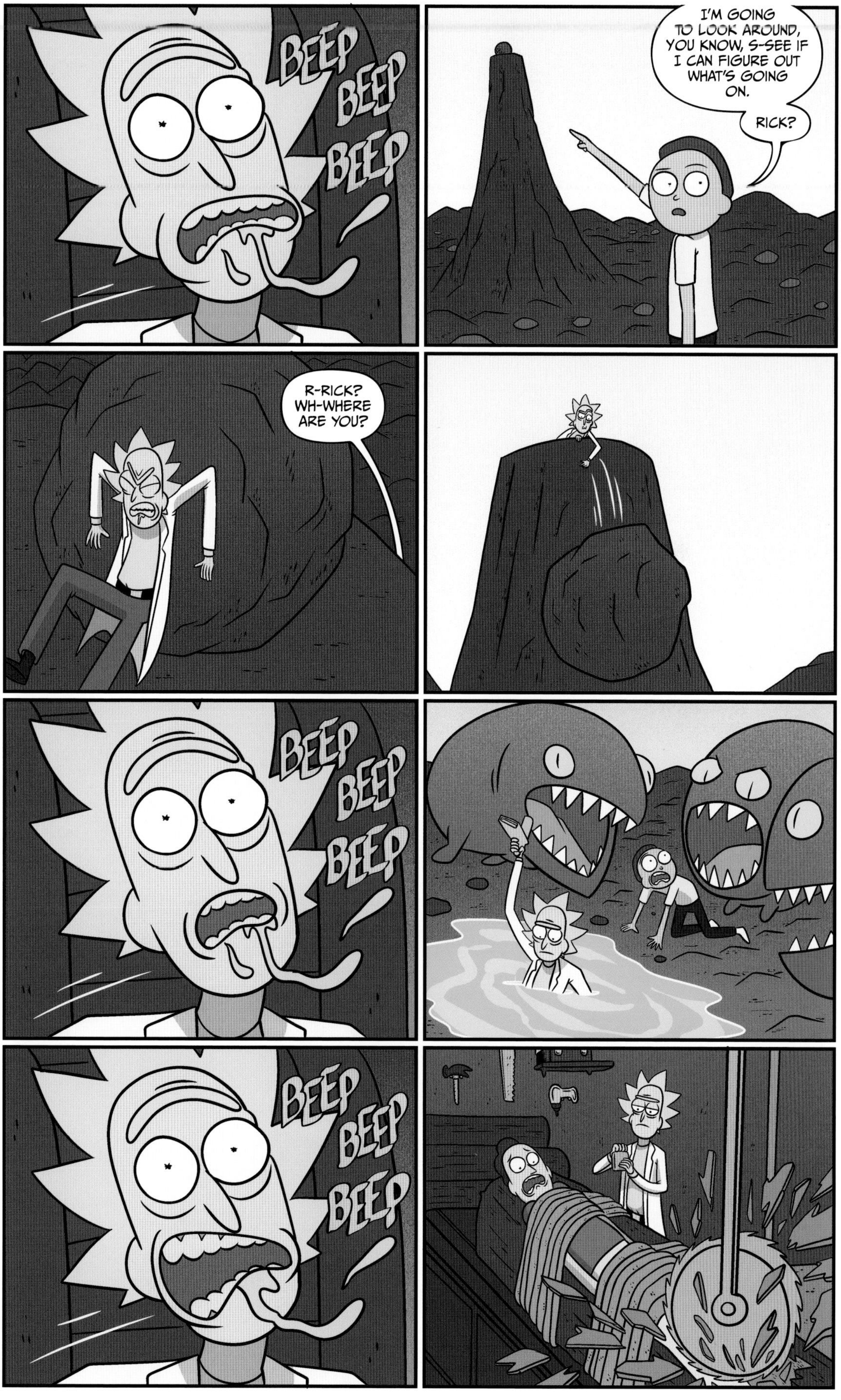
BEEP
BEEP
BEEP
I'M GOING TO LOOK AROUND, YOU KNOW, S-SEE IF I CAN FIGURE OUT WHAT'S GOING ON.
RICK?
R-RICK? WH-WHERE ARE YOU?
BEEP
BEEP
BEEP
BEEP
BEEP
BEEP

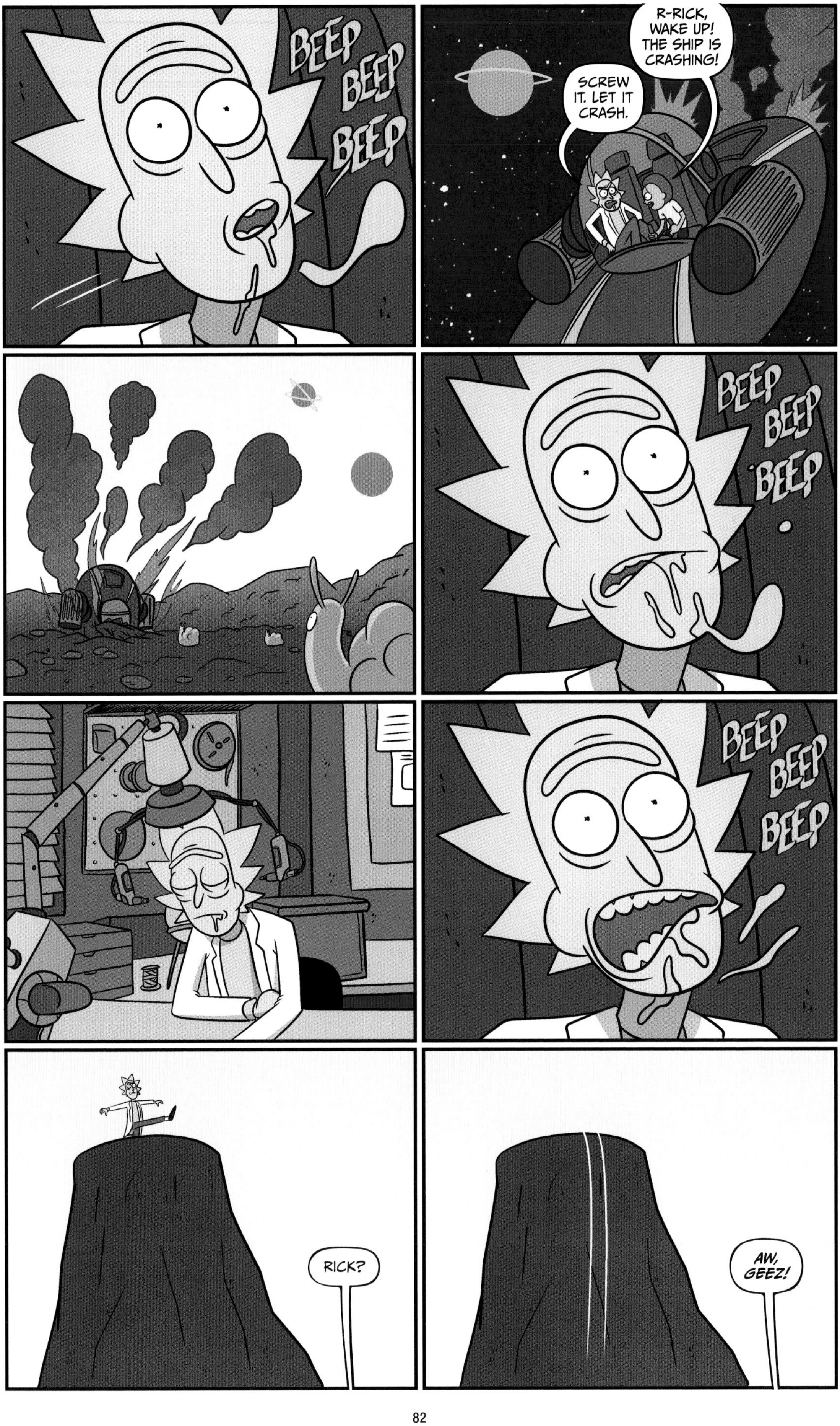
BEEP
BEEP
BEEP
R-RICK, WAKE UP! THE SHIP IS CRASHING!
SCREW IT. LET IT CRASH.
BEEP
BEEP
BEEP
BEEP
BEEP
BEEP
RICK?
AW, GEEZ!

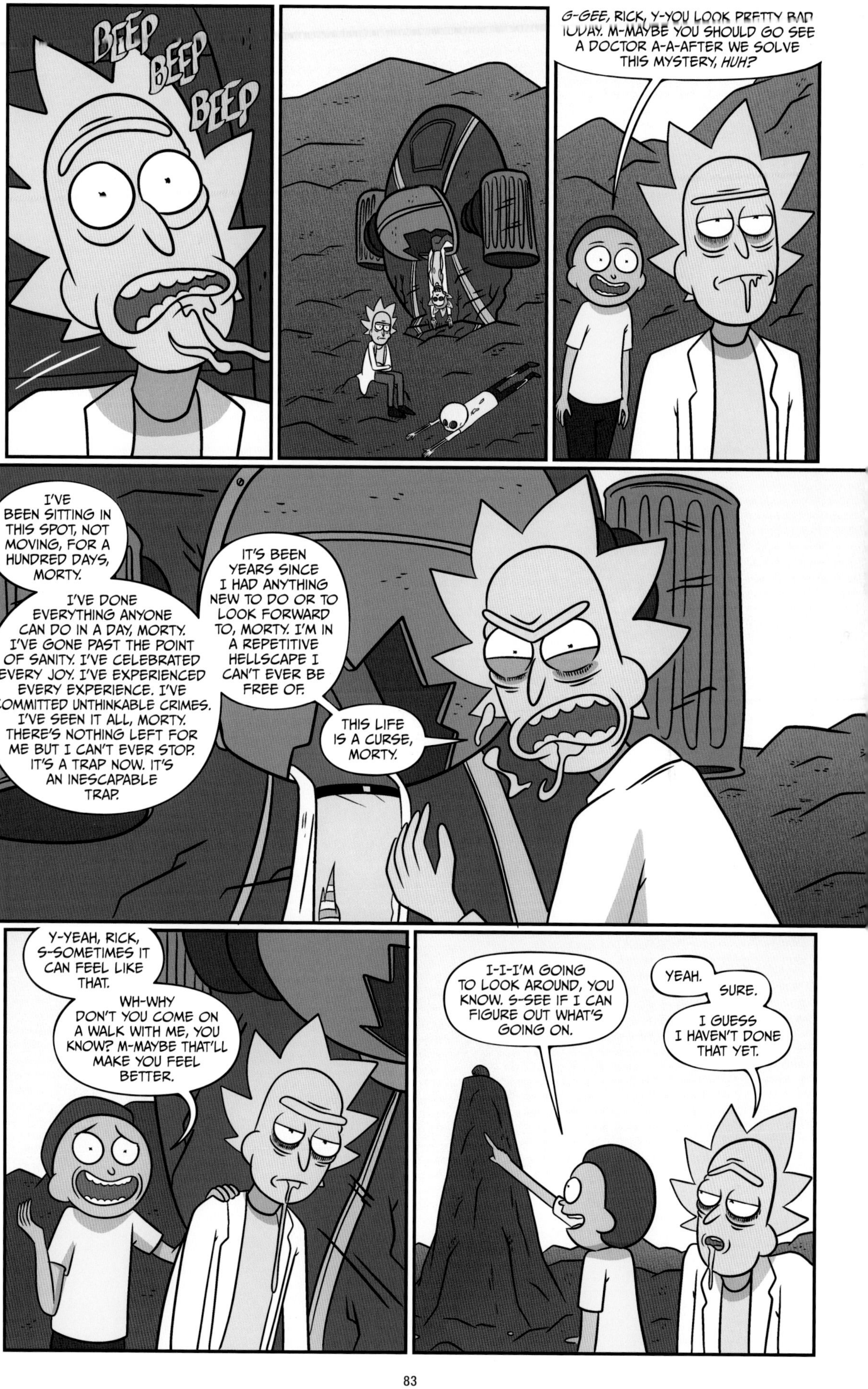
BEEP BEEP BEEP
G-GEE, RICK, Y-YOU LOOK PRETTY BAD TODAY. M-MAYBE YOU SHOULD GO SEE A DOCTOR A-A-AFTER WE SOLVE THIS MYSTERY, HUH?
I'VE BEEN SITTING IN THIS SPOT, NOT MOVING, FOR A HUNDRED DAYS, MORTY.
I'VE DONE EVERYTHING ANYONE CAN DO IN A DAY, MORTY. I'VE GONE PAST THE POINT OF SANITY. I'VE CELEBRATED EVERY JOY. I'VE EXPERIENCED EVERY EXPERIENCE. I'VE COMMITTED UNTHINKABLE CRIMES. I'VE SEEN IT ALL, MORTY. THERE'S NOTHING LEFT FOR ME BUT I CAN'T EVER STOP. IT'S A TRAP NOW. IT'S AN INESCAPABLE TRAP.
IT'S BEEN YEARS SINCE I HAD ANYTHING NEW TO DO OR TO LOOK FORWARD TO, MORTY. I'M IN A REPETITIVE HELLSCAPE I CAN'T EVER BE FREE OF.
THIS LIFE IS A CURSE, MORTY.
Y-YEAH, RICK, S-SOMETIMES IT CAN FEEL LIKE THAT.
WH-WHY DON'T YOU COME ON A WALK WITH ME, YOU KNOW? M-MAYBE THAT'LL MAKE YOU FEEL BETTER.
I-I-I'M GOING TO LOOK AROUND, YOU KNOW. S-SEE IF I CAN FIGURE OUT WHAT'S GOING ON.
YEAH.
SURE.
I GUESS I HAVEN'T DONE THAT YET.

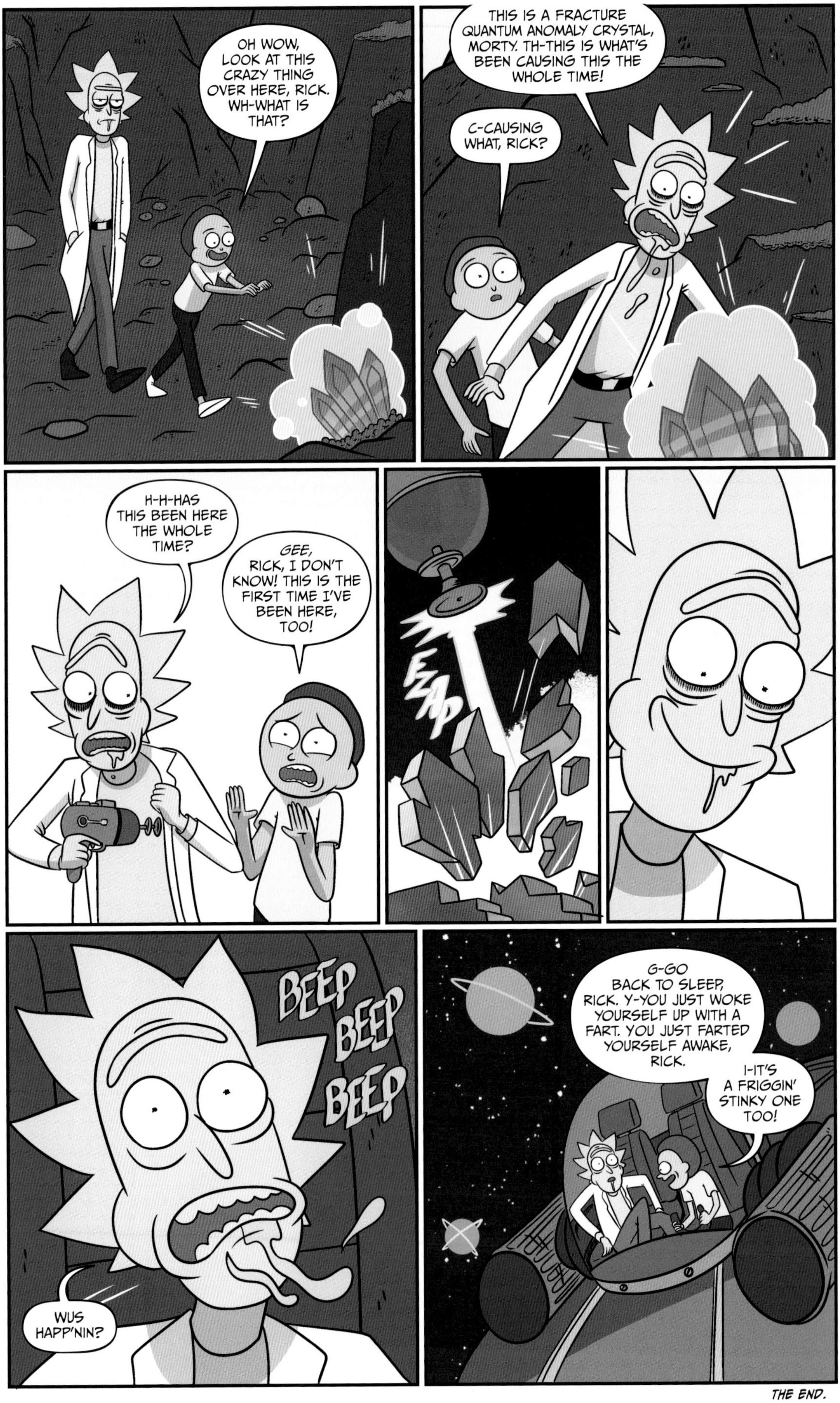
OH WOW, LOOK AT THIS CRAZY THING OVER HERE, RICK. WH-WHAT IS THAT?
THIS IS A FRACTURE QUANTUM ANOMALY CRYSTAL, MORTY. TH-THIS IS WHAT'S BEEN CAUSING THIS THE WHOLE TIME!
C-CAUSING WHAT, RICK?
H-H-HAS THIS BEEN HERE THE WHOLE TIME?
GEE, RICK, I DON'T KNOW! THIS IS THE FIRST TIME I'VE BEEN HERE, TOO!
ZZAP
BEEP
BEEP
BEEP
WUS HAPP'NIN?
G-GO BACK TO SLEEP, RICK. Y-YOU JUST WOKE YOURSELF UP WITH A FART. YOU JUST FARTED YOURSELF AWAKE, RICK.
I-IT'S A FRIGGIN' STINKY ONE TOO!

THE END.

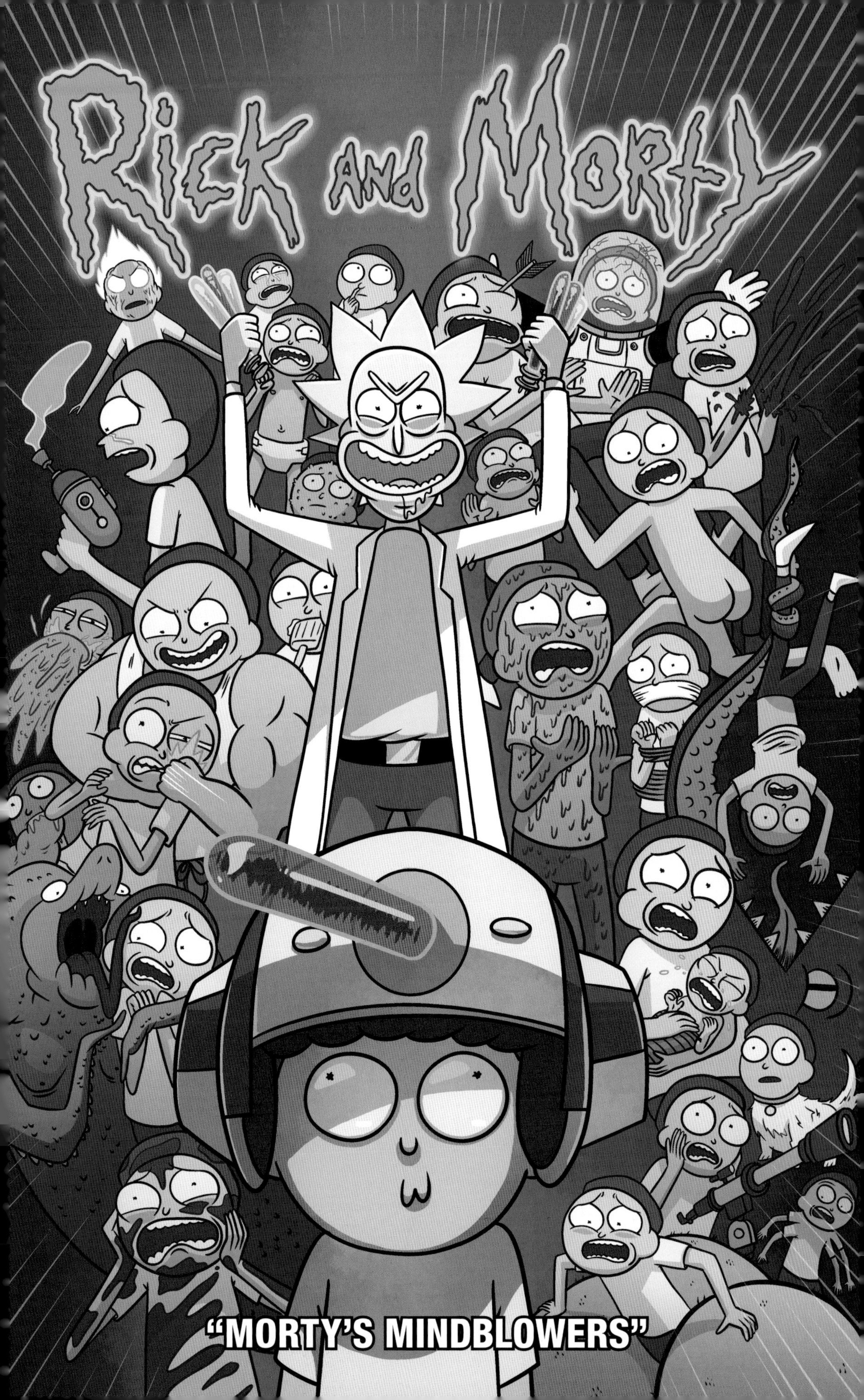
Rick and Morty
"MORTY'S MINDBLOWERS"

"MORTY'S MINDBLOWERS"

PAGES 87-93, 98, 110-111, 116-117, 122-126
WRITTEN BY **KYLE STARKS**   ILLUSTRATED BY **MARC ELLERBY**   COLORED BY **SARAH STERN**

PAGES 94-97
WRITTEN BY **KYLE STARKS**   ILLUSTRATED BY **ANDREW MACLEAN**   COLORED BY **NICK FILARDI**

PAGES 99-103
WRITTEN BY **TINI HOWARD**   ILLUSTRATED BY **JARRETT WILLIAMS**   COLORED BY **SARAH STERN**

PAGES 104-105
WRITTEN, ILLUSTRATED, AND COLORED BY **SARAH GRALEY**

PAGES 106-109
WRITTEN BY **MARC ELLERBY**   ILLUSTRATED BY **KYLE STARKS**   COLORED BY **SARAH STERN**

PAGES 112-115
WRITTEN, ILLUSTRATED, AND COLORED BY **BENJAMIN DEWEY**

PAGES 118-121
WRITTEN BY **JOSH TRUJILLO**   ILLUSTRATED BY **RII ABREGO**   COLORED BY **SARAH STERN**

ALL PAGES LETTERED BY **CRANK!**

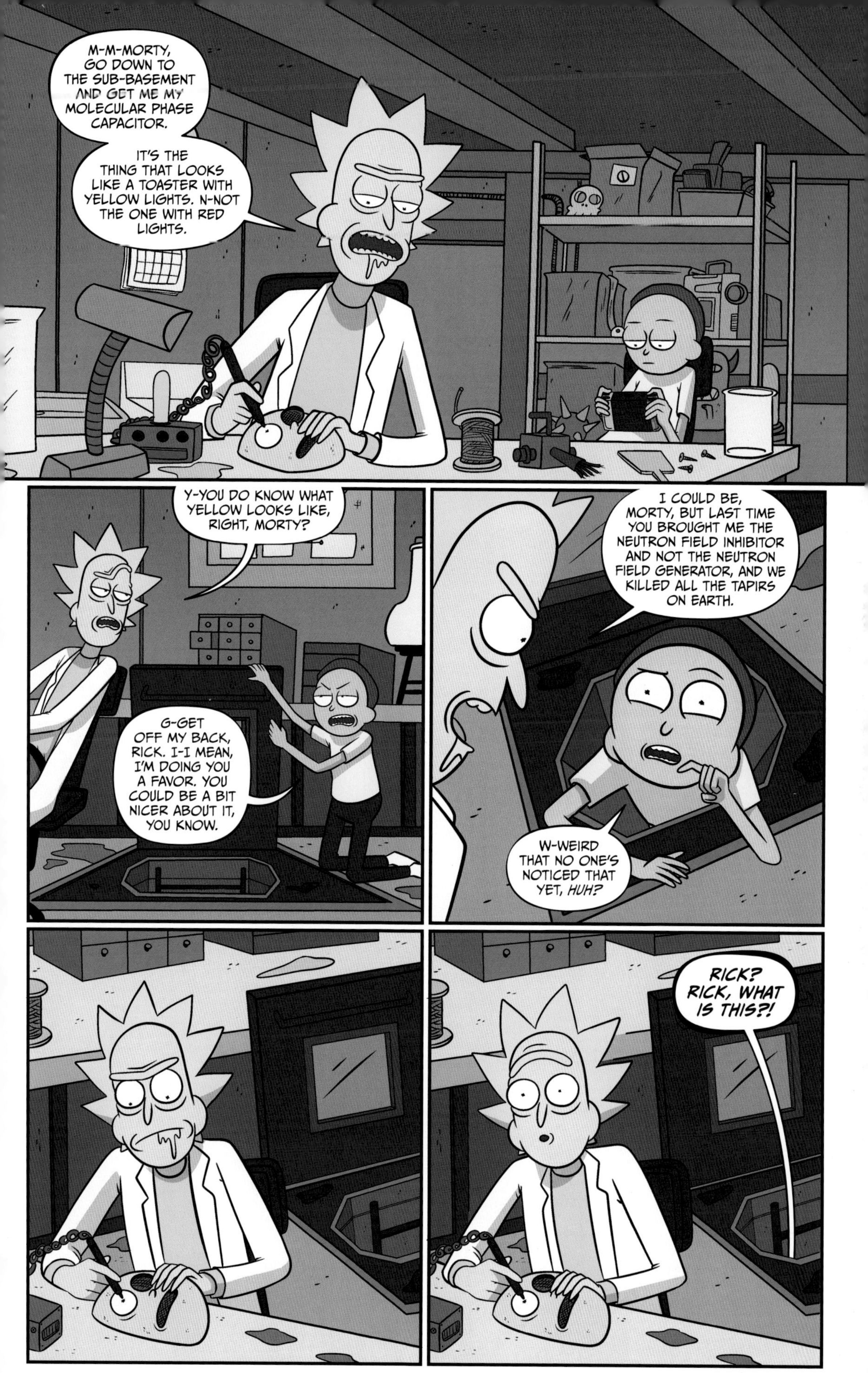
M-M-MORTY, GO DOWN TO THE SUB-BASEMENT AND GET ME MY MOLECULAR PHASE CAPACITOR.
IT'S THE THING THAT LOOKS LIKE A TOASTER WITH YELLOW LIGHTS. N-NOT THE ONE WITH RED LIGHTS.
Y-YOU DO KNOW WHAT YELLOW LOOKS LIKE, RIGHT, MORTY?
G-GET OFF MY BACK, RICK. I-I MEAN, I'M DOING YOU A FAVOR. YOU COULD BE A BIT NICER ABOUT IT, YOU KNOW.
I COULD BE, MORTY, BUT LAST TIME YOU BROUGHT ME THE NEUTRON FIELD INHIBITOR AND NOT THE NEUTRON FIELD GENERATOR, AND WE KILLED ALL THE TAPIRS ON EARTH.
W-WEIRD THAT NO ONE'S NOTICED THAT YET, *HUH?*
RICK? RICK, WHAT IS THIS?!

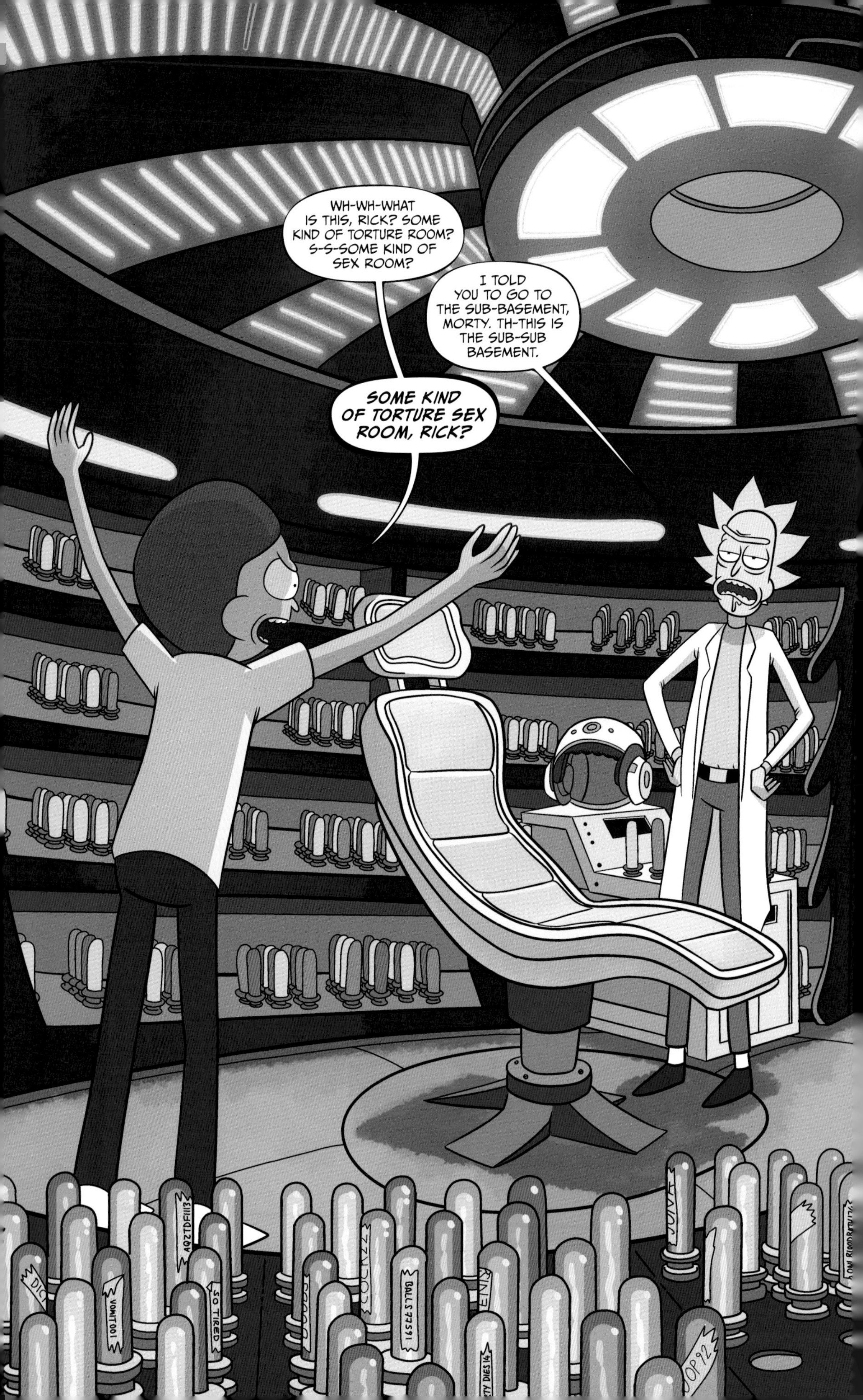
WH-WH-WHAT IS THIS, RICK? SOME KIND OF TORTURE ROOM? S-S-SOME KIND OF SEX ROOM?
SOME KIND OF TORTURE SEX ROOM, RICK?
I TOLD YOU TO GO TO THE SUB-BASEMENT, MORTY. TH-THIS IS THE SUB-SUB BASEMENT.

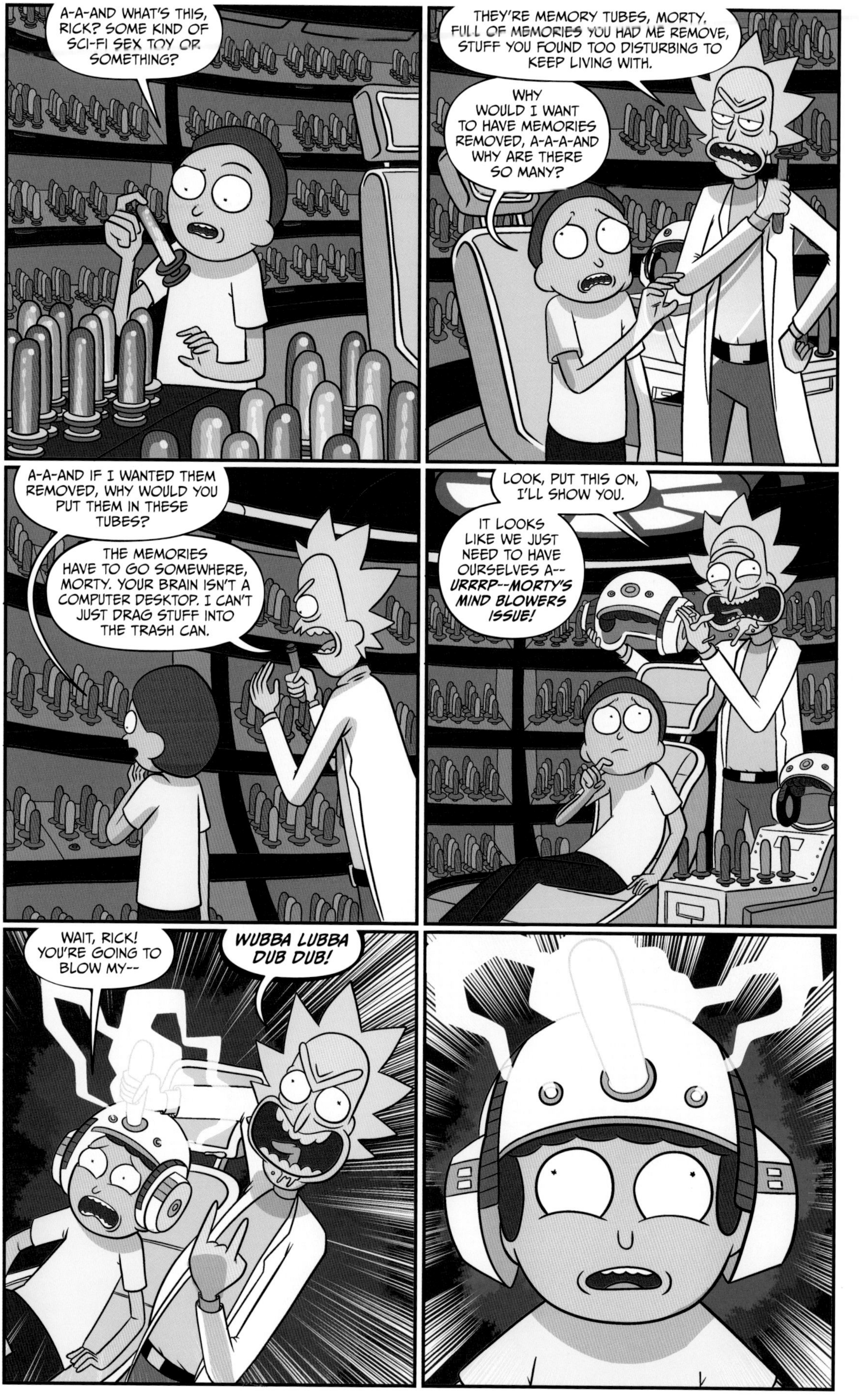
A-A-AND WHAT'S THIS, RICK? SOME KIND OF SCI-FI SEX TOY OR SOMETHING?
THEY'RE MEMORY TUBES, MORTY. FULL OF MEMORIES YOU HAD ME REMOVE, STUFF YOU FOUND TOO DISTURBING TO KEEP LIVING WITH.
WHY WOULD I WANT TO HAVE MEMORIES REMOVED, A-A-A-AND WHY ARE THERE SO MANY?
A-A-AND IF I WANTED THEM REMOVED, WHY WOULD YOU PUT THEM IN THESE TUBES?
THE MEMORIES HAVE TO GO SOMEWHERE, MORTY. YOUR BRAIN ISN'T A COMPUTER DESKTOP. I CAN'T JUST DRAG STUFF INTO THE TRASH CAN.
LOOK, PUT THIS ON, I'LL SHOW YOU.
IT LOOKS LIKE WE JUST NEED TO HAVE OURSELVES A-- URRRP--MORTY'S MIND BLOWERS ISSUE!
WAIT, RICK! YOU'RE GOING TO BLOW MY--
WUBBA LUBBA DUB DUB!

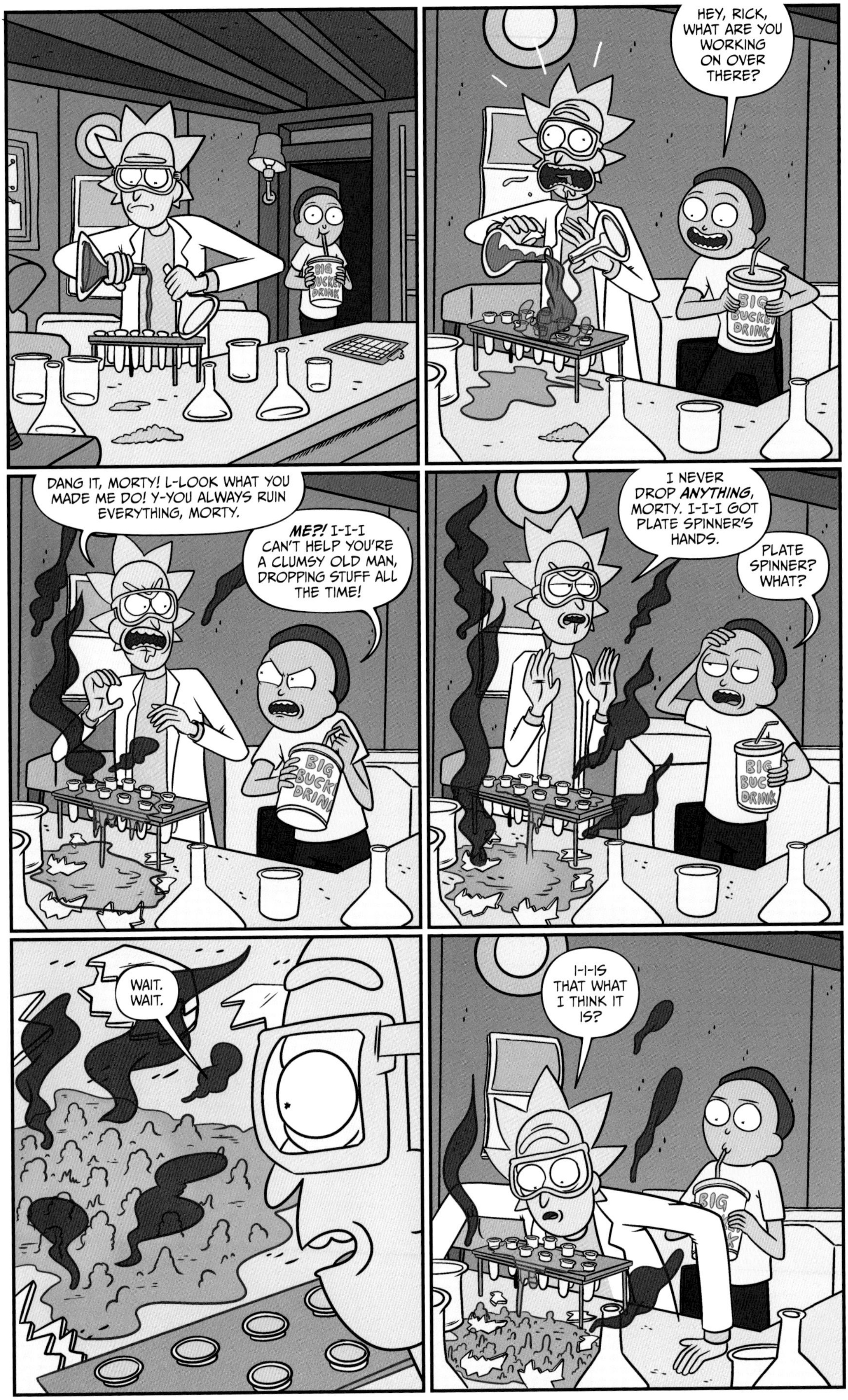

BIG BUCKET DRINK
HEY, RICK, WHAT ARE YOU WORKING ON OVER THERE?
DANG IT, MORTY! L-LOOK WHAT YOU MADE ME DO! Y-YOU ALWAYS RUIN EVERYTHING, MORTY.
ME?! I-I-I CAN'T HELP YOU'RE A CLUMSY OLD MAN, DROPPING STUFF ALL THE TIME!
I NEVER DROP ANYTHING, MORTY. I-I-I GOT PLATE SPINNER'S HANDS.
PLATE SPINNER? WHAT?
WAIT. WAIT.
I-I-IS THAT WHAT I THINK IT IS?

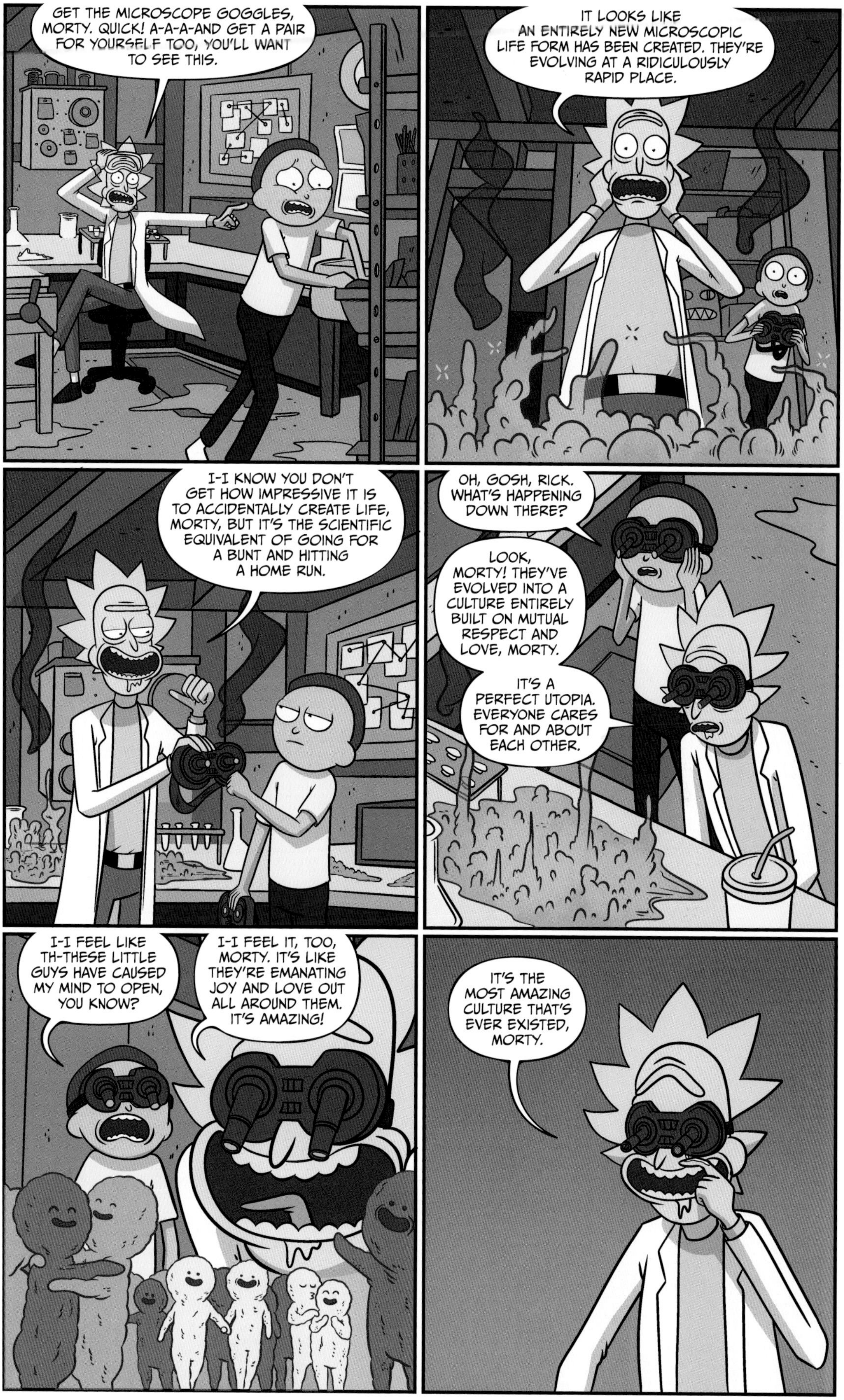
GET THE MICROSCOPE GOGGLES, MORTY. QUICK! A-A-A-AND GET A PAIR FOR YOURSELF TOO, YOU'LL WANT TO SEE THIS.
IT LOOKS LIKE AN ENTIRELY NEW MICROSCOPIC LIFE FORM HAS BEEN CREATED. THEY'RE EVOLVING AT A RIDICULOUSLY RAPID PLACE.
I-I KNOW YOU DON'T GET HOW IMPRESSIVE IT IS TO ACCIDENTALLY CREATE LIFE, MORTY, BUT IT'S THE SCIENTIFIC EQUIVALENT OF GOING FOR A BUNT AND HITTING A HOME RUN.
OH, GOSH, RICK. WHAT'S HAPPENING DOWN THERE?
LOOK, MORTY! THEY'VE EVOLVED INTO A CULTURE ENTIRELY BUILT ON MUTUAL RESPECT AND LOVE, MORTY.
IT'S A PERFECT UTOPIA. EVERYONE CARES FOR AND ABOUT EACH OTHER.
I-I FEEL LIKE TH-THESE LITTLE GUYS HAVE CAUSED MY MIND TO OPEN, YOU KNOW?
I-I FEEL IT, TOO, MORTY. IT'S LIKE THEY'RE EMANATING JOY AND LOVE OUT ALL AROUND THEM. IT'S AMAZING!
IT'S THE MOST AMAZING CULTURE THAT'S EVER EXISTED, MORTY.

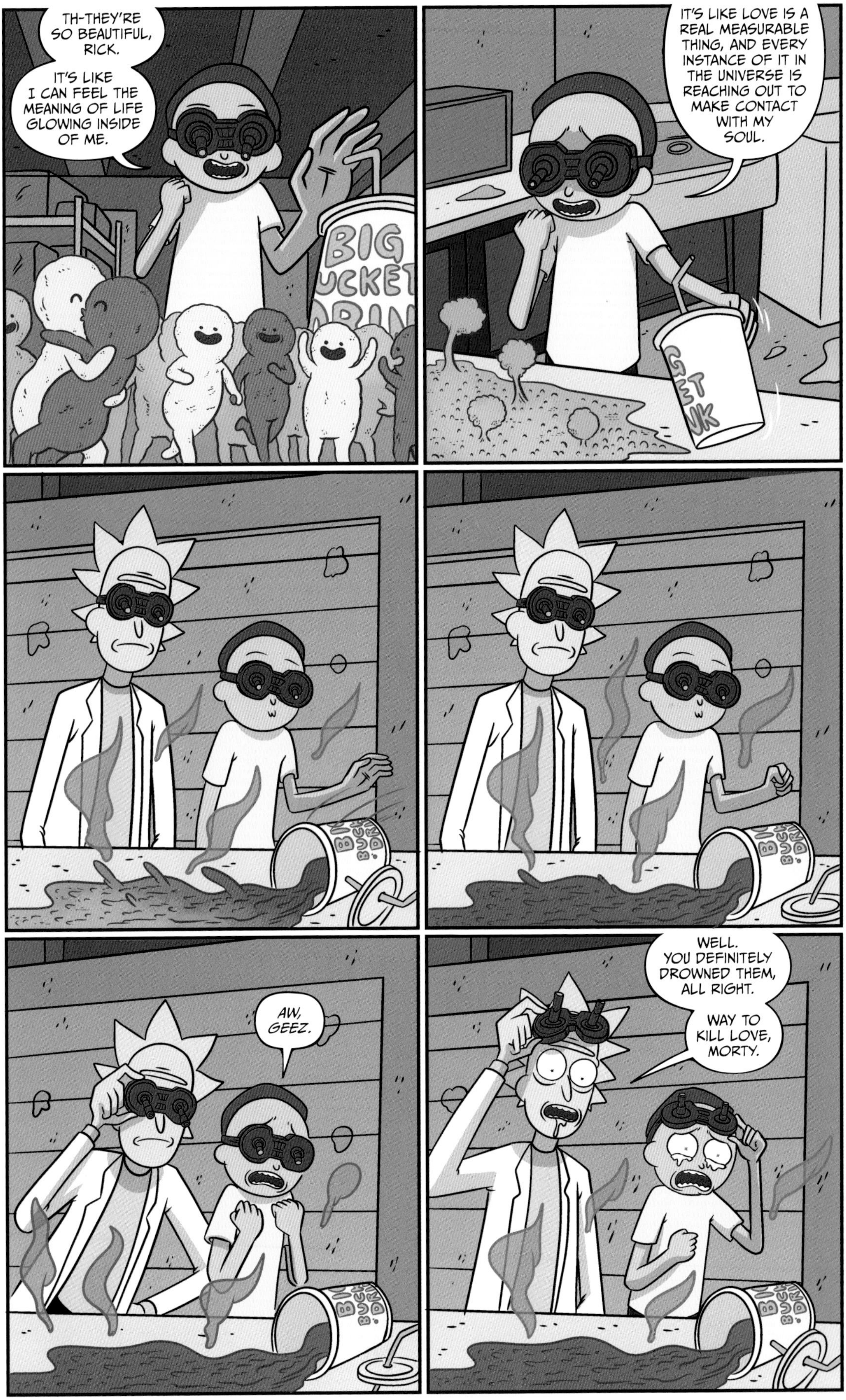
TH-THEY'RE SO BEAUTIFUL, RICK.
IT'S LIKE I CAN FEEL THE MEANING OF LIFE GLOWING INSIDE OF ME.
BIG BUCKET DRIN
IT'S LIKE LOVE IS A REAL MEASURABLE THING, AND EVERY INSTANCE OF IT IN THE UNIVERSE IS REACHING OUT TO MAKE CONTACT WITH MY SOUL.
AW, GEEZ.
WELL. YOU DEFINITELY DROWNED THEM, ALL RIGHT.
WAY TO KILL LOVE, MORTY.

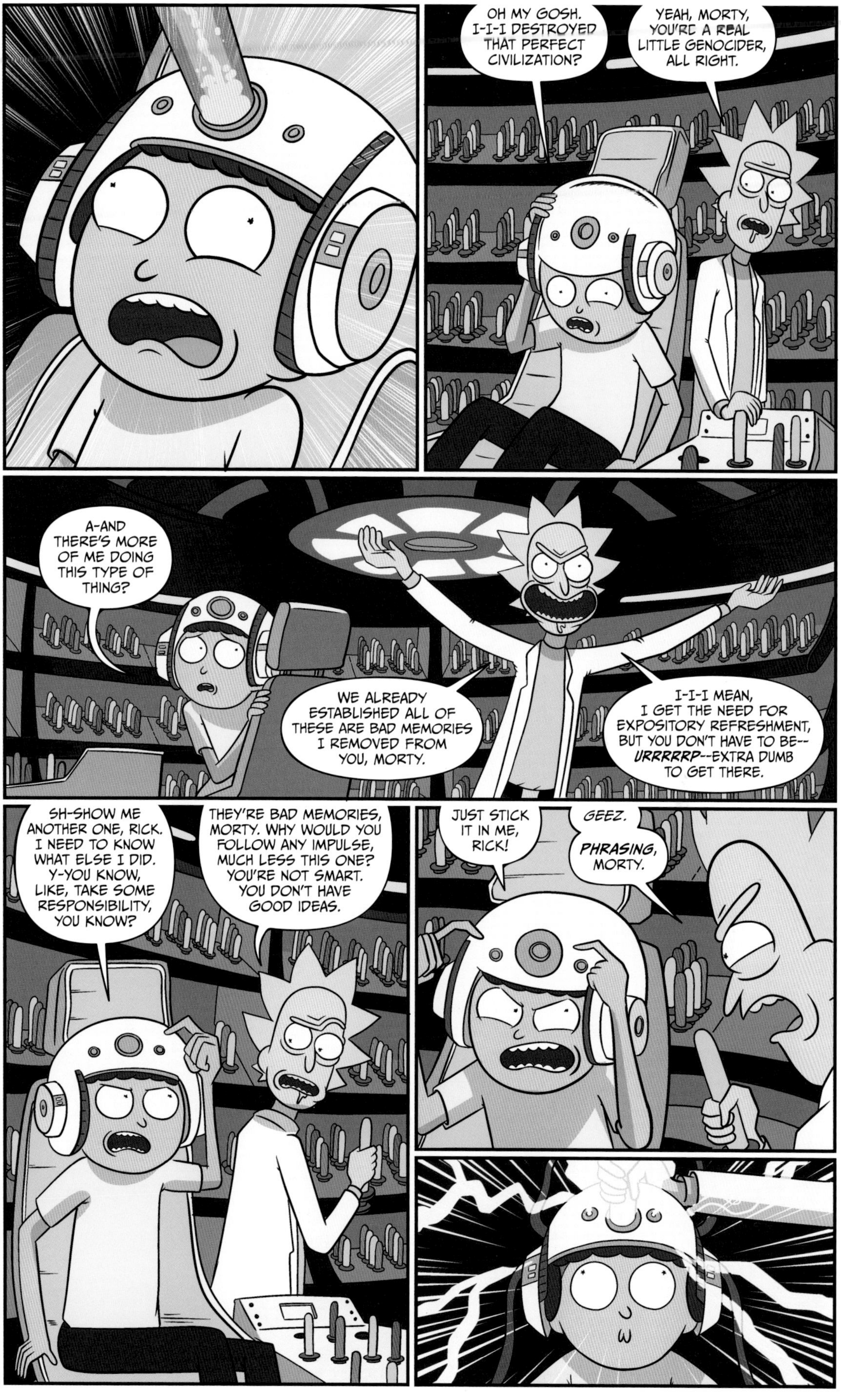
OH MY GOSH. I-I-I DESTROYED THAT PERFECT CIVILIZATION?
YEAH, MORTY, YOU'RE A REAL LITTLE GENOCIDER, ALL RIGHT.
A-AND THERE'S MORE OF ME DOING THIS TYPE OF THING?
WE ALREADY ESTABLISHED ALL OF THESE ARE BAD MEMORIES I REMOVED FROM YOU, MORTY.
I-I-I MEAN, I GET THE NEED FOR EXPOSITORY REFRESHMENT, BUT YOU DON'T HAVE TO BE-- ***URRRRRP***--EXTRA DUMB TO GET THERE.
SH-SHOW ME ANOTHER ONE, RICK. I NEED TO KNOW WHAT ELSE I DID. Y-YOU KNOW, LIKE, TAKE SOME RESPONSIBILITY, YOU KNOW?
THEY'RE BAD MEMORIES, MORTY. WHY WOULD YOU FOLLOW ANY IMPULSE, MUCH LESS THIS ONE? YOU'RE NOT SMART. YOU DON'T HAVE GOOD IDEAS.
JUST STICK IT IN ME, RICK!
GEEZ.
PHRASING, MORTY.

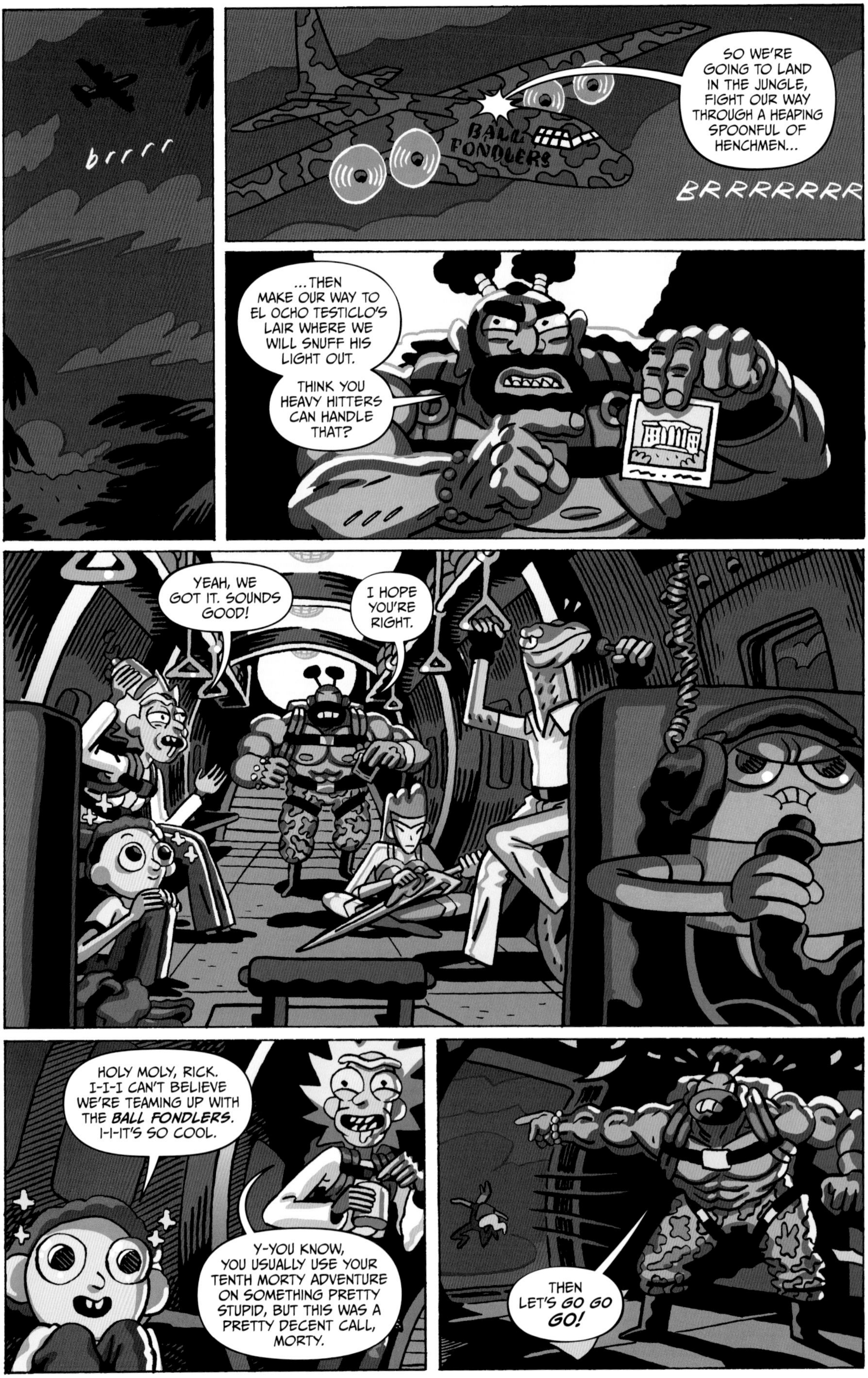
brrrr
BALL FONDLERS
SO WE'RE GOING TO LAND IN THE JUNGLE, FIGHT OUR WAY THROUGH A HEAPING SPOONFUL OF HENCHMEN...
BRRRRRRR
...THEN MAKE OUR WAY TO EL OCHO TESTICLO'S LAIR WHERE WE WILL SNUFF HIS LIGHT OUT.
THINK YOU HEAVY HITTERS CAN HANDLE THAT?
YEAH, WE GOT IT. SOUNDS GOOD!
I HOPE YOU'RE RIGHT.
HOLY MOLY, RICK. I-I-I CAN'T BELIEVE WE'RE TEAMING UP WITH THE ***BALL FONDLERS.*** I-I-IT'S SO COOL.
Y-YOU KNOW, YOU USUALLY USE YOUR TENTH MORTY ADVENTURE ON SOMETHING PRETTY STUPID, BUT THIS WAS A PRETTY DECENT CALL, MORTY.
THEN LET'S ***GO GO GO!***

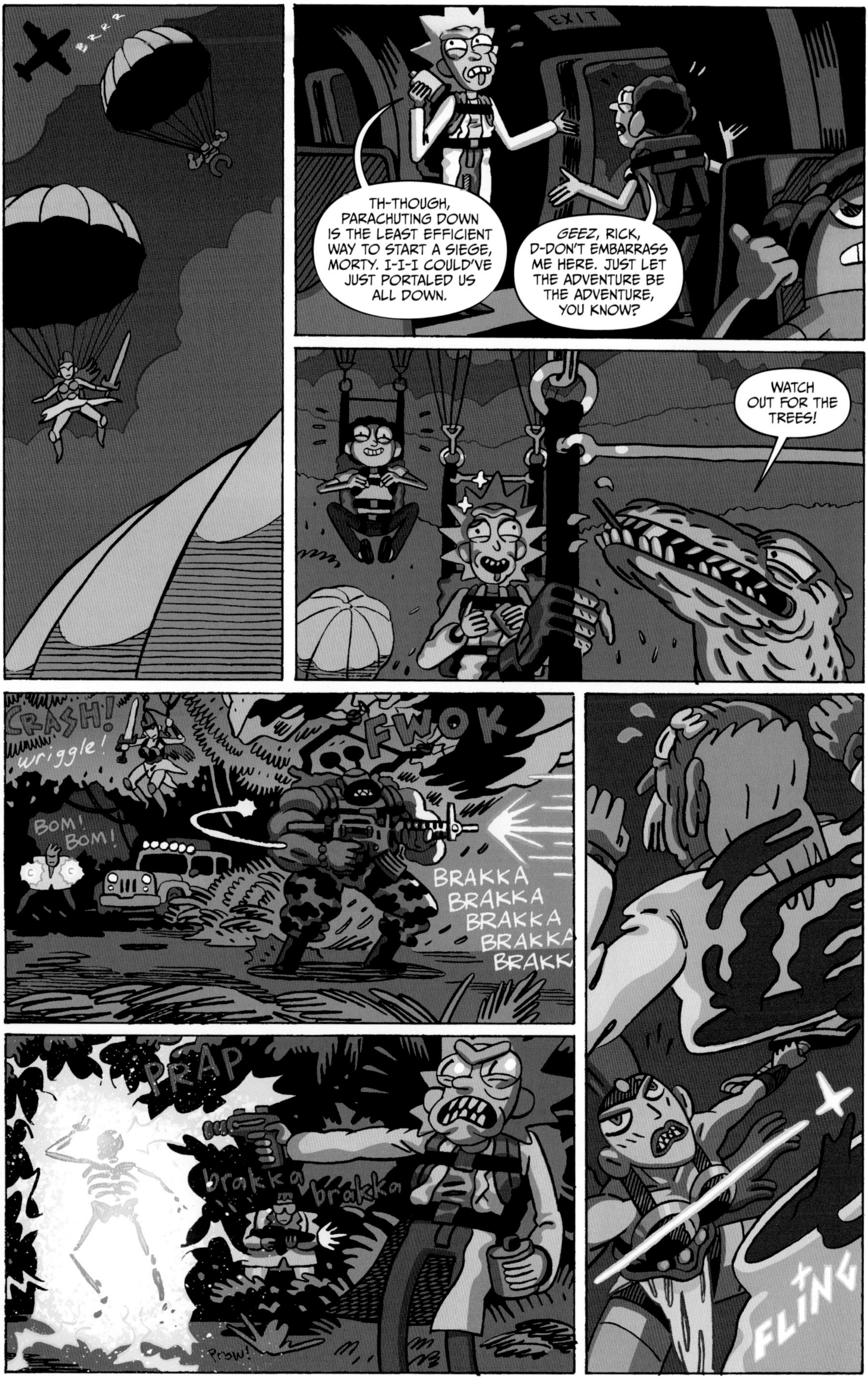

BZZZ
EXIT
TH-THOUGH, PARACHUTING DOWN IS THE LEAST EFFICIENT WAY TO START A SIEGE, MORTY. I-I-I COULD'VE JUST PORTALED US ALL DOWN.
GEEZ, RICK, D-DON'T EMBARRASS ME HERE. JUST LET THE ADVENTURE BE THE ADVENTURE, YOU KNOW?
WATCH OUT FOR THE TREES!
CRASH!
wriggle!
FWOK
BOM! BOM!
BRAKKA BRAKKA BRAKKA BRAKKA BRAKK
PRAP
brakka brakka
Prow!
FLING

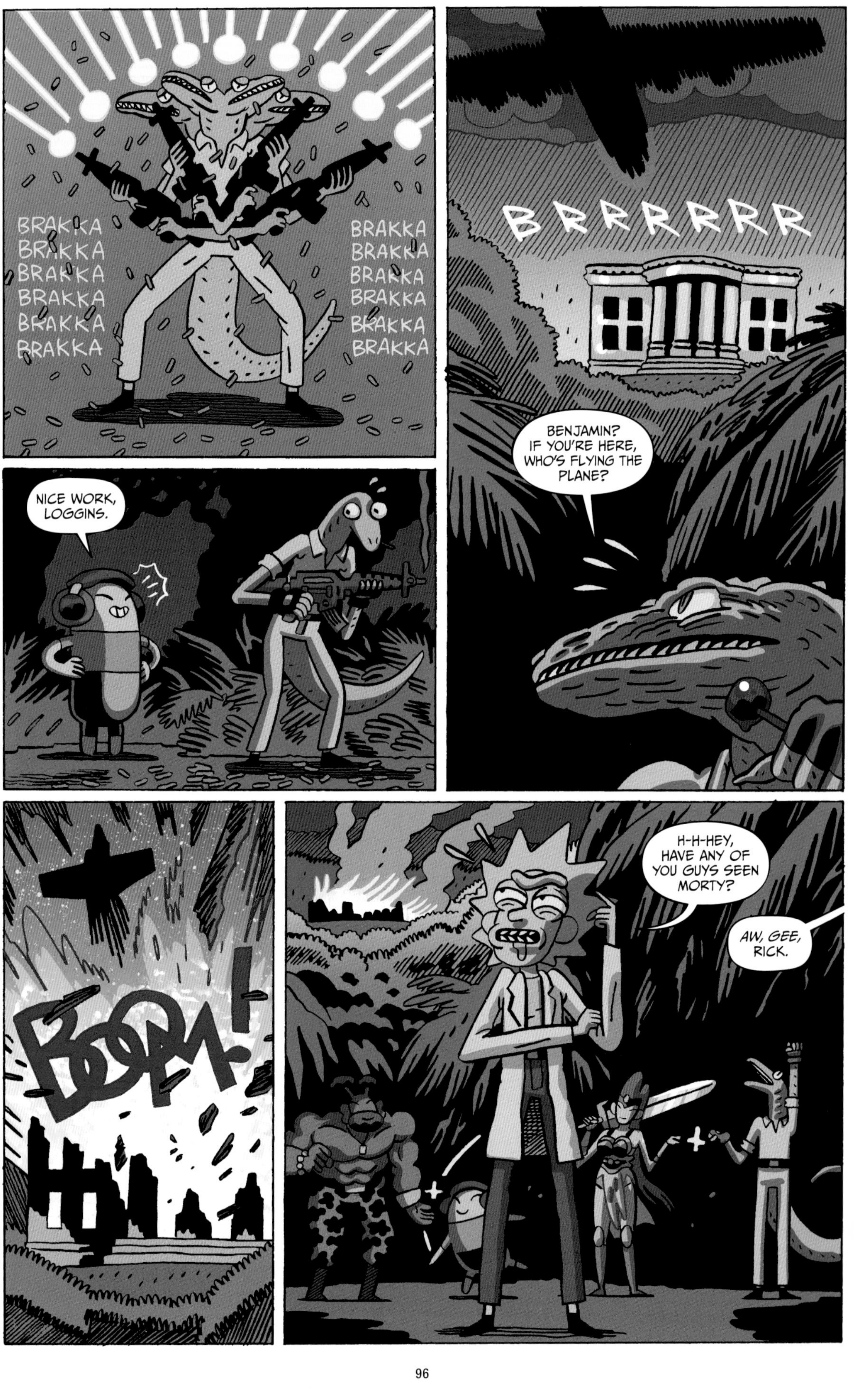
BRAKKA
BRAKKA
BRAKKA
BRAKKA
BRAKKA
BRAKKA
BRAKKA
BRAKKA
BRAKKA
BRAKKA
BRAKKA
BRAKKA
NICE WORK, LOGGINS.
BRRRRRRR
BENJAMIN? IF YOU'RE HERE, WHO'S FLYING THE PLANE?
BOOM!
H-H-HEY, HAVE ANY OF YOU GUYS SEEN MORTY?
AW, GEE, RICK.

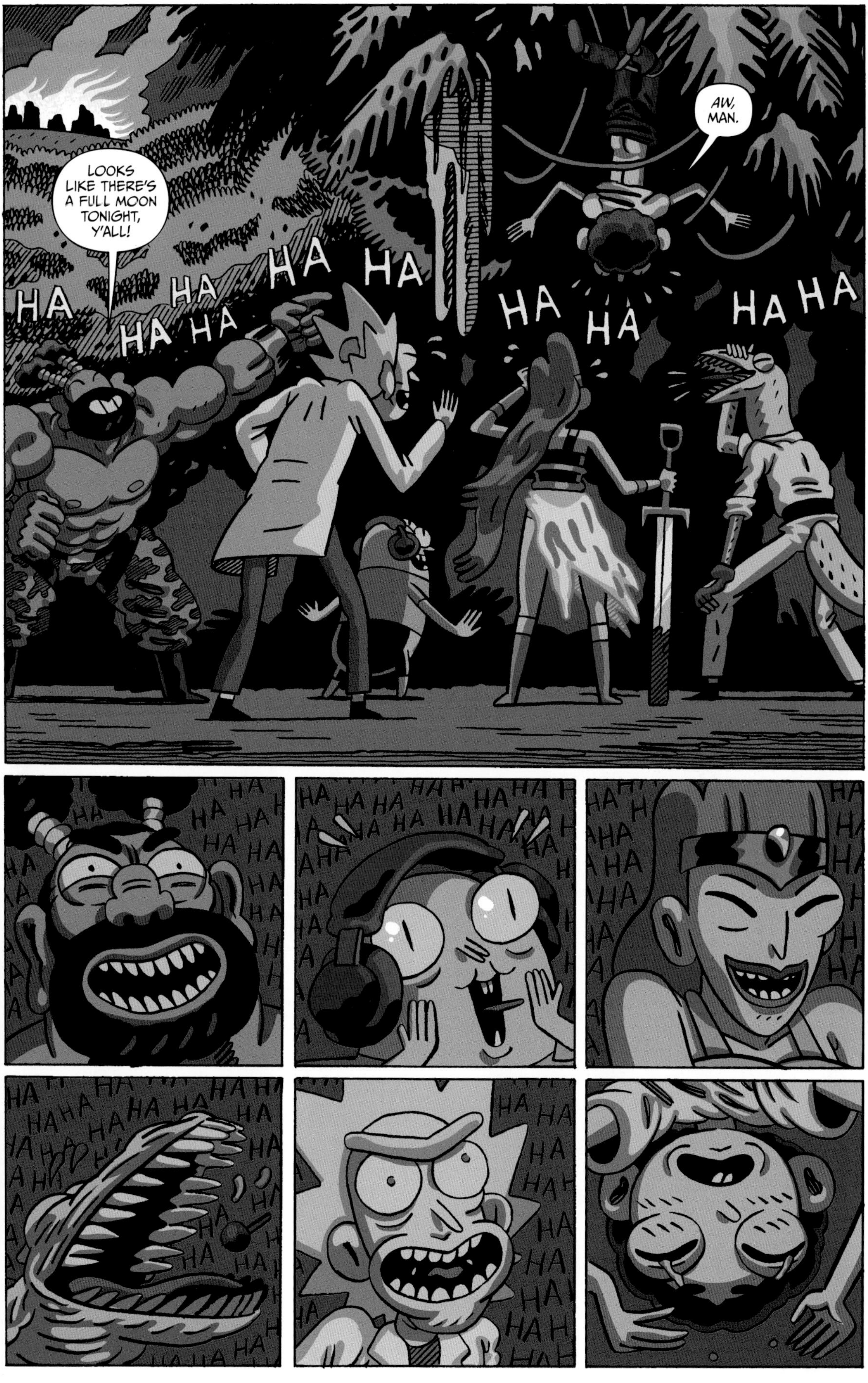
LOOKS LIKE THERE'S A FULL MOON TONIGHT, Y'ALL!
AW, MAN.
HA HA HA HA HA HA HA HA HA HA HA

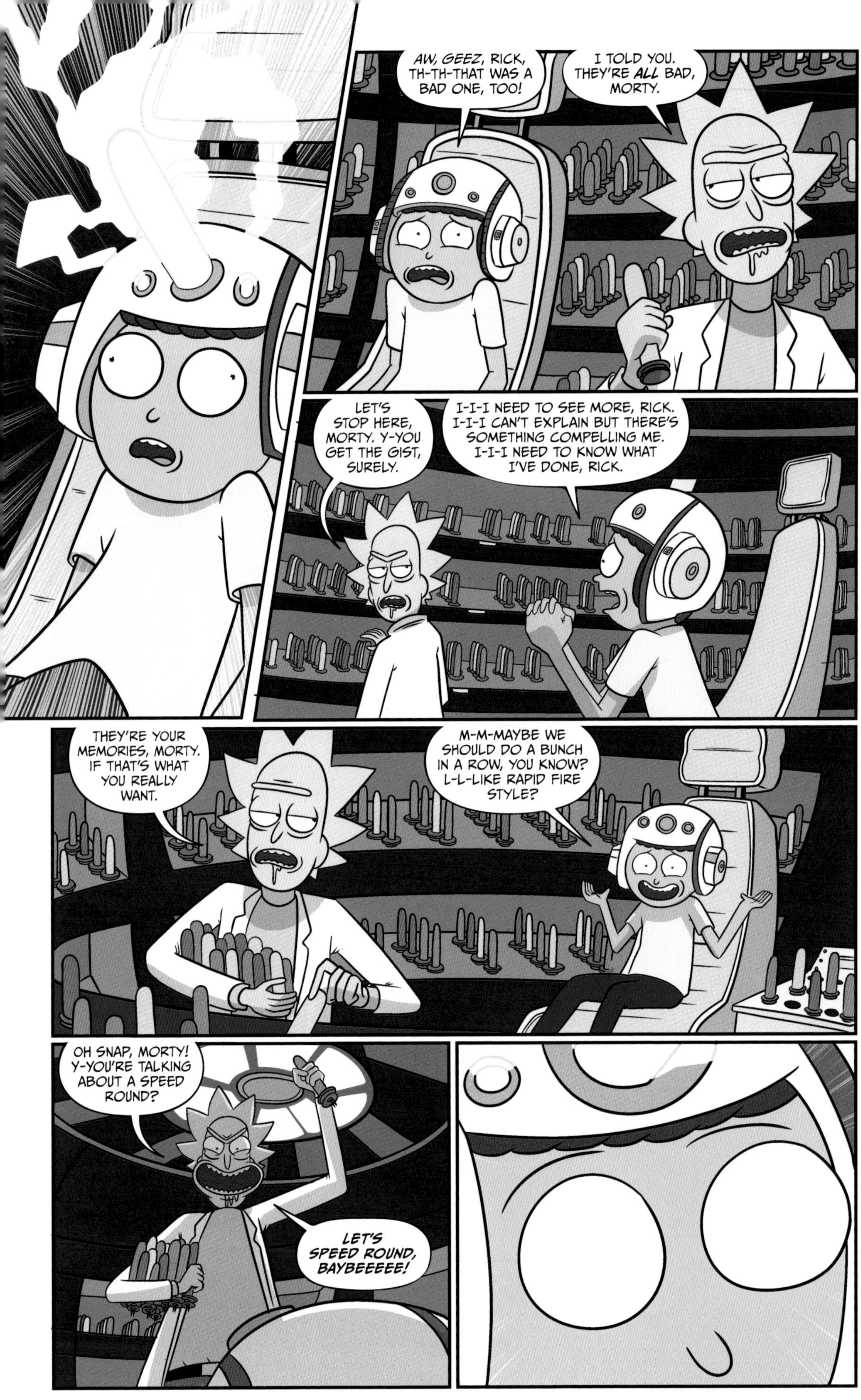
AW, GEEZ, RICK, TH-TH-THAT WAS A BAD ONE, TOO!
I TOLD YOU. THEY'RE ***ALL*** BAD, MORTY.
LET'S STOP HERE, MORTY. Y-YOU GET THE GIST, SURELY.
I-I-I NEED TO SEE MORE, RICK. I-I-I CAN'T EXPLAIN BUT THERE'S SOMETHING COMPELLING ME. I-I-I NEED TO KNOW WHAT I'VE DONE, RICK.
THEY'RE YOUR MEMORIES, MORTY. IF THAT'S WHAT YOU REALLY WANT.
M-M-MAYBE WE SHOULD DO A BUNCH IN A ROW, YOU KNOW? L-L-LIKE RAPID FIRE STYLE?
OH SNAP, MORTY! Y-YOU'RE TALKING ABOUT A SPEED ROUND?
LET'S SPEED ROUND, BAYBEEEEE!

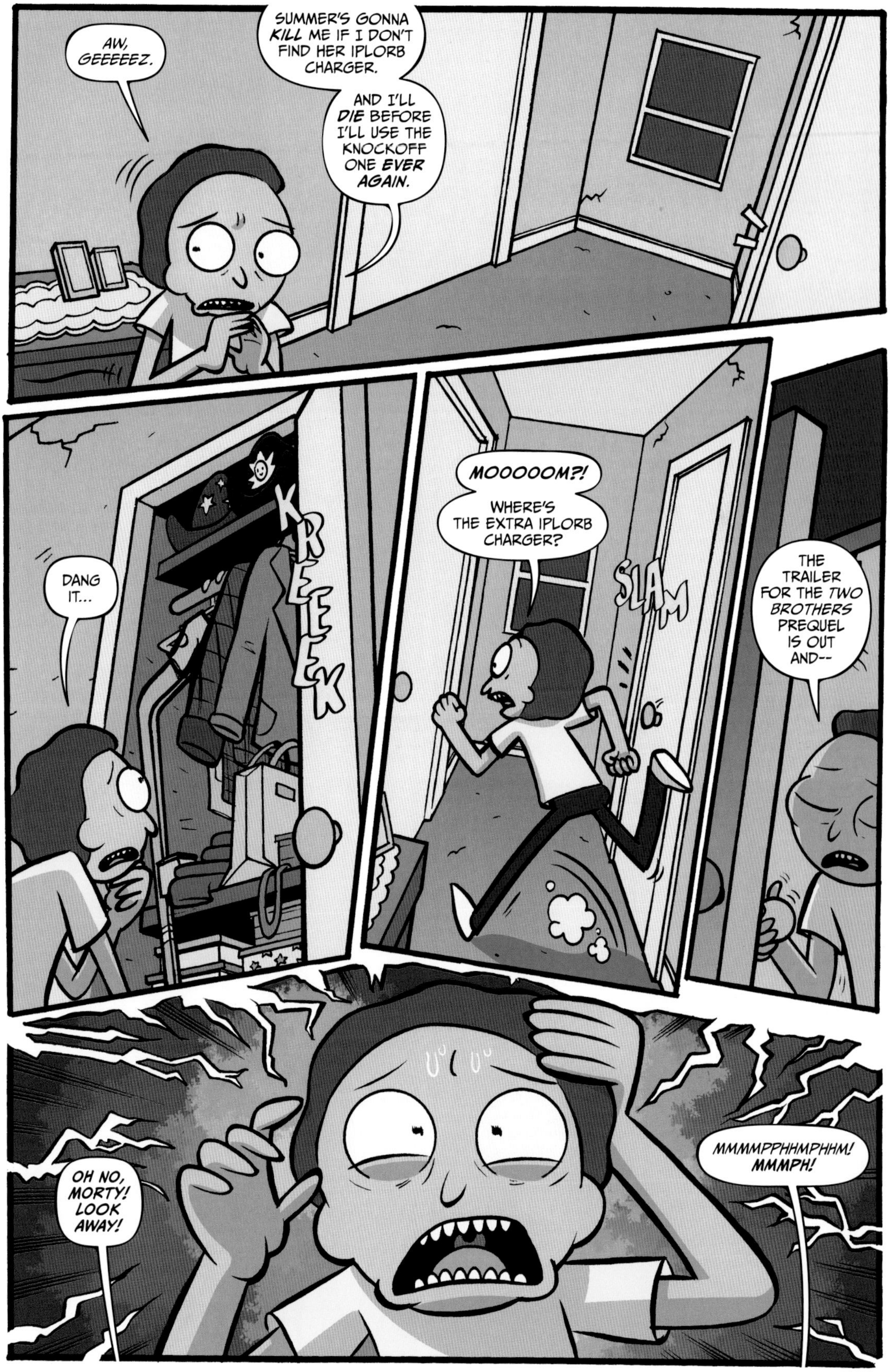
AW, GEEEEEZ.
SUMMER'S GONNA KILL ME IF I DON'T FIND HER IPLORB CHARGER.
AND I'LL DIE BEFORE I'LL USE THE KNOCKOFF ONE EVER AGAIN.
DANG IT...
KREEEEK
MOOOOOM?!
WHERE'S THE EXTRA IPLORB CHARGER?
SLAM
THE TRAILER FOR THE TWO BROTHERS PREQUEL IS OUT AND--
OH NO, MORTY! LOOK AWAY!
MMMMPPHHMPHHM! MMMPH!

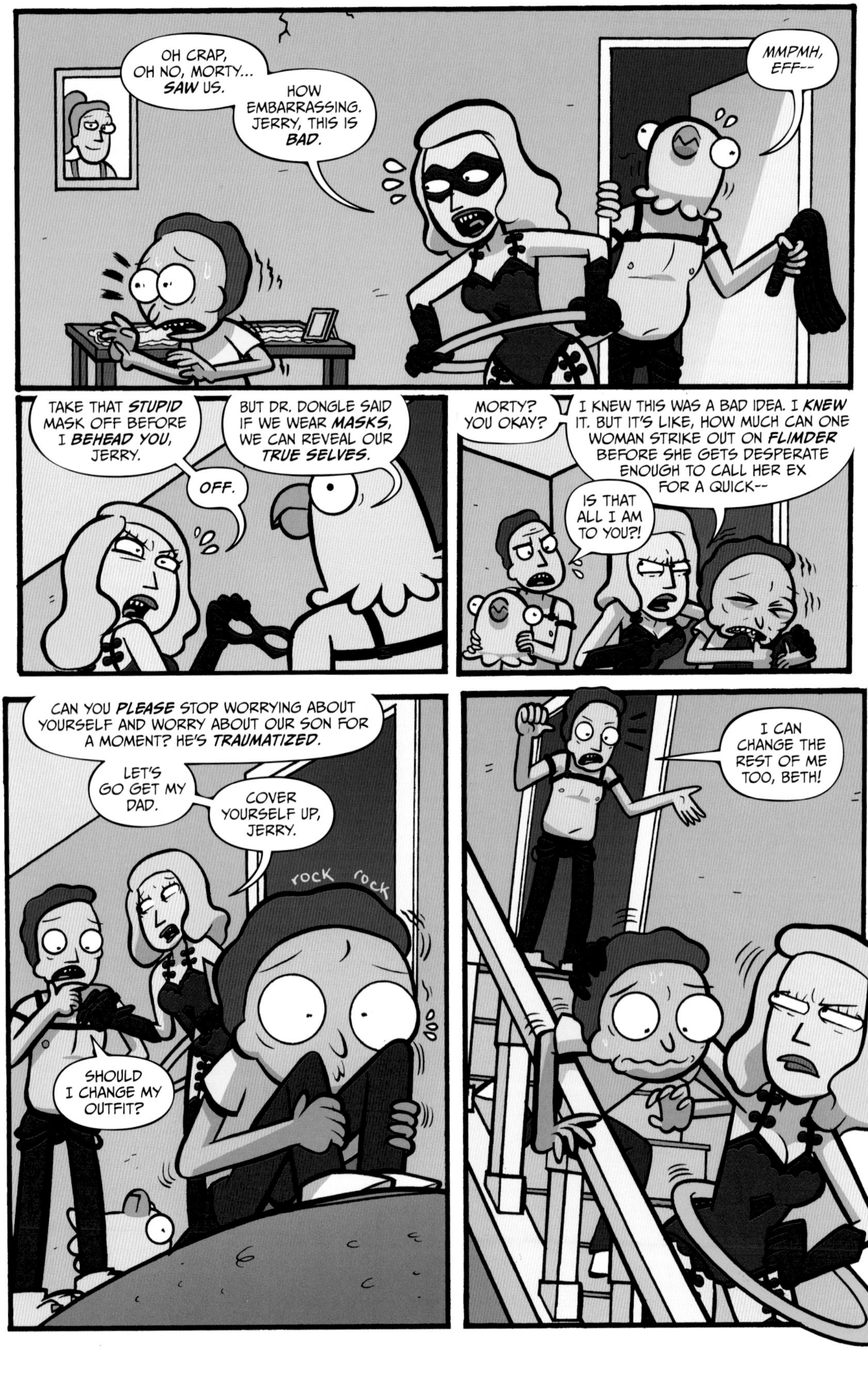
OH CRAP, OH NO, MORTY... SAW US.
HOW EMBARRASSING. JERRY, THIS IS BAD.
MMPMH, EFF--
TAKE THAT STUPID MASK OFF BEFORE I BEHEAD YOU, JERRY.
BUT DR. DONGLE SAID IF WE WEAR MASKS, WE CAN REVEAL OUR TRUE SELVES.
OFF.
MORTY? YOU OKAY?
I KNEW THIS WAS A BAD IDEA. I KNEW IT. BUT IT'S LIKE, HOW MUCH CAN ONE WOMAN STRIKE OUT ON FLIMDER BEFORE SHE GETS DESPERATE ENOUGH TO CALL HER EX FOR A QUICK--
IS THAT ALL I AM TO YOU?!
CAN YOU PLEASE STOP WORRYING ABOUT YOURSELF AND WORRY ABOUT OUR SON FOR A MOMENT? HE'S TRAUMATIZED.
LET'S GO GET MY DAD.
COVER YOURSELF UP, JERRY.
rock rock
SHOULD I CHANGE MY OUTFIT?
I CAN CHANGE THE REST OF ME TOO, BETH!

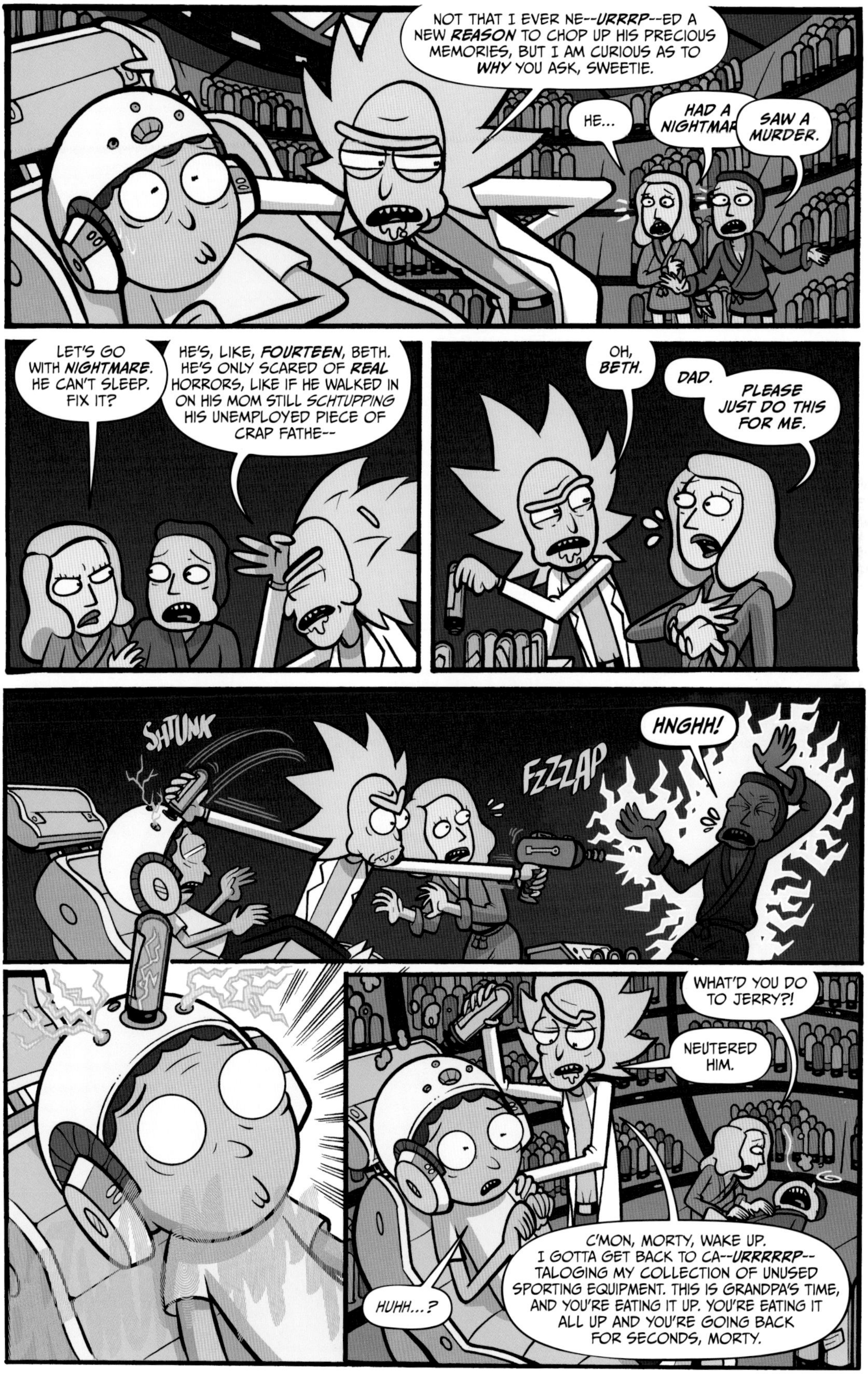
NOT THAT I EVER NE--URRRP--ED A NEW REASON TO CHOP UP HIS PRECIOUS MEMORIES, BUT I AM CURIOUS AS TO WHY YOU ASK, SWEETIE.
HE...
HAD A NIGHTMAR
SAW A MURDER.
LET'S GO WITH NIGHTMARE. HE CAN'T SLEEP. FIX IT?
HE'S, LIKE, FOURTEEN, BETH. HE'S ONLY SCARED OF REAL HORRORS, LIKE IF HE WALKED IN ON HIS MOM STILL SCHTUPPING HIS UNEMPLOYED PIECE OF CRAP FATHE--
OH, BETH.
DAD.
PLEASE JUST DO THIS FOR ME.
SHTUNK
FZZZAP
HNGHH!
WHAT'D YOU DO TO JERRY?!
NEUTERED HIM.
C'MON, MORTY, WAKE UP. I GOTTA GET BACK TO CA--URRRRRP--TALOGING MY COLLECTION OF UNUSED SPORTING EQUIPMENT. THIS IS GRANDPA'S TIME, AND YOU'RE EATING IT UP. YOU'RE EATING IT ALL UP AND YOU'RE GOING BACK FOR SECONDS, MORTY.
HUHH...?

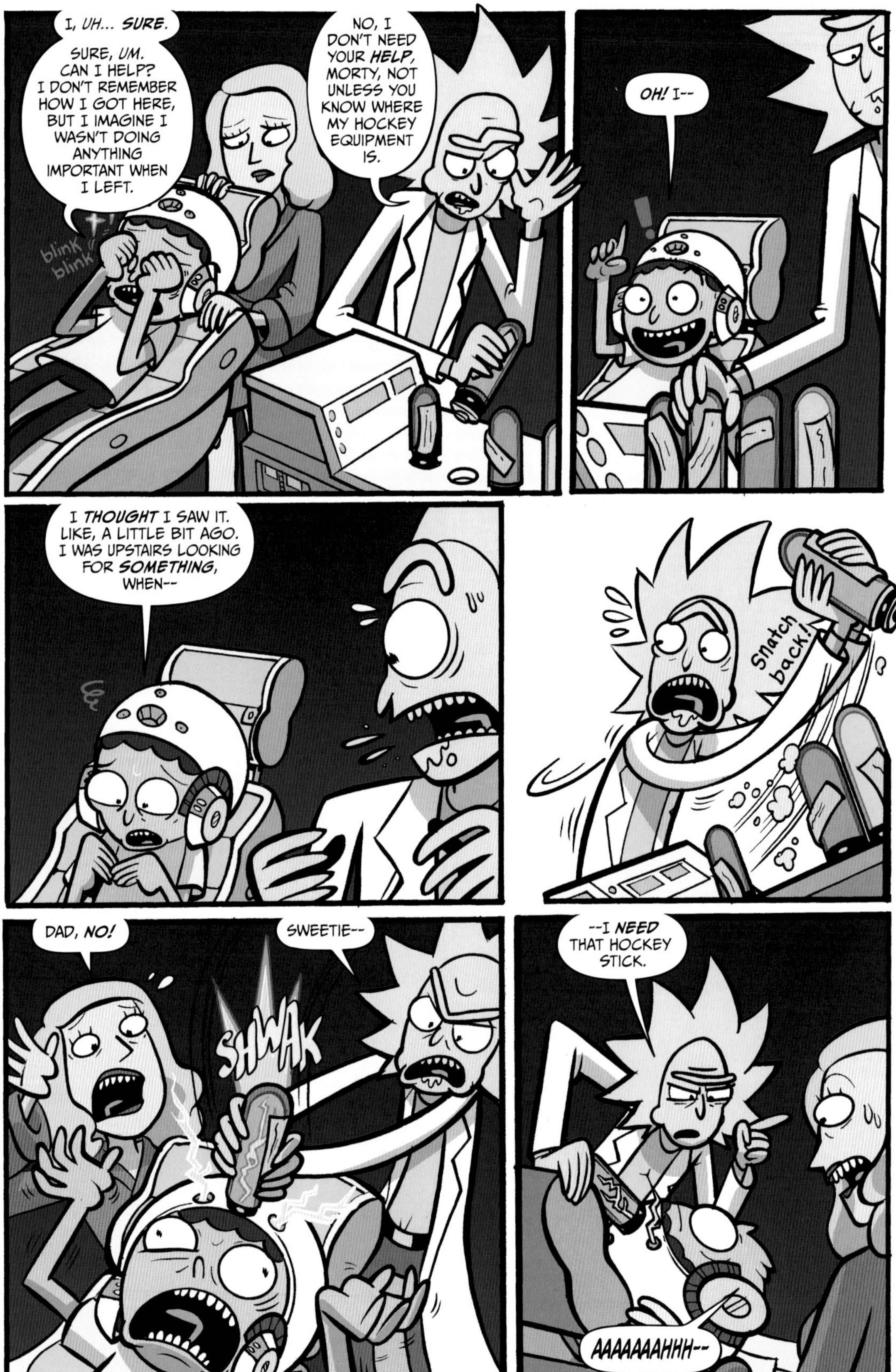
I, UH... SURE.
SURE, UM. CAN I HELP? I DON'T REMEMBER HOW I GOT HERE, BUT I IMAGINE I WASN'T DOING ANYTHING IMPORTANT WHEN I LEFT.
blink blink
NO, I DON'T NEED YOUR HELP, MORTY, NOT UNLESS YOU KNOW WHERE MY HOCKEY EQUIPMENT IS.
OH! I--
I THOUGHT I SAW IT. LIKE, A LITTLE BIT AGO. I WAS UPSTAIRS LOOKING FOR SOMETHING, WHEN--
Snatch back!
DAD, NO!
SWEETIE--
SHWAK
--I NEED THAT HOCKEY STICK.
AAAAAAAHHH--

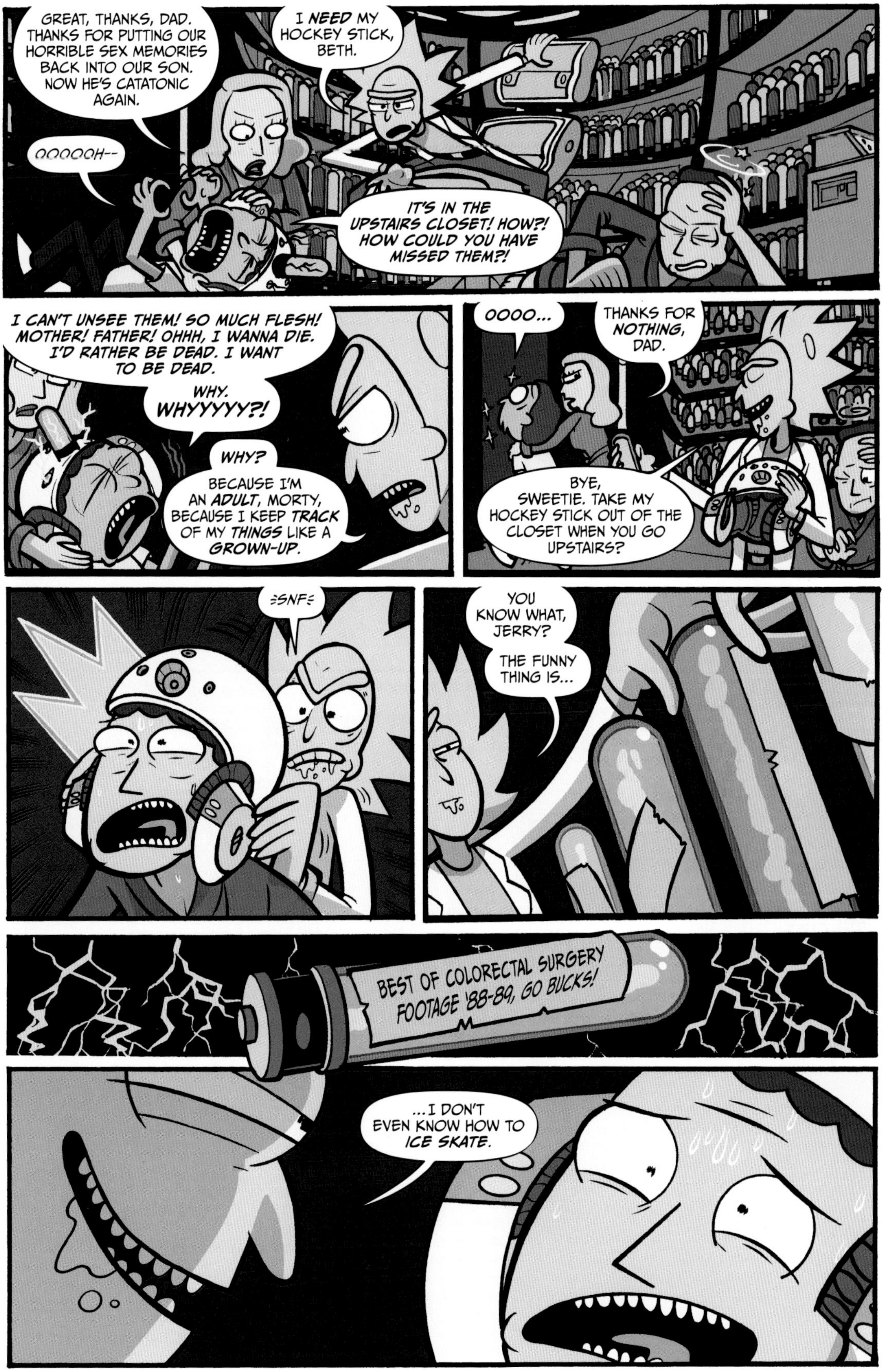
GREAT, THANKS, DAD. THANKS FOR PUTTING OUR HORRIBLE SEX MEMORIES BACK INTO OUR SON. NOW HE'S CATATONIC AGAIN.
I *NEED* MY HOCKEY STICK, BETH.
OOOOOH--
IT'S IN THE UPSTAIRS CLOSET! HOW?! HOW COULD YOU HAVE MISSED THEM?!
I CAN'T UNSEE THEM! SO MUCH FLESH! MOTHER! FATHER! OHHH, I WANNA DIE. I'D RATHER BE DEAD. I WANT TO BE DEAD.
WHY. WHYYYYY?!
WHY?
BECAUSE I'M AN *ADULT*, MORTY, BECAUSE I KEEP *TRACK* OF MY *THINGS* LIKE A *GROWN-UP*.
OOOO...
THANKS FOR *NOTHING*, DAD.
BYE, SWEETIE. TAKE MY HOCKEY STICK OUT OF THE CLOSET WHEN YOU GO UPSTAIRS?
SNF
YOU KNOW WHAT, JERRY?
THE FUNNY THING IS...
BEST OF COLORECTAL SURGERY FOOTAGE '88-89, GO BUCKS!
...I DON'T EVEN KNOW HOW TO *ICE SKATE*.

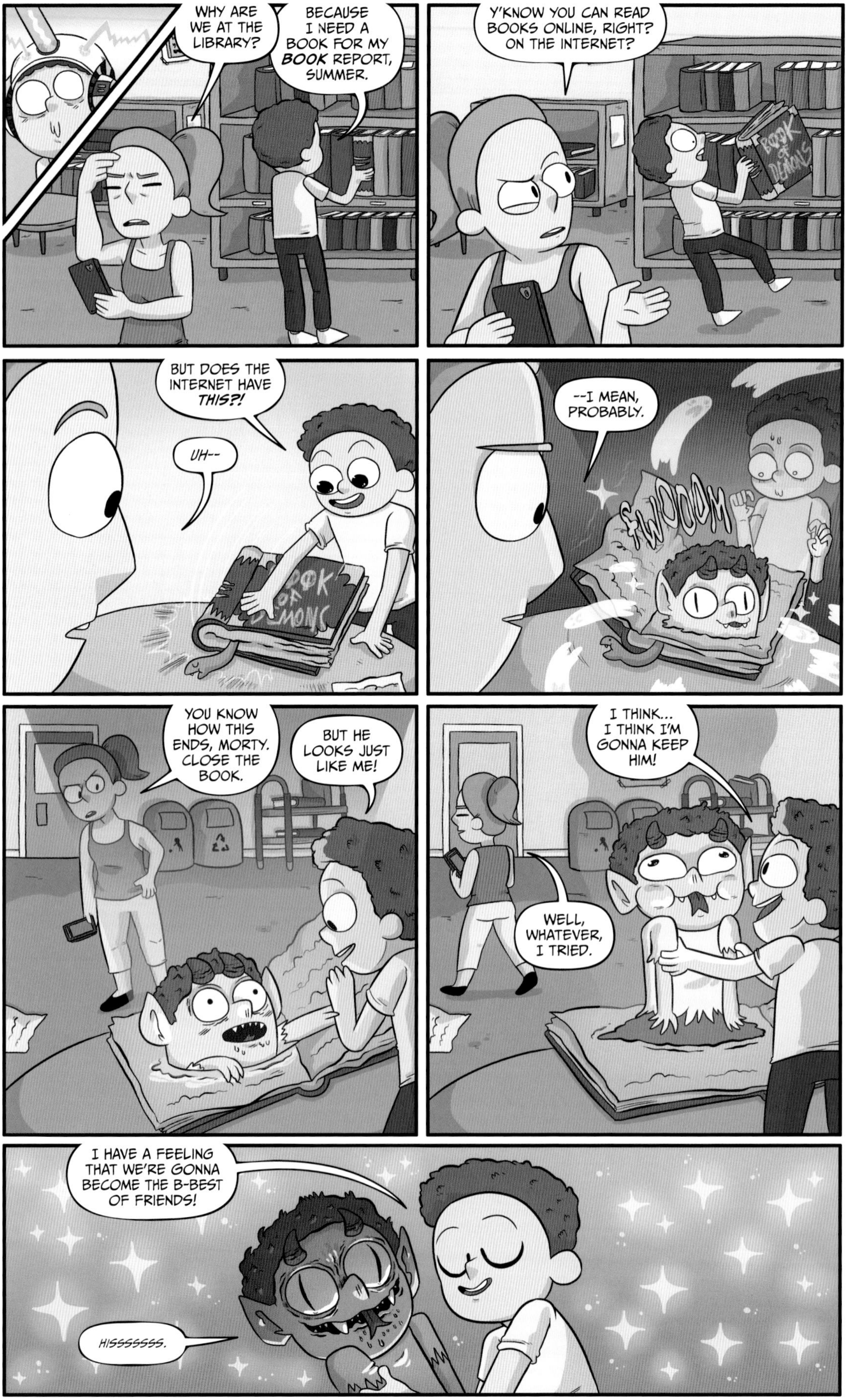
WHY ARE WE AT THE LIBRARY?
BECAUSE I NEED A BOOK FOR MY BOOK REPORT, SUMMER.
Y'KNOW YOU CAN READ BOOKS ONLINE, RIGHT? ON THE INTERNET?
BOOK OF DEMONS
BUT DOES THE INTERNET HAVE THIS?!
UH--
BOOK OF DEMONS
--I MEAN, PROBABLY.
SWOOOM
YOU KNOW HOW THIS ENDS, MORTY. CLOSE THE BOOK.
BUT HE LOOKS JUST LIKE ME!
I THINK... I THINK I'M GONNA KEEP HIM!
WELL, WHATEVER, I TRIED.
I HAVE A FEELING THAT WE'RE GONNA BECOME THE B-BEST OF FRIENDS!
HISSSSSSS.

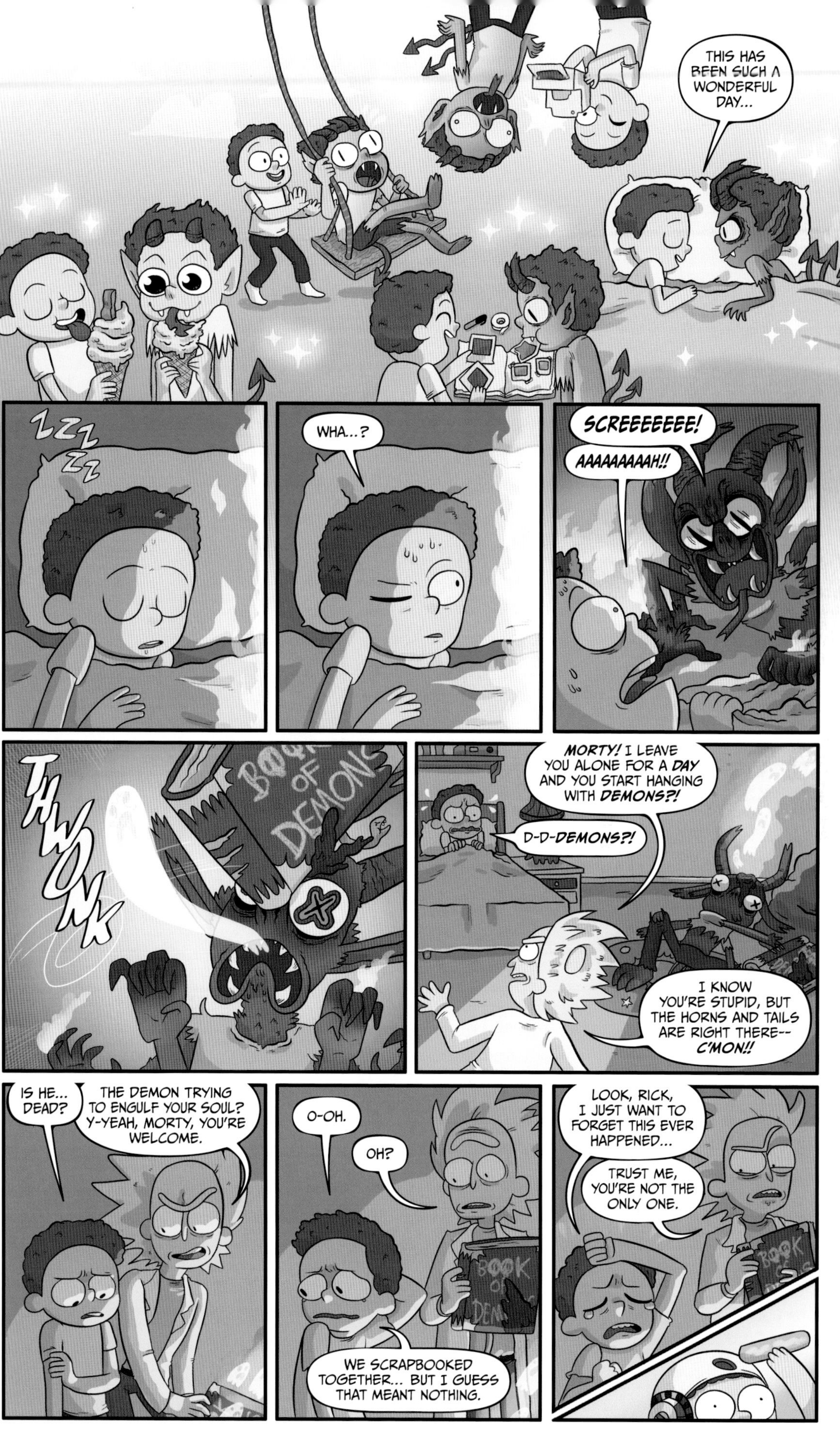
THIS HAS BEEN SUCH A WONDERFUL DAY...
ZZZ ZZZ
WHA...?
SCREEEEEEEE!
AAAAAAAAAH!!
THWONK
BOOK OF DEMONS
MORTY! I LEAVE YOU ALONE FOR A DAY AND YOU START HANGING WITH DEMONS?!
D-D-DEMONS?!
I KNOW YOU'RE STUPID, BUT THE HORNS AND TAILS ARE RIGHT THERE-- C'MON!!
IS HE... DEAD?
THE DEMON TRYING TO ENGULF YOUR SOUL? Y-YEAH, MORTY, YOU'RE WELCOME.
O-OH.
OH?
WE SCRAPBOOKED TOGETHER... BUT I GUESS THAT MEANT NOTHING.
LOOK, RICK, I JUST WANT TO FORGET THIS EVER HAPPENED...
TRUST ME, YOU'RE NOT THE ONLY ONE.

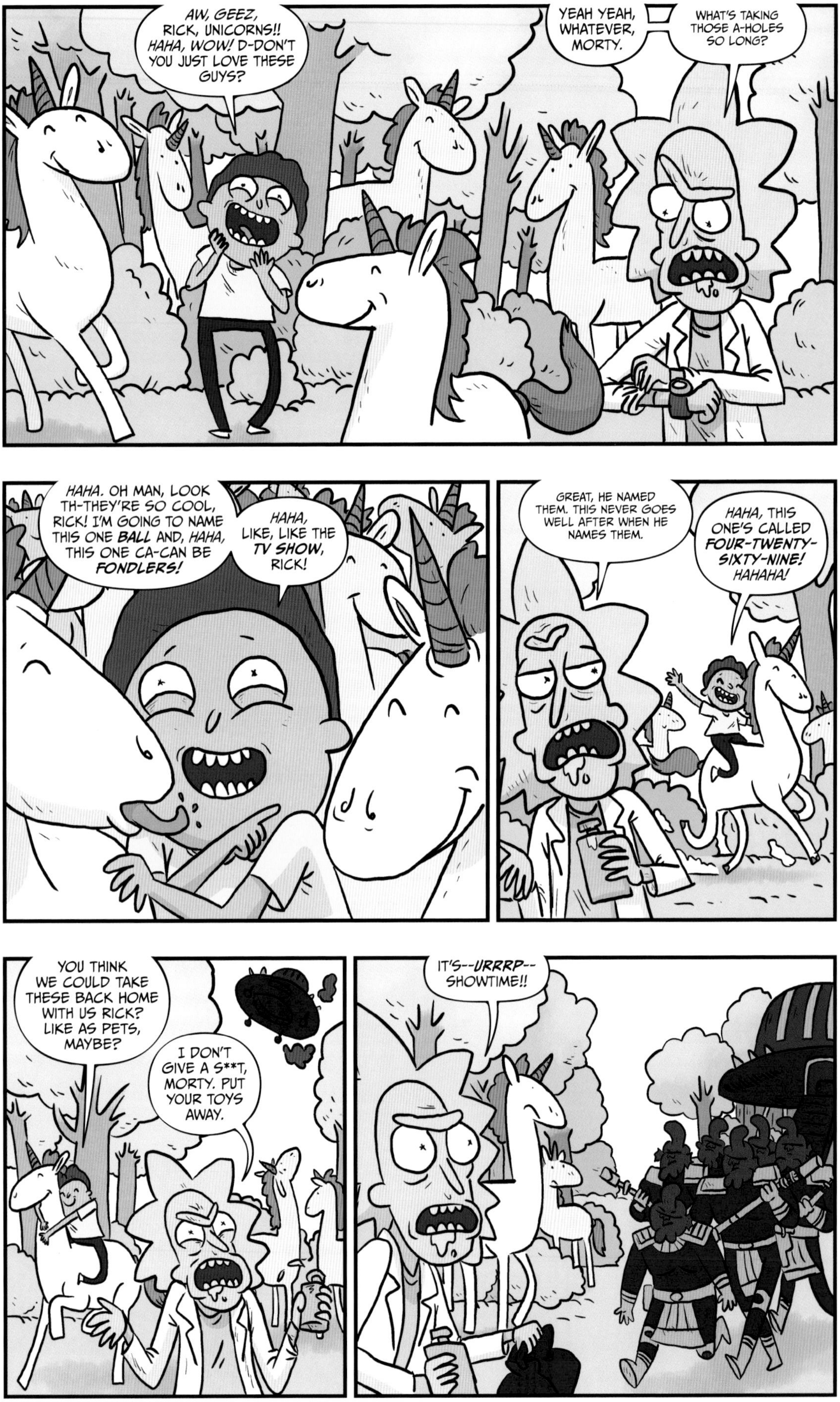
AW, GEEZ, RICK, UNICORNS!! HAHA, WOW! D-DON'T YOU JUST LOVE THESE GUYS?
YEAH YEAH, WHATEVER, MORTY.
WHAT'S TAKING THOSE A-HOLES SO LONG?
HAHA. OH MAN, LOOK TH-THEY'RE SO COOL, RICK! I'M GOING TO NAME THIS ONE BALL AND, HAHA, THIS ONE CA-CAN BE FONDLERS!
HAHA, LIKE, LIKE THE TV SHOW, RICK!
GREAT, HE NAMED THEM. THIS NEVER GOES WELL AFTER WHEN HE NAMES THEM.
HAHA, THIS ONE'S CALLED FOUR-TWENTY-SIXTY-NINE! HAHAHA!
YOU THINK WE COULD TAKE THESE BACK HOME WITH US RICK? LIKE AS PETS, MAYBE?
I DON'T GIVE A S**T, MORTY. PUT YOUR TOYS AWAY.
IT'S--URRRP--SHOWTIME!!

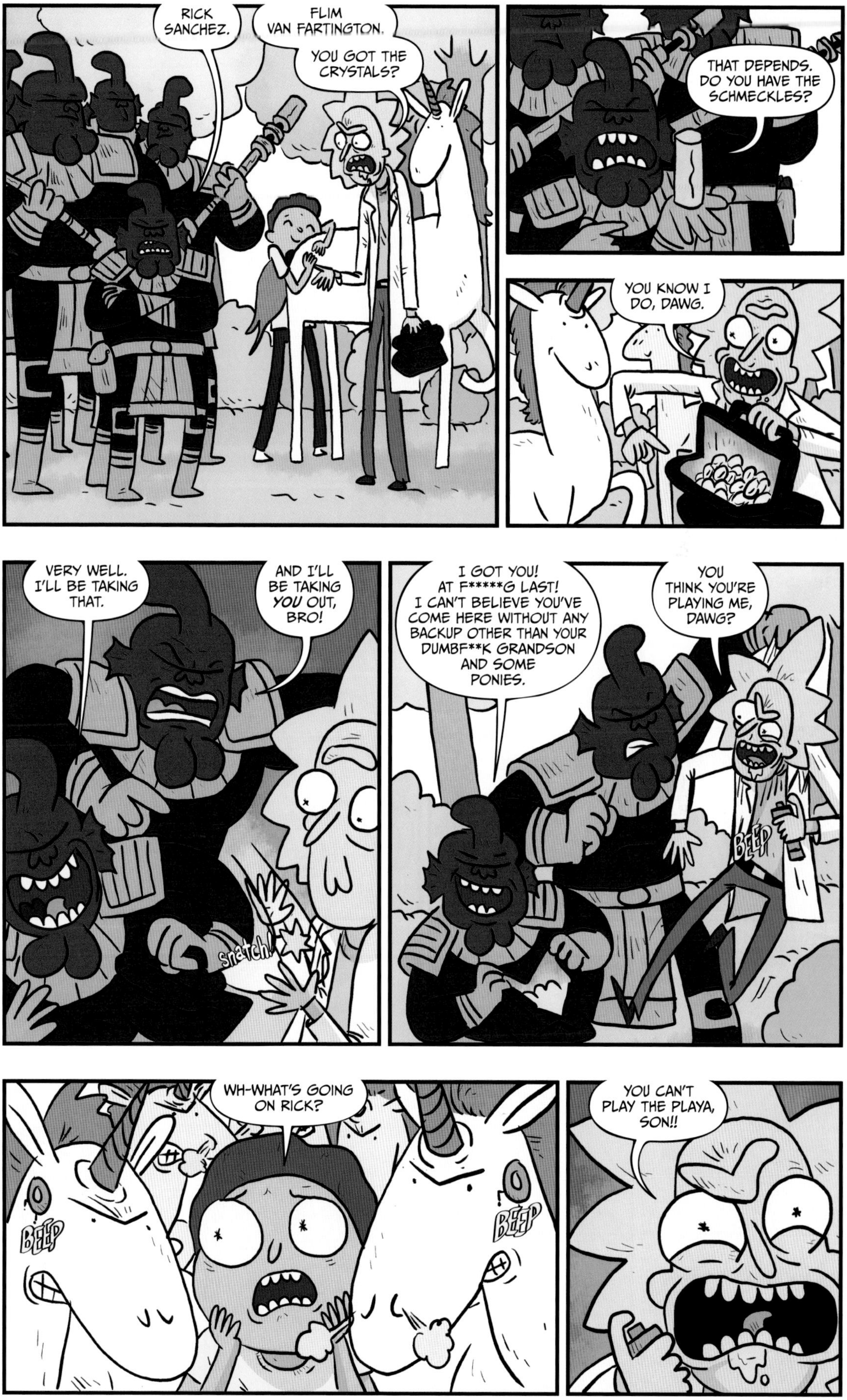
RICK SANCHEZ.
FLIM VAN FARTINGTON.
YOU GOT THE CRYSTALS?
THAT DEPENDS. DO YOU HAVE THE SCHMECKLES?
YOU KNOW I DO, DAWG.
VERY WELL. I'LL BE TAKING THAT.
AND I'LL BE TAKING *YOU* OUT, BRO!
snatch!
I GOT YOU! AT F*****G LAST! I CAN'T BELIEVE YOU'VE COME HERE WITHOUT ANY BACKUP OTHER THAN YOUR DUMBF**K GRANDSON AND SOME PONIES.
YOU THINK YOU'RE PLAYING ME, DAWG?
BEEP
WH-WHAT'S GOING ON RICK?
BEEP
BEEP
YOU CAN'T PLAY THE PLAYA, SON!!

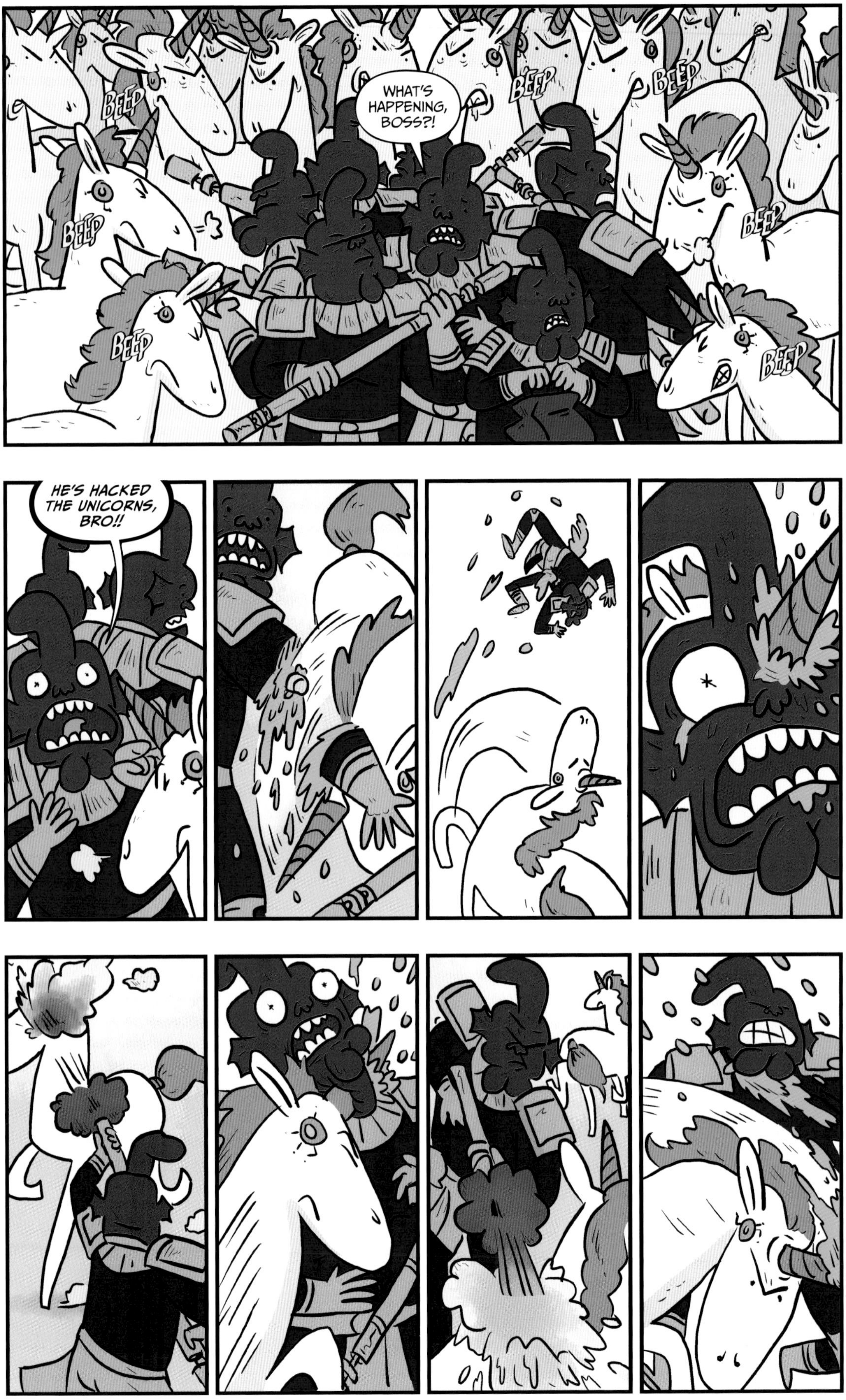
WHAT'S HAPPENING, BOSS?!
BEEP
BEEP
BEEP
BEEP
BEEP
BEEP
BEEP
HE'S HACKED THE UNICORNS, BRO!!

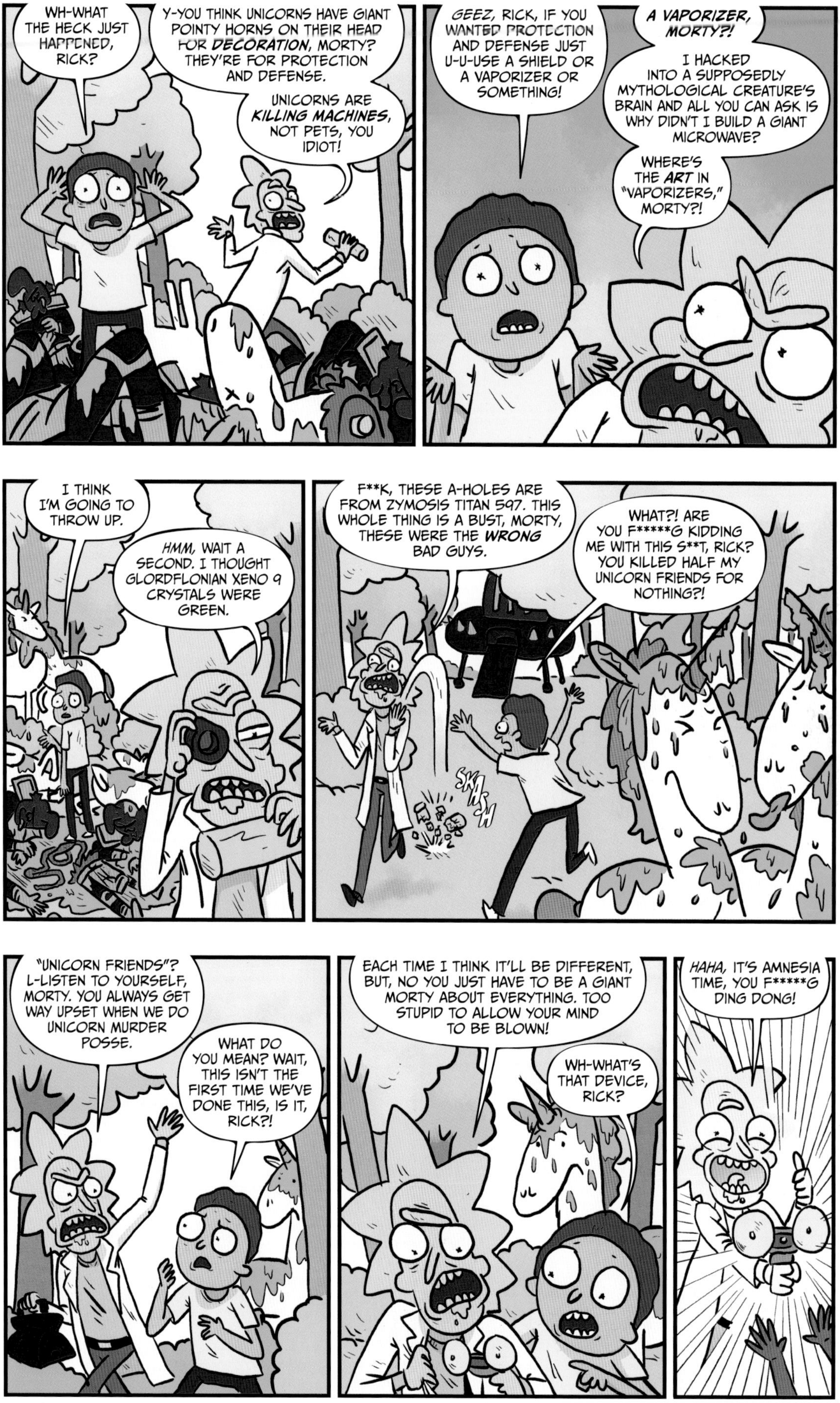
WH-WHAT THE HECK JUST HAPPENED, RICK?
Y-YOU THINK UNICORNS HAVE GIANT POINTY HORNS ON THEIR HEAD FOR DECORATION, MORTY? THEY'RE FOR PROTECTION AND DEFENSE.
UNICORNS ARE KILLING MACHINES, NOT PETS, YOU IDIOT!
GEEZ, RICK, IF YOU WANTED PROTECTION AND DEFENSE JUST U-U-USE A SHIELD OR A VAPORIZER OR SOMETHING!
A VAPORIZER, MORTY?!
I HACKED INTO A SUPPOSEDLY MYTHOLOGICAL CREATURE'S BRAIN AND ALL YOU CAN ASK IS WHY DIDN'T I BUILD A GIANT MICROWAVE?
WHERE'S THE ART IN "VAPORIZERS," MORTY?!
I THINK I'M GOING TO THROW UP.
HMM, WAIT A SECOND. I THOUGHT GLORDFLONIAN XENO 9 CRYSTALS WERE GREEN.
F**K, THESE A-HOLES ARE FROM ZYMOSIS TITAN 597. THIS WHOLE THING IS A BUST, MORTY, THESE WERE THE WRONG BAD GUYS.
WHAT?! ARE YOU F*****G KIDDING ME WITH THIS S**T, RICK? YOU KILLED HALF MY UNICORN FRIENDS FOR NOTHING?!
SKASH
"UNICORN FRIENDS"? L-LISTEN TO YOURSELF, MORTY. YOU ALWAYS GET WAY UPSET WHEN WE DO UNICORN MURDER POSSE.
WHAT DO YOU MEAN? WAIT, THIS ISN'T THE FIRST TIME WE'VE DONE THIS, IS IT, RICK?!
EACH TIME I THINK IT'LL BE DIFFERENT, BUT, NO YOU JUST HAVE TO BE A GIANT MORTY ABOUT EVERYTHING. TOO STUPID TO ALLOW YOUR MIND TO BE BLOWN!
WH-WHAT'S THAT DEVICE, RICK?
HAHA, IT'S AMNESIA TIME, YOU F*****G DING DONG!

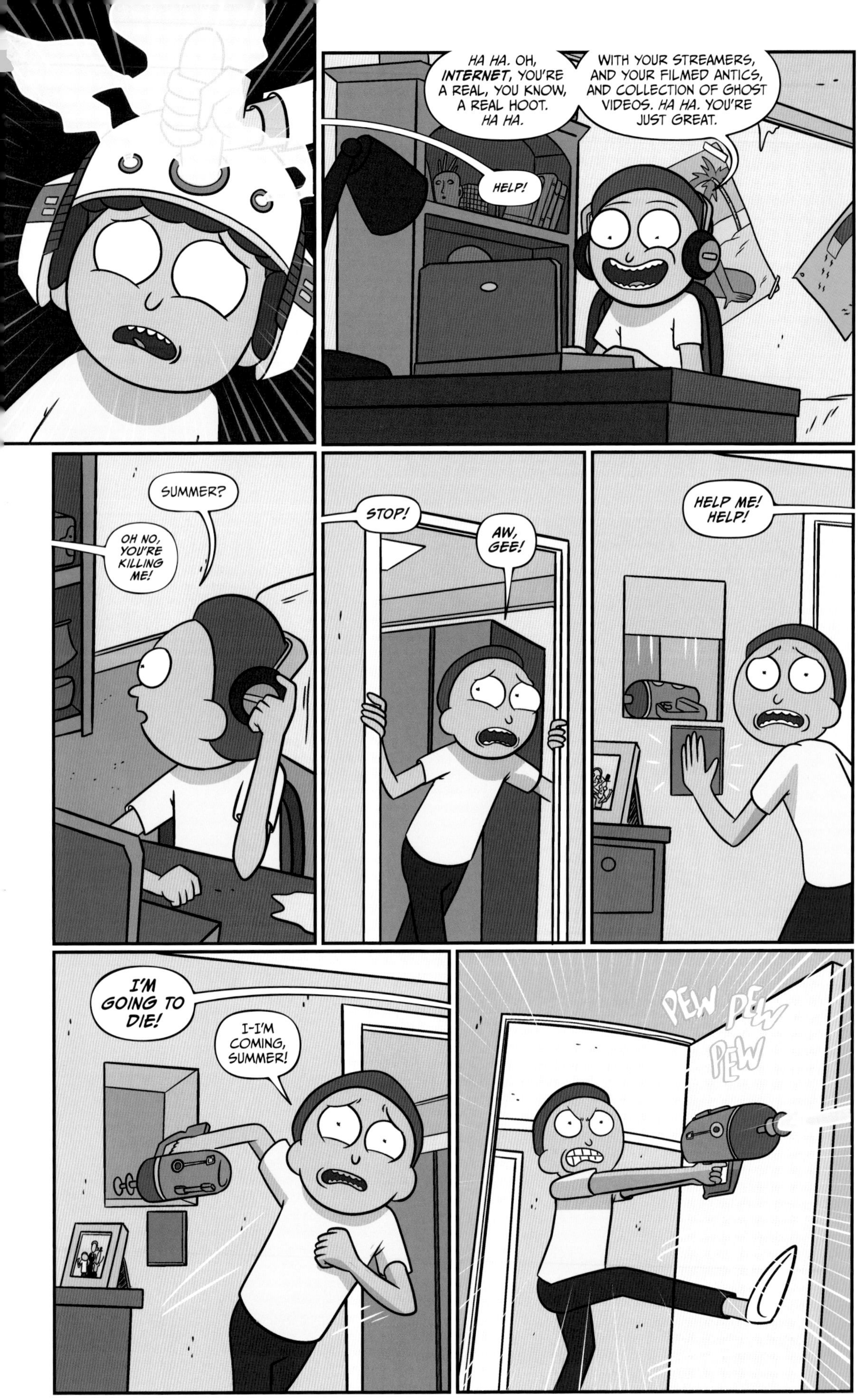
HA HA. OH, INTERNET, YOU'RE A REAL, YOU KNOW, A REAL HOOT. HA HA.
WITH YOUR STREAMERS, AND YOUR FILMED ANTICS, AND COLLECTION OF GHOST VIDEOS. HA HA. YOU'RE JUST GREAT.
HELP!
SUMMER?
OH NO, YOU'RE KILLING ME!
STOP!
AW, GEE!
HELP ME! HELP!
I'M GOING TO DIE!
I-I'M COMING, SUMMER!
PEW PEW
PEW

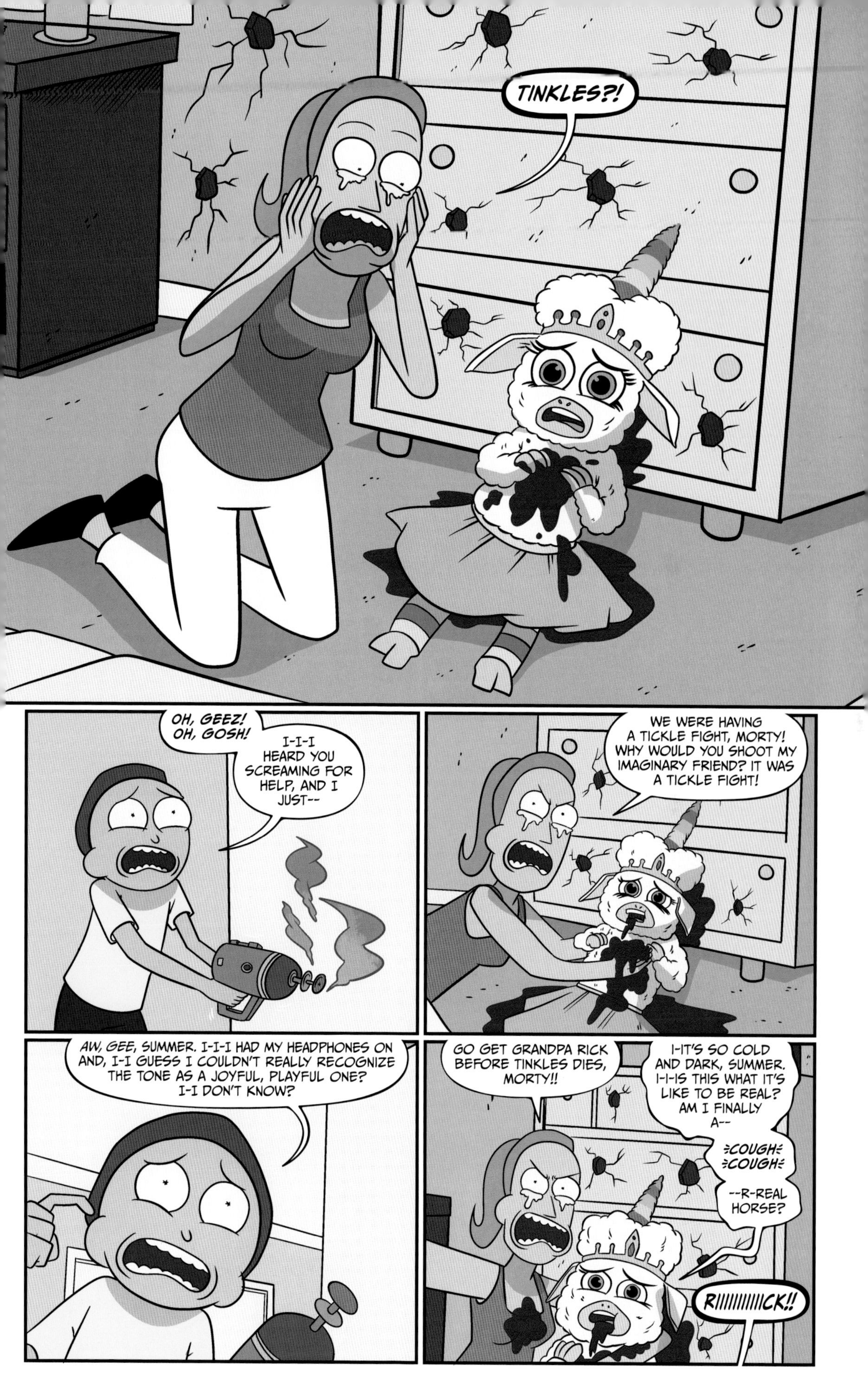
TINKLES?!
OH, GEEZ! OH, GOSH!
I-I-I HEARD YOU SCREAMING FOR HELP, AND I JUST--
WE WERE HAVING A TICKLE FIGHT, MORTY! WHY WOULD YOU SHOOT MY IMAGINARY FRIEND? IT WAS A TICKLE FIGHT!
AW, GEE, SUMMER. I-I-I HAD MY HEADPHONES ON AND, I-I GUESS I COULDN'T REALLY RECOGNIZE THE TONE AS A JOYFUL, PLAYFUL ONE? I-I DON'T KNOW?
GO GET GRANDPA RICK BEFORE TINKLES DIES, MORTY!!
I-IT'S SO COLD AND DARK, SUMMER. I-I-IS THIS WHAT IT'S LIKE TO BE REAL? AM I FINALLY A--
COUGH
COUGH
--R-REAL HORSE?
RIIIIIIIIICK!!

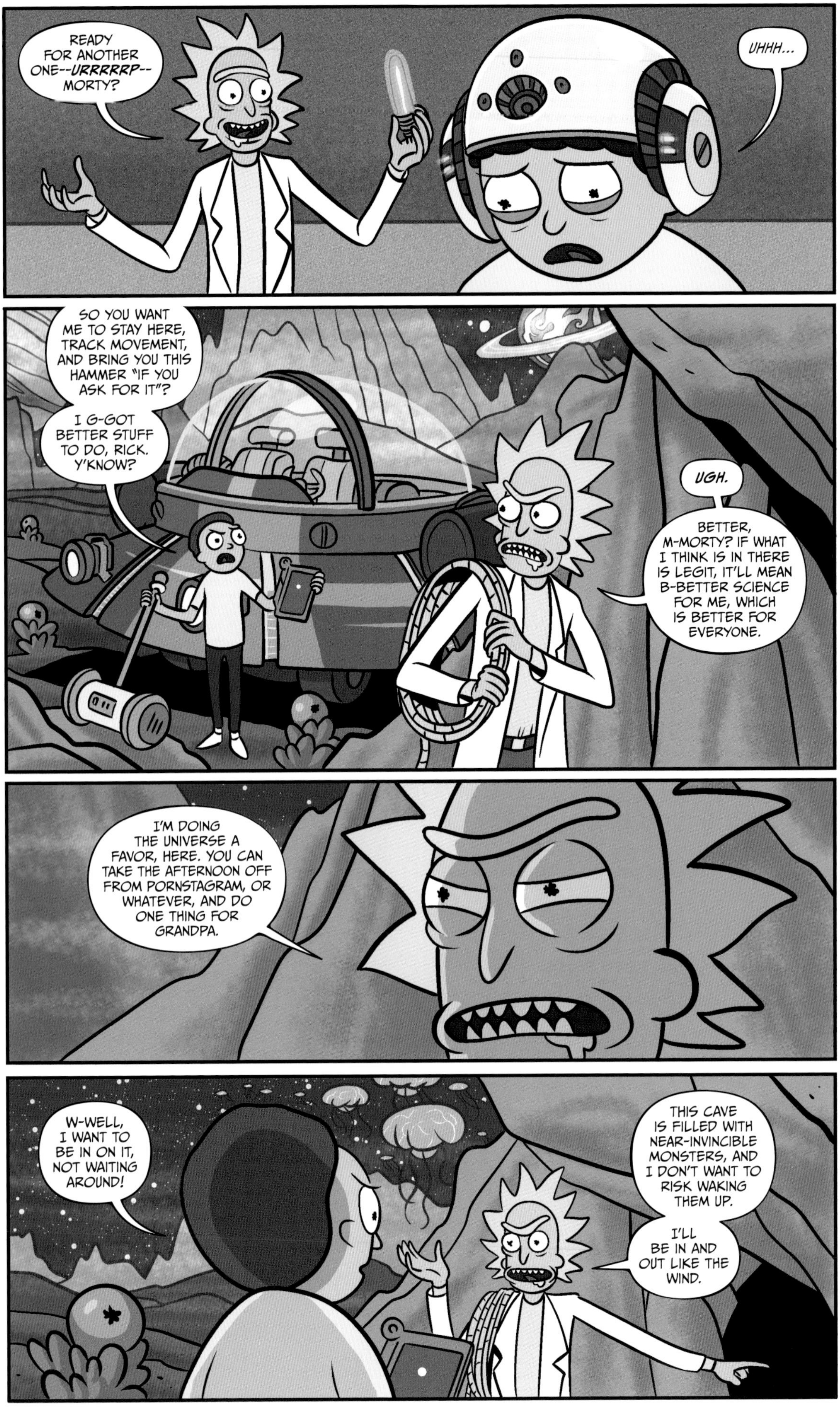
READY FOR ANOTHER ONE--URRRRRP--MORTY?
UHHH...
SO YOU WANT ME TO STAY HERE, TRACK MOVEMENT, AND BRING YOU THIS HAMMER "IF YOU ASK FOR IT"?
I G-GOT BETTER STUFF TO DO, RICK. Y'KNOW?
UGH.
BETTER, M-MORTY? IF WHAT I THINK IS IN THERE IS LEGIT, IT'LL MEAN B-BETTER SCIENCE FOR ME, WHICH IS BETTER FOR EVERYONE.
I'M DOING THE UNIVERSE A FAVOR, HERE. YOU CAN TAKE THE AFTERNOON OFF FROM PORNSTAGRAM, OR WHATEVER, AND DO ONE THING FOR GRANDPA.
W-WELL, I WANT TO BE IN ON IT, NOT WAITING AROUND!
THIS CAVE IS FILLED WITH NEAR-INVINCIBLE MONSTERS, AND I DON'T WANT TO RISK WAKING THEM UP.
I'LL BE IN AND OUT LIKE THE WIND.

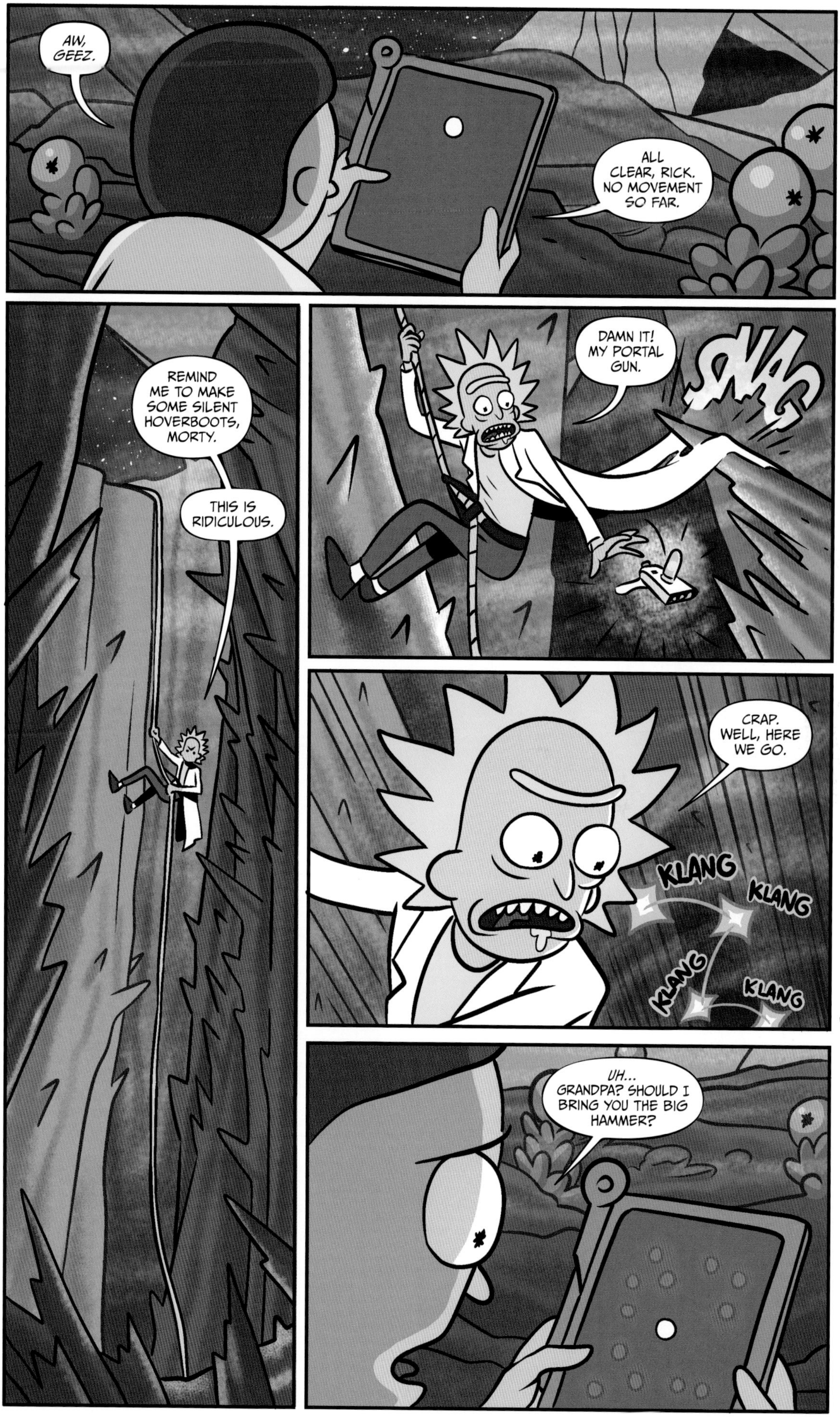
AW, GEEZ.
ALL CLEAR, RICK. NO MOVEMENT SO FAR.
REMIND ME TO MAKE SOME SILENT HOVERBOOTS, MORTY.
THIS IS RIDICULOUS.
DAMN IT! MY PORTAL GUN.
SNAG
CRAP. WELL, HERE WE GO.
KLANG
KLANG
KLANG
KLANG
UH... GRANDPA? SHOULD I BRING YOU THE BIG HAMMER?

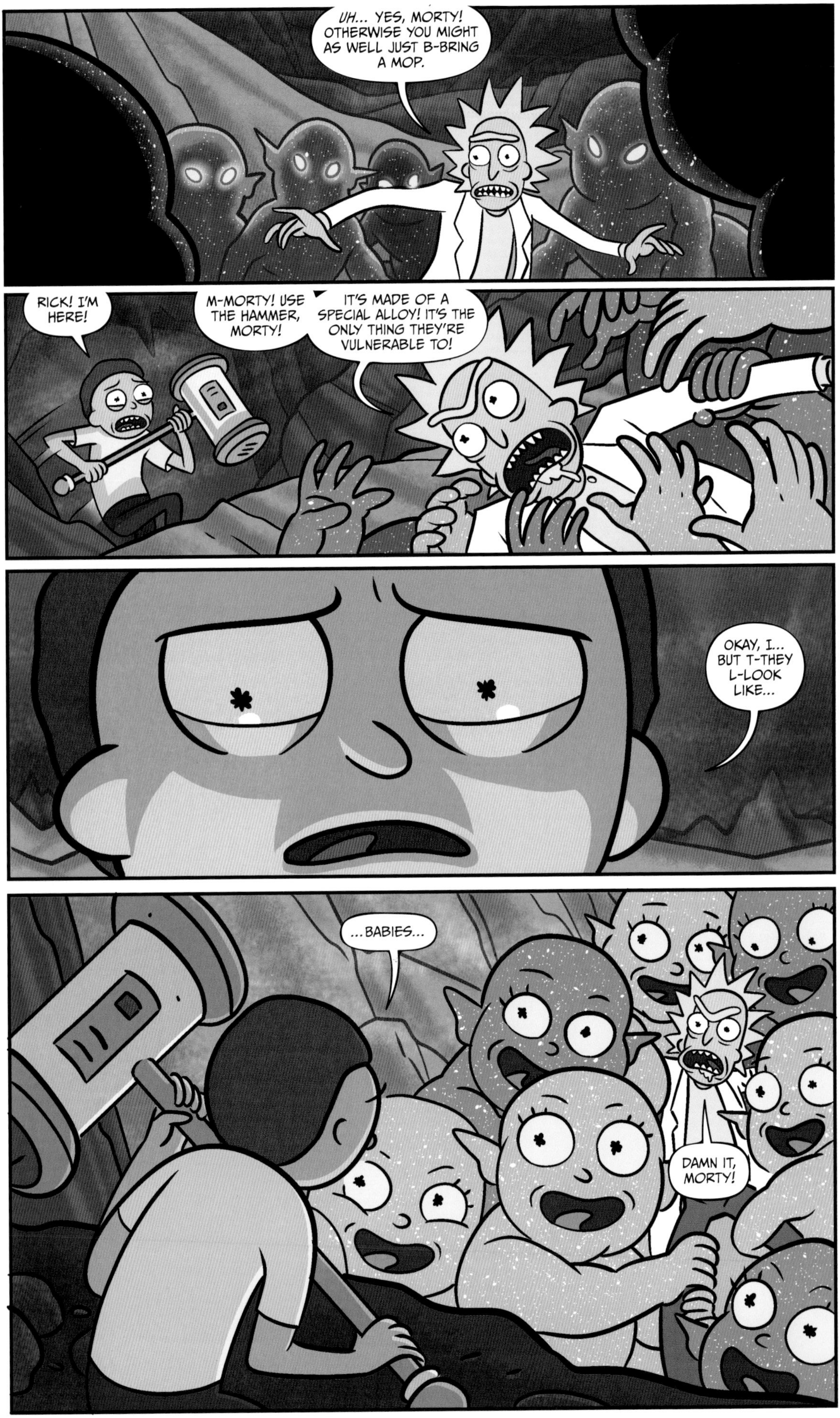
UH... YES, MORTY! OTHERWISE YOU MIGHT AS WELL JUST B-BRING A MOP.
RICK! I'M HERE!
M-MORTY! USE THE HAMMER, MORTY!
IT'S MADE OF A SPECIAL ALLOY! IT'S THE ONLY THING THEY'RE VULNERABLE TO!
OKAY, I... BUT T-THEY L-LOOK LIKE...
...BABIES...
DAMN IT, MORTY!

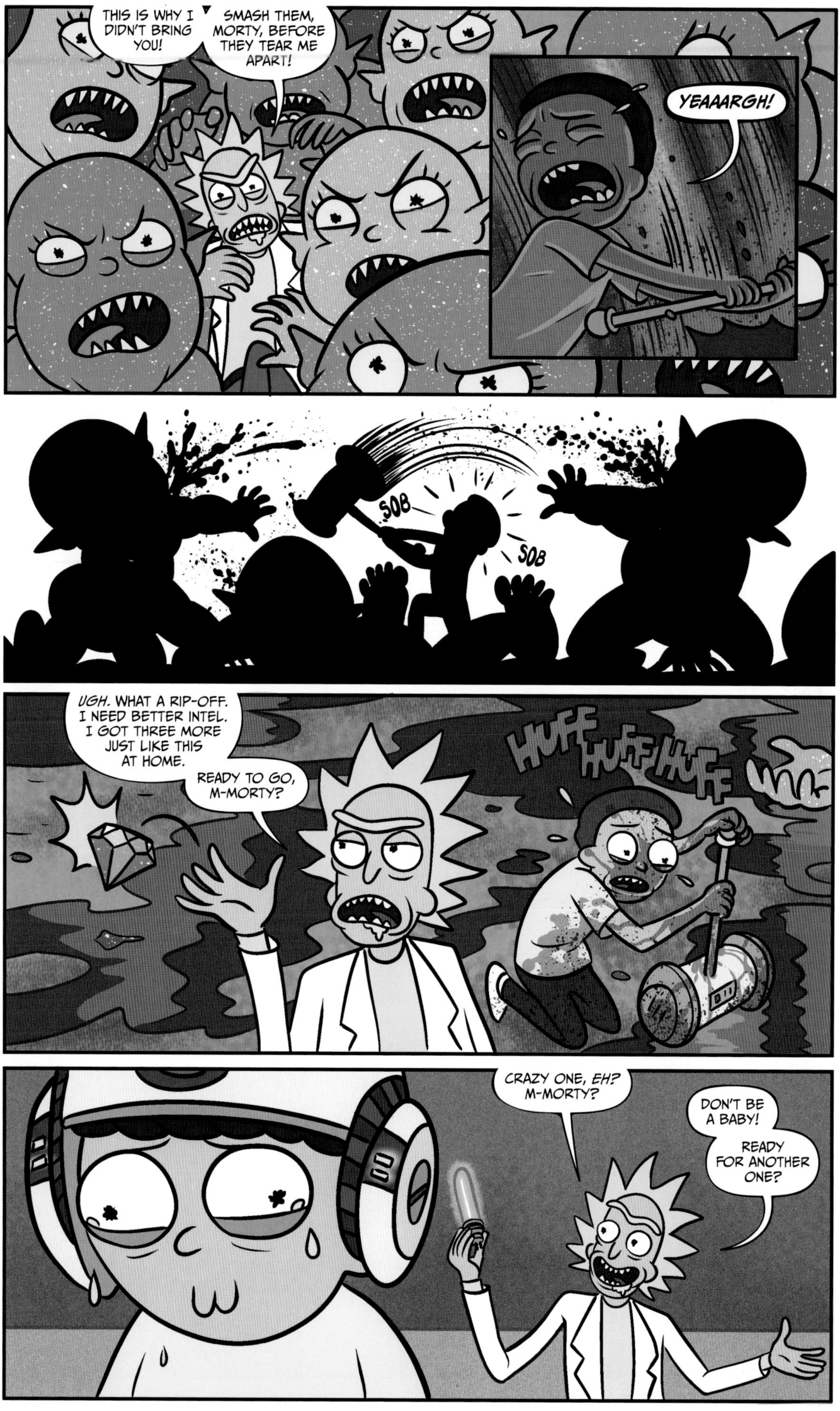
THIS IS WHY I DIDN'T BRING YOU!
SMASH THEM, MORTY, BEFORE THEY TEAR ME APART!
YEAAARGH!
SOB
SOB
UGH. WHAT A RIP-OFF. I NEED BETTER INTEL. I GOT THREE MORE JUST LIKE THIS AT HOME.
READY TO GO, M-MORTY?
HUFF HUFF HUFF
CRAZY ONE, EH? M-MORTY?
DON'T BE A BABY!
READY FOR ANOTHER ONE?

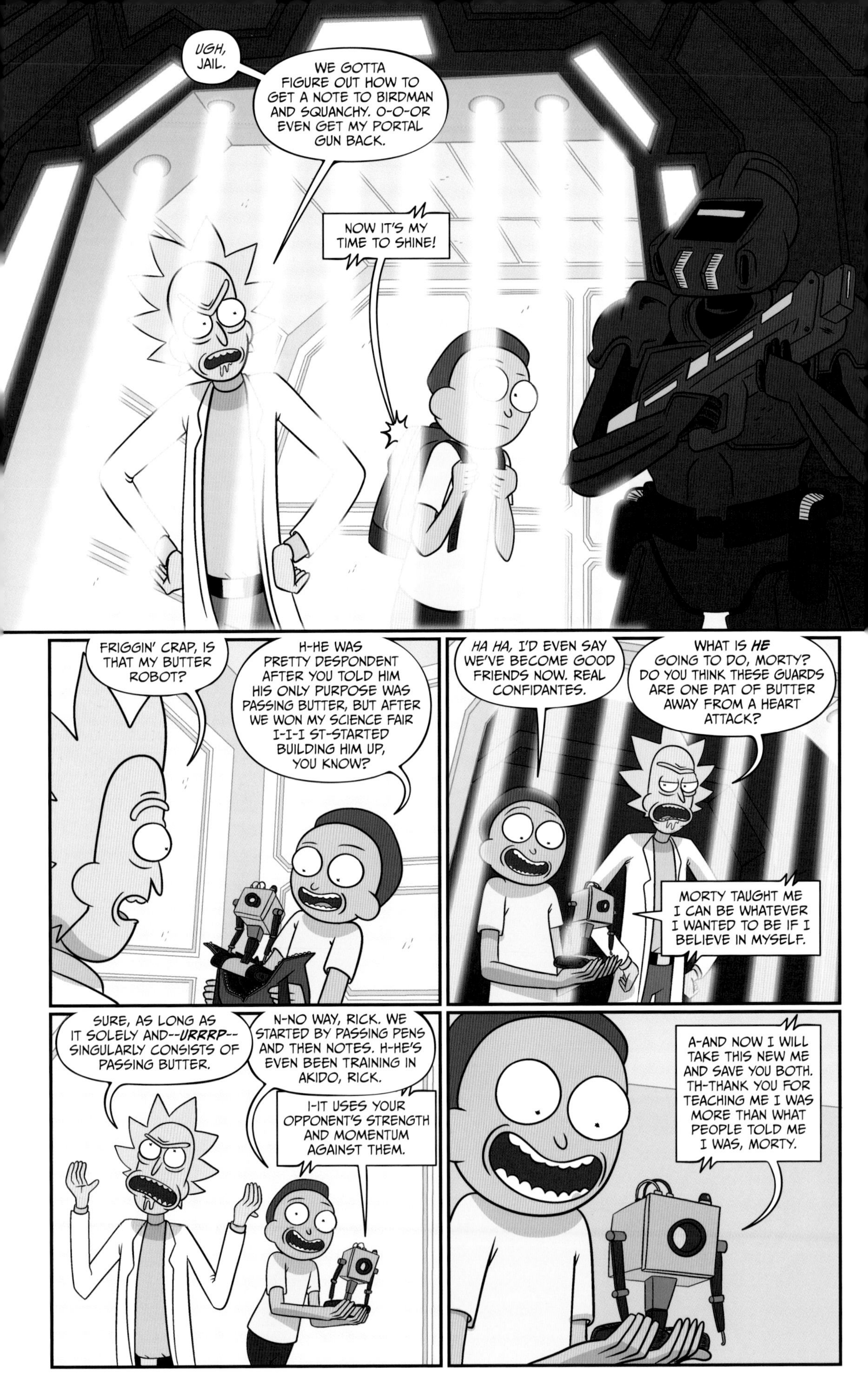
UGH, JAIL.
WE GOTTA FIGURE OUT HOW TO GET A NOTE TO BIRDMAN AND SQUANCHY. O-O-OR EVEN GET MY PORTAL GUN BACK.
NOW IT'S MY TIME TO SHINE!
FRIGGIN' CRAP, IS THAT MY BUTTER ROBOT?
H-HE WAS PRETTY DESPONDENT AFTER YOU TOLD HIM HIS ONLY PURPOSE WAS PASSING BUTTER, BUT AFTER WE WON MY SCIENCE FAIR I-I-I ST-STARTED BUILDING HIM UP, YOU KNOW?
HA HA, I'D EVEN SAY WE'VE BECOME GOOD FRIENDS NOW. REAL CONFIDANTES.
WHAT IS HE GOING TO DO, MORTY? DO YOU THINK THESE GUARDS ARE ONE PAT OF BUTTER AWAY FROM A HEART ATTACK?
MORTY TAUGHT ME I CAN BE WHATEVER I WANTED TO BE IF I BELIEVE IN MYSELF.
SURE, AS LONG AS IT SOLELY AND--URRRP--SINGULARLY CONSISTS OF PASSING BUTTER.
N-NO WAY, RICK. WE STARTED BY PASSING PENS AND THEN NOTES. H-HE'S EVEN BEEN TRAINING IN AKIDO, RICK.
I-IT USES YOUR OPPONENT'S STRENGTH AND MOMENTUM AGAINST THEM.
A-AND NOW I WILL TAKE THIS NEW ME AND SAVE YOU BOTH. TH-THANK YOU FOR TEACHING ME I WAS MORE THAN WHAT PEOPLE TOLD ME I WAS, MORTY.

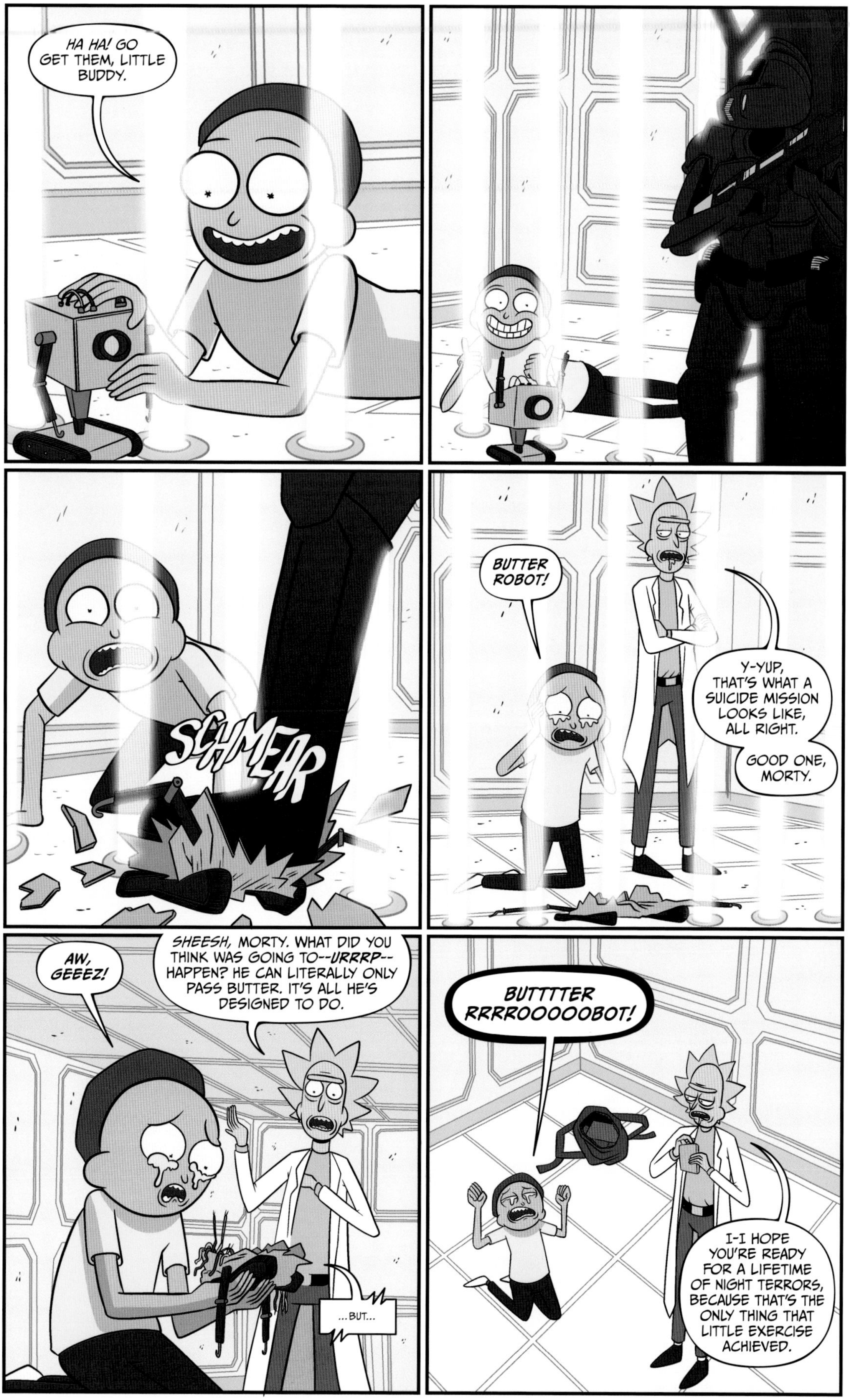
HA HA! GO GET THEM, LITTLE BUDDY.
SCHMEAR
BUTTER ROBOT!
Y-YUP, THAT'S WHAT A SUICIDE MISSION LOOKS LIKE, ALL RIGHT.
GOOD ONE, MORTY.
AW, GEEEZ!
SHEESH, MORTY. WHAT DID YOU THINK WAS GOING TO--URRRP--HAPPEN? HE CAN LITERALLY ONLY PASS BUTTER. IT'S ALL HE'S DESIGNED TO DO.
...BUT...
BUTTTTER RRRROOOOOBOT!
I-I HOPE YOU'RE READY FOR A LIFETIME OF NIGHT TERRORS, BECAUSE THAT'S THE ONLY THING THAT LITTLE EXERCISE ACHIEVED.

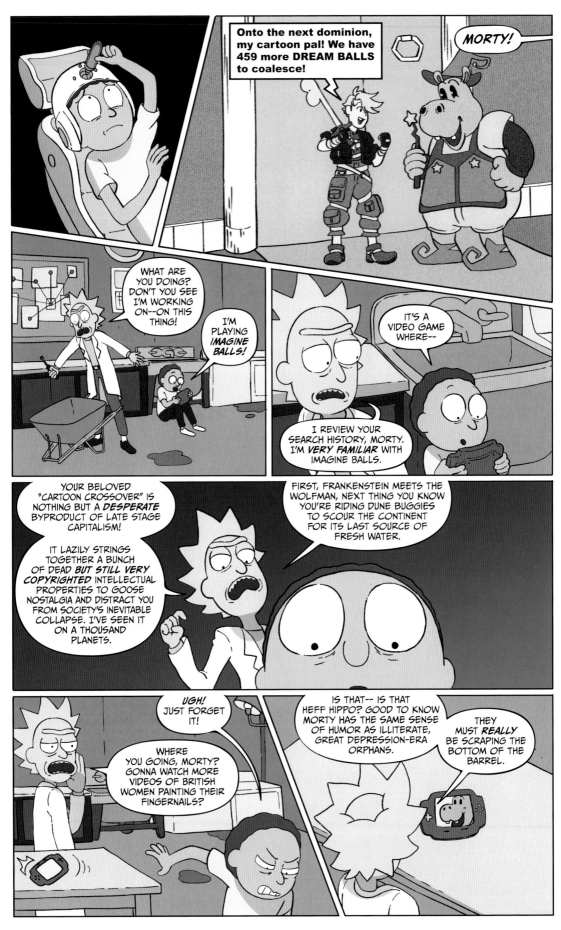

Onto the next dominion, my cartoon pal! We have 459 more DREAM BALLS to coalesce!

MORTY!

WHAT ARE YOU DOING? DON'T YOU SEE I'M WORKING ON--ON THIS THING!

I'M PLAYING *IMAGINE BALLS!*

IT'S A VIDEO GAME WHERE--

I REVIEW YOUR SEARCH HISTORY, MORTY. I'M *VERY FAMILIAR* WITH IMAGINE BALLS.

YOUR BELOVED "CARTOON CROSSOVER" IS NOTHING BUT A *DESPERATE* BYPRODUCT OF LATE STAGE CAPITALISM!

IT LAZILY STRINGS TOGETHER A BUNCH OF DEAD *BUT STILL VERY COPYRIGHTED* INTELLECTUAL PROPERTIES TO GOOSE NOSTALGIA AND DISTRACT YOU FROM SOCIETY'S INEVITABLE COLLAPSE. I'VE SEEN IT ON A THOUSAND PLANETS.

FIRST, FRANKENSTEIN MEETS THE WOLFMAN, NEXT THING YOU KNOW YOU'RE RIDING DUNE BUGGIES TO SCOUR THE CONTINENT FOR ITS LAST SOURCE OF FRESH WATER.

UGH! JUST FORGET IT!

WHERE YOU GOING, MORTY? GONNA WATCH MORE VIDEOS OF BRITISH WOMEN PAINTING THEIR FINGERNAILS?

IS THAT-- IS THAT HEFF HIPPO? GOOD TO KNOW MORTY HAS THE SAME SENSE OF HUMOR AS ILLITERATE, GREAT DEPRESSION-ERA ORPHANS.

THEY MUST *REALLY* BE SCRAPING THE BOTTOM OF THE BARREL.

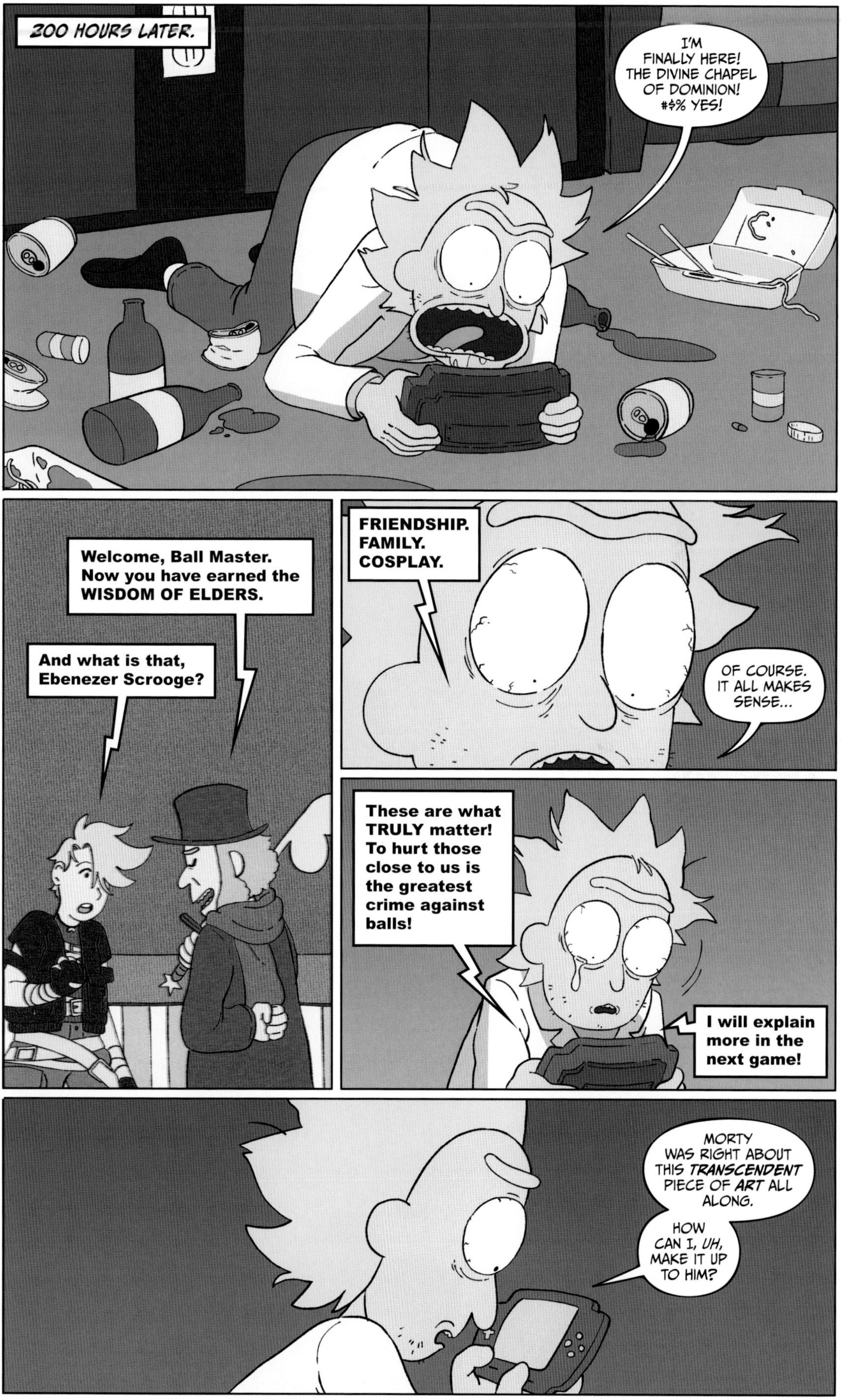
200 HOURS LATER.
I'M FINALLY HERE! THE DIVINE CHAPEL OF DOMINION! #$% YES!
Welcome, Ball Master. Now you have earned the WISDOM OF ELDERS.
And what is that, Ebenezer Scrooge?
FRIENDSHIP. FAMILY. COSPLAY.
OF COURSE. IT ALL MAKES SENSE...
These are what TRULY matter! To hurt those close to us is the greatest crime against balls!
I will explain more in the next game!
MORTY WAS RIGHT ABOUT THIS *TRANSCENDENT* PIECE OF *ART* ALL ALONG.
HOW CAN I, *UH*, MAKE IT UP TO HIM?

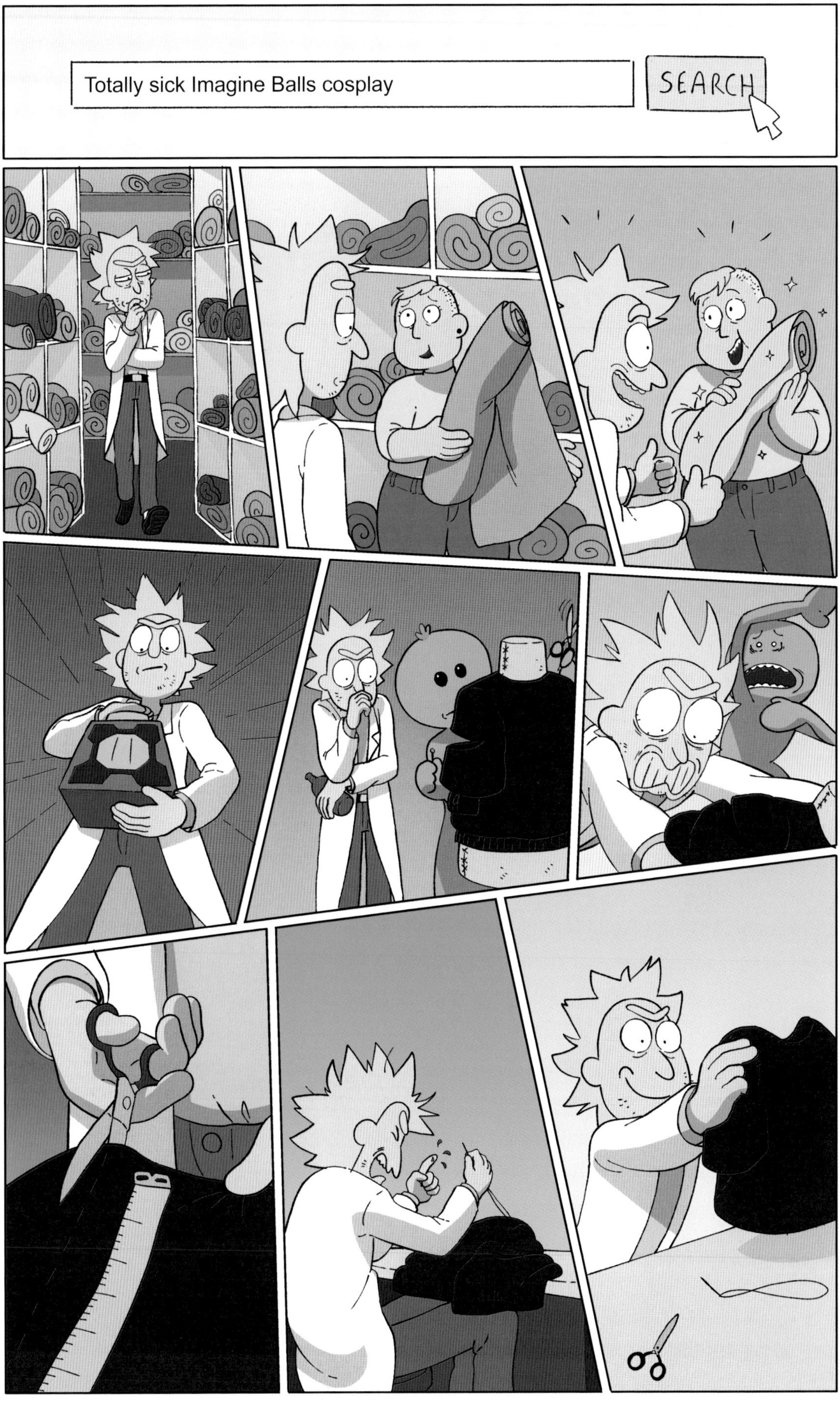
Totally sick Imagine Balls cosplay
SEARCH

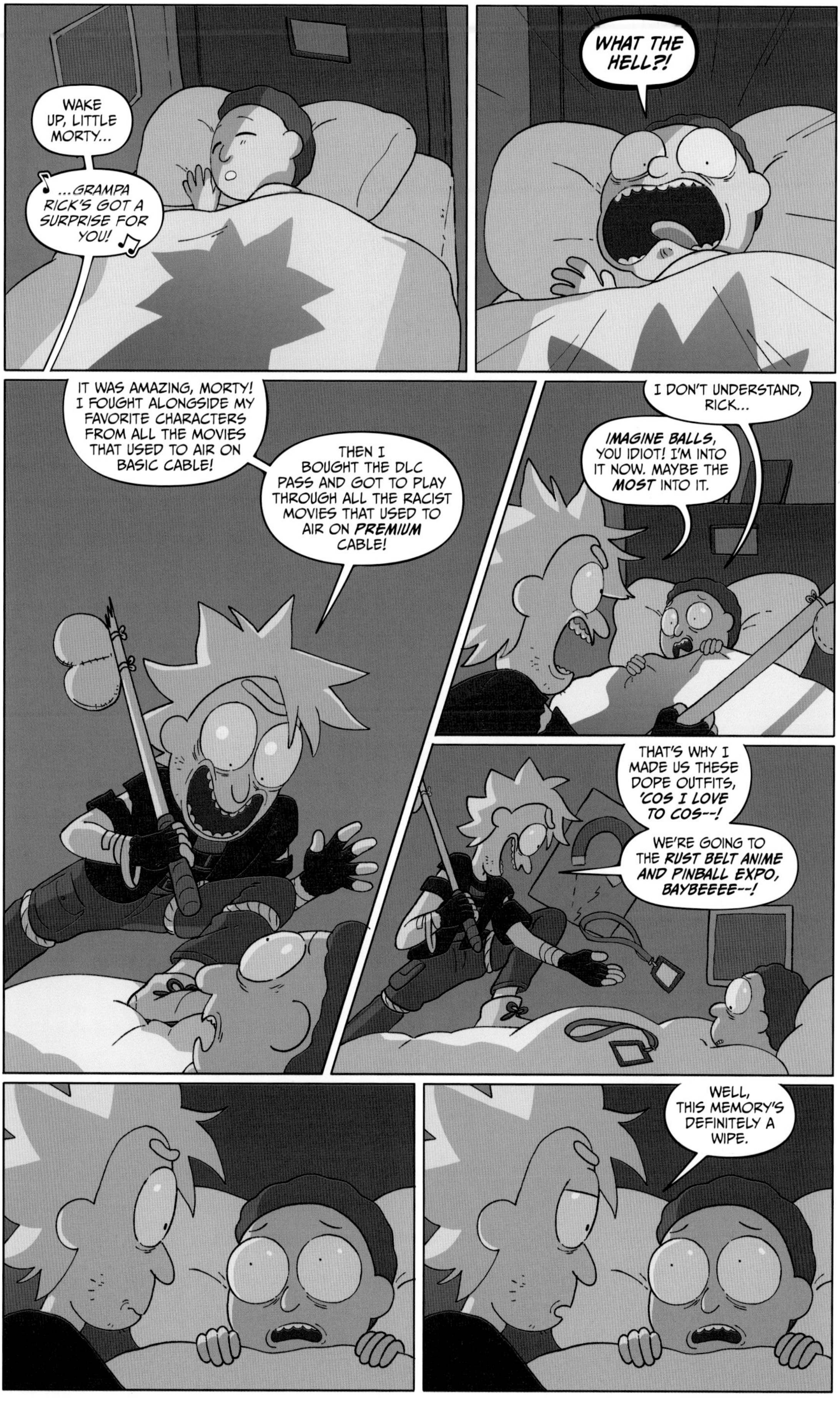
WAKE UP, LITTLE MORTY...
...GRAMPA RICK'S GOT A SURPRISE FOR YOU!
WHAT THE HELL?!
IT WAS AMAZING, MORTY! I FOUGHT ALONGSIDE MY FAVORITE CHARACTERS FROM ALL THE MOVIES THAT USED TO AIR ON BASIC CABLE!
THEN I BOUGHT THE DLC PASS AND GOT TO PLAY THROUGH ALL THE RACIST MOVIES THAT USED TO AIR ON PREMIUM CABLE!
I DON'T UNDERSTAND, RICK...
IMAGINE BALLS, YOU IDIOT! I'M INTO IT NOW. MAYBE THE MOST INTO IT.
THAT'S WHY I MADE US THESE DOPE OUTFITS, 'COS I LOVE TO COS--!
WE'RE GOING TO THE RUST BELT ANIME AND PINBALL EXPO, BAYBEEEE--!
WELL, THIS MEMORY'S DEFINITELY A WIPE.

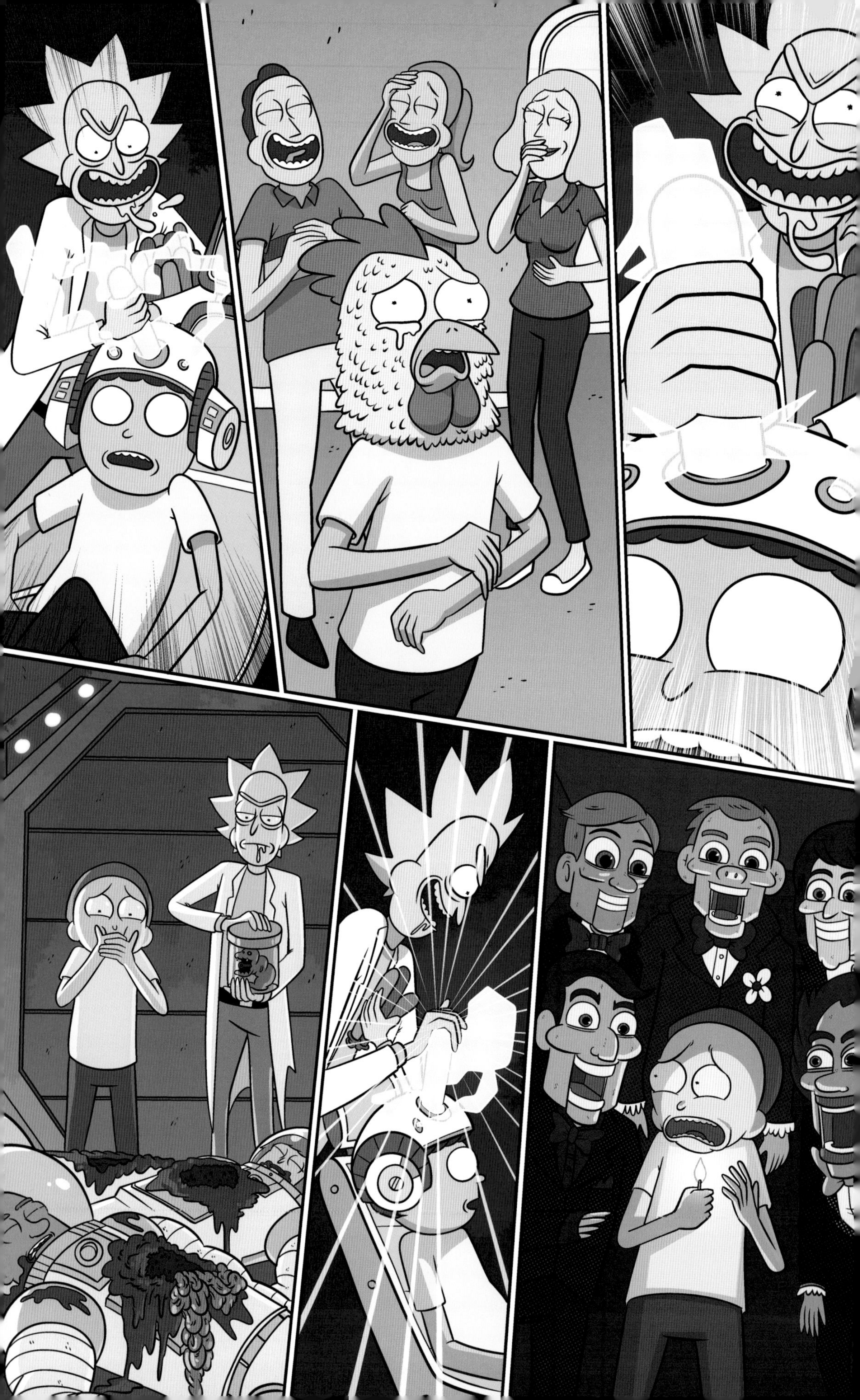

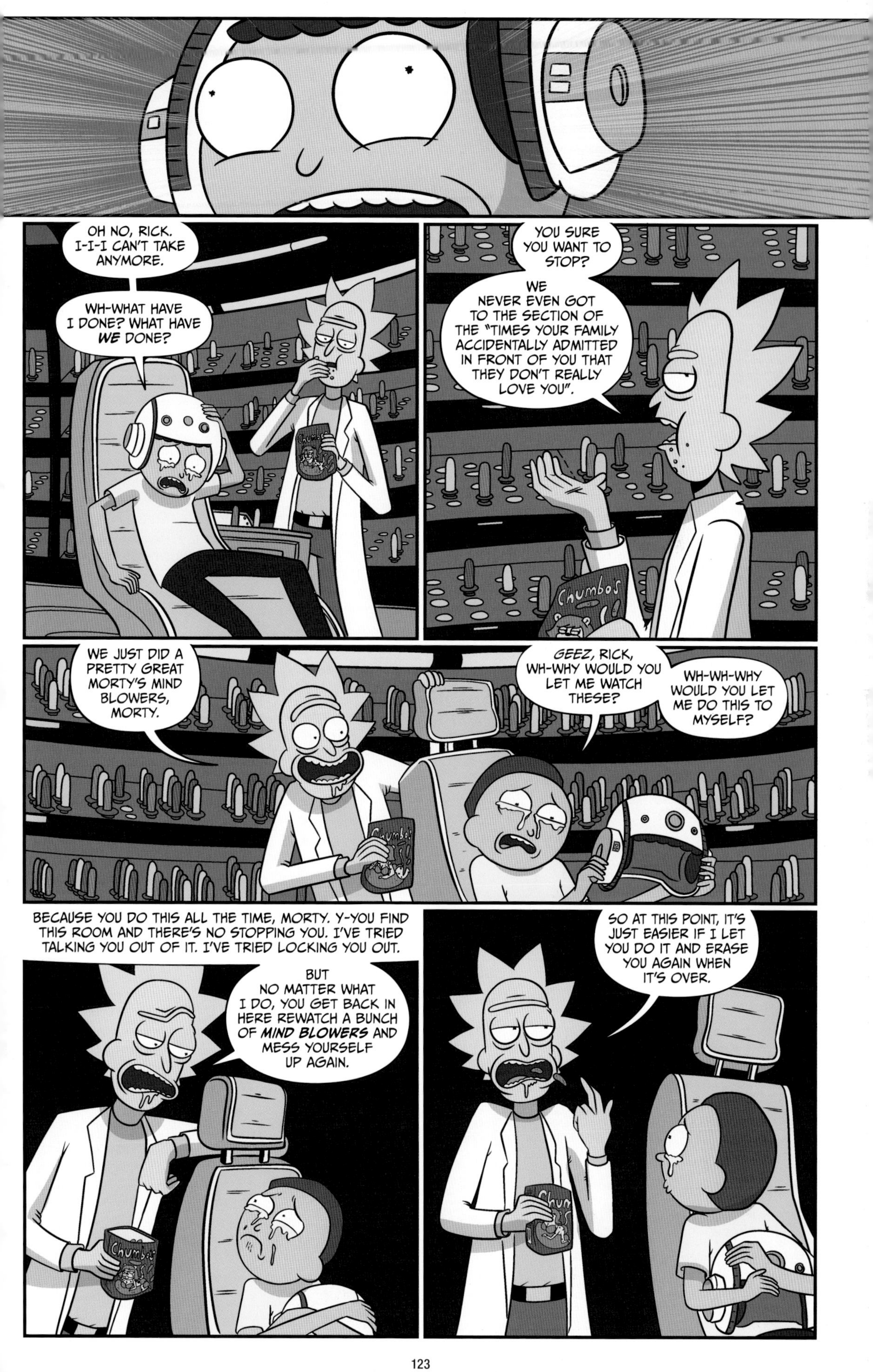
OH NO, RICK. I-I-I CAN'T TAKE ANYMORE.
WH-WHAT HAVE I DONE? WHAT HAVE *WE* DONE?
YOU SURE YOU WANT TO STOP?
WE NEVER EVEN GOT TO THE SECTION OF THE "TIMES YOUR FAMILY ACCIDENTALLY ADMITTED IN FRONT OF YOU THAT THEY DON'T REALLY LOVE YOU".
Chumbo's
WE JUST DID A PRETTY GREAT MORTY'S MIND BLOWERS, MORTY.
GEEZ, RICK, WH-WHY WOULD YOU LET ME WATCH THESE?
WH-WH-WHY WOULD YOU LET ME DO THIS TO MYSELF?
BECAUSE YOU DO THIS ALL THE TIME, MORTY. Y-YOU FIND THIS ROOM AND THERE'S NO STOPPING YOU. I'VE TRIED TALKING YOU OUT OF IT. I'VE TRIED LOCKING YOU OUT.
BUT NO MATTER WHAT I DO, YOU GET BACK IN HERE REWATCH A BUNCH OF ***MIND BLOWERS*** AND MESS YOURSELF UP AGAIN.
SO AT THIS POINT, IT'S JUST EASIER IF I LET YOU DO IT AND ERASE YOU AGAIN WHEN IT'S OVER.

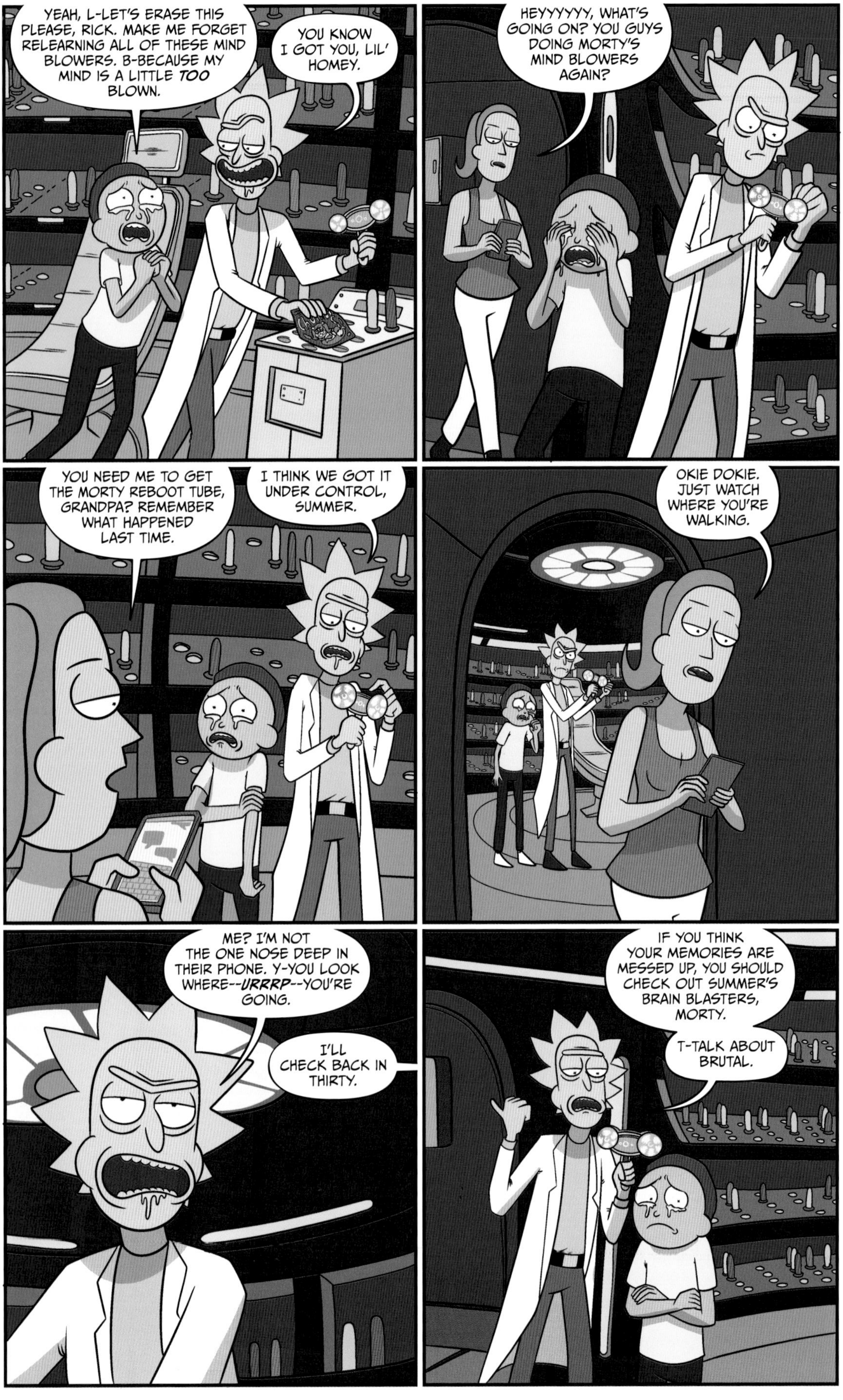
YEAH, L-LET'S ERASE THIS PLEASE, RICK. MAKE ME FORGET RELEARNING ALL OF THESE MIND BLOWERS. B-BECAUSE MY MIND IS A LITTLE *TOO* BLOWN.
YOU KNOW I GOT YOU, LIL' HOMEY.
HEYYYYYY, WHAT'S GOING ON? YOU GUYS DOING MORTY'S MIND BLOWERS AGAIN?
YOU NEED ME TO GET THE MORTY REBOOT TUBE, GRANDPA? REMEMBER WHAT HAPPENED LAST TIME.
I THINK WE GOT IT UNDER CONTROL, SUMMER.
OKIE DOKIE. JUST WATCH WHERE YOU'RE WALKING.
ME? I'M NOT THE ONE NOSE DEEP IN THEIR PHONE. Y-YOU LOOK WHERE--*URRRP*--YOU'RE GOING.
I'LL CHECK BACK IN THIRTY.
IF YOU THINK YOUR MEMORIES ARE MESSED UP, YOU SHOULD CHECK OUT SUMMER'S BRAIN BLASTERS, MORTY.
T-TALK ABOUT BRUTAL.

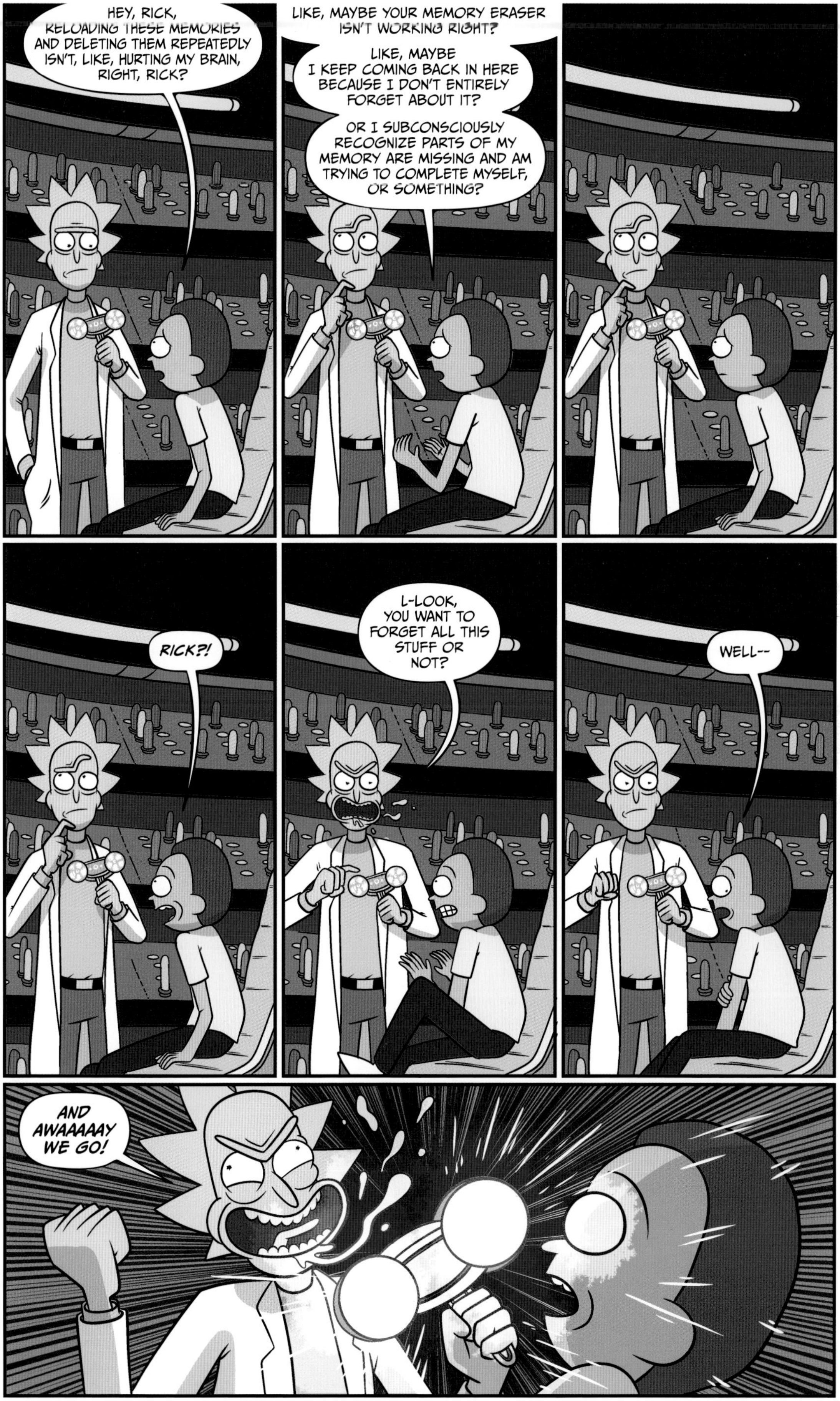

HEY, RICK, RELOADING THESE MEMORIES AND DELETING THEM REPEATEDLY ISN'T, LIKE, HURTING MY BRAIN, RIGHT, RICK?
LIKE, MAYBE YOUR MEMORY ERASER ISN'T WORKING RIGHT?
LIKE, MAYBE I KEEP COMING BACK IN HERE BECAUSE I DON'T ENTIRELY FORGET ABOUT IT?
OR I SUBCONSCIOUSLY RECOGNIZE PARTS OF MY MEMORY ARE MISSING AND AM TRYING TO COMPLETE MYSELF, OR SOMETHING?
RICK?!
L-LOOK, YOU WANT TO FORGET ALL THIS STUFF OR NOT?
WELL--
AND AWAAAAAY WE GO!

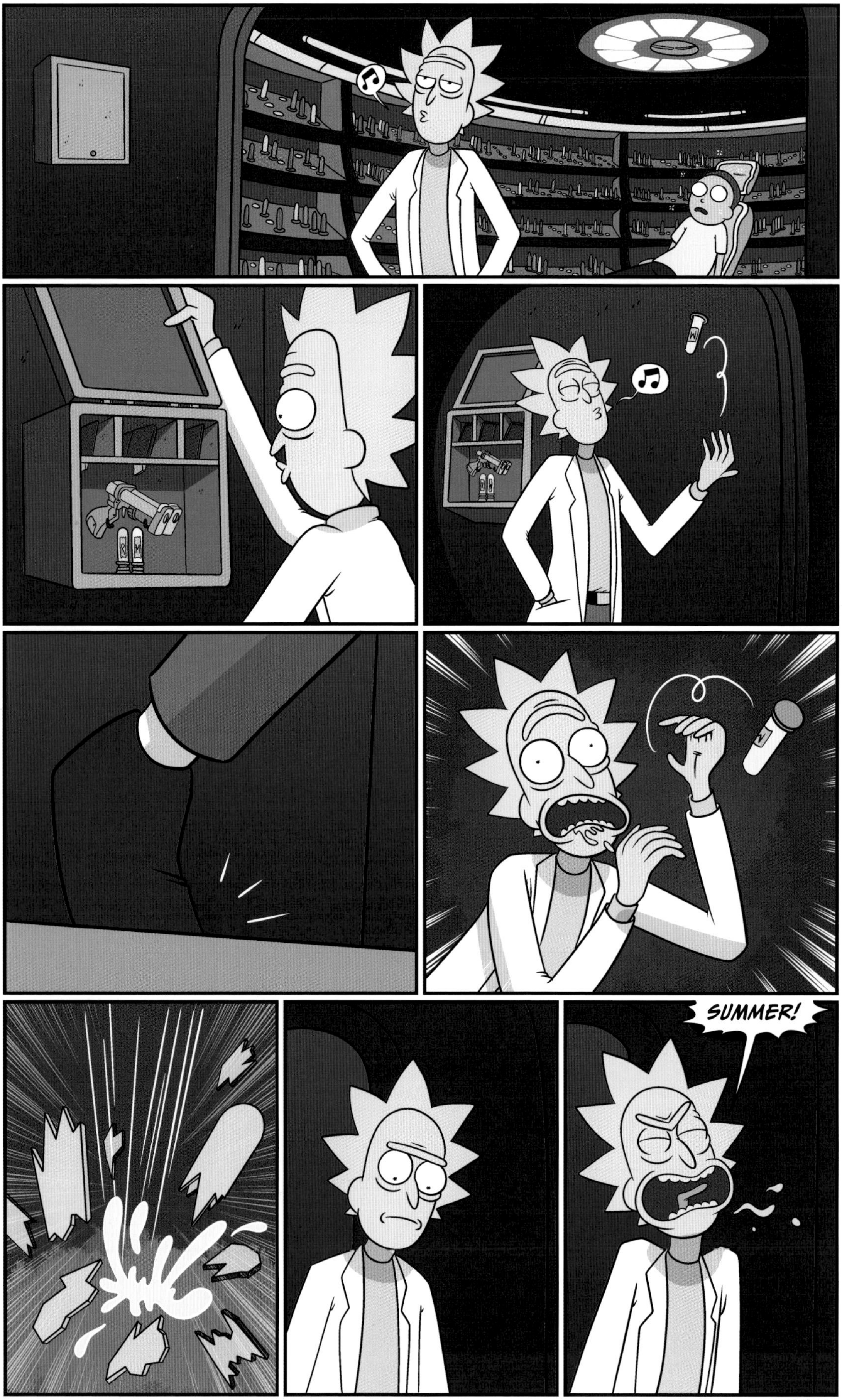
SUMMER!

THE END.

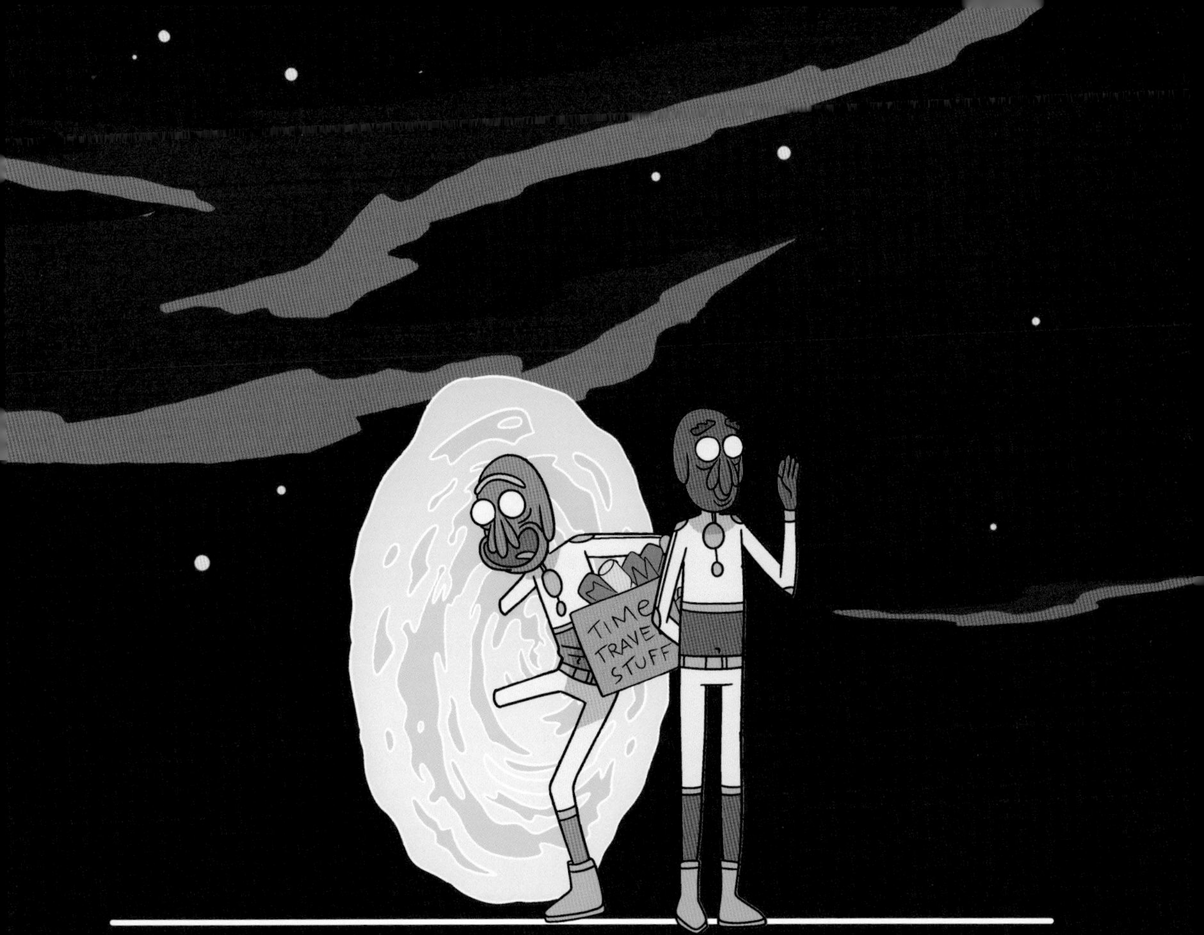
TIME
TRAVE
STUFF

BONUS STORIES

WRITTEN BY **KARLA PACHECO**

BIG PENPIN

AND

U-Tō, BRUTE?

ILLUSTRATED BY **CJ CANNON**

TEENAGE WASTELAND

AND

DON'T TELL RICK THE JERRYSITTER'S DEAD

ILLUSTRATED BY **IAN MCGINTY**

COLORED BY **SARAH STERN** LETTERED BY **CRANK!**

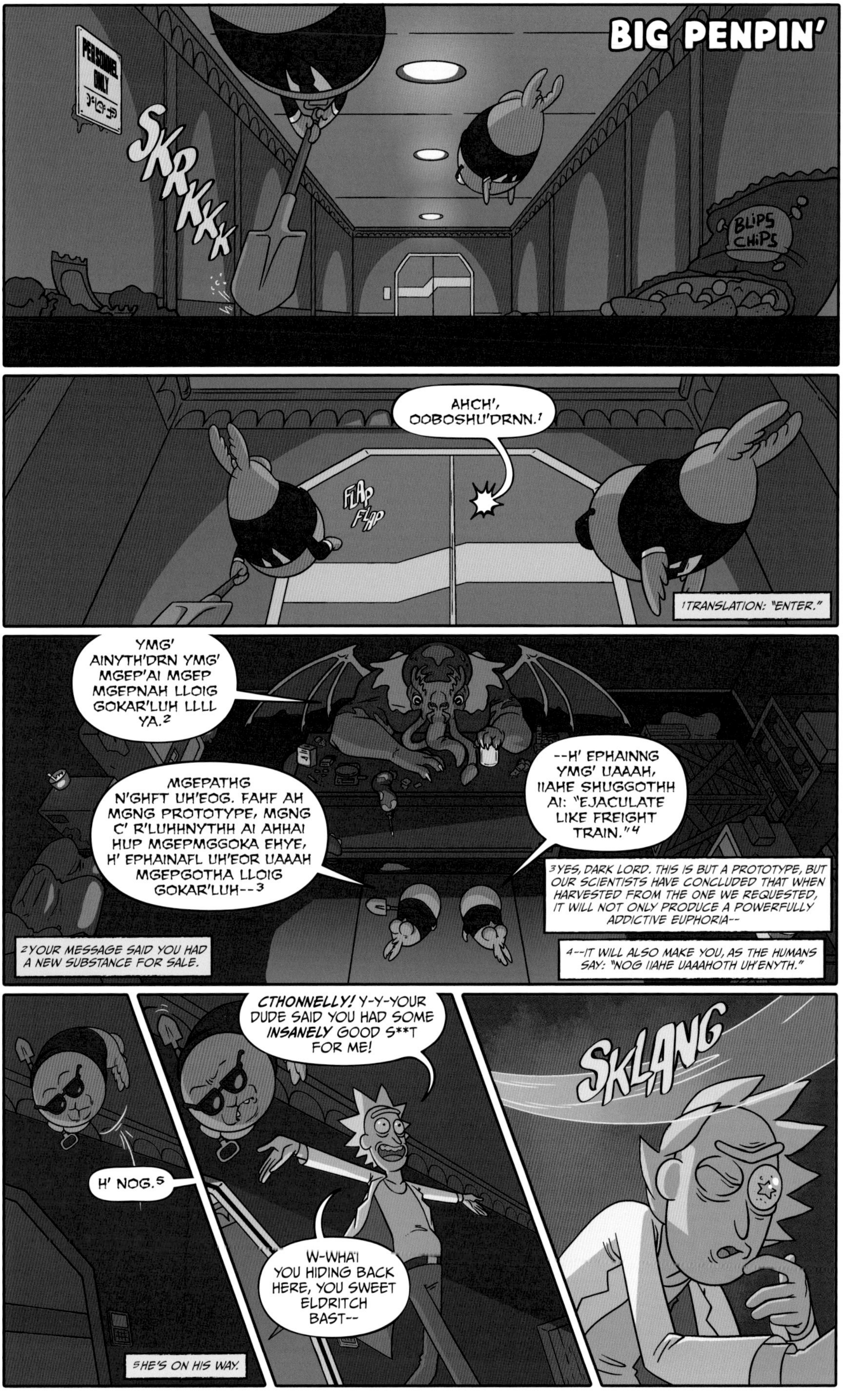
BIG PENPIN'
PERSONNEL ONLY
SKRKKKK
BLIPS CHIPS
AHCH', OOBOSHU'DRNN.[1]
FLAP FLAP
[1]TRANSLATION: "ENTER."
YMG' AINYTH'DRN YMG' MGEP'AI MGEP MGEPNAH LLOIG GOKAR'LUH LLLL YA.[2]
[2]YOUR MESSAGE SAID YOU HAD A NEW SUBSTANCE FOR SALE.
MGEPATHG N'GHFT UH'EOG. FAHF AH MGNG PROTOTYPE, MGNG C' R'LUHHNYTHH AI AHHAI HUP MGEPMGGOKA EHYE, H' EPHAINAFL UH'EOR UAAAH MGEPGOTHA LLOIG GOKAR'LUH--[3]
[3]YES, DARK LORD. THIS IS BUT A PROTOTYPE, BUT OUR SCIENTISTS HAVE CONCLUDED THAT WHEN HARVESTED FROM THE ONE WE REQUESTED, IT WILL NOT ONLY PRODUCE A POWERFULLY ADDICTIVE EUPHORIA--
--H' EPHAINNG YMG' UAAAH, IIAHE SHUGGOTHH AI: "EJACULATE LIKE FREIGHT TRAIN."[4]
[4]--IT WILL ALSO MAKE YOU, AS THE HUMANS SAY: "NOG IIAHE UAAAHOTH UH'ENYTH."
H' NOG.[5]
[5]HE'S ON HIS WAY.
CTHONNELLY! Y-Y-YOUR DUDE SAID YOU HAD SOME INSANELY GOOD S**T FOR ME!
W-WHAT YOU HIDING BACK HERE, YOU SWEET ELDRITCH BAST--
SKLANG

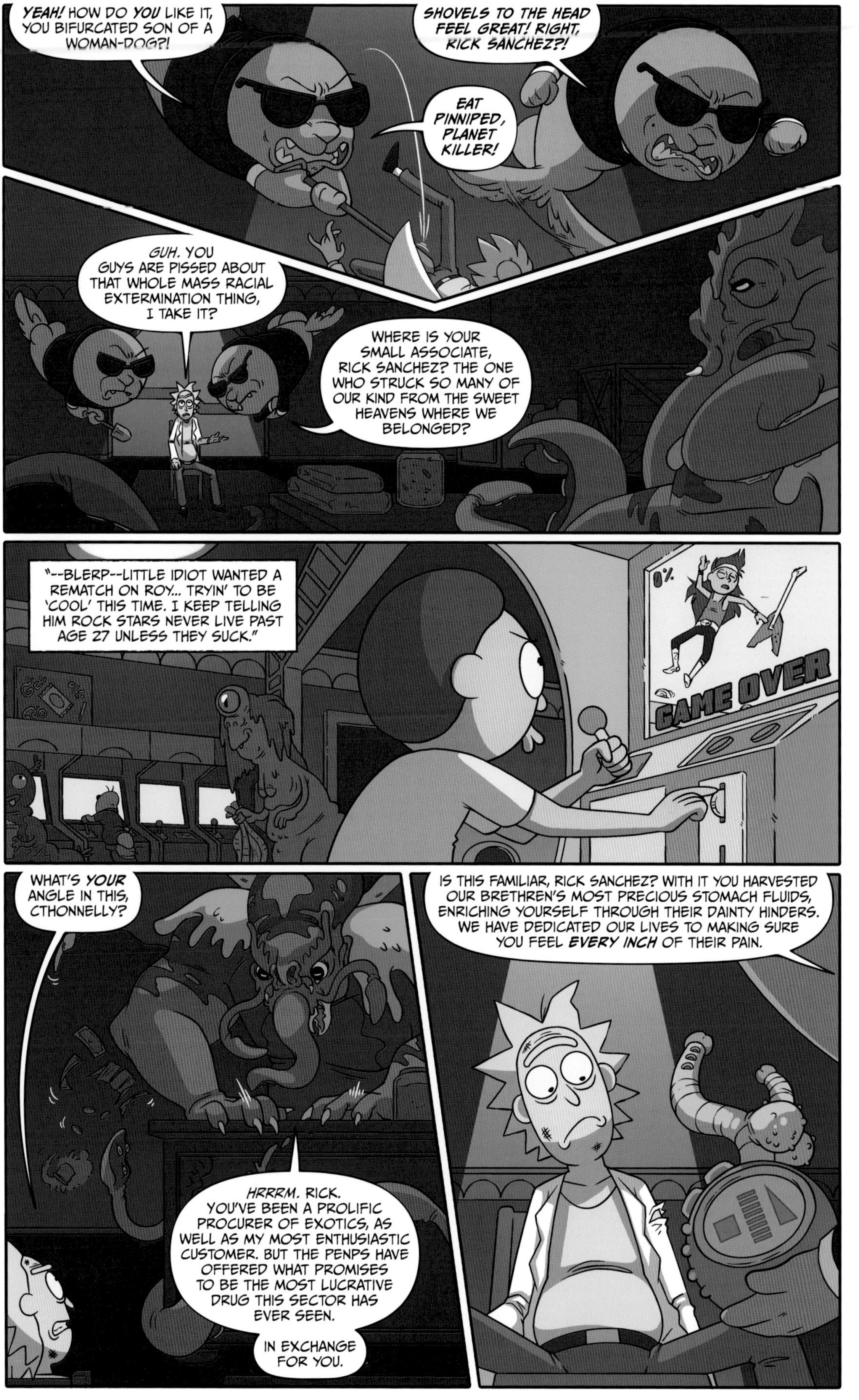
YEAH! HOW DO YOU LIKE IT, YOU BIFURCATED SON OF A WOMAN-DOG?!
SHOVELS TO THE HEAD FEEL GREAT! RIGHT, RICK SANCHEZ?!
EAT PINNIPED, PLANET KILLER!
GUH. YOU GUYS ARE PISSED ABOUT THAT WHOLE MASS RACIAL EXTERMINATION THING, I TAKE IT?
WHERE IS YOUR SMALL ASSOCIATE, RICK SANCHEZ? THE ONE WHO STRUCK SO MANY OF OUR KIND FROM THE SWEET HEAVENS WHERE WE BELONGED?
"--BLERP--LITTLE IDIOT WANTED A REMATCH ON ROY... TRYIN' TO BE 'COOL' THIS TIME. I KEEP TELLING HIM ROCK STARS NEVER LIVE PAST AGE 27 UNLESS THEY SUCK."
0%
GAME OVER
WHAT'S YOUR ANGLE IN THIS, CTHONNELLY?
HRRRM. RICK. YOU'VE BEEN A PROLIFIC PROCURER OF EXOTICS, AS WELL AS MY MOST ENTHUSIASTIC CUSTOMER. BUT THE PENPS HAVE OFFERED WHAT PROMISES TO BE THE MOST LUCRATIVE DRUG THIS SECTOR HAS EVER SEEN.
IN EXCHANGE FOR YOU.
IS THIS FAMILIAR, RICK SANCHEZ? WITH IT YOU HARVESTED OUR BRETHREN'S MOST PRECIOUS STOMACH FLUIDS, ENRICHING YOURSELF THROUGH THEIR DAINTY HINDERS. WE HAVE DEDICATED OUR LIVES TO MAKING SURE YOU FEEL EVERY INCH OF THEIR PAIN.

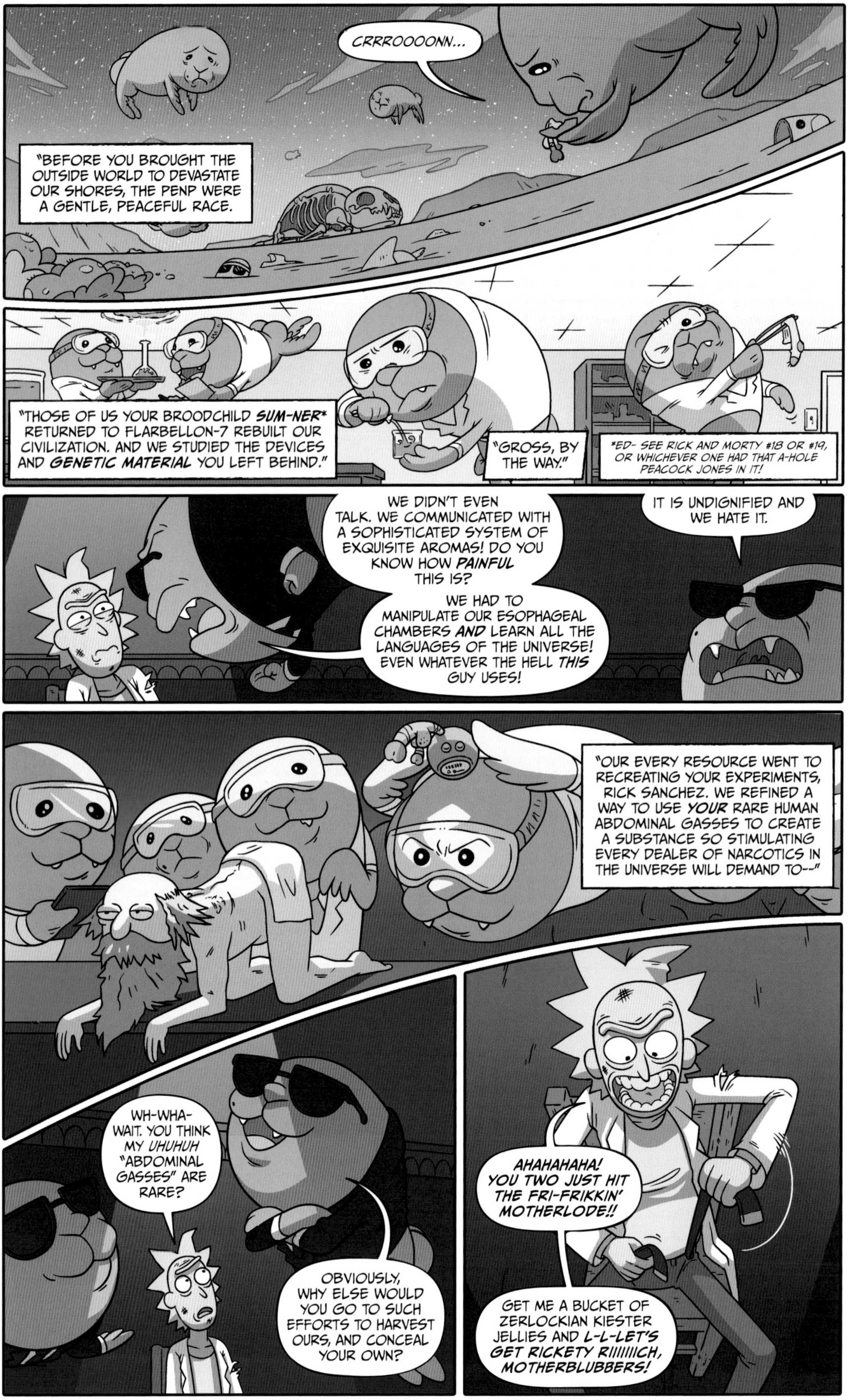
CRRROOOONN...
"BEFORE YOU BROUGHT THE OUTSIDE WORLD TO DEVASTATE OUR SHORES, THE PENP WERE A GENTLE, PEACEFUL RACE.
"THOSE OF US YOUR BROODCHILD SUM-NER* RETURNED TO FLARBELLON-7 REBUILT OUR CIVILIZATION. AND WE STUDIED THE DEVICES AND GENETIC MATERIAL YOU LEFT BEHIND."
"GROSS, BY THE WAY."
*ED- SEE RICK AND MORTY #18 OR #19, OR WHICHEVER ONE HAD THAT A-HOLE PEACOCK JONES IN IT!
WE DIDN'T EVEN TALK. WE COMMUNICATED WITH A SOPHISTICATED SYSTEM OF EXQUISITE AROMAS! DO YOU KNOW HOW PAINFUL THIS IS?
WE HAD TO MANIPULATE OUR ESOPHAGEAL CHAMBERS AND LEARN ALL THE LANGUAGES OF THE UNIVERSE! EVEN WHATEVER THE HELL THIS GUY USES!
IT IS UNDIGNIFIED AND WE HATE IT.
"OUR EVERY RESOURCE WENT TO RECREATING YOUR EXPERIMENTS, RICK SANCHEZ. WE REFINED A WAY TO USE YOUR RARE HUMAN ABDOMINAL GASSES TO CREATE A SUBSTANCE SO STIMULATING EVERY DEALER OF NARCOTICS IN THE UNIVERSE WILL DEMAND TO--"
WH-WHA-WAIT. YOU THINK MY UHUHUH "ABDOMINAL GASSES" ARE RARE?
OBVIOUSLY, WHY ELSE WOULD YOU GO TO SUCH EFFORTS TO HARVEST OURS, AND CONCEAL YOUR OWN?
AHAHAHAHA! YOU TWO JUST HIT THE FRI-FRIKKIN' MOTHERLODE!!
GET ME A BUCKET OF ZERLOCKIAN KIESTER JELLIES AND L-L-LET'S GET RICKETY RIIIIIICH, MOTHERBLUBBERS!

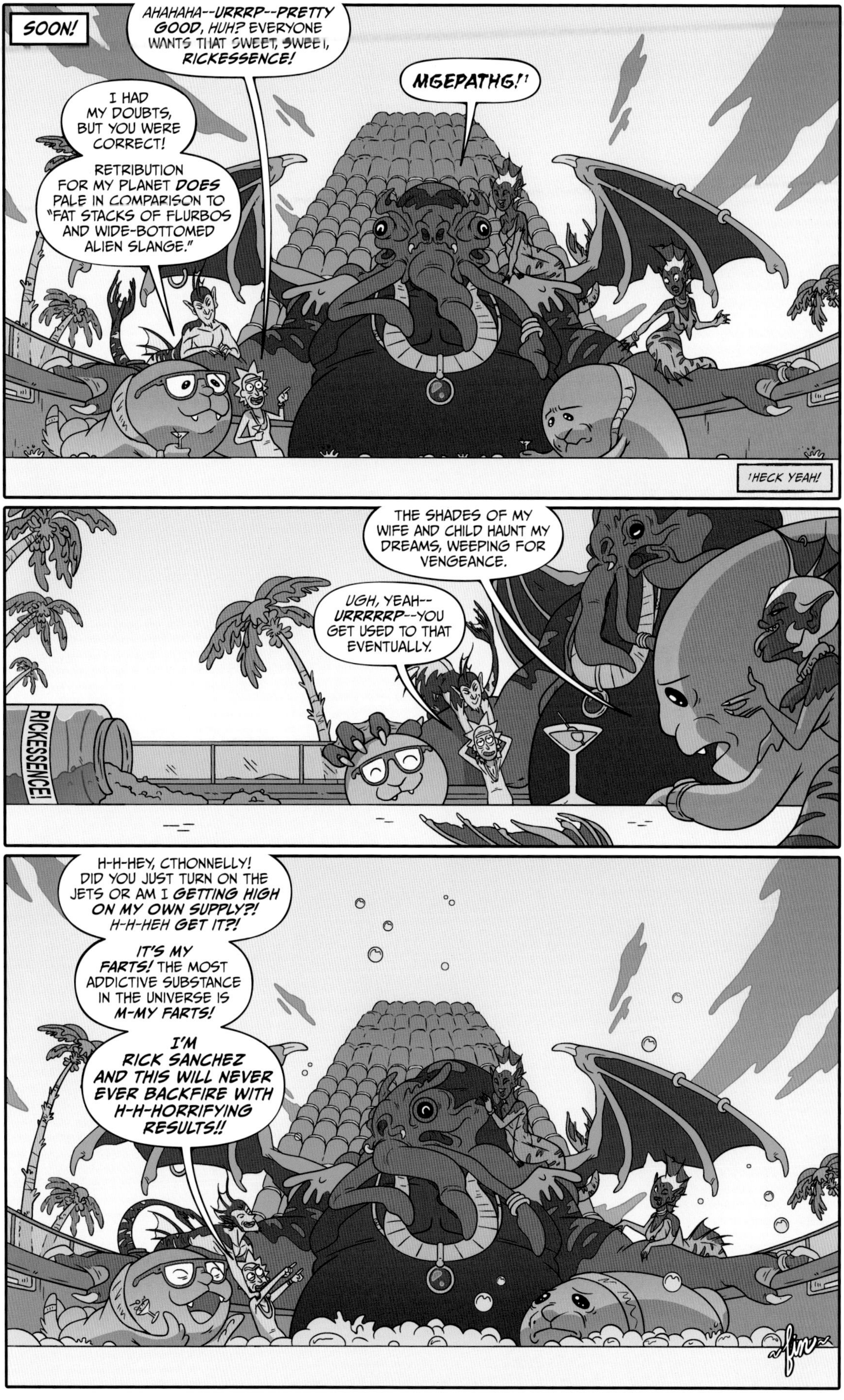

SOON!
AHAHAHA--URRRP--PRETTY GOOD, HUH? EVERYONE WANTS THAT SWEET, SWEET, RICKESSENCE!
I HAD MY DOUBTS, BUT YOU WERE CORRECT!
RETRIBUTION FOR MY PLANET DOES PALE IN COMPARISON TO "FAT STACKS OF FLURBOS AND WIDE-BOTTOMED ALIEN SLANGE."
MGEPATHG![1]
[1]HECK YEAH!
THE SHADES OF MY WIFE AND CHILD HAUNT MY DREAMS, WEEPING FOR VENGEANCE.
UGH, YEAH--URRRRP--YOU GET USED TO THAT EVENTUALLY.
RICKESSENCE!
H-H-HEY, CTHONNELLY! DID YOU JUST TURN ON THE JETS OR AM I GETTING HIGH ON MY OWN SUPPLY?! H-H-HEH GET IT?!
IT'S MY FARTS! THE MOST ADDICTIVE SUBSTANCE IN THE UNIVERSE IS M-MY FARTS!
I'M RICK SANCHEZ AND THIS WILL NEVER EVER BACKFIRE WITH H-H-HORRIFYING RESULTS!!
~fin~

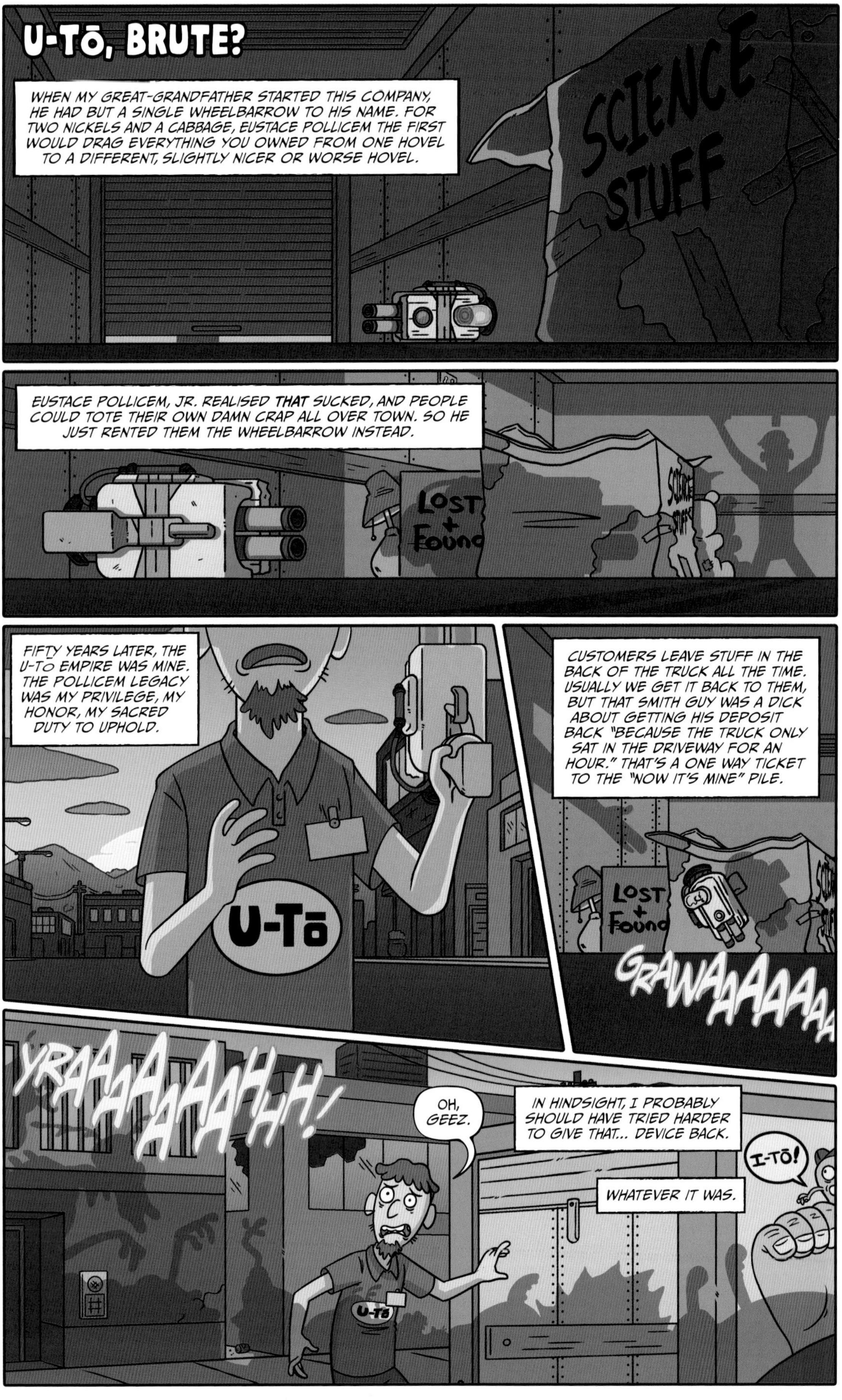
U-Tō, BRUTE?
WHEN MY GREAT-GRANDFATHER STARTED THIS COMPANY, HE HAD BUT A SINGLE WHEELBARROW TO HIS NAME. FOR TWO NICKELS AND A CABBAGE, EUSTACE POLLICEM THE FIRST WOULD DRAG EVERYTHING YOU OWNED FROM ONE HOVEL TO A DIFFERENT, SLIGHTLY NICER OR WORSE HOVEL.
SCIENCE STUFF
EUSTACE POLLICEM, JR. REALISED **THAT** SUCKED, AND PEOPLE COULD TOTE THEIR OWN DAMN CRAP ALL OVER TOWN. SO HE JUST RENTED THEM THE WHEELBARROW INSTEAD.
LOST + FOUND
FIFTY YEARS LATER, THE U-Tō EMPIRE WAS MINE. THE POLLICEM LEGACY WAS MY PRIVILEGE, MY HONOR, MY SACRED DUTY TO UPHOLD.
U-Tō
CUSTOMERS LEAVE STUFF IN THE BACK OF THE TRUCK ALL THE TIME. USUALLY WE GET IT BACK TO THEM, BUT THAT SMITH GUY WAS A DICK ABOUT GETTING HIS DEPOSIT BACK "BECAUSE THE TRUCK ONLY SAT IN THE DRIVEWAY FOR AN HOUR." THAT'S A ONE WAY TICKET TO THE "NOW IT'S MINE" PILE.
LOST + FOUND
GRAWAAAAAAA
YRAAAAAAAHHH!
OH, GEEZ.
IN HINDSIGHT, I PROBABLY SHOULD HAVE TRIED HARDER TO GIVE THAT... DEVICE BACK.
I-Tō!
WHATEVER IT WAS.

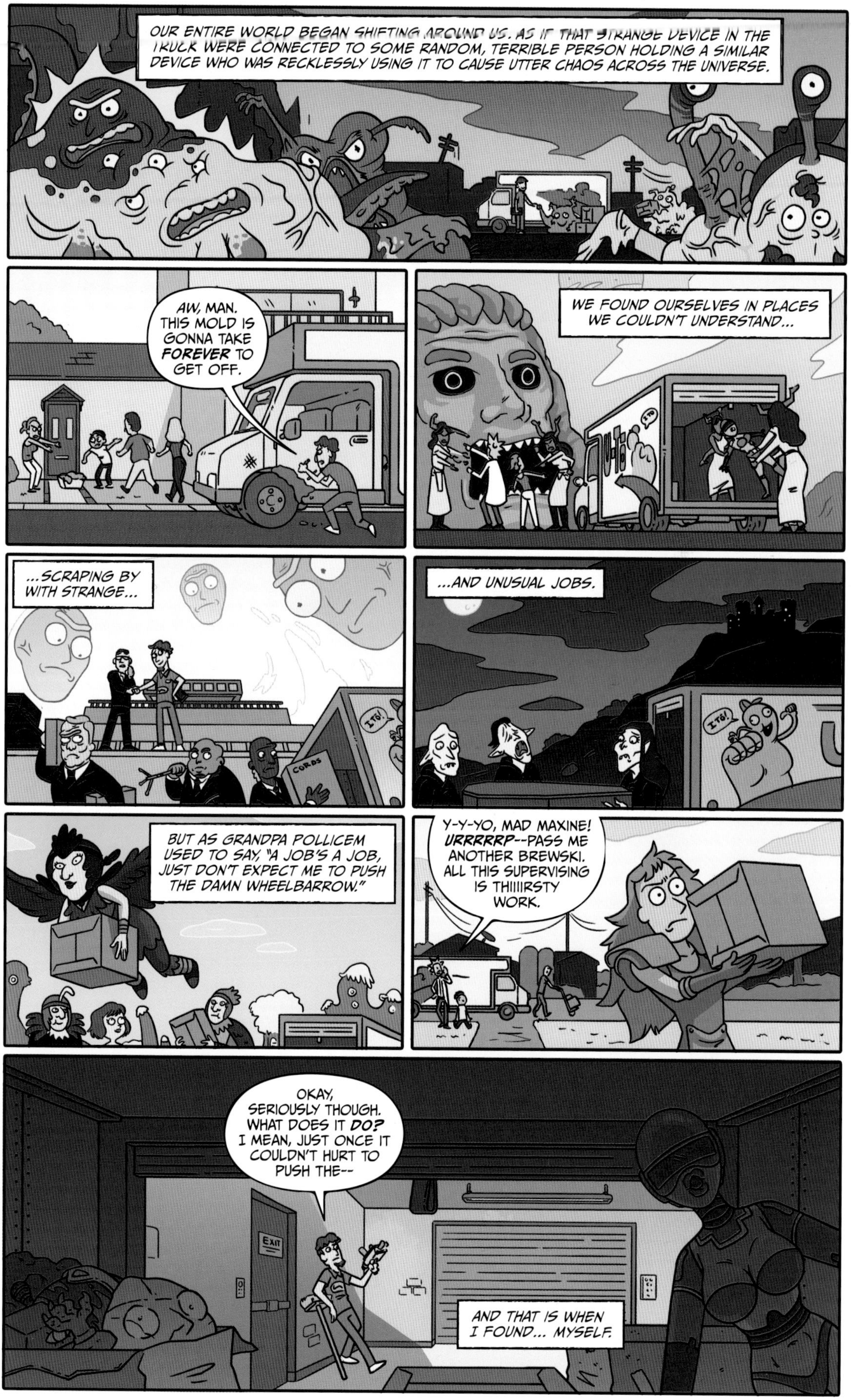

OUR ENTIRE WORLD BEGAN SHIFTING AROUND US. AS IF THAT STRANGE DEVICE IN THE TRUCK WERE CONNECTED TO SOME RANDOM, TERRIBLE PERSON HOLDING A SIMILAR DEVICE WHO WAS RECKLESSLY USING IT TO CAUSE UTTER CHAOS ACROSS THE UNIVERSE.
AW, MAN. THIS MOLD IS GONNA TAKE **FOREVER** TO GET OFF.
WE FOUND OURSELVES IN PLACES WE COULDN'T UNDERSTAND...
...SCRAPING BY WITH STRANGE...
CORDS
...AND UNUSUAL JOBS.
BUT AS GRANDPA POLLICEM USED TO SAY, "A JOB'S A JOB, JUST DON'T EXPECT ME TO PUSH THE DAMN WHEELBARROW."
Y-Y-YO, MAD MAXINE! **URRRRRP**--PASS ME ANOTHER BREWSKI. ALL THIS SUPERVISING IS THIIIIRSTY WORK.
OKAY, SERIOUSLY THOUGH. WHAT DOES IT **DO?** I MEAN, JUST ONCE IT COULDN'T HURT TO PUSH THE--
EXIT
AND THAT IS WHEN I FOUND... MYSELF.

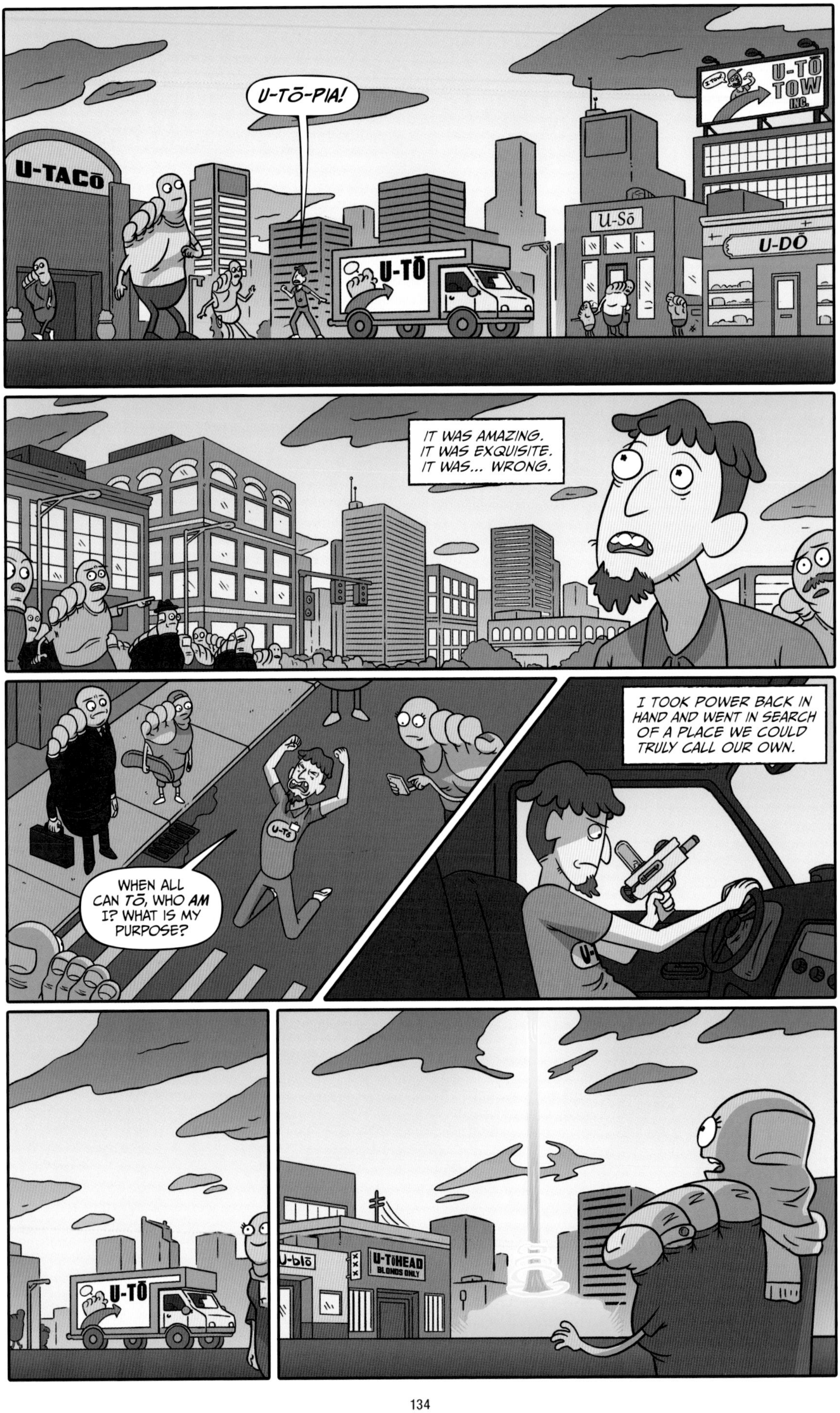
U-TŌ-PIA!
U-TACŌ
U-TŌ TOW INC.
U-Sō
U-DŌ
U-TŌ
IT WAS AMAZING. IT WAS EXQUISITE. IT WAS... WRONG.
WHEN ALL CAN TŌ, WHO AM I? WHAT IS MY PURPOSE?
I TOOK POWER BACK IN HAND AND WENT IN SEARCH OF A PLACE WE COULD TRULY CALL OUR OWN.
U-TŌ
U-blō
U-TōHEAD BLONDS ONLY

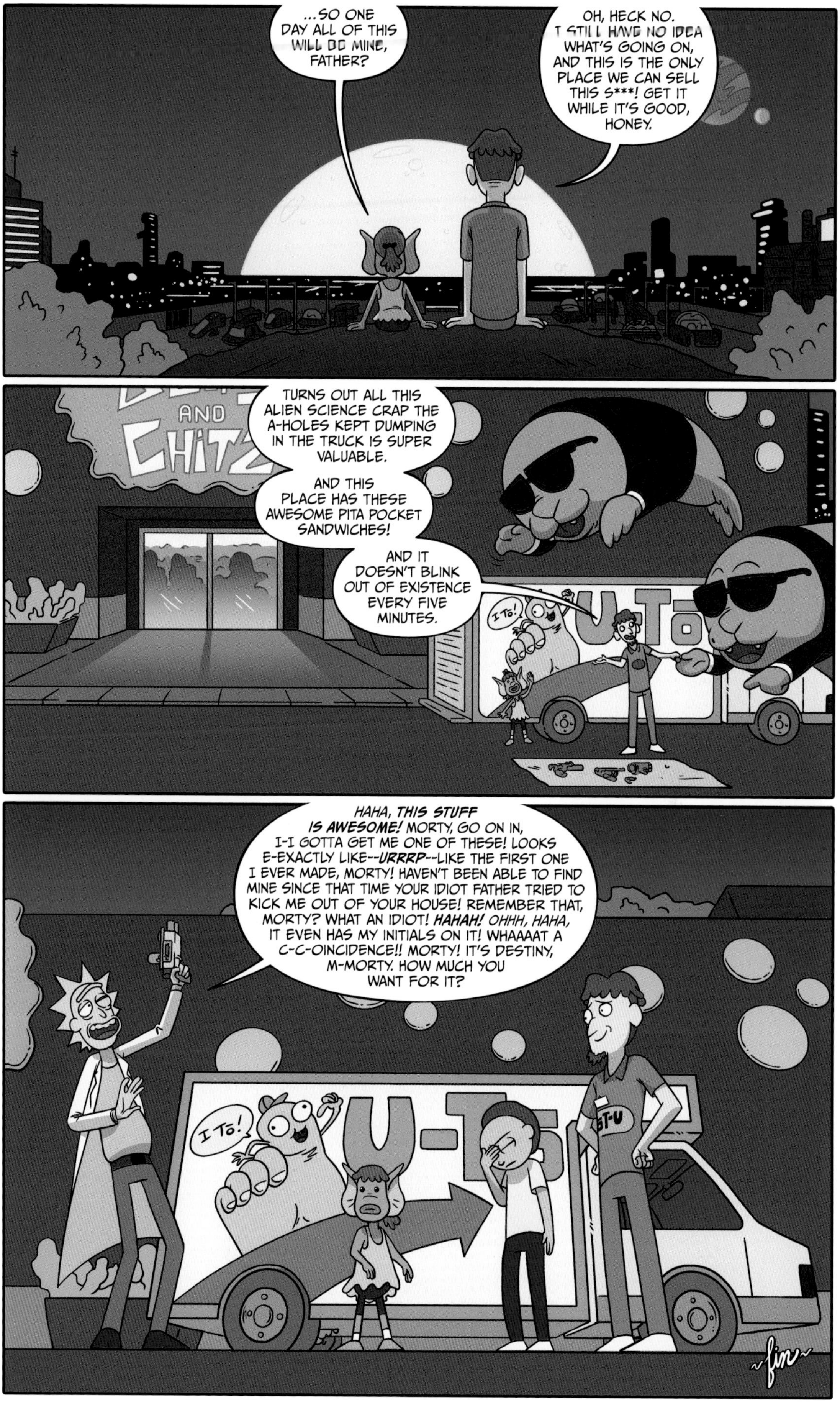
...SO ONE DAY ALL OF THIS WILL BE MINE, FATHER?
OH, HECK NO. I STILL HAVE NO IDEA WHAT'S GOING ON, AND THIS IS THE ONLY PLACE WE CAN SELL THIS S***! GET IT WHILE IT'S GOOD, HONEY.
AND CHITZ
TURNS OUT ALL THIS ALIEN SCIENCE CRAP THE A-HOLES KEPT DUMPING IN THE TRUCK IS SUPER VALUABLE.
AND THIS PLACE HAS THESE AWESOME PITA POCKET SANDWICHES!
AND IT DOESN'T BLINK OUT OF EXISTENCE EVERY FIVE MINUTES.
I To!
U-To
HAHA, THIS STUFF IS AWESOME! MORTY, GO ON IN, I-I GOTTA GET ME ONE OF THESE! LOOKS E-EXACTLY LIKE--URRRP--LIKE THE FIRST ONE I EVER MADE, MORTY! HAVEN'T BEEN ABLE TO FIND MINE SINCE THAT TIME YOUR IDIOT FATHER TRIED TO KICK ME OUT OF YOUR HOUSE! REMEMBER THAT, MORTY? WHAT AN IDIOT! HAHAH! OHHH, HAHA, IT EVEN HAS MY INITIALS ON IT! WHAAAAT A C-C-OINCIDENCE!! MORTY! IT'S DESTINY, M-MORTY. HOW MUCH YOU WANT FOR IT?
I To!
U-To
ST-U
~fin~

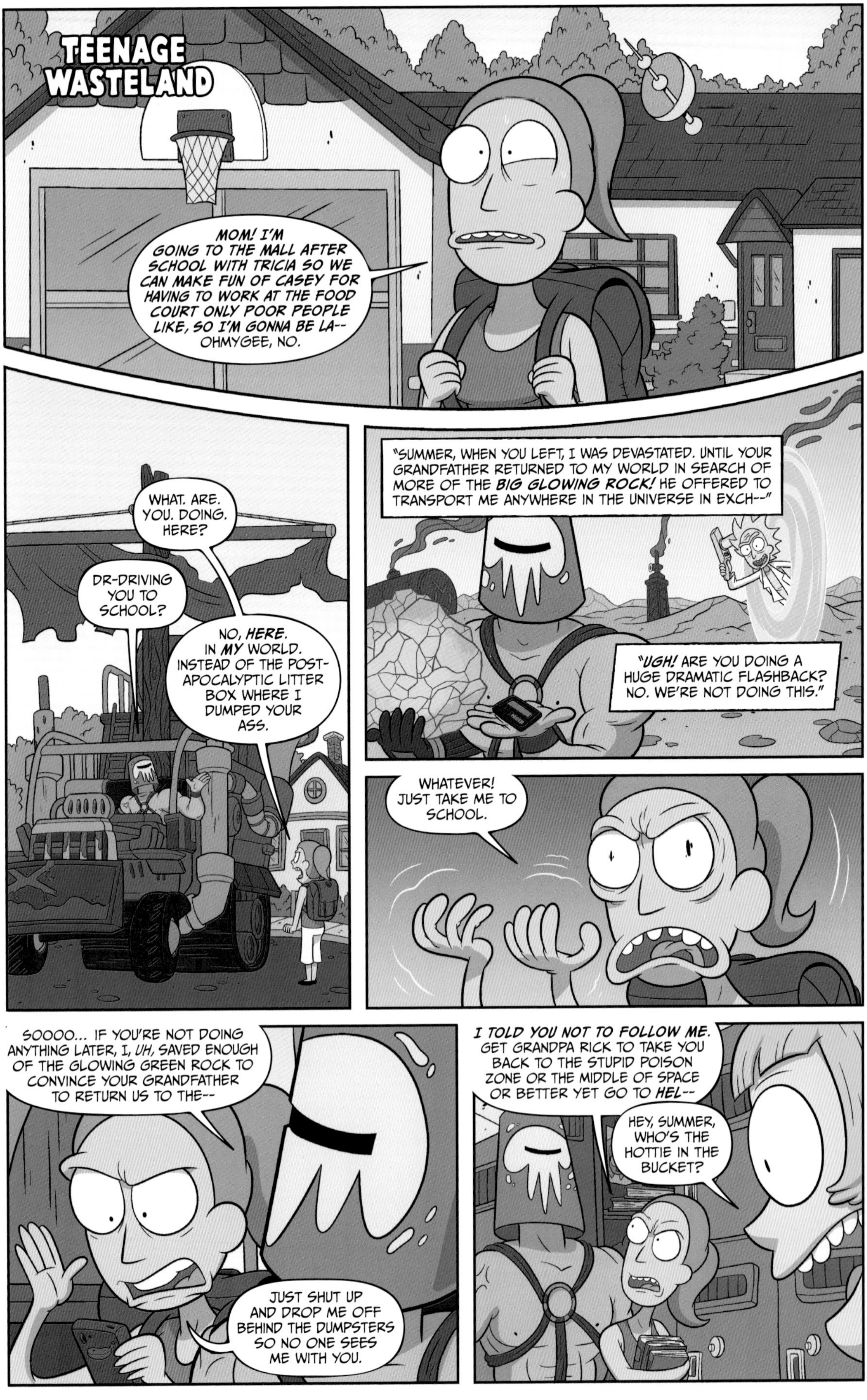
TEENAGE WASTELAND
MOM! I'M GOING TO THE MALL AFTER SCHOOL WITH TRICIA SO WE CAN MAKE FUN OF CASEY FOR HAVING TO WORK AT THE FOOD COURT ONLY POOR PEOPLE LIKE, SO I'M GONNA BE LA-- OHMYGEE, NO.
WHAT. ARE. YOU. DOING. HERE?
DR-DRIVING YOU TO SCHOOL?
NO, HERE. IN MY WORLD. INSTEAD OF THE POST-APOCALYPTIC LITTER BOX WHERE I DUMPED YOUR ASS.
"SUMMER, WHEN YOU LEFT, I WAS DEVASTATED. UNTIL YOUR GRANDFATHER RETURNED TO MY WORLD IN SEARCH OF MORE OF THE BIG GLOWING ROCK! HE OFFERED TO TRANSPORT ME ANYWHERE IN THE UNIVERSE IN EXCH--"
"UGH! ARE YOU DOING A HUGE DRAMATIC FLASHBACK? NO. WE'RE NOT DOING THIS."
WHATEVER! JUST TAKE ME TO SCHOOL.
SOOOO... IF YOU'RE NOT DOING ANYTHING LATER, I, UH, SAVED ENOUGH OF THE GLOWING GREEN ROCK TO CONVINCE YOUR GRANDFATHER TO RETURN US TO THE--
JUST SHUT UP AND DROP ME OFF BEHIND THE DUMPSTERS SO NO ONE SEES ME WITH YOU.
I TOLD YOU NOT TO FOLLOW ME. GET GRANDPA RICK TO TAKE YOU BACK TO THE STUPID POISON ZONE OR THE MIDDLE OF SPACE OR BETTER YET GO TO HEL--
HEY, SUMMER, WHO'S THE HOTTIE IN THE BUCKET?

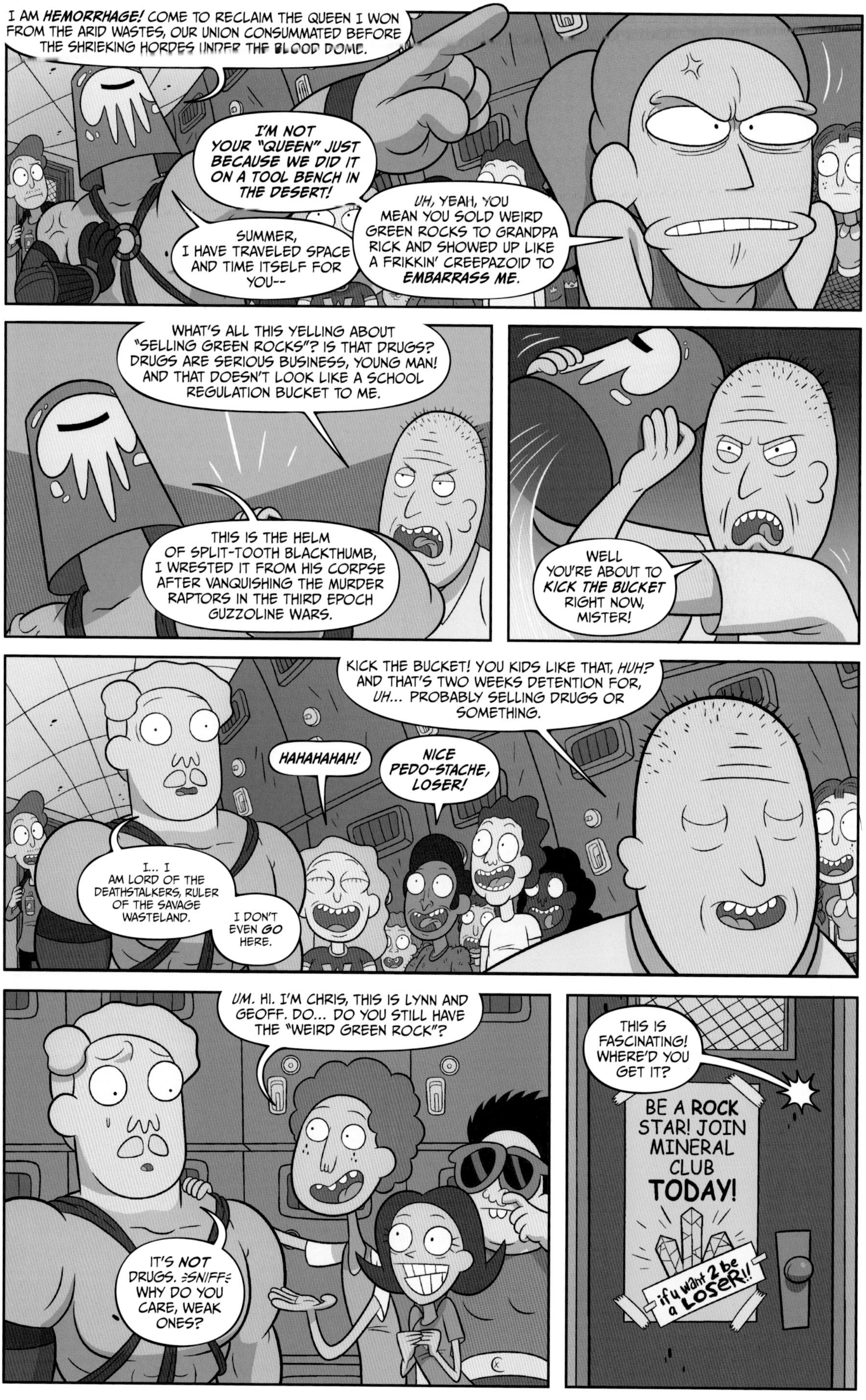

I AM *HEMORRHAGE!* COME TO RECLAIM THE QUEEN I WON FROM THE ARID WASTES, OUR UNION CONSUMMATED BEFORE THE SHRIEKING HORDES UNDER THE BLOOD DOME.
I'M NOT YOUR "QUEEN" JUST BECAUSE WE DID IT ON A TOOL BENCH IN THE DESERT!
SUMMER, I HAVE TRAVELED SPACE AND TIME ITSELF FOR YOU--
UH, YEAH, YOU MEAN YOU SOLD WEIRD GREEN ROCKS TO GRANDPA RICK AND SHOWED UP LIKE A FRIKKIN' CREEPAZOID TO *EMBARRASS ME.*
WHAT'S ALL THIS YELLING ABOUT "SELLING GREEN ROCKS"? IS THAT DRUGS? DRUGS ARE SERIOUS BUSINESS, YOUNG MAN! AND THAT DOESN'T LOOK LIKE A SCHOOL REGULATION BUCKET TO ME.
THIS IS THE HELM OF SPLIT-TOOTH BLACKTHUMB, I WRESTED IT FROM HIS CORPSE AFTER VANQUISHING THE MURDER RAPTORS IN THE THIRD EPOCH GUZZOLINE WARS.
WELL YOU'RE ABOUT TO *KICK THE BUCKET* RIGHT NOW, MISTER!
KICK THE BUCKET! YOU KIDS LIKE THAT, *HUH?* AND THAT'S TWO WEEKS DETENTION FOR, *UH...* PROBABLY SELLING DRUGS OR SOMETHING.
HAHAHAHAH!
NICE PEDO-STACHE, LOSER!
I... I AM LORD OF THE DEATHSTALKERS, RULER OF THE SAVAGE WASTELAND.
I DON'T EVEN *GO* HERE.
UM. HI. I'M CHRIS, THIS IS LYNN AND GEOFF. DO... DO YOU STILL HAVE THE "WEIRD GREEN ROCK"?
IT'S *NOT* DRUGS. *SNIFF* WHY DO YOU CARE, WEAK ONES?
THIS IS FASCINATING! WHERE'D YOU GET IT?
BE A ROCK STAR! JOIN MINERAL CLUB TODAY!
if u want 2 be a LOSER!!

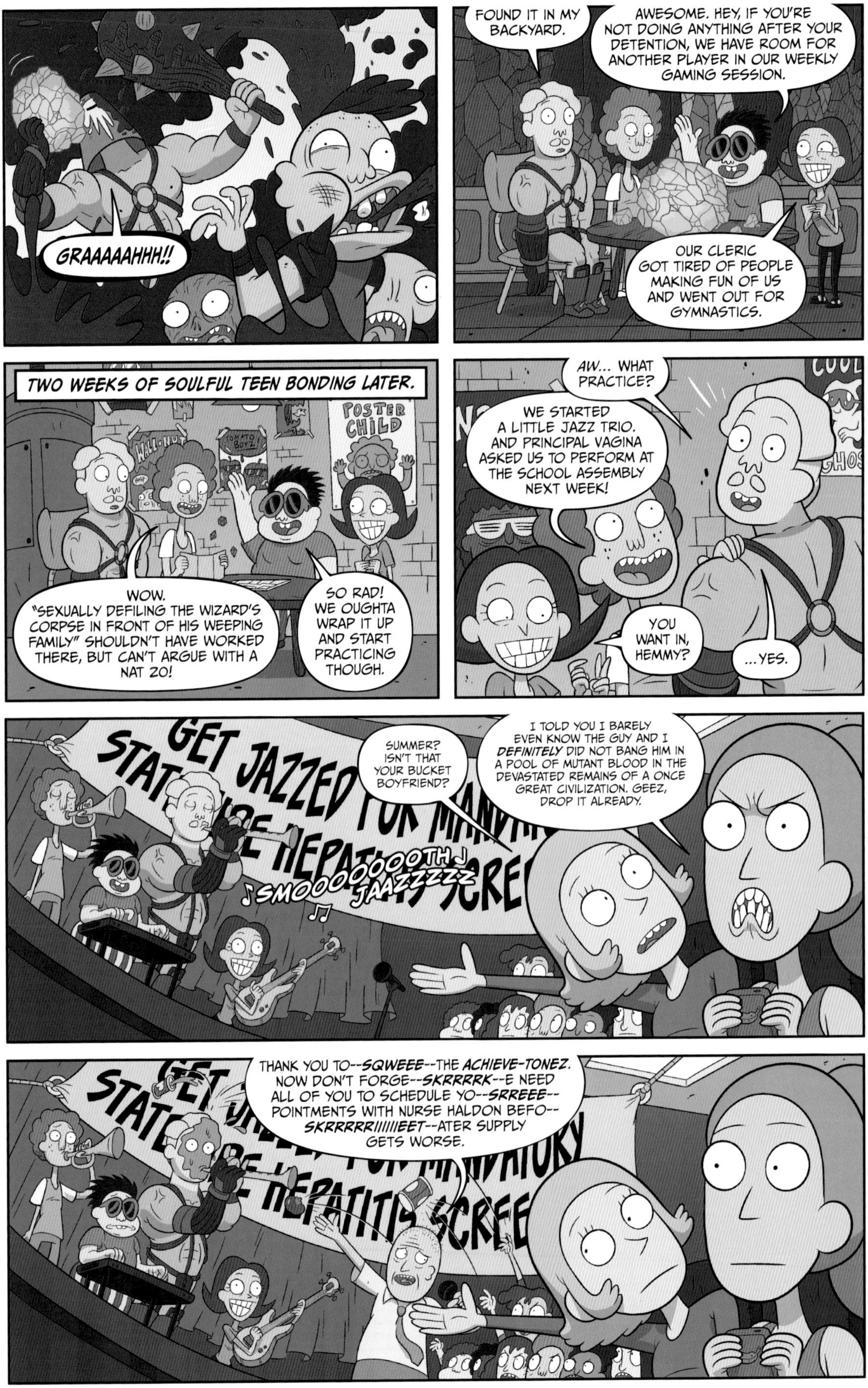
GRAAAAAHHH!!
FOUND IT IN MY BACKYARD.
AWESOME. HEY, IF YOU'RE NOT DOING ANYTHING AFTER YOUR DETENTION, WE HAVE ROOM FOR ANOTHER PLAYER IN OUR WEEKLY GAMING SESSION.
OUR CLERIC GOT TIRED OF PEOPLE MAKING FUN OF US AND WENT OUT FOR GYMNASTICS.
TWO WEEKS OF SOULFUL TEEN BONDING LATER.
POSTER CHILD
WOW. "SEXUALLY DEFILING THE WIZARD'S CORPSE IN FRONT OF HIS WEEPING FAMILY" SHOULDN'T HAVE WORKED THERE, BUT CAN'T ARGUE WITH A NAT 20!
SO RAD! WE OUGHTA WRAP IT UP AND START PRACTICING THOUGH.
AW... WHAT PRACTICE?
WE STARTED A LITTLE JAZZ TRIO. AND PRINCIPAL VAGINA ASKED US TO PERFORM AT THE SCHOOL ASSEMBLY NEXT WEEK!
YOU WANT IN, HEMMY?
...YES.
SMOOOOOOOOTH JAAZZZZZ
SUMMER? ISN'T THAT YOUR BUCKET BOYFRIEND?
I TOLD YOU I BARELY EVEN KNOW THE GUY AND I *DEFINITELY* DID NOT BANG HIM IN A POOL OF MUTANT BLOOD IN THE DEVASTATED REMAINS OF A ONCE GREAT CIVILIZATION. GEEZ, DROP IT ALREADY.
THANK YOU TO--*SQWEEE*--THE *ACHIEVE-TONEZ*. NOW DON'T FORGE--*SKRRRRK*--E NEED ALL OF YOU TO SCHEDULE YO--*SRREEE*--POINTMENTS WITH NURSE HALDON BEFO--*SKRRRRRIIIIIIEET*--ATER SUPPLY GETS WORSE.

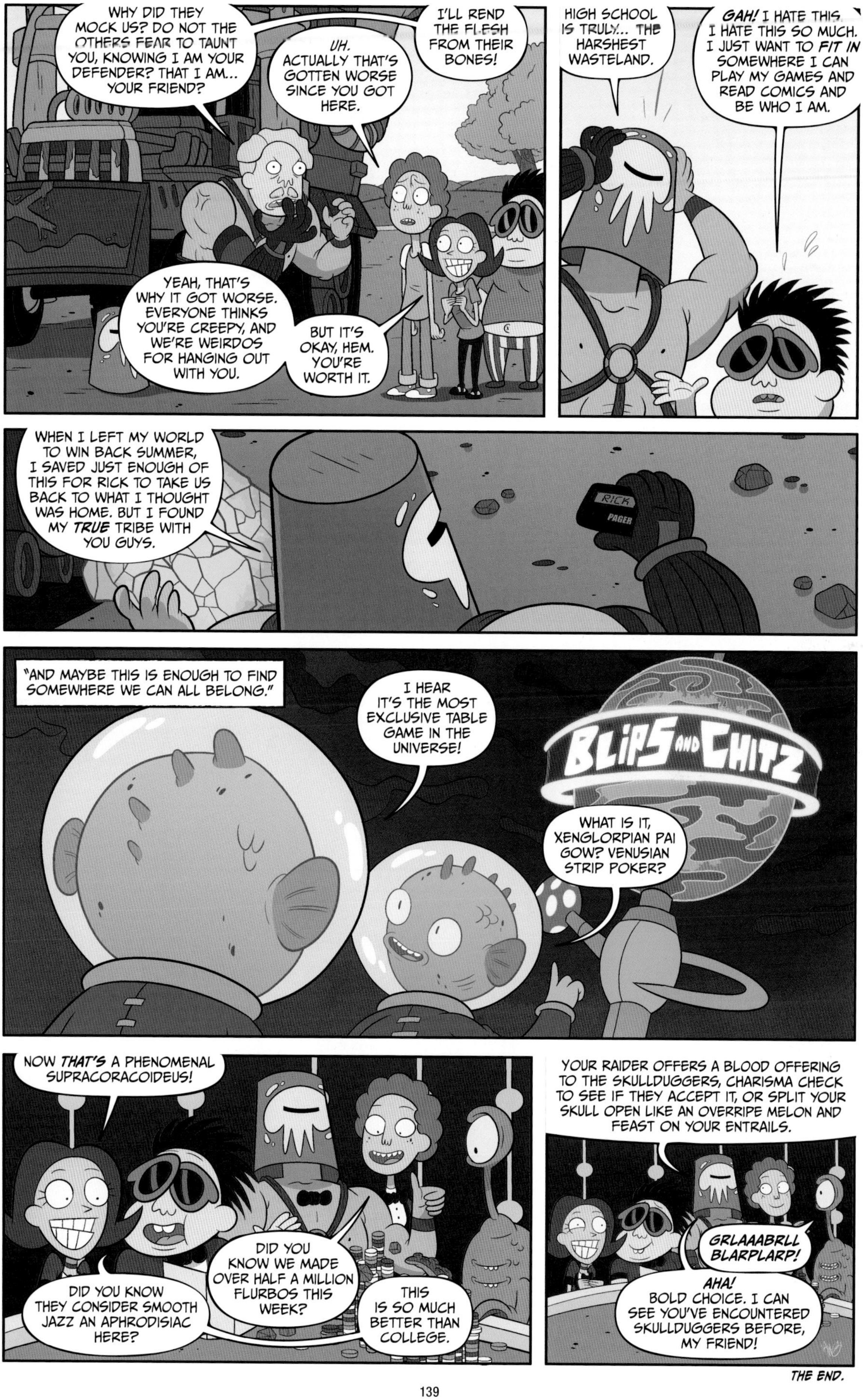
WHY DID THEY MOCK US? DO NOT THE OTHERS FEAR TO TAUNT YOU, KNOWING I AM YOUR DEFENDER? THAT I AM... YOUR FRIEND?
UH. ACTUALLY THAT'S GOTTEN WORSE SINCE YOU GOT HERE.
I'LL REND THE FLESH FROM THEIR BONES!
YEAH, THAT'S WHY IT GOT WORSE. EVERYONE THINKS YOU'RE CREEPY, AND WE'RE WEIRDOS FOR HANGING OUT WITH YOU.
BUT IT'S OKAY, HEM. YOU'RE WORTH IT.
HIGH SCHOOL IS TRULY... THE HARSHEST WASTELAND.
GAH! I HATE THIS. I HATE THIS SO MUCH. I JUST WANT TO FIT IN SOMEWHERE I CAN PLAY MY GAMES AND READ COMICS AND BE WHO I AM.
WHEN I LEFT MY WORLD TO WIN BACK SUMMER, I SAVED JUST ENOUGH OF THIS FOR RICK TO TAKE US BACK TO WHAT I THOUGHT WAS HOME. BUT I FOUND MY TRUE TRIBE WITH YOU GUYS.
RICK PAGER
"AND MAYBE THIS IS ENOUGH TO FIND SOMEWHERE WE CAN ALL BELONG."
I HEAR IT'S THE MOST EXCLUSIVE TABLE GAME IN THE UNIVERSE!
BLIPS AND CHITZ
WHAT IS IT, XENGLORPIAN PAI GOW? VENUSIAN STRIP POKER?
NOW THAT'S A PHENOMENAL SUPRACORACOIDEUS!
DID YOU KNOW THEY CONSIDER SMOOTH JAZZ AN APHRODISIAC HERE?
DID YOU KNOW WE MADE OVER HALF A MILLION FLURBOS THIS WEEK?
THIS IS SO MUCH BETTER THAN COLLEGE.
YOUR RAIDER OFFERS A BLOOD OFFERING TO THE SKULLDUGGERS, CHARISMA CHECK TO SEE IF THEY ACCEPT IT, OR SPLIT YOUR SKULL OPEN LIKE AN OVERRIPE MELON AND FEAST ON YOUR ENTRAILS.
GRLAAABRLL BLARPLARP!
AHA! BOLD CHOICE. I CAN SEE YOU'VE ENCOUNTERED SKULLDUGGERS BEFORE, MY FRIEND!
THE END.

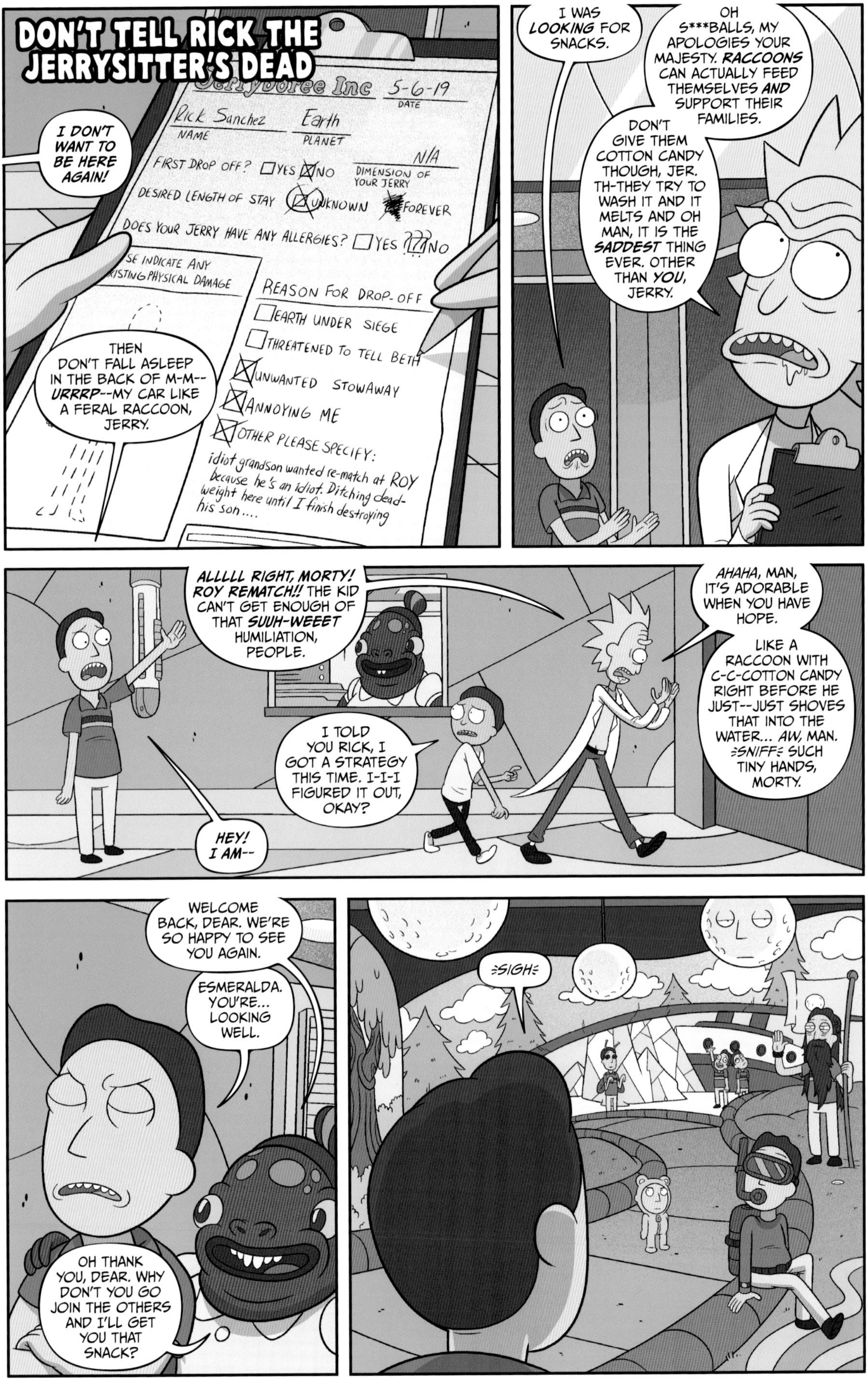
DON'T TELL RICK THE JERRYSITTER'S DEAD
Jerryboree Inc 5-6-19 DATE
Rick Sanchez NAME
Earth PLANET
FIRST DROP OFF? YES NO
N/A DIMENSION OF YOUR JERRY
DESIRED LENGTH OF STAY UNKNOWN FOREVER
DOES YOUR JERRY HAVE ANY ALLERGIES? YES ??? NO
REASON FOR DROP-OFF
EARTH UNDER SIEGE
THREATENED TO TELL BETH
UNWANTED STOWAWAY
ANNOYING ME
OTHER PLEASE SPECIFY:
idiot grandson wanted re-match at ROY because he's an idiot. Ditching dead-weight here until I finish destroying his son....
I DON'T WANT TO BE HERE AGAIN!
THEN DON'T FALL ASLEEP IN THE BACK OF M-M-- URRRP--MY CAR LIKE A FERAL RACCOON, JERRY.
I WAS LOOKING FOR SNACKS.
OH S***BALLS, MY APOLOGIES YOUR MAJESTY. RACCOONS CAN ACTUALLY FEED THEMSELVES AND SUPPORT THEIR FAMILIES.
DON'T GIVE THEM COTTON CANDY THOUGH, JER. TH-THEY TRY TO WASH IT AND IT MELTS AND OH MAN, IT IS THE SADDEST THING EVER. OTHER THAN YOU, JERRY.
ALLLLL RIGHT, MORTY! ROY REMATCH!! THE KID CAN'T GET ENOUGH OF THAT SUUH-WEEET HUMILIATION, PEOPLE.
HEY! I AM--
I TOLD YOU RICK, I GOT A STRATEGY THIS TIME. I-I-I FIGURED IT OUT, OKAY?
AHAHA, MAN, IT'S ADORABLE WHEN YOU HAVE HOPE.
LIKE A RACCOON WITH C-C-COTTON CANDY RIGHT BEFORE HE JUST--JUST SHOVES THAT INTO THE WATER... AW, MAN. SNIFF SUCH TINY HANDS, MORTY.
WELCOME BACK, DEAR. WE'RE SO HAPPY TO SEE YOU AGAIN.
ESMERALDA. YOU'RE... LOOKING WELL.
OH THANK YOU, DEAR. WHY DON'T YOU GO JOIN THE OTHERS AND I'LL GET YOU THAT SNACK?
SIGH

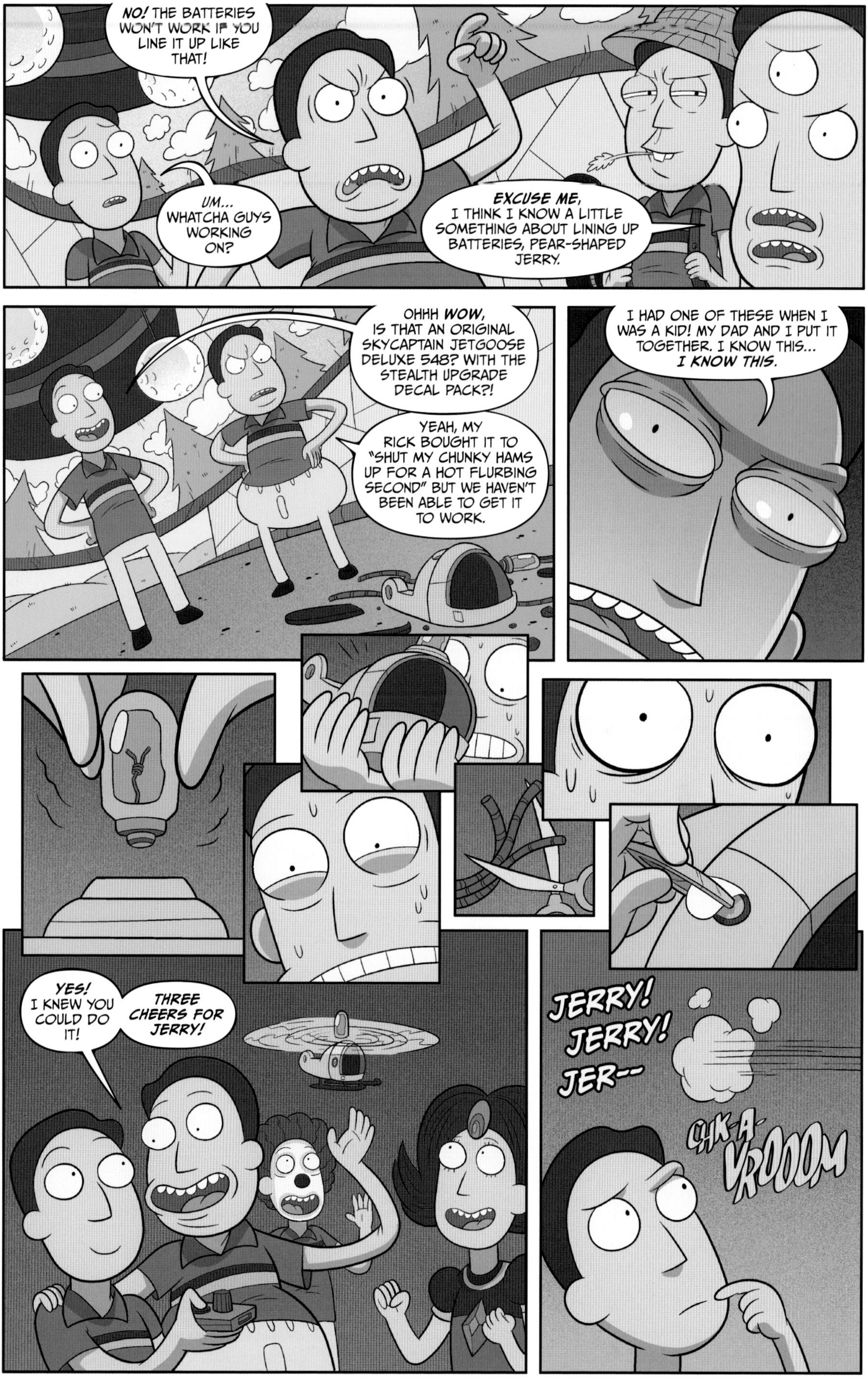
NO! THE BATTERIES WON'T WORK IF YOU LINE IT UP LIKE THAT!
UM... WHATCHA GUYS WORKING ON?
EXCUSE ME, I THINK I KNOW A LITTLE SOMETHING ABOUT LINING UP BATTERIES, PEAR-SHAPED JERRY.
OHHH WOW, IS THAT AN ORIGINAL SKYCAPTAIN JETGOOSE DELUXE 548? WITH THE STEALTH UPGRADE DECAL PACK?!
YEAH, MY RICK BOUGHT IT TO "SHUT MY CHUNKY HAMS UP FOR A HOT FLURBING SECOND" BUT WE HAVEN'T BEEN ABLE TO GET IT TO WORK.
I HAD ONE OF THESE WHEN I WAS A KID! MY DAD AND I PUT IT TOGETHER. I KNOW THIS... I KNOW THIS.
YES! I KNEW YOU COULD DO IT!
THREE CHEERS FOR JERRY!
JERRY! JERRY! JER--
CHK-A-VROOOM

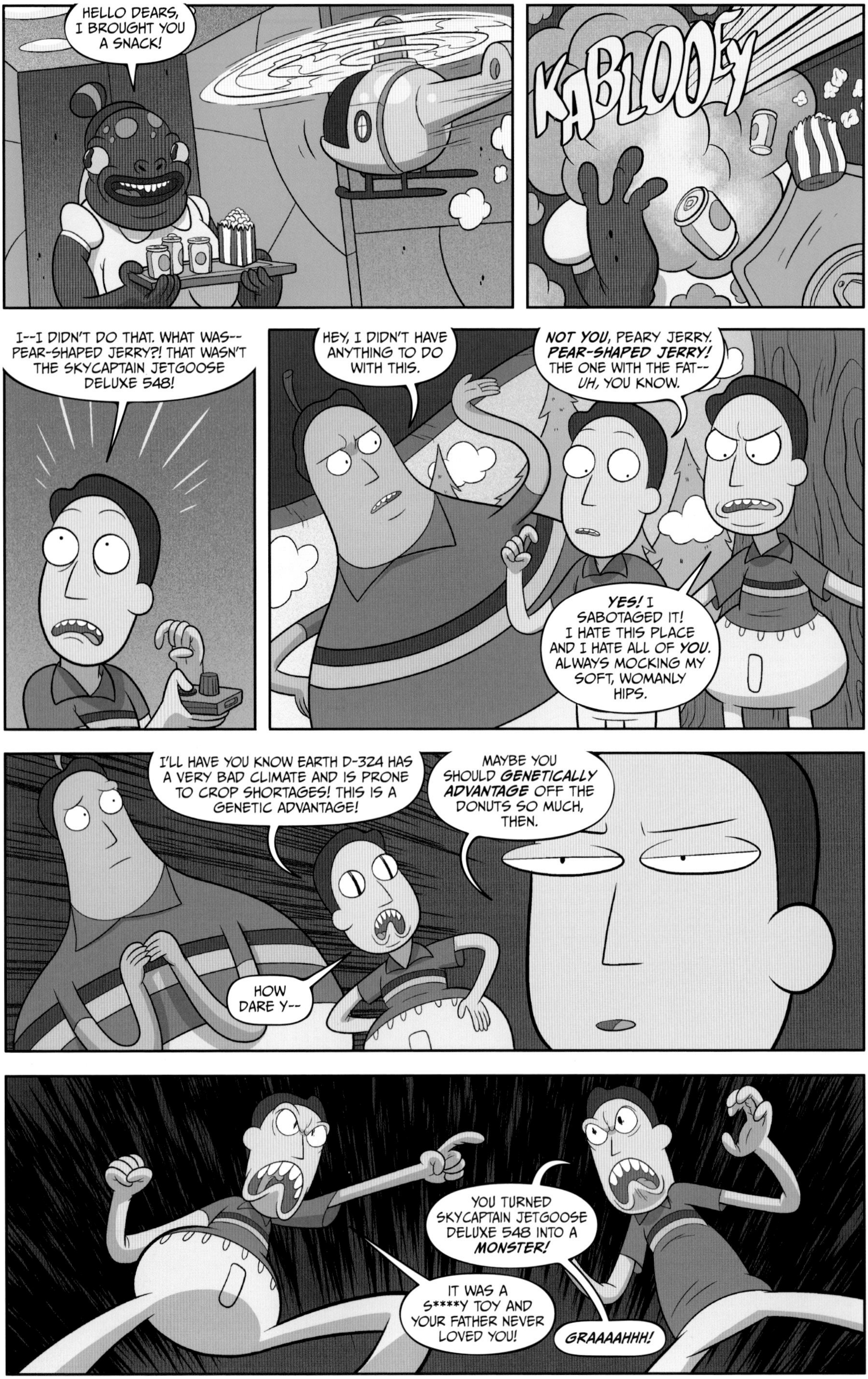
HELLO DEARS, I BROUGHT YOU A SNACK!
KABLOOEY
I--I DIDN'T DO THAT. WHAT WAS-- PEAR-SHAPED JERRY?! THAT WASN'T THE SKYCAPTAIN JETGOOSE DELUXE 548!
HEY, I DIDN'T HAVE ANYTHING TO DO WITH THIS.
NOT YOU, PEARY JERRY. PEAR-SHAPED JERRY! THE ONE WITH THE FAT-- UH, YOU KNOW.
YES! I SABOTAGED IT! I HATE THIS PLACE AND I HATE ALL OF YOU. ALWAYS MOCKING MY SOFT, WOMANLY HIPS.
I'LL HAVE YOU KNOW EARTH D-324 HAS A VERY BAD CLIMATE AND IS PRONE TO CROP SHORTAGES! THIS IS A GENETIC ADVANTAGE!
MAYBE YOU SHOULD GENETICALLY ADVANTAGE OFF THE DONUTS SO MUCH, THEN.
HOW DARE Y--
YOU TURNED SKYCAPTAIN JETGOOSE DELUXE 548 INTO A MONSTER!
IT WAS A S****Y TOY AND YOUR FATHER NEVER LOVED YOU!
GRAAAAHHH!

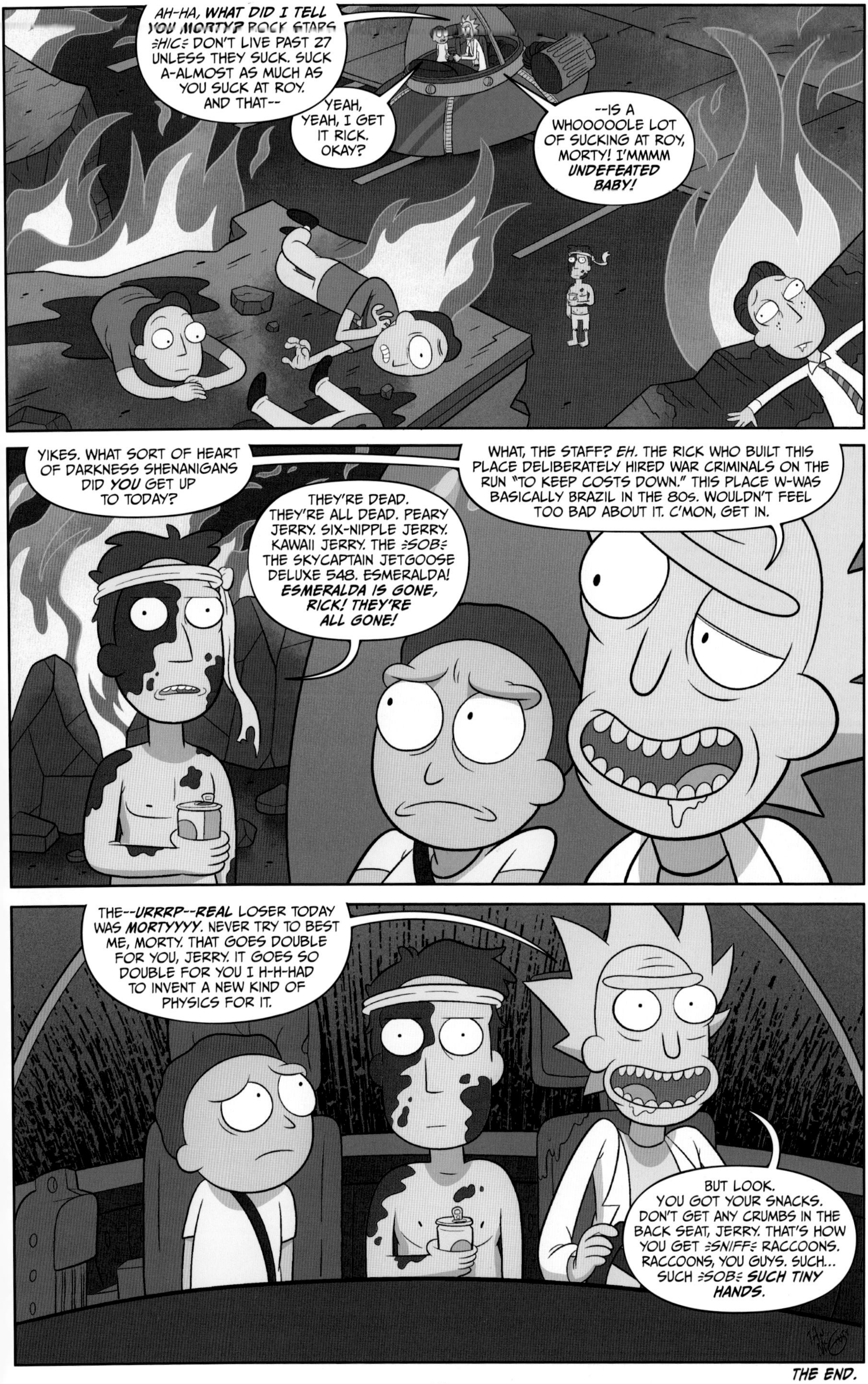
AH-HA, WHAT DID I TELL YOU MORTY? ROCK STARS ≡HIC≡ DON'T LIVE PAST 27 UNLESS THEY SUCK. SUCK A-ALMOST AS MUCH AS YOU SUCK AT ROY. AND THAT--
YEAH, YEAH, I GET IT RICK. OKAY?
--IS A WHOOOOOLE LOT OF SUCKING AT ROY, MORTY! I'MMMM UNDEFEATED BABY!
YIKES. WHAT SORT OF HEART OF DARKNESS SHENANIGANS DID YOU GET UP TO TODAY?
THEY'RE DEAD. THEY'RE ALL DEAD. PEARY JERRY. SIX-NIPPLE JERRY. KAWAII JERRY. THE ≡SOB≡ THE SKYCAPTAIN JETGOOSE DELUXE 548. ESMERALDA! ESMERALDA IS GONE, RICK! THEY'RE ALL GONE!
WHAT, THE STAFF? EH. THE RICK WHO BUILT THIS PLACE DELIBERATELY HIRED WAR CRIMINALS ON THE RUN "TO KEEP COSTS DOWN." THIS PLACE W-WAS BASICALLY BRAZIL IN THE 80s. WOULDN'T FEEL TOO BAD ABOUT IT. C'MON, GET IN.
THE--URRRP--REAL LOSER TODAY WAS MORTYYYY. NEVER TRY TO BEST ME, MORTY. THAT GOES DOUBLE FOR YOU, JERRY. IT GOES SO DOUBLE FOR YOU I H-H-HAD TO INVENT A NEW KIND OF PHYSICS FOR IT.
BUT LOOK. YOU GOT YOUR SNACKS. DON'T GET ANY CRUMBS IN THE BACK SEAT, JERRY. THAT'S HOW YOU GET ≡SNIFF≡ RACCOONS. RACCOONS, YOU GUYS. SUCH... SUCH ≡SOB≡ SUCH TINY HANDS.

THE END.

DAN HARMON is the Emmy® winning creator/executive producer of the comedy series Community as well as the co-creator/executive producer of Adult Swim's *Rick and Morty*™.

JUSTIN ROILAND grew up in Manteca, California where he did the basic stuff children do. Later in life he traveled to Los Angeles. Justin also really hates writing about himself in the third person. I hate this. That's right. It's me. I've been writing this whole thing. Hi. The cat's out of the bag. It's just you and me now. There never was a third person.

KYLE STARKS is an Eisner-nominated comic creator from Southern Indiana, where he resides with his beautiful wife and two amazing daughters. Check out his creator-owned work: *Assaination Nation, Kill Them All*, and *Sexcastle*.

KARLA PACHECO lives in the Pacific Northwest on a boat named The Slippery Pig. She once won the Exxon Valdez from Waterworld fighting in the Thunderdome. She wrote a children's book about murders. She's the worst. Find her online at @THEkarlapacheco.

TINI HOWARD is a writer and swamp witch from the Carolina Wilds. Her work includes *Rick and Morty*™: *Pocket Like You Stole It, Assassinistas, Euthanauts*, and she is now a Marvel Exclusive writer. She lives with her husband, Blake, and her son, Orlando, who is a cat.

JOSH TRUJILLO is a writer, editor, and comic book creator based in San Rafael, California. You can remain updated on his work by following Josh on Twitter @LostHisKeysMan.

MARC ELLERBY is a comics illustrator living in Essex, UK. He has worked on such titles as *Doctor Who, Regular Show* and *The Amazing World of Gumball*. His own comics are *Chloe Noonan: Monster Hunter* and *Ellerbisms*.

CJ CANNON is a self-taught artist living in Nashville, Tennessee. When they're not working on comics, outside riding their bike, or drumming, they're almost always in the house drawing fanart.

IAN MCGINTY is an Artist, Writer, and Designer. He is the creator of *Welcome to Showside* and worked on Nickelodeon's *INVADER ZIM* movie, *Rocko's Modern Life, Adventure Time* and more.

ANDREW MACLEAN is an american comic book writer and artist. He's worked for Oni Press, Image Comics, Marvel, DC, and Dark Horse. He is the creator of the YALSA nominated graphic novel, *ApocalyptiGirl* (Dark Horse), and the Diamond Gem award winning series, *HEAD LOPPER* (Image Comics).

BENJAMIN DEWEY draws fun stuff for a living. He loves his wife, cats, science, guitars and fantasy RPG games.

JARRETT WILLIAMS was born in New Orleans, Louisiana and graduated from the Savannah College of Art & Design (MFA). He has three volumes of his pro-wrestling/adventure series *Super Pro K.O.!* for Oni Press. He has also completed *Hyper Force Neo* for Z2 Comics.

SARAH GRALEY is a comic writer and artist based in the UK. She's been drawing *Our Super Adventure* and posting it online since 2012, and is also the author of the ever-spooky *Kim Reaper*, and the *Rick and Morty*™: *Lil' Poopy Superstar* miniseries.

RII ABREGO is a southern USA-based illustrator who has contributed to titles such as Steven Universe, Adventure Time, and Rick and Morty™. They can be found at twitter.com/riibrego — just follow the rat emoji.

SARAH STERN is a comic artist and colorist from New York. Find her at sarahstern.com or follow her on Twitter at @worstwizard.

NICK FILARDI grew up in New London, Connecticut listening to Small Town Hero and watching *Batman: The Animated Serie*s. He is currently living in Gainesville, Florida with his three-legged dog, DeNiro.

CHRIS CRANK letters a bunch of books put out by Image, Dark Horse and Oni Press. He also has a podcast with Mike Norton (crankcast.net) and makes music (sonomorti.bandcamp.com).

PUESTE is an artist living and working in Spain.